KNOW STEALING

"If you are wondering where we have gone wrong as a country, then read this book. Shane Coley does a great job of getting to the very core of the problem. The media and talking heads we hear every day are so fixated on the symptoms that we forget to search for the root cause. This book peels the onion back layer by layer and explains in detail where the problem is. This book is a MUST read for anyone interested in restoring individual liberty in America!"

~ **Clay Ortiz**

"Rarely does a book not only challenge, but revolutionize the manner in which you view the world. Upon finishing such works, it's as if you've been given a lens to better identify the functions of society that are right in front of you, but have been too small to see. Frederic Bastiat's classic, The Law, comes to mind. Know Stealing is one such book. Shane Coley takes on the daunting task of explaining some of the most complex issues facing our world today and succeeds with concise and astute brilliance. His solution, rooted in historical, economical, and Biblical foundations is a single rule: No Stealing. His insights on the significance and protection of life, liberty, and property are desperately needed and a pleasure to read."

~ **Drew Martin**, Columnist, RevoluTimes.com

"Shane Coley has succeeded in methodically correcting the most dangerous errors modern American society has in understanding economics, politics, government & Christian theology. A 15-year project with more to show for it than most entire lives. Transformational!"

~ **Jimmy Norman**, Executive Director,
Georgians For Constitutional Government

"I am forced to say that in all my years of formal education, I had never learned of the Austrian School of Economics. All of those good 1970 era dollars spent in vain sitting in micro and macro economic classes, principles and theory of banking, all culminating in a degree in accounting, and I never heard of Ludwig Von Mises until I met Shane. [...] Complete with charts and illustrations, readers are led on a journey to rediscover the elementary fact that words have meaning, or, more specifically, accurate meanings! I was pleasantly surprised that even an old goat like me could still discover some words with a nuanced meaning a little different than what I had thought. Who knew? Once the foundational understandings of the key words are in place, topics are explored to weave together the knowledge that will allow you to KnoW Stealing. "

~ **Rick McQueen**

"Armed with wisdom, knowledge and an aptitude for teaching, Shane Coley skillfully disperses the fog of economic, political and moral complexities which tend to make our nation's problems seem insurmountable. Shane brings to light long ignored principles, which must be understood if we are to have any chance of restoring the liberty, peace, and prosperity, which our country enjoyed in former times. Information contained in this excellent work is invaluable."

~ **Linda Morrow**

"If Know Stealing were written in the 1840s philosopher, economist, and author Frederic Bastiat would be the perfect person to write the foreword. This book is excellent reading for anyone from the high school student to the would-be-politician. If this book were required reading in high schools, we could restore our Nation in a matter of a generation or less."

~ **Walt Holton**

"I'd buy a copy for all my friends if they had Kindles... Lots of ideas in this book that I have had in my head for a while but don't have the skill to convey to others the way Mr. Coley does (and there's plenty here I hadn't thought of or didn't really understand too.) As a previous reviewer stated, this book does an excellent job of getting to the core of our problems, and leaves me hopeful they can be solved."

~ **Luke Albers**

In response to Luke Albers statement *"I'd buy a copy for all my friends if they had Kindles,"* Valerie James wrote: "I was just thinking the same thing after reading Know Stealing this morning. Previously, I was familiar with sound money principles, but have had a difficult time 'translating' these concepts to my friends and family. Thank you for writing in a simple manner, with straightforward analogies that can be more easily passed on.

"Know Stealing" should be passed along to every library, school, neighbor, pastor, family member, and friend—this book may open their eyes, give them hope, and save our children. 'Bastiat's "The Law" has been my #1 book to gift, but not everybody "gets it" who gets it—Shane Coley's book will now be #1 to gift, and is much simpler to understand."

~ **Valerie James**

"Rarely is the written work able to methodically unravel centuries of deceit and to lay the thieving emperor bare for all to see. Know Stealing accomplishes this and more, offering a necessary corrective to the theft at the root of modern society. Such is the power of truth simply stated. Arm yourself with the ideas herein to become a true defender of liberty."

~ **Christopher David**
Candidate for Congress [CA-33]

"Shane Coley's Know Stealing is a breakthrough, must-read work which uncovers hidden causes of America's "boom and bust" economic cycles, as well as generational economic and societal decay. Know Stealing provides keys to how "We the People" will be able to save America from the brink, while creating a solid, stable foundation of both individual behavior and just government, resulting in economic and individual prosperity. Shane clearly, factually, and meticulously demonstrates how our costless fiat money system, along with other systems of state control, like energy policy, media, regulation, and taxation, are designed to pillage America's citizens and the broader economy, leading to certain tyranny and destruction. Know Stealing reminds us that stealing violates the 8th Commandment, and that, as a nation founded upon Judeo-Christian principles, we must confront stealing head on and return our financial and governmental systems to an honorable, Constitutional, truth-based foundation before we will ever be able to avoid financial catastrophes, let alone ensure America's liberties, freedoms, and prosperity are maintained into the future. I highly recommend Know Stealing as a foundational work for those involved in economic, industrial, and public policy, as well as for all who desire to restore America to her foundational roots and greatness."

~ **David M Chaney**
CEO, Role1
CEO/CxO, Solutions
President and Founder, CEOs for Liberty

Know Stealing should be in everyone's library and should be discussed and taught regularly in our homes, churches, schools, and businesses."

~ **Cody Murray**

Read other reviews at http://www.knowstealing.com

KNOW STEALING

M. Shane Coley

YAV PUBLICATIONS
ASHEVILLE, NORTH CAROLINA

First Edition

ISBN: 978-1-937449-02-5 (hardbound)
ISBN: 978-1-937449-04-9 (soft cover)
ISBN: 978-1-937449-03-2 (eBook)

Published by:

YAV PUBLICATIONS

ASHEVILLE, NORTH CAROLINA

YAV books may be purchased in bulk for educational, business, or promotional use. For information, contact Books@yav.com or phone toll-free 888-693-9365.
Visit our website: www.InterestingWriting.com

3 5 7 9 10 8 6 4 2
Assembled in the United States of America
Published February 2012

To all who live thankful and productive lives

Table of Contents

Foreword

Since our first meeting in 2005, I have enjoyed conversations with Shane regarding many of the ideas presented in Know Stealing. It has been exciting to watch him shape and refine them. Reading this book has given me the opportunity to consider again, in an integrated and comprehensive way, many of the ideas we explored in conversation.

The author's productive work presented here is scholarly and of the highest quality. More importantly, the ideas presented here have been refined in the crucible of passion. The author's passion for discovering, understanding, and sharing the truth about money sets this book apart from many others which deal with the same subject. Truth seekers who read and study the ideas and arguments captured in these pages will not be disappointed.

Money is one of the most pervasive ingredients in modern life. At the same time, money is one of the most misunderstood concepts of modern life. Definitions and discussions of macroeconomics and "money and banking" are common in academic textbooks. These are also common topics of discussion among businesses and individuals. The media always has coverage that is somehow linked to money. Yet these definitions and discussions rarely explore the reality of what is commonly called money. Without precise definitions and an objective study of 'true money,' those who control the definition and exchange of money will exploit those who do not. Theft is the inevitable result. The facts and rigorous analysis of the concept of money presented herein can inform and undergird policy alternatives aimed at preventing such theft.

One may find passionate, thorough, and carefully reasoned discussions on a number of critical ideas in Know Stealing. Beginning with the important idea of money, Shane then considers the essential ideas of power, authority, production and more, as pieces of a grand puzzle. These concepts are grounded in Biblical truth and an honest study of history, rather than the all-to-common intellectual fabrication of those formally trained in the study of economics or politics. At a minimum, this book will challenge the reader to clarify his or her understanding of these important concepts. At a maximum, this book will spark a passion, which will motivate the reader to seek out, and support policy alternatives aimed at preventing the current broad-scale theft arising from what is loosely called 'money' today. I strongly encourage you to - K**no**w Stealing.

~ **John Feezell, PhD.**
Professor of Economics
School of Business at LeTourneau University

1. Getting Started

1.1 Introduction

A people or nation that does not understand liberty cannot defend it.

I work late and rise early thinking about liberty, production and the nature of things. The stakes are high. Your time is valuable. Please permit me to be direct. We have been deceived, and I know *how* it was done.

The reader with an open mind, who actively questions everything including the ideas recorded here, will get the most out of *Know Stealing*. When you reach the last page, it is my hope that you will have demanded, and that I will have delivered, solid arguments capable of standing under scrutiny and pressure.

Consider the following brief statements:

We have problems that do not have to exist. They can be resolved.

Western civilization is crumbling financially at the level of the individual, the family, the business and the government. This is no small issue. Why is there a uniform worldwide collapse of economies?

We all know of some bad ideas that the other guy accepts. But it turns out that there are a few simple, important, highly destructive ideas, which have been commonly accepted by most people for several hundred years. This confusion and error is causing us serious problems.

Certain commonly accepted ideas are measurably and objectively wrong. These ideas encourage destructive actions, which lead to *bad outcomes.*

Just like in a garden, we are reaping what we sow. It is time for us to clear away centuries of brush and debris, and it is definitely time to stop planting more bad seeds.

Consider these *outcomes*:

Job loss
Home foreclosure
Business bankruptcy
People have debt not savings
Retirements grow and disappear *on paper*
Big government

Government bankruptcy
Worldwide economic meltdown

The list goes on.

Ideas guide *actions*, which have *outcomes*. Therefore, if society as a whole has common problems, then whatever ideas are commonly accepted about the world are suspect. There are several institutions that people claim are essential to modern civilization because of the good they do. It is true that there are institutions that do good work and have significant influence. However, if an institution is considered to be genuinely influential in society, then it must also be open to scrutiny and critical review.

In other words, how can a person say that institution A is all that is holding things together, and then suggest that the problems that exist are not the fault of the institution? Either the institution is weak and really not very influential, or the institution is influential and has a share in the blame for the global economic, moral and social decay in which we find ourselves.

There was a time when I would have argued against certain negative claims about my religion, my country, our marketplace and our government. But I knew something wasn't right, so I went on a journey of sorts to discover the truth about things.

Please accept the following short story as an allegory.

I once went on a journey seeking answers. After many years I found an old chest in a forgotten place that was overflowing with good things, including lost knowledge. I studied the contents carefully.

Once I understood the reality, cause and nature of the problems we face, I looked back to tell my friends what I had learned. But they were far away and there was a great wasteland between us. No matter how hard I tried, people could not understand, unless they were able to go back with me over rugged terrain to see what I had found.

What a strange predicament to be in. I loved my friends and people in general and I was sitting before a treasure that would benefit us all. In fact, the value to each individual is much greater if this treasure is shared.

But I couldn't tell people about it, I was too far away. I couldn't show them because the trip over the wasteland was too long and difficult. I had learned enough to understand what was happening in the world, but that is an altogether different thing from showing others. So I set my next goal.

I determined to learn how to effectively share a more complete understanding of the world with others. I set about building trails, roads and bridges. I started drawing maps for the journey. I labored until a dangerous, expensive, painful, fifteen-year journey was turned into a few days of safe travel. That travel guide is in your hand.

Come with me. You will never see the world the same again.

So how does this trip begin? We need to look for common ground.

By training, our thinking is dangerously twisted so that we learn to perceive friends as enemies and enemies as friends. Our first step is to genuinely put all persons into one big category. Propaganda shouts about differences between people everyday. Is there anything that all people have in common?

Attributing Creation to God, the Bible states the obvious.

"for He causes His sun to rise on the evil and the good, and sends rain on the righteous and the unrighteous." (Matthew 5:45b, NASB95)

We are all subject to a common enemy. For fifteen years I have studied to understand why American families and businesses are being pushed from *savings* and *prosperity* toward *debt* and *loss*. Besides the sun and rain, it turns out people have much more in common than many of us realize.

The course we are on as a nation is unsustainable. No great civilization expects to collapse, yet they all have. There are specific reasons for their collapse, which are discussed in these pages. The good news is that the powerful tools for restoring our individual wealth and prosperity are recorded here. The bad news is that the powerful tools for restoring our individual wealth and prosperity are not automatically clear and correct in the hearts and minds of people. In order to establish and maintain a free and prosperous society, each person must understand how the world actually works, and then teach others. Businessmen, pastors, politicians, professors, blue-collar, white-collar, young, old, wealthy, poor… We are all together deceived. I will prove this.

Understanding the simple idea that *people depend on production* is required to restore our liberty and personal wealth. When that idea settles in alongside a few others, a new and valuable framework of understanding comes into view.

The Bible verse above observes a simple fact about the world. The sun rises and the rain falls on every perspective, attitude and religion.

What if there is a small bit of common ground between all people, regardless of worldview?

For instance, I may not know you, but I still know the sun rises and the rain falls on you.

People have different religions, but religion should not be a test for public office, except from the voting booth where it should always be a test. Even though Romans 13 is often poorly translated and wrongly applied, it does state that a Christian must be subject to higher authorities, regardless of religion, political affiliation or worldview. At the same time, the power and actions of authority must be limited based on just law. Getting this basic relationship right in our thinking is essential.[1]

Perhaps there are other similar basics that can help restore our freedom. In fact, I am pleased to report that there are. I found these treasures by rejecting the false teaching commonly dressed in peer review, conventional wisdom and "it's always been that way." For example, we all *eat food and use things.* Since food and things must be produced, we all have at least that in common. Oppressive power comes primarily from control of production. Power structures cannot exist without the labor and property of producers. A clear understanding of these and a few other essential ideas may forever change the way you perceive the world.

I hope those who already understand these ideas will find this a useful teaching tool. I am thankful for the centuries of great thinkers, writers and teachers who have produced more detailed work on liberty, production and wealth than any one person will ever exhaust. Even so, there may be important ideas here that are genuinely new to most people, regardless of education or worldview.

I labored to make this very basic writing as short as possible, while still being careful to cover essential ideas, so that these ideas can travel quickly. Restoring our liberty and prosperity depends on the speed with

1 Romans 13:1-7 is quoted and discussed in significant detail in the section on Authority.

which these misplaced old ideas become commonplace again in our society. Every chapter has a purpose and role supporting that end.

One of the great challenges is engaging the audience. I want to engage the economist, scientist and pastor. I also want to engage the cattleman, mechanic and truck driver. I want to draw in the grandfather and his grandchildren. I am hopeful that these ideas will become the buzz in middle school, high school and college. I want mothers and daughters to be informed and encouraged.

In order to genuinely engage such a diverse audience, there must be a common denominator. One would think that an interesting common denominator that speaks to the educated man and the working man, as well as the young and the old would not exist. But it does.

In some ways I am uniquely qualified to present these ideas. You will see from my biography that I am at home with young and old, formally educated or not, grease and dirt or suit and tie, chewing the fat or presenting formal testimony. At every opportunity, I gladly advance the ideas of liberty and openly debate those who hold a different view, whether around the campfire or in the classroom, boardroom or in some public venue.

One of my challenges is to explain where we are wrong in our thinking without unnecessarily offending people. At the same time, I would debate any citizen, businessman, pastor, professor, teacher, leader, political activist, elected official or journalist on these ideas at any time, in any place. The bottom line is that our thinking is extremely mixed up and, in many important areas, just flat out wrong. The errors in our thinking and understanding are costing us our liberty, our homes, our jobs, our retirements and our children's future.

Liberty and prosperity are always at stake in every nation for every generation. Eventually bad decisions in the past force a generation to come to terms with the truth about what is necessary to sustain a free society. We are one of those generations. In our case, we can no longer naively depend on past production, new land, old-style immigration, industrialization, available cheap energy and paper wealth to maintain our standard of living.

We must learn how the world actually works.
We must learn to identify root causes.
We must learn how to defend our individual rights and property.
We must understand how power is developed and aggregated.
We must understand how nations are built and how they fall.
We must understand liberty, production, and the nature of things.

These pages contain *keys* to understanding that will enable a person to see through the errors that surround us daily. We have the power to overcome destructive ideas that exist in business, politics and religion.

My single objective is to share the very best of what I've learned with those who are willing to open their minds and think, in order to understand how to restore and preserve our great nation as a land of liberty and production. I welcome all challenges with regard to these ideas.

Of course the reader will find in these pages opinion, preference, analogy, anecdote, hyperbole, allegory and other literary devices, which aid in conveying ideas and communicating meaning. When I claim that something is objectively true, it will be clearly stated as such.

The Bible is referenced as a guiding document for those to whom the book is Holy and as literature for others. Since Christian beliefs significantly impact the culture for both Christians and non-Christians, understanding how the Bible influences society is useful for all. While there are significant sections which deal with typically misinterpreted Bible passages, the main case can be made using math, reason, logic, and history. The Bible passages and teaching are necessary to help resolve certain problematic conflict in Christian teaching and thought.

The material in this book is powerful. It will teach a bold middle school student all that is necessary to debate and defeat a formally educated economist or an experienced politician. Imagine a magnificent skyscraper that is built on a lie. If a person, even a child, can show that the foundation is a lie, then the whole building has to be an illusion. Many things we believe are true are no more than illusions. Children who study the ideas presented in this book will have a better understanding of the world we live in than most successful and formally educated adults.

Sadly, we will discover that for the past 1600 years the Christian community has maintained at least one specific error in Christian thought which makes Christians largely responsible for the disaster we currently face as a nation. Amazingly I've been unable to find any person or literature that makes the specific case that you will read here. Neither have I met anyone who would even make the effort to present a reasoned argument against these claims. I'll be most appreciative if a reader can connect me with literature on any of these uncommon topics.[2]

---

2 My argument here is multifaceted. First, these concepts are critical and basic which

The goal of this book is to restore sound thinking about liberty, production, and the nature of things so that a growing number of people may experience the blessings of liberty. In order to do that we have to cover a lot of ground without getting bogged down on any one point. This is a slow starting, then faster-moving book of ideas which will point the interested reader to a wealth of literature which goes deeper into related theory and detail.

Liberty and prosperity are the prizes. So let's get started.

1.2 The Puzzle

"Educate and inform the whole mass of the people... They are the only sure reliance for the preservation of our liberty." —Thomas Jefferson

I am only asking you to fundamentally change how you see the world... How hard could that be?

Just kidding!!

I hope you will smile while you read. I find that when tackling something like this a little humor is often a helpful ingredient. Please understand that for most of my life I have been pouring out thoughts and questions on anyone who would slow down long enough to listen. As I learned more, the conversations became more interesting for me and more challenging for the unsuspecting leaders I questioned on various topics. Because I speak to people from various walks of life having all sorts of different worldviews, I have an idea about how people respond to new ideas in general and these ideas specifically.

My goal is for the reader to start here, learn, finish, keep learning and get others on the same track. That is a tall order for challenging material. Somehow I want for you as the reader to understand that this material is highly valuable to you personally. I want to convey that if you

---

means they should be common knowledge. No search should be necessary. Second, I have physically and electronically searched many resources where these ideas should be present, and they are either not present, or at least not obvious enough for me to find. Third, I have asked many well educated people from various disciplines and have met no one who has been previously aware of these facts and ideas. Fourth, the commentaries and writing I have found include error which the information presented here illuminates as error.

wait a few months or years to read this, you will be unhappy about the decision. If I am correct, there should be strong word-of-mouth referrals confirming this claim.

Part of my experience in sharing these ideas one-on-one is finding that people are more or less beside themselves as these ideas sink in. People start talking about how this affects their own ideas, ranging from the most basic to the most in depth. Better yet, one day they realize their worldview and understanding has been radically changed, in a valuable way that the honest man or the saint would approve.

I don't know how to tailor an appeal to you personally, but if I did, I would. Different people have different experience, knowledge and preferences. Early chapters are basic and a little redundant. There is a reason for that.

Imagine that the information in *Know Stealing* is located at the peak of a mountain. Those who are skilled and well trained climbers can head straight for the peak. Those who are great at other things, but not skilled and trained in mountain climbing have to take an easier and longer route.

Because of the importance of these ideas, my goal is to produce a common document that skilled and unskilled alike can use to begin conversations that are capable of leading to restoration. People have no reason to work toward common solutions until they can see common problems. The goal is to get everyone up to the peak so that from a common vantage point we can begin working together toward restoring liberty, prosperity and individual rights.

In a challenging attempt to balance the document for a wide audience, the book is organized as follows:

Parts and Pieces Make a Picture

The chapters are written to convey ideas as though the ideas are pieces of a puzzle. We all know that puzzles are solved by assembling pieces. This book contains the pieces of a puzzle that explain what is necessary to sustain a free and prosperous society.

Thinking of a real puzzle, most puzzle pieces are little *mysteries* until they are fit together with other pieces. Parts of the scene become clearer as each small mystery is solved. The pieces eventually combine to form an easily understood scene. Along the way, it is often difficult to determine where a particular piece goes and it is often difficult to locate the next piece for a particular spot. This is especially true if the scene is unknown or, even worse, if the wrong scene is envisioned.

It is worth noting that in the real puzzle business the clear picture began as a scene that someone cut into little pieces to make a profit. When talking about real puzzles, that is a good thing. However, there are many *unjust* forces in society that are intentionally used to turn clear pictures into scattered pieces of a puzzle, also in order to make a profit.

The real puzzle business is about producing wealth by producing a product and challenging people to think. The social puzzle business is about transferring wealth and teaching people not to think.

In the real puzzle business, the goal is to tell people about the product and invite them to assemble the pieces. In the social puzzle business, the goal is to hide the pieces and tell people there is no puzzle.

Like a puzzle, these chapters fit together to present a clear picture that has been lost to us for at least several hundred years. The reader may think this statement is a bit extreme, but among these ideas are genuine treasures, which can change the general balance of power in the world.

Please understand that this is a book of practical, profitable knowledge, not a book of secrets. However, it is also essential to understand that some people profit when the knowledge and ideas written about here are confused or unknown.

Please remember, as with a physical puzzle, some pieces may seem unimportant until they become part of the whole. Some pieces serve as simple connections to fill in the background. Other pieces are rich in detail and information. Sometimes it takes several pieces to bring an important part of the scene into clear view. But along the way and in the end, understanding increases and the world we live in becomes clearer. Solutions become possible in our thinking.

I wish these ideas could be organized as a real puzzle. If you were to put such a puzzle together, I think you would immediately call your best friends and say "Come as soon as you can. This you have to see."

2. Removing Obstacles

Sometimes old ideas interfere with new ones.
Sometimes a false belief takes the place of true reality.

2.1 A Ship Story

We have so many problems. Which problem is most important?

Someone says: Well clearly, my problem is the one we need to fix first... Otherwise I would be working on something else...

May I encourage you to think with me on this?

What if there actually is a way to solve ninety-five percent of our problems by working together to solve a certain root cause of all our problems? I know this can be done.

Join me in recognizing that problems should be prioritized. Let's see if there is such a thing as a highest priority problem.

Let's use a ship analogy

Suppose there is a large, sophisticated, 4,000-passenger ship designed to sail from one continent to another over the course of three months. Suppose this ship has several problems, including a rude captain, four thieves, a murderer, a pirate, a lazy crew, poorly prepared food, severely damaged dishes, crumbling paint and lumpy mattresses.

Which problem would you address first? And when would this happen?

Suppose there are three groups who each identify the problems they consider most important.

Suppose they divide their energies and go to work. Let's say that they all succeed or that some succeed or that none succeed. You choose the outcome you prefer.

One Other Problem

Let's also suppose that there is one other problem. The ship has a large hole that takes on water at a rate of 500 gallons per minute. Using every available resource, only 250 gallons per minute can be pumped out of the ship. At this rate, the ship will sink somewhere over the deep ocean about halfway to its destination.

While all the issues are important, only the hole in the ship unavoidably and seriously affects every person on the ship. Only one problem absolutely must be solved or all is lost for the passengers.

But Some Gain

The same problem will provide gain for the pirate and his associates.

They like the hole.

The pirate who drilled the hole will have a vessel waiting to collect the loot and carry him on to the next adventure. He knows that the mathematical reality of water flow guarantees the ship will sink.

Functional Root Cause

The only hope for the passengers is for them to know about the hole in the ship and plug it.

While they cannot remove the water fast enough, there will be no need to remove any water if they simply plug the hole before they leave. If the hole is plugged along the way, then once the hole is plugged, they have time, resources and opportunity to save themselves and the ship.

If they have knowledge of the hole and understand its effect, they will plug the hole and the remaining problems will matter again. If for any reason they do not plug the hole, nothing else matters because good food and soft mattresses are not needed by people who have been looted and left to die.

Ideological Root Cause

Now let's see if there is such thing as an ideological root cause.

Suppose the pirate offered safe passage and part of the loot to the captain, part of the crew, the murderer, thieves and the ship owner.

Now we see clearly that the passenger's loss is their gain. We also see that the danger we face, this group does not face.

We can also see that the reason this group of people has gathered on the ship is to steal, kill and destroy.

Stop Thief!

If the passengers were aware of what was coming, they would patch the hole and deal with the pirate. However, thieves don't advertise their plans. They operate in secret.

Applied Principle – Know Leaking

But let's just suppose that the passengers know to look for holes in ships and they know holes are bad, so they patch the hole without realizing that this plan was in motion. The pirate can say nothing because he has no power over the passengers and their associates while the ship is in port. His relative power increases only after taking away the resources necessary for the passengers to resist. Between the port and the middle of the ocean, the balance of power changes in favor of the pirate, because of the hole. With the hole repaired in port, the situation changes.

With hope of success gone, the pirate, murderer, thieves, captain and lousy crew would leave.

Since now there will be no insurance settlement, the ship owner would again need to provide a valuable product and service to stay in business. To prevent loss, he would ensure that the food and other comforts were at least adequate and he would hire a dependable captain and crew.

Now we see that the hole in the ship was part of a plan to capture wealth. When the hope of gain through theft was gone, the criminals disbanded, the owner protected his property and employed his capital to gain a return. The passengers were safe and recipients of good service.

The Lesson

Some problems, like the hole, make all other problems meaningless and unimportant. Some problems are a higher priority.

Some problems, like the hole and the plan to steal, are the hidden cause of other problems, like lumpy mattresses, lousy service and insurance fraud. The secondary problems that we see divert our attention and keep us busy while our ship is sinking. Solving the Functional Root Cause is an efficient, uncontroversial, cost effective way to deter thieves and resolve secondary problems.

If the passengers know as a matter of principle that the ship must not have a hole, their attention to the ship's hull and its condition would take away the tools the thieves depend on for success.

Likewise, if we understand that stealing transfers power from the many to the few, we know that we must stop the thief by taking away the tools and systems of theft the thieves depend on for success. It is certain that stolen resources will always be used in ways that are destructive to individual life, liberty and property. It is certain that some people will steal, given the opportunity. They must not have the opportunity.

The United States is like this ship. We are nearing the deep waters. We must plug the hole. If we plug the hole, the problem you are most concerned about will probably disappear.

We must all know and understand the hole.

2.2 American Apathy?

The destructive bipartisan consensus to ignore principle has suffocated American political life for many years. Anyone who tries to ask fundamental questions instead of cosmetic ones is ridiculed or ignored.

It is common to hear that the problems we face in the United States are caused by *"the apathy of the American people."* I disagree with this assessment. I have more confidence in Americans than that.

Government at every level is large, intrusive, wasteful and corrupt. Government intervention is destroying wealth, jobs, manufacturing, agriculture, savings, retirement, education and the basic moral fiber of our society. These are the kinds of problems that we say people are apathetic about. But are they really?

We pit defenseless, uncoordinated individual action against a massive integrated system with relatively unlimited resources which have been pillaged from the American people. We teach people to focus on the effects that they see and feel while ignoring hidden root causes. We should not be surprised when our problems are not solved and people feel defeated.

In common language today, if we hear that a person is apathetic, we understand that they just don't care. But more than that, we are conveying the idea that they don't care about something that they *should* care about. So before we can call the American people apathetic, we need to identify what it is that the individual American citizen should care about.

In simplest terms, it is the right and responsibility of each individual to defend his life, liberty and property. Furthermore *just* government is established to assist the individual in defending his life, liberty and property. In such a system, stealing in all its forms would be illegal and would be punished, preferably by restitution whenever possible. Every individual would either be the recipient of charity, or would exercise his liberty to be productive. He would care for his property and produce that which first sustains his own life and then leads to abundance and prosperity, so that he has enough to share with others if he so chooses.

The one who produces would learn to cooperate with others and would become a good steward and an efficient user of resources. The one who receives charity would learn to do what he or she could in exchange for the help that they would gratefully receive.

For a person to be disinterested in certain things is called preference, not apathy, and is completely acceptable. We accuse people of being apathetic about things they should not even have to think about, much less care deeply about.

This may seem trivial at first, but the only thing that we need the individual American citizen to care about is that life, liberty and property will be defended and stealing will not be tolerated, including when government and favored business are the thieves.

Whether wealthy or poor, a person's self interest, beginning with hunger, will drive him to action.[3] If stealing is not an option, then the individual will become a productive and responsible member of society or be the recipient of private charity.

All government depends on resources confiscated from producers for its very existence. Therefore, in a system where life, liberty and property are defended, government would necessarily be small and limited.

Our large, intrusive, destructive government does not exist because the American people are apathetic. Our large, intrusive, destructive government exists because the people have been deceived and robbed. It exists because we have unwittingly permitted legal plunder.

I am one of many people who are rationally disinterested in our national three-ring circus called politics. I don't know anyone who is apathetic about knowingly being robbed.

The American people are in many ways deceived and may be resigned to defeat, but I refuse to believe they are apathetic.

2.3 People Eat Food and Use Things

Production and Liberty cannot be separated for long. Those who give up industry and agriculture plant seeds of poverty and oppression.

The idea that *people eat food and use things* may seem like a simple, pointless concept, but it is a critical element in understanding how wealth is transferred, how the middle class is wiped out and how nations fall. In fact, starting here in thought will often quickly illuminate and

---

3 "For even when we were with you, we used to give you this order: if anyone is not willing to work, then he is not to eat, either." (2 Thessalonians 3:10, NASB95) and "A worker's appetite works for him, For his hunger urges him on." (Proverbs 16:26, NASB95)

clarify otherwise confusing issues. Please test this idea to see if it can be profitable for you in your thoughts and conversations.

Our culture and daily life is filled with categories and labels that are designed to explain how people are different from one another. We are taught to think about all of our problems in terms of divisions between groups. "Woe is me! Those people are *different*! I lost my job and it's all their fault!"

It is true that there are differences between people, but diversity is good not bad. In a free society diverse people will associate based on coordination and preference.

Imagine a blacksmith who dislikes farming and a farmer who doesn't like to do the work of a blacksmith. Even though they would not trade jobs, the blacksmith eats corn and the farmer's horse needs to be shod. When they have spare time they both like to fish. In the market they coordinate their diverse interest, skills, labor and property. In recreation they enjoy their profits and common interests by exercising their liberty and freedom of association, based on preference.

Today we are conditioned to divide people into categories based on race, sex, age, religion, occupation, income, and of course the various political categories. Once divided, we are taught that the other group is the cause of some problem we have. Of course much could be written about the error of lumping people together in groups, but the purpose of this chapter is much less ambitious. The objective of *Know Stealing* is to correctly identify the functional causes of the problems we face today so that we can find real solutions. One critical piece of the puzzle is to set aside differences and look for things people have in common.

The subtitle of *Know Stealing* is *"solutions for people who eat food and use things."* Regardless of any and all other categories, if you are a living person, I know for certain that you eat food and use things.

We all eat food and use things; food and things must be produced.

Production is the fruit of labor and property; labor and property belong to individuals.

Individuals have rights according to justice; property rights must be respected so that people have the opportunity to be productive.

Under those conditions we can prosper together. During a recent political campaign I often made the following observation:

"Many of us notice that people depend on production. People eat food and use things. Food and things must be produced. Government produces nothing and unlawful government wastes much. Since people depend on production and unlawful government interferes with production, there is

no way that such government has any solutions for us. We must remember that every promise made today by a government official has to be kept by a producer. There is no other way."

To be clear, just and limited government is healthy and valuable. However just and limited government still doesn't produce anything, doesn't participate in the market, and doesn't steal from citizens or otherwise transfer wealth. Just government is a partner in defending life, liberty and property.

You may have noticed that some form of the word production occurs six times in the preceding quote. Production is the just or righteous mixture of life, liberty and property combined in a way that the output is more valuable than the input.

There is no way that we can even understand our problems, much less find meaningful solutions, unless we understand the massive degree to which people depend on production, every minute of every day. In fact, everything we do or use depends on production. Those who believe there is a Creator would consider creation itself to be the result of production. However, setting aside the notion of a Creator and observing things as they are, it is clear, for example, that there is a productive exchange of carbon dioxide and oxygen between plants and animals. Even our thoughts depend on production. Please consider the following logical progression:

If a person doesn't *eat*, he *dies*.

If a person is *dead*, he doesn't *think*.[4]

Therefore *thought* relies on *food*.

Food must be produced.

Restated, *thought* relies on *food*, which must be *produced*.

Therefore *thought* relies on *production*.

Since thought relies on production, then clearly everything we do or use relies on production.

Not only is it certain that people depend on production, but we will observe that power comes from production. We will also discover that authority is power which is primarily distributed through labor, property and production. Authority is the power to act, not the right to

4 That is, temporally speaking, a dead person doesn't think.

act. The importance of understanding the source, nature and limits of authority cannot be overstated. A clear and correct view of authority is essential to understanding life and liberty.

Once again, the subtitle of *Know Stealing* is *"solutions for people who eat food and use things."* Eating food and using things is something that every living person has in common. People depend on production for everything from their basic needs to their most extravagant wants. In the chapter titled *Production and the Prodigal Son* we observe the firm relationship between physical and spiritual wants and needs.

Consider Matthew 6. Jesus tells us not to worry about food and things, but He closes by noting that God knows we need them. People eat food and use things because God organized creation that way.

"For this reason I say to you, do not be worried about your life, as to what you will eat or what you will drink; nor for your body, as to what you will put on. Is not life more than food, and the body more than clothing?" (Matthew 6:25, NASB95)

"For the Gentiles eagerly seek all these things; for your heavenly Father knows that you need all these things." (Matthew 6:32, NASB95)

We are not to worry about these things, but we are to work. Based on Scripture, according to Jesus, God the Son and God the Father are workers.

"But He answered them, "My Father is working until now, and I Myself am working." (John 5:17, NASB95)

"For even when we were with you, we used to give you this order: if anyone is not willing to work, then he is not to eat, either." (2 Thessalonians 3:10, NASB95)

Since our most pressing needs, our most distant dreams and the force of authority all depend on production, we will think in terms of production while considering the problems we face as a society. This is a powerful key to understanding. *In fact, as we continue developing our framework for analyzing our problems and looking for real solutions, you will see that every problem can be significantly answered in terms of production.*

Much more could be said about eating food and using things, but after all this is just one piece of the puzzle.

2.4 Turning Dreams into Stories

Those who value leisure above liberty will lose both.

Sometimes it helps to think about what we are giving up. We have already established that people eat food and use things. It turns out these very same people also have hopes, dreams and desires.

A person who has been cold and hungry all of his life is likely to dream of things like a meal every day or a pair of shoes. On the other hand, a person who has plenty of food, clothes and shelter may dream about cars, houses, vacations and exciting things to do.

But all people dream of something.

Some are very creative thinkers, having imaginations illuminated with goals and desires far beyond their present conditions. But most people dream of something that is just a little better than today. Their vision ends in the shadows bordering their present circumstances. Their hope is small.

We fail to dream of better things because we are so busy, so debt burdened, so burned out, so stressed and confused about what is happening to us that better dreams don't have a chance to enter our minds.

The practical and essential knowledge in this book has the power to restore our hope and help us turn dreams into stories. When dreams become stories, new and better dreams take their place. Hope increases and new opportunities in life are discovered, cherished and pursued.

When people are able to live free, their *liberty under justice leads to production, which leads to abundance, which leads to prosperity.* Prosperity means that most needs are met and our opportunities abound. When people have abundance and prosperity, they begin to dream, not just the kinds of dreams that we dream today, but better dreams of better things.

The hungry man would count it progress and blessing to have the opportunity to produce food for himself and his family. After they are fed, perhaps the new dream is of a home.

I suspect our society is currently filled with dreams of a stable home and family that is whole, close, supportive and prospering. Families are prospering when they have savings and no debt. Imagine that stable, prosperous families were not dreams but instead were the typical result for hardworking people. With essential knowledge added to hard work, this can be the case again.

Imagine a secure retirement being a measurable reality based on real property, rather than a precarious or lost dream based on paper promises from Social Security, a stock portfolio or increasingly worthless dollars.

Think for a moment. What are your dreams?

Some of us dream of fishing. If you save enough to go fishing, but the purchasing power of your savings are taken away, then your fishing trip is stolen. If you have to sell your boat to pay taxes, your boat and labor are stolen. If your dream is a quiet vacation, but your profit is confiscated, your vacation is stolen.

Suppose your dream is to spend peaceful time with family. A society that mocks respect and hard work will cause relationships to be damaged. Because our labor is taxed and wasted, we have to work more so that we lose time with our spouse, children, parents and friends. We lose downtime for ourselves. We are robbed of the beautiful things we dream of and work for in life.

Given the opportunity, our hard work and sacrifice would have already turned many of our dreams into stories of things already done. When dreams of the past are realized, new dreams and new plans fill our imagination, and guide our labor, thoughts and time. This book explains exactly why many of our dreams and plans are not yet stories, and what each of us can do about it.

Remember that stolen dreams are stolen labor, profits, wealth. The thief is enjoying your savings, your retirement and he is fishing in your boat. He is enjoying your dream.

Let's pull our dreams off the shelf and learn to dream boldly again. It is time that we armed ourselves with knowledge and once again dream the American Dream. The opportunity to prosper is our heritage and our right and we are duty bound to defend it.

2.5 Stealing Defined

The title of this book is intended to convey two important ideas. The first idea is *no stealing* because stealing will utterly destroy the liberty and prosperity of any society. The second idea is *know stealing*, which is to say we must have a clear understanding of stealing and the forms it takes in order to recognize and stop it.

Most people would agree that stealing is wrong and should not be allowed. However sometimes what one person would call theft another person would call acceptable, or perhaps even say the action is smart and sophisticated. For this reason we need to define the term. Once we have a clear definition of stealing, we will need to look for places where theft is occurring, often without being noticed. This search for hidden theft will be developed throughout the book.

Our working definition for Steal: To take away or withhold without right or permission.

Two Boys and a Ball

Let's analyze our definition by considering an example beginning with two eight year old boys. Suppose Joe and Steve are playing with Joe's ball.

Clearly, if Steve takes Joe's ball, then that would be stealing.

If Steve throws Joe's ball into a fire so that it burns up, that would also be stealing. This is important because stealing occurs whenever a person is deprived of something that is rightfully his, including the *opportunity* to produce things of value. Even though Steve does not have the ball, it was still stolen from Joe and Steve did the stealing. Some might incorrectly say that Steve is not a thief since he did not get any benefit from the ball.

But maybe there were indirect benefits for Steve. Steve may have a closet full of balls such that his gain was simply the satisfaction of depriving Joe of also having a ball. This would be theft from something like pride or envy.

Or maybe Steve rents his ball to the boys in the community and he did not want Joe as a competitor. This would be theft based on something like greed.

If Steve did not intend for Joe to be deprived of his ball, then Steve would have taken responsibility for Joe's loss and replaced Joe's ball. This would be an accident followed by restitution, which is good.

Finally, it could have been burned up by Steve just out of meanness. This is theft based on something like bitterness, envy and disrespect.

Permission

Consider the idea of permission. Suppose Joe gives Steve permission to take his ball.

If Joe gave Steve the ball willingly with no threat of force involved, then it would be a gift from Joe to Steve. However, if Joe was placed under any form of unjust pressure that would only be relieved if he gave Steve his ball, then it is theft. In other words, if Joe gave Steve the ball to keep Steve from beating him up or burning the only ball on the playground, then that is not permission. It is coercion and theft.

Property Rights and Authority

Now we need to think about Joe's right to own the ball. Suppose Joe worked raking leaves to earn the money tokens to purchase the ball. Clearly he has the right of ownership of the ball. But what if we bring Dad into the picture?

We will look at this in terms of authority, property and production. In this relationship Dad is the producer and provider. For this reason, as a boy who eats food and uses things, Joe is perpetually in his Dad's debt. This means that while Joe is a dependent child, Dad can always call in a payment against Joe's account. Therefore, as producer and provider, Dad has an economic right to take young Joe's ball at any time, for any reason. Dad also has the authority or power to take Joe's ball. According to Scripture, children are to honor their father and mother, which is a law of God. Violating just law is a basis for the use of force in response, which could then be a basis for taking Joe's ball. Since the father is responsible to nurture and teach his son good lessons, taking Joe's ball without a good cause will be a counterproductive lesson and will damage their relationship.

Now, suppose Joe maliciously threw his ball through the window of the house. In this case, Joe has put his ownership of the ball in jeopardy. His dad is the authority who could remove the ball from his possession and should cause him to be accountable for the broken window. Joe has in effect stolen the window, which is a violation of just law. Joe should have to pay for and help replace the window, after which his ownership of the ball would be secure again. Only if he made a habit of breaking windows would he permanently lose his ball under the power of Dad's authority according to the standard of just law, based on theft and failing to honor his parents. Repeated offenses would indicate willingness to steal and to dishonor (withhold honor from) his parents.

If it was an accident and Joe had a good attitude about his responsibility in this, his Dad might graciously decide to pay the price for Joe. Notice that ownership of the ball is not necessarily forfeit by the accident, but property equal to at least the value of the replacement of the window is forfeit by either Joe, or perhaps his Dad. He may have cost himself the value of fifty balls. In any case, someone has to pay the full price for the window. Therefore we can easily see why exacting the price of Joe's ball would be more than just, since he will remain a debtor with regard to the window. More can be said and the ideas will be further communicated as the chapters unfold.

Recap

So far we have determined that stealing is when something is taken away or withheld from its rightful owner, regardless of whether the theft was accidental or the thief is benefited. In addition we see that sometimes a thief is benefited in ways that are indirect and difficult to see. We also see that a dependent is subject to his provider as a simple matter of accounting and we begin to see that authority should exercise power according to the standard of just law. Finally we see that we can forfeit our own property rights by certain actions we take, as a matter of accounting under just law.

Government as Parent

Some people believe that government has the authority and the right to take property from its citizens. Some people would even look at government as being like the parent and citizens like the child. Let's begin by considering the parent/child analogy, but instead of thinking of the government as being like the dad, let's think of the dad being like government. Let's talk about dad as though he were government.

First of all, since people create government, the dad would be created by the son and his fellows. The son would be creating the dad in order to defend each and every person's individual right to life, liberty and property. Of course it's absurd to think of the son creating the father... *Our analogy has already failed, but, with a hat tip to irrational thought, we press on!*

Secondly, since government produces nothing, the dad would not be the provider and teacher. Dad would be completely dependent on the labor, property and production of the son for everything.

Because the son has to actually produce in order to survive, the son is the one who understands how things actually work and therefore he is the one who is the teacher.

We know the real dad should love his son and desire to see his son succeed. The real dad should sacrifice himself for the benefit of his son. *However, if dad were like government, then he would consume his son to benefit himself and his associates.*

Now some might still say that government has a right and authority to take the property of its citizens in order to benefit its citizens. This argument falls apart for any action performed by government that goes beyond its proper role, which is to be a partner in defending the life, liberty and property of the individual. This is true for two reasons.

First, since people depend on production and government produces nothing and wastes much, then when government does anything that is in conflict with natural law or inappropriately depends on human nature, it can only be causing loss and harm to its citizens. This is a logical reality.

Secondly, the reality of government intervention is that some men in the society are benefited, by theft, at the expense of other men. In other words, to think in terms of the absurd parent analogy, a government that loves its citizens like a father loves his children, would not forcefully benefit some citizens (children) at the expense of other citizens (children). But this is what unlawful (unjust) government always does. Since recognizing unlawful government is essential, one of the goals of *Know Stealing* is to help clearly identify unlawful government.

The Role of Government

Lawful government is measured by how well it abides by its prime directive. The prime directive of government in the United States of America is expressed as follows: Defense of individual Life, Liberty and Property.

Life and liberty cannot be separated. Without life, liberty has no meaning. Our first property is our own person, therefore liberty and property cannot be separated. All additional property is acquired and maintained through the exercise of life and liberty. Just law will always be opposed to theft, which prevents property from being stolen. Therefore, *liberty encompasses life, liberty and property.*

Consider the following paraphrase from the Declaration of Independence:

"[people are] endowed by their Creator with certain unalienable Rights… among these are Life, Liberty and the pursuit of Happiness. … To secure these rights, Governments are instituted among Men, deriving their just powers from the consent of the governed… [and government's] foundation [must be laid] on such principles and [have its powers organized] in such form, as to [the People] shall seem most likely to effect their [Individual] Safety and Happiness."

The Declaration of Independence is about individual liberty and the role of government as a partner or agent organized to assist in defending individual liberty. Why would the people of a nation form a government for any other reason?

Consider the US Constitution:

From the Preamble: "*secure the blessings of liberty to ourselves and our posterity*"

From Amendment 5: "*nor be deprived of life, liberty, or property, without due process of law.*"

Consider the CONSTITUTION OF THE STATE OF GEORGIA:

From the Preamble: "*promote the interest and happiness of the citizen and of the family, and transmit to posterity the enjoyment of liberty,*"

ARTICLE 1, BILL OF RIGHTS, SECTION 1, RIGHTS OF PERSONS

Paragraph 1: Life, liberty, and property. No person shall be deprived of life, liberty, or property except by due process of law.

The Declaration of Independence, the preamble to the US Constitution, the Fifth Amendment, the preamble to the Georgia Constitution and Article One, Section One of the Georgia Constitution are all about defending the life, liberty and property of the individual.

Not so clearly seen is the reality that those who were forming these guiding documents wanted far greater powers for government, far fewer rights for people, and more wealth transfers for those favored by government. The sad fact is that these kinds of powers have been seized for most of human history, even during the settlement of this continent beginning in at least 1607. The manipulators skilled in transferring wealth have been very successful, but their success does not have to continue.

Knowledge Is Required

Our founders knew defending Life, Liberty and Property is dangerous and difficult work.

"Government is not reason. It is not eloquence. It is force. Like fire, government is a dangerous servant and a fearful master." — George Washington

"If a nation expects to be ignorant and free in a state of civilization, it expects what never was and never will be." — Thomas Jefferson

"All the perplexities, confusion and distress in America arise, not from defects in their Constitution or Confederation, not from want of honor or virtue, so much as from the downright ignorance of the nature of coin, credit and circulation." — John Adams

John Adams made a point that indirectly explains the problem. When we don't understand how stealing is done, we don't know how to defend against it. When we don't understand the nature of production, authority, power, justice, law and money, we are deceived into supporting the institutions, which crush good things in society.

We must always remember that people depend on production. People eat food and use things. Food and things must be produced. Government produces nothing and wastes much. Every promise made by a government official has to be kept by a producer.

Government is charged with the prime directive of defending the life, liberty and property of all citizens. This cannot be accomplished by taking positive actions to "make things happen," because positive actions by government consume resources which can only be confiscated from individuals. Confiscation of life, liberty and property by force to fuel positive government action violates the prime directive of our government and is therefore unjust and unlawful. Only by defending property rights can government fulfill the prime directive. Instead our government defends wealth transfers and "entitlement rights." This must end.

To test the idea that power comes from the control of production, try to identify and explain any other source of temporal power in this world. The only way for government to have the power to act is by confiscating production from individuals. Production is the fruit of life (in the form of labor), liberty and property. *Therefore our government steals individual life, liberty and property.*

For those who may wonder if the government really steals from productive citizens, the proof is easy.

Inflation takes away purchasing power that has been saved over a lifetime of work. Inflation eventually destroys the purchasing power of financial instruments, like stocks or insurance policies, which are denominated in an inflated currency.

The Central Banking System forces individuals and small business into debt, so that today few people really own any property. The banks hold title to nearly everything. In 1910, 70% of all business expansion was self-funded because people had savings. The Federal Reserve System was established in 1913 and now nearly everyone has debt. This is not a coincidence.

Home foreclosures are caused by government intervention and the process is making favored business wealthy through bailouts. The debt based system forces people to pay interest on their own purchasing power[5], but few people recognize this is the case, as noted by the John Adams quote above.

Farms and factories are bankrupt, yet the entire economy depends on these essential wealth-producing properties. Only by being robbed can an entire class of producers that are the foundation of an economy fail, while dependent sectors become wealthy. Until people stop eating food and using things, farms and factories are essential to wealth production. The product of our banks is deceptive wealth transfer. Until banks start producing something of value, they can only plunder producers. Banks having the legal privilege to create money tokens from thin air contribute nothing to wealth production.

And these examples are before getting into anything controversial like which actions of government are just and lawful.

Finally, remember that if we pay for a product and the seller doesn't deliver, we are entitled to get our money tokens back. Otherwise the seller is guilty of theft by taking. We have paid a high price for government to defend our life, liberty and property. But someone has stolen a large part of our life, liberty and property. Regardless of who is the thief, government has not done its job. The thieves should pay restitution under law, whoever they are. We need a refund.

Ten Commandments

We are defining stealing in this chapter. Our working definition for Steal is *to take away or withhold without right or permission.*

---

5 Purchasing power, money, money tokens

This will be further developed in the following chapter titled *One Law*, but to close out our definition chapter I want to make two observations about the Ten Commandments from the Bible.

1. Thou shalt have no other gods before me.
2. Thou shalt not make unto thee any graven image
3. Thou shalt not take the name of the LORD thy God in vain
4. Remember the Sabbath day, to keep it holy.
5. Honour thy father and thy mother
6. Thou shalt not kill.
7. Thou shalt not commit adultery.
8. Thou shalt not steal.
9. Thou shalt not bear false witness against thy neighbour.
10. Thou shalt not covet

At least the eighth and tenth commandments would make no sense unless people have a right to own private property.

A violation of any of the last six commandments involves withholding or taking something away from another person. In addition to withholding honor, dishonoring parents may lead to loss of property in any number of ways. The loss could be from something like lost production or fines and fees paid by parents on behalf of an unruly child. The last five commandments clearly involve theft or attitudes and thoughts which lead to theft.

Steal: To take away or withhold without right or permission.

Defining stealing is one more piece of the puzzle.

2.6 One Law

I will not waste time with statistics about how many laws there are in the United States or any of the other super-states around the world. We all know we have too many laws, regulations and rules. Instead I want us to think about the nature and purpose of law.

As you read this chapter, please remember that the goal is to identify one law that will satisfy everyone and provide a foundation for a healthy society. If the Bible and the common experience of many people are correct, then a person's conscience should support or reject the conclusion.

Law is a standard, not a force

One of the observations that we begin with is that authority is a force, not a standard. Next we observe that law is a standard, not a force.

We often incorrectly think of authority as a standard and law as a force. These are subtle ideas, which are developed later, but are worth mentioning here. For example we sometimes refer to the "force of law," but law is not capable of exerting any force. Law never takes an action. Instead, law is the standard that determines which actions are acceptable and often which actions are taken in response to lawless behavior.

In order for a body of law to be just it must be based on a consistent standard. Law must be applied in the same way to every person. Since our state and federal constitutions are obviously organized to defend the life, liberty and property of the individual, the boundaries of law are easy for us to set.

No person or entity may infringe on the life, liberty or property of another person.

When the standard of law is to defend the life, liberty and property of the individual, then a lawbreaker is one who violates another person's rights. Therefore the lawbreaker forfeits his rights to a degree relative to his violation of another person's rights. The lawbreaker has used force or deception to violate the rights of another person. Therefore the power of authority is able to satisfy justice by using force in response.

The penalty for violating another person's rights should be restitution whenever possible. Restitution may be to return the property that was taken, or it may be to return the property along with a penalty. In some cases, like murder or some forms of abuse, the thing that was taken, cannot be replaced. In certain of these cases the lawbreaker forfeits his life.

Before we get into the idea of the origin and definition of law, since our federal, state and local laws originate from definite places with specific jurisdictions, at the very minimum there must be a single guiding standard for any laws from a common source. In other words, there should never be conflict between any two laws from the same source, like a federal, state or local government.

It turns out that what we call law, which is then the basis for rules and regulations, often is unjust, treats people differently and is in conflict with itself. Since law is supposed to be just, impartial and based on a single standard, what we call law in modern society is an utter disaster and disgrace. In fact, much of the writing in the legal books is lies, not laws. We accept these disastrous standard-violating lies in part because we wrongly believe that authority is a standard.

Law and Scripture

The Bible tells us that if we love God and people then we will not be in violation of God's Law. It also states that the wicked are lawless and those who keep the law strive with the wicked. This information is helpful because it leads us toward a method of testing all law.

Consider the following Bible verses:

"In everything, therefore, treat people the same way you want them to treat you, for this is the Law and the Prophets." (Matthew 7:12, NASB95)

The Law is intended to remind people how to treat each other right. We know what is right by thinking of what we would want for ourselves. In addition, we are told that the Law of God is made known in the heart and conscience of people. In fact, it is God's nature that is the standard for law. A law is an expression of a particular assessment and application of actions that are consistent with God's nature. This includes assessing the violation and applying punishment.

"And He said to him, " 'You shall love the Lord your God with all your heart, and with all your soul, and with all your mind.' "This is the great and foremost commandment. "The second is like it, 'You shall love your neighbor as yourself.' "On these two commandments depend the whole Law and the Prophets." (Matthew 22:37–40, NASB95)

If we love God and love people, our thoughts and actions will not violate God's law.

"Owe nothing to anyone except to love one another; for he who loves his neighbor has fulfilled the law. For this, "You shall not commit adultery, You shall not murder, You shall not steal, You shall not covet," and if there

is any other commandment, it is summed up in this saying, "You shall love your neighbor as yourself." Love does no wrong to a neighbor; therefore love is the fulfillment of the law." (Romans 13:8–10, NASB95)

Because love does no wrong to another person, love is the fulfillment of the law.

"For the whole Law is fulfilled in one word, in the statement, "You shall love your neighbor as yourself." (Galatians 5:14, NASB95)

Again love fulfills the Law.

"But the fruit of the Spirit is love, joy, peace, patience, kindness, goodness, faithfulness, gentleness, self-control; against such things there is no law." (Galatians 5:22–23, NASB95)

If there is something called law that is against any of these things, then it is unlawful in itself. For example, arresting people for flying kites, selling lemonade, or directing traffic when a light is out is wrong[6]. Since the Bible teaches that God's law is known in our conscience, this passage suggests that law will not be contrary to our conscience. Something that claims to be law, yet is contrary to the human sense of justice, is actually unlawful.

"If, however, you are fulfilling the royal law according to the Scripture, "You shall love your neighbor as yourself," you are doing well. But if you show partiality, you are committing sin and are convicted by the law as transgressors." (James 2:8–9, NASB95)

This makes it clear that there is to be no partiality in anything, especially law. It also indicates that, when showing partiality, law is transgressed and the transgressors are convicted, but the conviction happens with no human official or court involved. This is likely a good example of the concepts in Galatians 6:7 or Romans 2:5.

6 These things have actually happened...

"Those who forsake the law praise the wicked, But those who keep the law strive with them. Evil men do not understand justice, But those who seek the Lord understand all things." (Proverbs 28:4–5, NASB95)

Lawless people praise other lawless people. ***People who want to keep the law will strive with those who do not.*** This also states that evil men do not understand justice.

This passage is particularly important. It indicates that a simple and clear test which will identify those who really desire to abide by the standard of law, and expose those who do not. The Bible clearly states that love is the fulfillment of the Law of God. The Law of God is recorded in detail in the Bible and also recorded in the conscience of each person.

But is there a way to identify a standard that will consistently expose lawless behavior for those who reject the Law of God as a standard?

Rejecting Bad Law

There are so many more things to say about law, but for the present purpose a focused and limited commentary will be more valuable.

The only way for the king or government to issue an unlawful decree and call it law is for the people to be confused about the nature of authority and the nature of law. When the people misunderstand authority and law, those who possess authority and make the laws will plunder the people.

Logically, since by definition those who abide by the law of God will do no harm to their neighbor, if people forget or violate the law of God then they are necessarily doing harm to their neighbor. People are either blessed or harmed based on sowing and reaping. Therefore if we sow ignorance we will reap destruction. If we sow lawlessness we will store up wrath for ourselves and will not reap blessings for ourselves or our children.

"My people are destroyed for lack of knowledge. Because you have rejected knowledge, I also will reject you from being My priest. Since you have forgotten the law of your God, I also will forget your children." (Hosea 4:6, NASB95)

On the other hand, if people have a clear understanding of the nature of authority and the nature of law, then they will recognize unlawful decrees and reject them. Or perhaps it would be more correct to say that with knowledge, the society would be organized in such a way that no wise ruler would dare to issue an unlawful decree. If a ruler behaved oppressively in a well-balanced society, the people would simply reject his decrees and replace him as ruler.

One Law for All

In the previous chapter we observed that at least the last six of the Ten Commandments involve stealing. We also know that people depend on production and production is the fruit of labor and property. When the Bible says that love does no wrong to a neighbor, this has to include honoring property rights. We cannot steal from a neighbor and claim to be loving. Of course the Eighth Commandment is "You shall not steal."

Suppose on the next July 4th in the United States we wiped the books clean of all laws, rules, regulations, executive orders or any other thing that might be called law, except the US Constitution. Once that was done, imagine that we have a ceremony where we write our first and only additional law on a parchment: No Stealing.

After that, we would amend the Constitution in every place that violated this law.

Would this serve us well, or fail the test? Let's think about that.

Can One Law Do The Job?

If someone murders, he steals a life.

If someone sexually assaults, he steals physically, emotionally and he steals time and health during the healing process. He also steals from relationship. Many books have been written which describe various aspects of the theft involved in such an act.

Adultery implies a violation of trust, which involves at least stealing things like love, joy and peace, and likely including theft of productivity and property.

If a property owner dumps chemicals in a stream or on the ground, he steals from the quality and health of the property he affects, especially that of his neighbor.

If a manufacturer is dumping waste when he should be cleaning up, he steals profits from the responsible producer who is a good steward of his manufacturing process.

If an unruly child disrupts a classroom, he is stealing from the teacher and other students. If his behavior is bad enough that his parents have to come and deal with the behavior, he is stealing their honor and their time and resources by wasting them.

Libel or slander is bearing false witness and steals a person's honor and good name.

Physical assault would steal a person's time, thoughts, sense of security, ability to work to some degree, cost of medical care, and general health for some period of time.

Of course stealing property would be stealing.

False advertising of a product would be stealing. In fact, false advertising would be a case of employing differing weights and/or differing measures in order to steal. If a quantity or value of a product is represented at a value higher than it actually is, then something of too great a value would be exchanged for the product.

Selling company stock worth $10 at a price of $100 would be fraud and therefore stealing. Of course a person could choose to exchange $100 for the stock because he believes that the company stock will be worth more than that in the future. However, when we study the nature of production we realize that no physical asset will produce beyond a certain margin of profit in a given year. This means that the only way for the stock with an underlying physical value of $10 to eventually sell for greater than the $100 purchase price is to once again misrepresent the value of the company stock. The purchaser is hoping for another opportunity to employ differing weights or differing measures in marketing his stock to the next purchaser. He is hoping to steal.

Alexander Hamilton employed differing weights and differing measures in order to confuse the people and corrupt legislature. Alexander Hamilton was permitted to violate our law against No Stealing.

Inflation of the money supply steals purchasing power. Therefore bills of credit, paper money, token money, debased currency or diluted commodities are all deceptive forms of stealing.

Unpaid debts are also stealing, provided the debts are based on genuine exchanges of value that remain out of balance.

When government regulation prevents a farmer from producing whatever he chooses on his property, his freedom of choice is taken away. If he is forced to leave land fallow, his opportunity to produce this year's crop is taken away. If the government pays the farmer to not grow food, other producers bear the cost of the payments directly and in terms of higher prices for food. Notice the phrase "other producers bear the cost." If a person consumes more than he produces, he will eventually run out of stuff, unless producers give gifts or are robbed to replenish the food and things used by Mr. Consume-more-than-I-produce.

Since people depend on production, the bills can only be paid by people who are net productive. Everything else is wealth transfer.

Tariffs

One of the important ideas to get settled in our minds is that in an honest system of exchange, producers exchange with producers. Which producer will give up what he has worked hard to produce in exchange for empty promises? None that I know. Producers value their life, liberty and property.

However, when a producer is trained to believe *there is no puzzle* or that certain harmful actions are actually to his benefit, then he will trade for an intermediary like paper money or subsidies. Paper money, subsidies and the system that enables them will always eventually crush producers and then overall production.

Before I explain the next point, remember that I am for strong and prosperous American citizens. I am for genuine wealth producing jobs here in the USA. I stand for all of the kinds of honest actions and choices that will cause Americans to prosper. With that in mind, another form of theft is the tariff.

When a tariff is imposed, inefficient local businesses are able to charge local buyers higher prices. That is a case of government enabled stealing. We are taught to think that the tariff protects local jobs, but that is only the case in a false economy driven by paper based wealth transfer and market manipulation. In an honest system of exchange, no matter how cheap an imported good is, unless the local people produce something of value to exchange for the cheap goods, there will be no local market for the cheap goods. The market will coordinate to produce things of value that can be exchanged in complex ways. With tariffs, favored business prospers at the expense of other people. With free trade in an honest system of exchange, the hardworking people prosper, and along with them even the poorest in the society are better off. I, Pencil written in 1958 by Leonard E. Read is a great short essay explaining the wonders of market coordination.

Implications of One Law

If our one law was ***No Stealing*** and the members of a society were able to ***Know Stealing*** when they saw it, then there would be no room for partiality and the society would prosper.

In the following chapters we will discover that because of the natural order of things, having one law against stealing would lead to ***a healthy balance of power*** in society.

3. Money

Said the tyrant to his son,
We will rob the people with their dictionary.

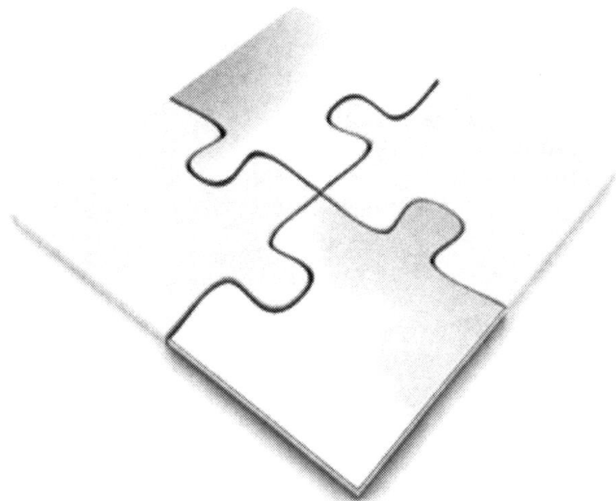

3.1 Words Have Meaning

Poorly defined words are shackles and chains.

I had planned to drop this chapter, but discovered that it was a required step in communicating part of our problem. Words are powerful, for good or for evil. Poorly defined words are shackles and chains.

Words have meaning, but the meaning of some words is so varied and distorted that the word becomes an effective tool of oppression. *Authority*, *Judgment*, *Justice*, *Law* and *Money* are all words that are misunderstood and misused in ways that unlawfully rule people and capture wealth.

When buying gasoline or milk, do people want the unit of measure to be correct and unchanging? Is an estimate good enough? Would people mind if the gallon or liter is smaller by a tiny percentage from one week to the next, so that grandpa's gallon or liter was larger? Would people mind if a gallon or liter gets smaller, but keeps the old price?

Units of measure must be precise, consistent and unchanging.

When paid for work, or crops or other production, do people expect a precise accounting of time and value?

Exchange requires a proper accounting based on weights and measures.

Does the percentage of water in a mixture matter?

Would a person drink a glass of battery acid and a glass of tea, since they both contain water...?

Do people always refuse to drink water mixed with acid? Maybe some people like grapefruit juice. Grapefruit juice includes water and citric acid, but that is different than water and battery acid.

Little things matter. Precise ingredients matter.

If your mom made your favorite chocolate chip cookies, but added just a little dog manure, would you care about that tiny added ingredient?

Brown and soft isn't good enough. People expect <u>all</u> the chips to be chocolate.

The *meaning* mixed into words is like weights, measures and ingredients. Definitions are like recipes or formulas. The *meaning* we mix into our words can cook up good cookies or poison. The *meaning* mixed into our words can *secure* individual life, liberty and property or *steal* individual life, liberty and property.

"No one sues righteously and no one pleads honestly. They trust in confusion and speak lies; They conceive mischief and bring forth iniquity." (Isaiah 59:4, NASB95)

"When words are many, sin is not absent, but he who holds his tongue is wise." (Proverbs 10:19, NIV84)

Definitions

Dictionary and socially acceptable definitions of words may be distorted and confused, in whole or in part. Definitions may have added ingredients that turn our favorite cookies into repulsive garbage. The following definitions for the words in the following table are quoted in their entirety for easy reference.

Remember that words are like the end-result of a recipe.

The phrase "*Mom's chocolate chip cookies*" defines for us the specific cookies that mom makes the same way every time. We don't talk about the ingredients or the process because we are thinking of the end-result.

If mom made *chocolate chip cookies* differently every time, then our reference to "*Mom's chocolate chip cookies*" would be a way to describe a vaguely common, yet always uncertain end result. Sometimes they are good, sometimes they are bad and how they were made is anybody's guess.

We haven't paid attention to the meaning of a few specific words for several hundred years. Money is an important example. Our money began by *claiming* to be *Mom's loving chocolate chip cookies*, but soon became cookies with a little dog manure mixed in. Now the government serves up 100% pure dog manure cookies and we barely even notice.

Recipe for Security or Disaster

The following definitions and thesaurus entries are important to your job, savings and retirement.

Words like these are either *valuable* or *costly* to a free society. If these definitions are commonly known, productive citizens benefit. If these definitions are not commonly known, the government sanctioned thieves benefit.

Reading these definitions and thesaurus entries can be tiresome. However, understanding the ideas presented here is a *defense against words of plunder*.

Those who misunderstand will be plundered with these words.

There are at least three ways to use this chapter; for *detailed study*, for a *quick scan* or for *reference*. Scan and reference are probably most useful.

Remember this is a puzzle piece. Spend a little time here. It will be worthwhile and will help sharpen and clarify ideas that follow.

Two Choices

Understand these ideas; keep your life, liberty and property.

Misunderstand these ideas; continue being abused, pillaged and robbed.

Words To Review

The table below contains a list of words followed by the type of information included for each word. My comments about the definitions and thesaurus entries are set apart in a narrow box.

Precise	definition, synonyms
Imprecise	definition, synonyms
Thing	definition, synonyms
Money	definition, synonyms
Mint	definition, synonyms
Fortune	synonyms
Wealth	synonyms
Silver	definition, synonyms n/a, atomic weight
Gold	definition, synonyms, atomic weight
Metric System	definition, synonyms n/a
Meter	definition, synonyms n/a
Kilogram	definition, synonyms n/a

Precise

Definition of precise

pre•cise \pri-ˈsīs\ *adjective*

[Middle English, from Middle French *precis*, from Latin *praecisus*, past participle of *praecidere* to cut off, from *prae-* + *caedere* to cut] 15th century

1 : exactly or sharply defined or stated

2 : minutely exact

3 : strictly conforming to a pattern, standard, or convention

4 : distinguished from every other {at just that *precise* moment} ***synonym*** see CORRECT — pre•cise•ness *noun*[7]

The word *precise* requires a *distinguished standard*. For example, with lumber or leather, a precise cut in a location based on a unit of measure can be repeated. Without a unit of measure the cut is not precise. In terms of a standard, the cut is random. The cut cannot be repeated, except by preserving the original piece as the pattern, which then becomes the standard.

A Note

The following thesaurus entries are organized in subgroups headed by a number. Each group may contain *synonyms, related words, near antonyms* and *antonyms*.

Synonyms for precise

precise adjective

1 meeting the highest standard of accuracy <a machine which takes very precise measurements of brain tumors>

Synonyms accurate, close, delicate, exact, fine, hairline, mathematical, pinpoint, refined, rigorous, spot-on

Related Words correct, right, strict, true; definite, definitive; nice, subtle; careful, fastidious, finical, finicky, meticulous

Near Antonyms approximate, round; false, incorrect, untrue, wrong; careless, loose; indefinite, unclear, vague; doubtful, dubious, questionable, unreliable, untrustworthy

Antonyms coarse, imprecise, inaccurate, inexact, rough

2 being in agreement with the truth or a fact or a standard <gave very precise answers to the members of the investigative committee>

Synonyms accurate, bang on [chiefly British], dead-on, exact, good, on-target, precise, proper, right, so, spot-on, true, veracious

Related Words legitimate, logical, sound, valid; errorless, faultless, flawless, impeccable, inerrant, infallible, letter-perfect, perfect; rigorous, strict, stringent

Near Antonyms defective, faulty, flawed, imperfect

Antonyms false, improper, inaccurate, incorrect, inexact, off, untrue, wrong

3 being neither more nor less than a certain amount, number, or extent <gave him the precise amount that he owed him>

Synonyms exact, flat, precise, round

Near Antonyms approximate, comparative, near, relative; imprecise

4 following an original exactly <a precise translation of the original Greek>

Synonyms accurate, authentic, exact, precise, right, strict, true, veracious

Related Words lifelike, realistic; careful, conscientious, meticulous, punctilious, scrupulous; authoritative; bona fide, genuine, real, veridical

Near Antonyms careless, slack, slipshod, slovenly; erroneous, incorrect, invalid, off, unsound, untrue, untruthful, wrong

Antonyms corrupt, corrupted, false, imprecise, inaccurate, inauthentic, inexact, loose, unfaithful

5 of a particular or exact sort <at that precise moment the lights went out>

Synonyms concrete, distinct, especial, peculiar, precise, set, special, specific

Related Words lone, only, separate, single, sole, solitary; distinctive, exclusive, individual, unique; limited, restricted; differentiated, specialized; given, specified

Near Antonyms general, generalized, generic, nonexclusive, universal

Antonyms nonspecific[8]

7 Merriam-Webster, I. (2003). *Merriam-Webster's collegiate dictionary.* (Eleventh ed.). Springfield, Mass.: Merriam-Webster, Inc.

8 By permission. From Merriam-Webster's Collegiate Dictionary ©2011 by Merriam-Webster, Incorporated (www.merriam-webster.com)

Imprecise

When something is *imprecise* one can only guess at its weight, measure, ingredients or meaning.

Definition of imprecise

im•pre•cise \ˌim-pri-ˈsīs\ adjective

1805 : not precise : INEXACT, VAGUE {an *imprecise* estimate} — im•pre•cise•ly adverb — im•pre•cise•ness noun — im•pre•ci•sion \-ˈsi-zhən\ *noun*[9]

Synonyms for imprecise

imprecise adjective

not precisely correct <3.14 is an imprecise approximation of the value of pi>

Synonyms approximate, approximative, ballpark, imprecise, inaccurate, loose, squishy

Related Words erroneous, false, incorrect, off, wrong; general, indefinable, indefinite, indeterminate, indistinct, mushy, undefined, undetermined, unsettled, vague; faulty, flawed, mistaken; specious; distorted, fallacious, misleading; doubtful, dubious, questionable, uncertain; inconclusive, indecisive; debatable, disputable; invalidated, unconfirmed, unsubstantiated, unsupported

Near Antonyms certain, incontestable, indubitable, positive, sure, undeniable, unquestionable; correct, errorless, factual, right, sound, true, valid; clear-cut, decisive, definable, defined, definite; incontrovertible, indisputable, irrefutable; absolute, unqualified; confirmed, corroborated, determined, established, substantiated, supported, validated

Antonyms accurate, dead, dead-on, exact, precise, ultraprecise, veracious[10]

Thing

The word *Thing* is included because it is a good example of a word whose meaning is so broad that it means nothing in particular and everything, at the same time.

A word like *thing* is very useful when we understand that the meaning is never intended to be *precise*. An *imprecise* term that can be used for a variety of purposes is useful.

On the other hand, many of the problems that we face today are caused by using *imprecise* terms as though they are *precise*.

Definition of thing

thing \ˈthiŋ\ *noun*

[Middle English, from Old English, thing, assembly; akin to Old High German *ding* thing, assembly, Gothic *theihs* time] before 12th century

1 a : a matter of concern : AFFAIR {many *things* to do}

b *plural* : state of affairs in general or within a specified or implied sphere {*things* are improving}

c : a particular state of affairs : SITUATION {look at this *thing* another way}

d : EVENT, CIRCUMSTANCE {that shooting was a terrible *thing*}

2 a : DEED, ACT, ACCOMPLISHMENT {do great *things*}

b : a product of work or activity {likes to build *things*}

c : the aim of effort or activity {the *thing* is to get well}

3 a : a separate and distinct individual quality, fact, idea, or usually entity

b : the concrete entity as distinguished from its appearances

c : a spatial entity

d : an inanimate object distinguished from a living being

4 a *plural* : POSSESSIONS, EFFECTS {pack your *things*}

b : whatever may be possessed or owned or be the object of a right

c : an art of clothing {not a *thing* to wear}

d *plural* : equipment or utensils especially for a particular purpose {bring the tea *things*}

5 : an object or entity not precisely designated or capable of being designated {use this *thing*}

6 a : DETAIL, POINT {checks every little *thing*}

b : a material or substance of a specified kind {avoid fatty *things*}

7 a : a spoken or written observation or point

b : IDEA, NOTION {says the first *thing* he thinks of}

c : a piece of news or information {couldn't get a *thing* out of him}

8 : INDIVIDUAL {not a living *thing* in sight}

9 : the proper or fashionable way of

---

9 Merriam-Webster, I. (2003). *Merriam-Webster's collegiate dictionary.* (Eleventh ed.). Springfield, Mass.: Merriam-Webster, Inc.

10 By permission. From Merriam-Webster's Collegiate Dictionary ©2011 by Merriam-Webster, Incorporated (www.merriam-webster.com)

behaving, talking, or dressing — used with *the*

10 a : a mild obsession or phobia {has a *thing* about driving} *also* : the object of such an obsession or phobia

b : something (as an activity) that makes a strong appeal to the individual : FORTE, SPECIALTY {letting students do their own *thing* —*Newsweek*} {I think travelling is very much a novelist's *thing* —Philip Larkin}[11]

Synonyms for thing

thing *noun*

1 a member of the human race <you poor thing, you must be exhausted>

Synonyms baby, being, bird, bod [British], body, character, cookie (or cooky), creature, customer, devil, duck, egg, face, fish, guy, head, human being, individual, life, man, mortal, party, person, personage, scout, slob, sort, soul, specimen, stiff, thing, wight

Related Words hominid, homo, humanoid; brother, fellow, fellowman, neighbor; celebrity, personality, self, somebody

Near Antonyms animal, beast, beastie, brute, critter

2 one that has a real and independent existence <the thing to which the subject of the sentence refers>

Synonyms being, commodity, existent, individual, individuality, integer, object, reality, something, substance, thing

Related Words body, subject; material, matter, quantity, stuff

Near Antonyms nonentity

3 something done by someone <one of the things you can do is to help me clean up>

Synonyms act, deed, doing, exploit, feat, thing

Related Words accomplishment, achievement, attainment; adventure, experience; emprise, enterprise, initiative, undertaking; handiwork, performance, work; stunt, trick; activity, dealing; maneuver, measure, move, operation, procedure, proceeding, step, tactic; coaction

4 something material that can be perceived by the senses <can you hand me that thing over there?>

Synonyms thing

Related Words article, item, piece; being, entity, substance; commodity, good, ware; dingus, doohickey, thingamabob, thingamajig (or thingumajig), thingummy, whatchamacallit, whatnot; accessory (also accessary), accompaniment, bauble, curio; gaud, gewgaw (also geegaw), knickknack (also nicknack), novelty, ornamental, spangle, token, trinket

5 something produced by physical or intellectual effort <just the latest thing from her fertile imagination>

Synonyms affair, fruit, handiwork, labor, output, produce, production, thing, work, yield

Related Words article, commodity, entry, object; goods, line, merchandise, wares; handcraft, handicraft; aftereffect, aftermath, conclusion, consequence, corollary, development, effect, issue, outcome, result, resultant, sequel, sequence, upshot; by-product, derivative, offshoot, offspring, outgrowth, residual, side effect (also side reaction), spin-off

6 something that happens <the burglary was just one of those things that can happen anywhere>

Synonyms affair, circumstance, episode, hap, happening, incident, occasion, occurrence, thing

Related Words coincidence, co-occurrence, fluke, freak; landmark, milepost, milestone, page, phenomenon, turning point; adventure, experience, time; happenchance, happenstance; accident, crisis, emergency, juncture; achievement, deed, exploit, feat; news, tidings

7 something that one hopes or intends to accomplish <the important thing is that we get the project back on schedule>

Synonyms aim, ambition, aspiration, bourne (also bourn), design, dream, end, idea, ideal, intent, intention, mark, meaning, object, objective, plan, point, pretension, purpose, target, thing

Related Words grail, holy grail; plot, project, scheme; desire, hope, mind, wish; nirvana; destination, terminus

Near Antonyms means, method, way

8 something to be dealt with <I have lots of things to do this afternoon>

Synonyms affair, business, thing

Related Words consideration, issue, problem; crisis, crossroad(s), crunch, emergency, exigency, flash point, head, juncture, strait, zero hour; concern, trouble, worry; care, lookout, responsibility; deadlock, halt, impasse, stalemate, standstill; corner, fix, hole, hot water, jam, pickle, pinch, predicament, scrape, spot

things pl transportable items that one owns <gather your things and get out>

Synonyms belongings, chattels, duds, effects, gear, goods, holdings, movables (or moveables), paraphernalia, personal effects, personal property, personalty, plunder [chiefly dialect], stuff, things

Related Words treasures, valuables; appointments, fixtures, furnishings; estate,

---

11 Merriam-Webster, I. (2003). *Merriam-Webster's collegiate dictionary.* (Eleventh ed.). Springfield, Mass.: Merriam-Webster, Inc.

property, tangibles; collateral

Near Antonyms immovables, real estate

10 something for which a person shows a special talent <math just isn't my thing>

Synonyms long suit, métier (also metier), speciality, specialty, strong suit, thing

Related Words area, arena, bailiwick, business, circle, demesne, department, discipline, domain, fief, fiefdom, field, line, precinct, province, realm, sphere, terrain; element; aptitude, aptness, bent, faculty, flair, genius, gift, knack, talent; pursuit, racket, vocation; inclination, leaning, partiality, penchant, predilection, predisposition, proclivity, propensity, tendency[12]

Money

Next, as you read the following definition and synonyms for *money* consider whether the common, everyday use of the term *money* is *precise* or *imprecise*.

Since people are paid for labor and production with money tokens, it is important that the definition of money be very *precise*. But is it?

Note

Notice below that the term *money* is reported to be only about 700 years old.

Definition of money

ˈmon•ey \ˈmə-nē\ *noun*

plural moneys *or* mon•ies \ˈmə-nēz\ *often attributive* [Middle English *moneye*, from Anglo-French *moneie*, from Latin *moneta* mint, money — more at MINT] 14th century

1 : something generally accepted as a medium of exchange, a measure of value, or a means of payment: as

a : officially coined or stamped metal currency

b : money of account

c : paper money

2 a : wealth reckoned in terms of money

b : an amount of money

c *plural* : sums of money : FUNDS

3 : a form or denomination of coin or paper money

4 a : the first, second, and third place winners (as in a horse or dog race) — usually used in the phrases *in the money* or *out of the money*

b : prize money {his horse took third *money*}

5 a : persons or interests possessing or controlling great wealth

b : a position of wealth {born into *money*} —for one's money: according to one's preference or opinion —on the money: exactly right or accurate {her intuition was right *on the money*}[13]

This definition is not looking too good... I see serious problems.

The very first item in the preceding definition begins with the word *something*. As I recall, the word *thing* is *imprecise*. Now we are told that money is *something*, which also means money is *anything* that meets the criteria in the rest of this particular definition.

The next criterion is that money must be *generally accepted*, which is a very imprecise and subjective concept. Something generally accepted by whom? And on what terms? By free choice or by force?

The preceding point is very important.

The third element in the criteria is that this generally accepted something must be either "a medium of exchange, a measure of value, or a means of payment."

Therefore anything generally accepted that is used as a medium of exchange or a means of payment can be called money.

The third possibility is that *anything generally accepted* as *a measure of value* can be called money.

The problem with *anything generally accepted* being *a measure of value* is that there is no standard for the thing called *money*, against which *everything else* is valued. In other words, if money measures the value of everything else, how is the value of money measured? The reality is that the money "measures" its own value at best.

Have you noticed that the money price of everything rises together? This means that the relative value between goods and services is fairly consistent in the market[14]. All the items get more expensive together, but not because their value is increasing. The prices change because the value of the money token is decreasing.

Attempting to regulate relative value between goods and services is a fool's errand. Prices move based on supply and demand. Demand includes subjective valuation. One person may pay a high price

12 By permission. From Merriam-Webster's Collegiate Dictionary ©2011 by Merriam-Webster, Incorporated (www.merriam-webster.com)

13 Merriam-Webster, I. (2003). *Merriam-Webster's collegiate dictionary.* (Eleventh ed.). Springfield, Mass.: Merriam-Webster, Inc.

14 Changes in relative value are caused by a variety of things like innovation or demand.

(*Continued from previous page*)
for a good or service that another person would not take even if it were free of charge.

The final elements in this definition are lettered *a*, *b* and *c*. Officially coined or stamped metal currency is one of the specific things whose definition changes over time in order to plunder producers. *Money of Account* and *Paper Currency* are equally vague and meaningless terms which are used to plunder producers.

Notice that there is no item d: privately minted coins which must survive in the marketplace by reliably adhering to standards of weight and measure.

There are almost 200 different currencies around the world today. Which of these is the standard? On what basis is the *generally accepted something* a standard? If there is no *standard*, can the ***definition*** of the *generally accepted something* change, and if so, who will benefit from the change?

Notice that the dictionary entry on *money* refers the reader to *mint* for part of the history of the term *money*.

Now we turn to synonyms for money. Once again we need to try and determine if the word money is *precise* or *imprecise*.

The list of synonyms for money would be humorous if it were not for the fact that the confusion about money is destroying our individual life, liberty and property.

Worse yet, in the *Merriam-Webster's Collegiate Dictionary ©2011* the first synonym entry for *money* is also used for *gold*! Even the definition for *gold* is the same as for *money*. Are *gold* and *money* the same? No. Of course not.

Synonyms for money

money noun

1 *something (as pieces of stamped metal or printed paper) customarily and legally used as a medium of exchange, a measure of value, or a means of payment <are you sure you have enough money to buy all that?>*

Synonyms bread [slang], bucks, cabbage [slang], cash, change, chips, coin, currency, dough, gold, green, jack [slang], kale [slang], legal tender, lolly [British], long green [slang], loot, lucre, moola (or moolah) [slang], needful, pelf, scratch [slang], shekels (also sheqels or shekelim or shekalim or sheqalim), tender, wampum

Related Words coinage, specie; dead presidents [slang], folding money, paper money, scrip; banknote, cashier's check, check, draft, money order, note, promissory note; bill, dollar, greenback; bankroll, capital, finances, funds, roll [slang], wad, wallet; chump change, dibs [slang], dime, mite, peanuts, pittance, shoestring; big bucks, bomb [British], boodle, bundle, earth, fortune, king's ransom, megabucks, mint, packet [chiefly British], pile, pot; abundance, means, opulence, riches, treasure, wealth; resources, wherewithal; mad money, petty cash, pin money, pocket money, spending money

2 a wealthy person <she had always planned to marry money>

Synonyms Croesus, deep pocket, fat cat, have, money, moneybags, plutocrat, silk stocking

Related Words moneymaker, money-spinner [chiefly British]; magnate, nabob, tycoon; billionaire, gazillionaire, millionaire, multibillionaire, multimillionaire, multimillionairess, zillionaire; heir, heiress, jet-setter, jeunesse dorée

Near Antonyms bankrupt, beggar

Antonyms have-not, pauper[15]

In the 1996 edition, gold, silver and copper are not in the list of synonyms for *money*. Shekel is the only term even vaguely related to weight.

Honest money is always precise in the beginning and is exchanged on the basis of standard weight and measure. Yet in the 1996 list of *synonyms* and *related words* for money we find no reference to precious metals or standards of weight and measure.

This is very interesting, since the money system originated from commodities - primarily gold, silver and copper - which were traded by weight and the measure of fineness. In addition, Bible translators have often incorrectly used the term *money* as a synonym for *silver*. It is a rather unusual thing for translators to substitute *imprecise* terms for well known *precise* terms. This translation topic is covered in some detail in the chapter titled *Theft By Translation*.

So that explains a bit about the 1996 Merriam-Webster's collegiate thesaurus.

But wait! It is the year 2011 and we are smarter now. We have discovered lost synonyms...

Silver and *copper* have not yet made it into the list of synonyms for *money*, but *gold* has. And now the thesaurus definition, synonyms and related words are identical for *gold* and *money*, as you will see below. Gold, *precise* to the atom has somehow inherited the synonyms for *imprecise* money.

Poorly defined words are shackles and chains.

Mint

Definition of mint

[2]mint *noun*

[Middle English *mynt* coin, money, from

15 By permission. From Merriam-Webster's Collegiate Dictionary ©2011 by Merriam-Webster, Incorporated (www.merriam-webster.com)

Old English *mynet*, from Latin *moneta* mint, coin, from *Moneta*, epithet of Juno; from the fact that the Romans coined money in the temple of Juno Moneta] 15th century

1 : a place where coins, medals, or tokens are made

2 : a place where something is manufactured

3 : a vast sum or amount {worth a *mint*}

'mint verb transitive

circa 1520

1 : to make (as coins) out of metal : COIN

2 : create, produce

3 : to cause to attain an indicated status {newly *minted* doctors} — mint•er *noun*[16]

> Notice that the term *money* is derived from the Latin term *moneta*. The definition of the term *money* and the definition of the term *mint* have suggested the age of the term *money* is between 500 and 700 years.

Synonyms for mint

mint noun

1 a very large amount of money <she made a mint when the real estate market was hot>

Synonyms big bucks, bomb [British], boodle, bundle, earth, king's ransom, megabucks, mint, packet [chiefly British], pile, wad

Related Words heap, pot; bonanza, mine, treasure trove; assets, capital, means, property, riches, wealth, wherewithal; bread [slang], cash, chips, currency, dough, gold, jack [slang], legal tender, lucre, pelf, tender, wampum

Near Antonyms petty cash, pin money, pocket money, spending money

Antonyms mite, peanuts, pittance song

mint adjective

1being in an original and unused or unspoiled state <a mint baseball card that should be worth a lot to a collector>

Synonyms brand-new, mint, pristine, span-new, virgin, virginal

Related Words unaltered, unblemished, unbruised, uncontaminated, undamaged, undefiled, unharmed, unhurt, unimpaired, uninjured, unmarred, unpolluted, unsoiled, unspoiled, unsullied, untainted, untouched, unworn; new, spick-and-span (or spic-and-span)

Near Antonyms blemished, broken, bruised, damaged, defaced, defiled, disfigured, harmed, hurt, impaired, injured, marred, soiled, sullied, tainted; faded, shopworn, used, well-worn, worn; contaminated, polluted, spoiled; hand-me-down, second hand

Antonyms stale[17]

> Why isn't the definition of the noun *mint* about a manufacturing facility? Instead of a *mint* being a place where coins are made, a *mint* is a large amount of *money*. A minting facility is precise and has identity. Money is imprecise, which means a large amount of money could be worth a lot or a little, depending on the money system and date.
>
> One of the synonyms for *mint* is *fortune*.

Fortune

Synonyms for fortune

fortune *noun*

1 what is going to happen to someone in the time ahead <the telephone psychic proceeded to tell me my fortune—at great length>

Synonyms future

Related Words circumstance, destiny, doom, fate, hap, kismet, lot, portion; futurities, outlook, prospect

Near Antonyms present

Antonyms past

2 a very large amount of money <the billionaire's huge mansion must have cost a fortune>

Synonyms big bucks, bomb [British], boodle, bundle, earth, king's ransom, megabucks, mint, packet [chiefly British], pile, wad

Related Words heap, pot; bonanza, mine, treasure trove; assets, capital, means, property, riches, wealth, wherewithal; bread [slang], cash, chips, currency, dough, gold, jack [slang], legal tender, lucre, pelf, tender, wampum

Near Antonyms petty cash, pin money, pocket money, spending money

Antonyms mite, peanuts, pittance song

3 a state or end that seemingly has been decided beforehand <it was his fortune that he should wander in the wilderness before becoming king>

Synonyms circumstance, destiny, doom, fortune, kismet, lot, portion

Related Words accident, casualty [archaic],

---

16 Merriam-Webster, I. (2003). *Merriam-Webster's collegiate dictionary.* (Eleventh ed.). Springfield, Mass.: Merriam-Webster, Inc.

17 By permission. From Merriam-Webster's Collegiate Dictionary ©2011 by Merriam-Webster, Incorporated

chance, hap, happenchance, happenstance, hazard, luck; predestination; aftereffect, aftermath, conclusion, consequence, development, effect, fruit, issue, outcome, outgrowth, result, resultant, sequel, sequence, upshot

4 success that is partly the result of chance <in a streak of good fortune, she won the lottery twice that year>

Synonyms fortunateness, fortune, luckiness

Related Words blessing, boon, fluke, godsend, hit, serendipity, strike, windfall; break, chance, opportunity; coup, stroke

Near Antonyms knock, misadventure, mishap; adversity, curse, debacle, sorrow, tragedy, trouble; calamity, cataclysm, catastrophe, disaster; defeat, failure, fizzle, nonachievement, nonsuccess; accident, casualty; disappointment, lapse, letdown, reversal, reverse, setback, slipup; circumstance, destiny, doom, fate, lot, portion; hex, jinx

Antonyms mischance, misfortune, unluckiness

5 the total of one's money and property <the family fortune is mostly in rare paintings and real estate>

Synonyms assets, capital, fortune, means, opulence, riches, substance, wherewithal, worth

Related Words belongings, chattels, effects, holdings, paraphernalia, possessions, things; bankroll, deep pockets, finances, funds, money, wallet; abundance, affluence, prosperity, success; treasure, valuables; accession, acquisition, personal property, personalty, property; nest egg, reserve, resources, savings, treasury

Near Antonyms debts, liabilities; indebtedness[18]

> In the 1996 list of synonyms for *fortune*, *wealth* is listed without mentioning *money*. Now in 2011 *money* is included twice as related to *property* in item 5, while *wealth* is lost among other terms under item 2, *a very large amount of money*. None of the entries list *gold*, which is supposedly so synonymous with *money* that the synonyms and related words lists are exactly the same... This is extremely incoherent and illogical.

Wealth

Synonyms for wealth

wealth *noun*

1 the total of one's money and property <her wealth increased to the point where she could afford several luxurious homes>

Synonyms assets, capital, fortune, means, opulence, riches, substance, wherewithal, worth

Related Words belongings, chattels, effects, holdings, paraphernalia, possessions, things; bankroll, deep pockets, finances, funds, money, wallet; abundance, affluence, prosperity, success; treasure, valuables; accession, acquisition, personal property, personalty, property; nest egg, reserve, resources, savings, treasury

Near Antonyms debts, liabilities; indebtedness

2 a considerable amount <a wealth of advice from all quarters on how they should spend their lottery winnings>

Synonyms abundance, barrel, basketful, boatload, bucket, bunch, bundle, bushel, carload, chunk, deal, dozen, fistful, gobs, good deal, heap, hundred, lashings (also lashins) [chiefly British], loads, mass, mess, mountain, much, multiplicity, myriad, oodles, pack, passel, peck, pile, plateful, plenitude, plentitude, plenty, pot, potful, profusion, quantity, raft, reams, scads, sheaf, shipload, sight, slew, spate, stack, store, ton, truckload, volume, wad, wealth, yard

Related Words epidemic, plague, rash; bonanza, embarrassment, excess, overabundance, overage, overkill, overmuch, oversupply, plethora, redundancy, superabundance, superfluity, surfeit, surplus; deluge, flood, overflow; army, bevy, cram, crowd, crush, drove, flock, herd, horde, host, legion, mob, multitude, press, score, sea, swarm, throng; gazillion, jillion, kazillion, million, thousands, trillion, zillion

Near Antonyms atom, crumb, dot, fleck, flyspeck, fragment, grain, granule, iota, jot, modicum, molecule, mote, nubbin, particle, ray, scintilla, scrap, shred, tittle, whit; smatter, smattering; dash, drop, morsel, shot; piece, portion, section; absence, dearth, famine, lack, paucity, poverty, scarceness, scarcity, shortage, undersupply, want; deficiency, deficit, inadequacy, insufficiency, meagerness, scantiness, scantness, skimpiness

Antonyms ace, bit, dab, dram, driblet, glimmer, handful, hint, lick, little, mite, mouthful, nip, ounce, peanuts, pinch, pittance, scruple, shade, shadow, smidgen (also smidgeon or smidgin or smidge), speck, spot, sprinkle, sprinkling, strain, streak, suspicion, tad, taste, touch, trace

3 an amount or supply more than sufficient to meet one's needs <a wealth of documentation to support her thesis>

Synonyms abundance, cornucopia, feast, plenitude, plentitude, plethora, superabundance, wealth

Related Words adequacy, competence, competency, sufficiency; ampleness, amplitude, liberality; excess, overdose, overflow, overkill, oversupply, redundancy, superfluity, superfluousness, surfeit, surplus; copiousness, fecundity, fertility, fruitfulness, opulence, richness; lavishness, luxuriance

18 Ibid.

Near Antonyms paucity, poverty, scarcity; barrenness, infertility, sterility

Antonyms deficiency, inadequacy, insufficiency, undersupply[19]

In the Merriam-Webster, I. (1996). *Merriam-Webster's collegiate thesaurus*, the synonyms for *wealth* does not list the term *money* even one time. Now in 2011 *money* is part of a definition and synonym for *wealth*.

Silver

Definition of silver

ˈsil•ver \ˈsil-vər\ noun

[Middle English, from Old English *seolfor*; akin to Old High German *silbar* silver, Lithuanian *sidabras*] before 12th century

1 : a white ductile very malleable metallic element that is capable of a high degree of polish, is chiefly monovalent in compounds, and has the highest thermal and electric conductivity of any substance — see ELEMENT table

2 : silver as a commodity {the value of *silver* has risen}

3 : coin made of silver

4 : articles (as hollowware or table flatware) made of or plated with silver *also* : similar articles and especially flatware of other metals (as stainless steel)

5 : a nearly neutral slightly brownish medium gray

6 : coho

7 : a silver medal awarded as the second prize in a competition[20]

Silver is first defined based on its intrinsic properties. The next reference is to the periodic table where the atomic number and atomic weight of the atom silver is listed.

The next three (2,3,4) definitions are *weights* or *shapes* of silver.

The last three are color, a fish and a rank which are expressed in relation to silver.

Everything in the definition is based on silver. The age of the term is listed as *before* the 12th century. It is in fact an ancient word.

Since silver is an element, it came with the earth. Man didn't create silver. Words for silver were present in ancient languages.

People living 5000, 4000, 3000, 2000, 1000, 500, 100 or one year ago, knew about silver.

On the other hand, money is created by man. The experts require computers to keep up with the definition and kinds of money systems and money tokens that exist today. How can there be a consistent definition of money over the course of 5000 years when money is a 700 year old ever-changing concept that is not connected to any standard? Even if we go back to around 600 BC and the beginning of coins, coinage is only about 2500 years old.[21]

Synonyms for silver

The Merriam-Webster, I. (1996). *Merriam-Webster's collegiate thesaurus* doesn't have any synonyms listed for *silver*. In the 2011 *Merriam-Webster's Collegiate Dictionary* the noun *silver* has several variations for *silverware, place setting*, etc. as the synonyms. There is no mention of coins or weights of silver used in exchange, even though various Bible translations regularly equate *silver* and *coins* or *money*.

Why would synonyms develop for a term that is precise down to the very protons, neutrons and electrons which define it? What is opposite of silver? All silver is metal, but all metal is not silver. Metal is too imprecise to be a word replacement for silver.

From the Table of Elements - silver

Element	Symbol	Atomic Number	Atomic Weight
Silver	Ag	47	107.87

19 Ibid.

20 Merriam-Webster, I. (2003). *Merriam-Webster's collegiate dictionary.* (Eleventh ed.). Springfield, Mass.: Merriam-Webster, Inc.

21 The chapter titled "Theft By Translation" provides a somewhat detailed explanation of this history and time-line.

Gold

Definition of gold

ˈgold \ˈgōld\ *noun*

often attributive [Middle English, from Old English; akin to Old High German *gold* gold, Old English *geolu* yellow — more at YELLOW] before 12th century

1 : a yellow malleable ductile metallic element that occurs chiefly free or in a few minerals and is used especially in coins, jewelry, and dentures — see ELEMENT table

2 a (1) : gold coins

(2) : a gold piece

b : money

c : gold standard 1

3 : a variable color averaging deep yellow

4 : something resembling gold *especially* : something valued as the finest of its kind {a heart of *gold*}

5 : a medal awarded as the first prize in a competition : a gold medal[22]

> Gold is much like silver in its definition. The intrinsic value and reliable characteristics of gold and silver permit us to think of things in relative order based on gold and silver. Gold is best and silver is second best.
>
> The *Gold Standard* in item 2c is a label to cover a lie, since the standard is not fixed.

Synonyms for gold

gold noun

something (as pieces of stamped metal or printed paper) customarily and legally used as a medium of exchange, a measure of value, or a means of payment <all the gold in the world won't buy happiness>

Synonyms bread [slang], bucks, cabbage [slang], cash, change, chips, coin, currency, dough, gold, green, jack [slang], kale [slang], legal tender, lolly [British], long green [slang], loot, lucre, moola (or moolah) [slang], needful, pelf, scratch [slang], shekels (also sheqels or shekelim or shekalim or sheqalim), tender, wampum

Related Words coinage, specie; dead presidents [slang], folding money, paper money, scrip; banknote, cashier's check, check, draft, money order, note, promissory note; bill, dollar, greenback; bankroll, capital, finances, funds, roll [slang], wad, wallet; chump change, dibs [slang], dime, mite, peanuts, pittance, shoestring; big bucks, bomb [British], boodle, bundle, earth, fortune, king's ransom, megabucks, mint, packet [chiefly British], pile, pot; abundance, means, opulence, riches, treasure, wealth; resources, wherewithal; mad money, petty cash, pin money, pocket money, spending money[23]

> Gold is precise enough that there are no synonyms, related words, contrasted words or antonyms listed in the Merriam-Webster, I. (1996). Merriam-Webster's collegiate thesaurus. Springfield, MA: Merriam-Webster thesaurus.
>
> Why would synonyms develop for a term that is precise down to the very protons, neutrons and electrons which define it? What is opposite of gold? All gold is metal, but all metal is not gold. Metal is too imprecise to be a word replacement for gold.
>
> But wait! It is the year 2011 and we are smarter now. We have discovered lost synonyms...
>
> Unfortunately, these synonyms for gold are an utter disgrace. This is akin to equating argentum, which is the Latin term for silver, with money, as evidenced in an 1860 Latin reader and dictionary I have in my possession.[24] This old dictionary incorrectly defines argentum as silver; silver money; money.[25]
>
> Here we can also see that gold is being equated with any and everything even remotely related to money. In fact, the preceding list uses ***exactly*** the definition and list of synonyms and related words which are used in item one under synonyms for money. That is a step that is intended to deceive your grandchildren. It is up to you to prevent that from happening by teaching your children to see these subtle changes and reject them.
>
> Compare the supposed synonyms for gold with the precise definition of gold listed in the chart on the following page. Notice that among all the supposed synonyms, every object is man-made or demands an imprecise definition of the word being referenced as a supposed synonym.

22 Ibid.

23 By permission. From Merriam-Webster's Collegiate Dictionary ©2011 by Merriam-Webster, Incorporated (www.merriam-webster.com)

24 Andrews, E. A., Sallust's History of the War Against Jugurtha, and of the Conspiracy of Catiline: with a Dictionary and Notes, Crocker and Brewster, 47 Washington Street, Boston, 1860. p. 149

25 This history and reasoning is explained in detail in following chapters.

From the Table of Elements - gold

Element	Symbol	Atomic Number	Atomic Weight
Gold	Au	79	196.97

How can one be sure to exchange the right amount of time, gasoline, milk, widgets, bolts, horsepower, cattle or gold? ***Only by using a consistent and unchanging standard of measure.***

Metric System

Definition of metric system

metric system *noun*

1864 : a decimal system of weights and measures based on the meter and on the kilogram[26]

Synonyms for metric system

The Merriam-Webster, I. (1996). *Merriam-Webster's collegiate thesaurus* doesn't have any synonyms listed for *metric system*. The *Merriam-Webster's Collegiate Dictionary* ©2011 by Merriam-Webster, Incorporated doesn't have any synonyms listed for *metric system*.

Meter

Definition of meter

[1]me•ter noun

[French *mètre*, from Greek *metron* measure] 1797 : the base unit of length in the International System of Units that is equal to the distance traveled by light in a vacuum in 1/299,792,458 second or to about 39.37 inches — see METRIC SYSTEM table[27]

Synonyms for meter

The Merriam-Webster, I. (1996). *Merriam-Webster's collegiate thesaurus* doesn't have any synonyms listed for *meter* as a measurement. The *Merriam-Webster's Collegiate Dictionary* ©2011 by Merriam-Webster, Incorporated doesn't have any synonyms listed for *meter* as a measurement.

Kilogram

Definition of kilogram

ki•lo•gram \-ˌgram\ noun

[French *kilogramme*, from *kilo-* + *gramme* gram] 1797

1 : the base unit of mass in the International System of Units that is equal to the mass of a prototype agreed upon by international convention and that is nearly equal to the mass of 1000 cubic centimeters of water at the temperature of its maximum density — see METRIC SYSTEM table

2 : a unit of force or weight equal to the weight of a kilogram mass under a gravitational attraction equal to that of the earth[28]

Synonyms for kilogram

The Merriam-Webster, I. (1996). *Merriam-Webster's collegiate thesaurus* doesn't have any synonyms listed for *kilogram*. The *Merriam-Webster's Collegiate Dictionary* ©2011 by Merriam-Webster, Incorporated doesn't have any synonyms listed for *kilogram*.

26 Ibid.
27 Ibid.
28 Ibid.

Summary

Summary

Words have meaning.

When words claim to be precise, yet have too many *meanings* or *ingredients*, they become meaningless and dangerous.

When cookies have bad ingredients, the cookies are bad. When words have bad ingredients, the words are bad.

Accepted meanings for certain words are a powerful force in society, for good or for evil.

We are being robbed with our dictionaries. The proof lies farther down the trail.

"Hear my words, you wise men, And listen to me, you who know. "For the ear tests words As the palate tastes food. "Let us choose for ourselves what is right; Let us know among ourselves what is good." (Job 34:2–4, NASB95)

"But I tell you that every careless word that people speak, they shall give an accounting for it in the day of judgment. "For by your words you will be justified, and by your words you will be condemned." (Matthew 12:36–37, NASB95)

"Be diligent to present yourself approved to God as a workman who does not need to be ashamed, accurately handling the word of truth." (2 Timothy 2:15, NASB95)

"For the word of God is living and active and sharper than any two-edged sword, and piercing as far as the division of soul and spirit, of both joints and marrow, and able to judge the thoughts and intentions of the heart." (Hebrews 4:12, NASB95)

"These things I have written to you concerning those who are trying to deceive you." (1 John 2:26, NASB95)

"Now I urge you, brethren, keep your eye on those who cause dissensions and hindrances contrary to the teaching which you learned, and turn away from them. For such men are slaves, not of our Lord Christ but of their own appetites; and by their smooth and flattering speech they deceive the hearts of the unsuspecting." (Romans 16:17–18, NASB95)

"Let no one deceive you with empty words, for because of these

things the wrath of God comes upon the sons of disobedience." (Ephesians 5:6, NASB95)

"But evil men and impostors will proceed from bad to worse, deceiving and being deceived." (2 Timothy 3:13, NASB95)

"Therefore seeing we have this ministry, as we have received mercy, we faint not; But have renounced the hidden things of dishonesty, not walking in craftiness, nor handling the word of God deceitfully; but by manifestation of the truth commending ourselves to every man's conscience in the sight of God." (2 Corinthians 4:1–2, KJV 1900)

3.2 Money Is A System

Money is not what people tend to think it is. General confusion about money opens the door for the earnings of producers to be silently stolen - in broad daylight.

Are Coins and Dollar Bills Money?

Coins and dollar bills are part of a money system, but they are not money. They are *money tokens.* Being a *money token* is like being a *car tire.*

A tire is not a car, but it is part of a car.

The definition of money based on practical reality prevents us from calling coins and dollar bills money. A token is not money. A token has no meaning outside of a money system. At the same time, the money system depends on money tokens to interact with people.

It is the token along with all other parts of the system that when combined together are money.

Tokens

Think about some of the ***tokens*** we regularly use...

If a quarter is twenty-five percent of a dollar, what does that mean? How can a metal token be twenty-five percent of a paper token? Is a sledgehammer twenty-five percent of a book? The question doesn't even make sense.

Is a quarter twenty-five percent of a silver dollar? A one ounce silver dollar is lately worth between $30 and $50. Does that mean that a current US quarter is worth between $7.50 and $12? No.

Why is the ounce of silver in a silver dollar worth a different amount than the value stamped on the coin? How can a 2011 silver American Eagle have $1 stamped on the outside, while the coins sell every day for $30 or more?

If you deposit a silver dollar in a bank your account will be credited $1. If you take the same dollar to a buyer of silver he will pay the silver price, which currently ranges from $30 to $50 an ounce.

Why is a one dollar bill valued differently than a five dollar bill, when they are just alike except for the number printed on the bill?

Tokens are ever-changing tools of plunder which are a small part of a *money system.*

Money Is Not...

To understand what money is, we need to first understand what money is ***not***.

Money is not a substance. If it were, then it could be weighed. If you were going to weigh money, what would you weigh? Would you weigh the paper or the coin? What would the weights mean?

Money is not an element. If it were an element, it would be defined by protons, neutrons and electrons.

Money is not an object. Most units of money are ledger entries or data on a computer hard drive.

A ledger entry can point to a cow or an acre of land. In that case, the entry is an item on an inventory list. But with money, the inventory is out of balance from the beginning.

If too many people come for their silver at the same time, the lie is exposed. That is known as a *bank run.* Eventually there is no inventory. That is known as *Central Banking.*

Magnetic *bits* on a computer hard drive store all data for a computer. *So which magnetic bit is money?* And when the *bit* is set for some other file, is that *bit* still money?

Of course the hard drive *bit* never was money. It is a part of the *record* of an *obligation* known as a *debt.* On one side of the obligation is *your home or car or business.* On the other side of the *obligation* is a *bit* on storage media that last week was an email or a picture of some banker's fishing trip. Today it is a record of your commitment of real property in exchange for a banker's commitment of nothing but a record keeping system that churns out money units from nothing.

Money has no clear definition. Money is loosely and deceptively defined as anything the bankers and government can convince people to use *as tokens in a record keeping system*. Remember the list of synonyms for money?

Money Is A System

Money is not an object.

Money is a system.

Money is a system of record keeping that is designed to capture wealth, centralize power, centralize authority and rule people. The objects we sometimes refer to as money are actually *tokens in a record-keeping system*. Without the system, the token would be worthless in exchange, except in terms of the tiny usefulness of the cheap material from which the token is made.

National currencies are tokens in a monetary system. A token from one country is rarely accepted in daily exchange for goods in other countries. Canadian dollars would not be accepted at McDonald's in South Carolina. The Canadian tokens only have meaning within the Canadian money system.

Only a small percentage of the trillions of US dollars are ever in the form of coins or paper bills. *The tokens are only a small part of the overall money system.*

Banks issue loans that create new units of money from nothing. These loans are *entries on a ledger* that indicate a borrower has agreed to either pay back the money units plus interest, or else *forfeit* his property which is pledged as collateral.

When checks are written or debit cards are used, the ledger entries change from bank to bank and customer to customer, but no tokens are ever involved. This is sometimes referred to as *checkbook money*.

What we tend to think of as money are only worthless *tokens*. The real power and nature of money is in the *system*.

Money is a system that uses an ever-changing combination of tokens and ledger entries to plunder productive people who are forced to use the system through illegitimate law.

3.3 Understanding Money

This chapter covers a range of essential ideas about money systems from a historical perspective.

Money is different than what we are taught in our social institutions, including our churches. In fact, the very idea of money is intentionally confused in our language and understanding. If you feel a bit confused as this chapter unfolds, you are not alone. Bringing clarity to a concept that is designed to confuse intelligent people is a challenge, but with a little patience, I am confident we can clear this up. Your hungry wallet and dreams of retirement will thank you.

Since people use money tokens daily to trade hard earned valuables with one another, understanding the truth about the system called *money* is essential for everyone.

Have you ever noticed that the money system is on one side of nearly all transactions? What thief could ask for a better setup? His wealth transfer system is silently present in every trade.

The things we regularly call money are actually tokens in a power and wealth transfer system that makes producers weak and poor, while making non-producers powerful and wealthy.

Imagine a few men standing in New York scanning the whole of the United States. They see the tremendous productive capacity and hard working American people and think to themselves, *"This should all be mine! I think I'll take it."* We think that is not possible to do, but it has been done.

Unjust transfer of wealth and power is the explicit purpose of the money system. Money systems and tokens are created specifically to plunder producers. This claim is measurably and objectively true.

In order to understand how money is used against a society to benefit some at the expense of others, we must understand that the definitions of money and money in real life are usually two totally separate things. In a few cases dictionary money is honest, while in other cases dictionary money is as deceptive as real life money. The trouble with honest dictionary money is that it doesn't exist. It's something from a fairy tale, like a unicorn.

We must learn to look beyond ***money tokens***, like dollars and base coins, and see the ***money function***, which is deceptive plunder.[29]

---

29 The idea behind the vain notion of honest money describes a ***function***, not an object. This function does not involve a *money system*. The function describes a

I have a first edition 1938 Webster's Students Dictionary. The first definition for money in this dictionary is "Metal, such as gold or silver, stamped and issued as a medium of exchange.[30]"

It is good that the first definition of money was stamped metal, but it is a partial definition because there is no mention of the system that defines the weights and measures to be used. In other words, what is the amount of metal? And what will that amount of metal have *stamped* on it? Will the stamped number remain constant while the amount of metal changes slowly over time, like in Rome?

In 1933 the US Government, with a few tiny exceptions, confiscated all the gold held by the American people. Violators were fined up to $10,000 or imprisoned for up to ten years. Based on current dollar to gold ratios, if you kept $5,000 in gold saved for retirement, the government could fine you $475,000 and send you to prison for ten years.

On January 31, 1934 a dollar was fixed in law to be 15.238 grains of gold, which was $35 to a fine ounce[31].

Therefore in order to indicate the system of plunder, the 1938 definition <u>should</u> <u>have</u> <u>been</u> "Metal, such as gold or silver, stamped and issued as a medium of exchange [according to an arbitrary system established by unjust law]."

Following is an image of the Executive Order that forced the American people to give up their gold.

---

system of honest exchange that depends on reliable *weights and measures* of real property, which has nothing to do with money.

30 *Webster's Students Dictionary for Upper School Levels 1938 p.527*

31 *Ibid.*

POSTMASTER: PLEASE POST IN A CONSPICUOUS PLACE. JAMES A. FARLEY, Postmaster General

UNDER EXECUTIVE ORDER OF THE PRESIDENT

Issued April 5, 1933

all persons are required to deliver

ON OR BEFORE MAY 1, 1933

all GOLD COIN, GOLD BULLION, AND GOLD CERTIFICATES now owned by them to a Federal Reserve Bank, branch or agency, or to any member bank of the Federal Reserve System.

Executive Order

FORBIDDING THE HOARDING OF GOLD COIN, GOLD BULLION, AND GOLD CERTIFICATES

[illegible]

FRANKLIN D. ROOSEVELT

THE WHITE HOUSE
April 5, 1933

Further Information Consult Your Local Bank

GOLD CERTIFICATES may be identified by the words "GOLD CERTIFICATE" appearing thereon. The serial number and the Treasury seal on the face of a GOLD CERTIFICATE are printed in YELLOW. Be careful not to confuse GOLD CERTIFICATES with other issues which are redeemable in gold but which are not GOLD CERTIFICATES. Federal Reserve Notes and United States Notes are "redeemable in gold" but are not "GOLD CERTIFICATES" and are not required to be surrendered.

Special attention is directed to the exceptions allowed under Section 2 of the Executive Order

CRIMINAL PENALTIES FOR VIOLATION OF EXECUTIVE ORDER

FDR made gold stamped and issued as a medium of exchange illegal. This means that a particular part of the money system was made illegal, but the money system remained. The 1938 Webster's Student Dictionary also has a fourth definition for money: "Any written or stamped certificate, such as a government paper note, which passes as a medium of exchange. "

Now a *government paper note* is being called both a certificate and money! A note is *debt*. A gold certificate is a claim to actual gold. Therefore money is defined as both stamped metal and worthless paper.

Money definitions can be confusing because the definitions for money keep changing and no good definition has ever been used in practice. It helps to understand that ***honest money*** is a mythical creature, like a unicorn. *Honest money* is like a *square wheel.* Honest money just doesn't exist, except maybe on the pages of a book. Money has properties that are always corrupt or soon corrupted.

The so-called ***honest money function*** can exist, but only for a moment. Once it leaves the pages of the dictionary, it is quickly corrupted because the deceptive word *money* is present. Depending on how degraded a money system is, if the system properties of money are removed, what remains is nothing at all, or a commodity by weight.

Money is an arbitrary and ever-changing ***system of plunder.***

Honest exchange is based on the stability of weights and measures.

Honest exchange requires the same precision and integrity on both sides of a trade. Home or business budgets don't have one line item: *goods and services.* A budget is somewhat general, but it is still broken down into categories. Purchases are for specific things like a gallon of milk, a house, or an automobile. What we exchange should be just as precise and tangible. For example, three ounces of fine silver is precise.

Following is the definition for ***money*** that attempts to incorporate honest exchange.

Honest Money (a mythical creature)
A medium of exchange
A unit of account
A store of value

Notice money is <u>not</u> defined above as an object. It is a ***function*** that various objects can perform. Since *honest money* is an oxymoron, I will attach this definition to an object that can perform the function.

Silver can be used as:
A medium of exchange
A unit of account
Because silver is:
A store of value

The moment the silver is called money, it has become a part of a system. The money system will rob you. Silver by weight will protect your life, liberty and property.

Silver

Let's begin sorting this out by considering silver. Silver has been useful in indirect exchange for thousands of years. For the people trading goods and services with silver, the silver functioned like what we call money today, with one exception. *When the silver was traded honestly by weight and purity, only the buyer and seller benefited from the transaction.* There was no mechanism for a third-party transfer of power and wealth. In other words, for thousands of years people used silver as a medium of exchange, a unit of account and a store of value, but without calling the silver *money.*[32]

If we decide to call silver *money*, then money becomes a label to describe a particular use or function of that silver within a system. For example, silver was also commonly used as jewelry. But even as jewelry a particular weight of silver could serve the exact same purpose as other silver that we might choose to call money, except it protects the buyer and seller. For example, suppose a buyer wants to make a purchase that has a price equal to three ounces of silver. He could make the purchase with a one ounce silver coin, a one ounce silver bar, and a one ounce silver bracelet. The only thing that may make the transaction difficult is determining the purity of the silver in each of the three objects. If each of the makers of the coin, bar and bracelet were trusted manufacturers who used 99.99% pure silver, then the transaction would be simple. Remember that silver is an atom of precious metal. Coins, bars and bracelets are simply shapes of the metal.

Now let's compare silver to the definition of the oxymoron honest money.

Since merchants would accept silver in exchange, we see that silver is a medium of exchange regardless of whether it is in the shape of a coin, bar or bracelet.

Since merchants priced goods and services in terms of commercial standard weights of silver, silver was a unit of account by weight.

---

32 The term money is from the Latin moneta which came into use around 1300 AD

Since silver is an atom with an exact atomic weight, and silver has a fixed quantity in the whole world and silver can only be increased by mining , silver is a store of value.

Therefore we can see that silver has properties that are associated with the function some people define as the oxymoron honest money, regardless of whether the silver is in the shape of a coin, bar or bracelet.

There is one more extremely important fact that we should notice here. The writing or images on the one ounce 99.99% pure silver coin, bar or bracelet have absolutely no effect on the value of the ounce of silver. In other words, these objects are valued for the silver content not for any label that may be stamped into the metal. Granted a stamp can add value in trade by being a trusted certification of weight and purity that the market can reject or discount if any deception is discovered. In this case the certified shapes would be subject to market forces just like horseshoes, nuts, bolts and engine parts.

Money is a *system* that can be manipulated. Rather than creating a definition that vainly attempts to put integrity into the idea of money, we should destroy the term money. Think of all the confusing things that fly around in our minds when we try to pin down what money is and what money is not.

Clear Definitions Secure Private Property

Money cannot be defined because it changes.

Silver is easily defined because it cannot be changed.

Every time money definitions change, rights are violated, producers are robbed, central power increases, and society crumbles a little more.

The US Dollar

Now let's see how the current US Dollar compares to this definition. We know that a dollar is a medium of exchange because dollars are exchanged by people everyday. We also know that a dollar is a unit of account because our banking accounts, paychecks and stock portfolios are measured in terms of dollars. However the US dollar is not a store of value. First I will explain why the US dollar is not a store of value and then we will consider what we should do with this definition of money since it does not seem to be accurate in relation to what we call money every day.

Store of Value?

For a time prior to 1968 the US one dollar bill was called a *silver certificate*. If you had a one-dollar bill that was a silver certificate you could exchange that certificate for an American Eagle silver dollar. In 1969 the paper dollar became a Federal Reserve *note* that could not be exchanged for any silver coin.

Imagine that in 1969 you did some work and were paid two dollars. One of the dollars was a Federal Reserve *note* and one of the dollars was an American Eagle *silver* dollar. Remember that one year earlier in 1968 a paper one-dollar bill could be exchanged for one American Eagle silver dollar. Now imagine that you saved those two dollars until today.

Today, the paper one-dollar bill has one dollar in *purchasing power*. However, the silver dollar has at least thirty-five dollars in *purchasing power* based on its silver content.

Who took your $68?

If you had been paid two paper dollars in 1969, today you would have two dollars in purchasing power.

If you had been paid two silver dollars in 1969, today you would have at least seventy dollars in purchasing power. So where did your sixty-eight dollars in purchasing power go?

If you take the American Eagle silver dollar to McDonald's to buy breakfast, they will accept it as a one dollar coin. This means that *you will lose* at least thirty-four dollars in purchasing power if you buy a biscuit with a silver dollar.

If you saved your two paper dollars from 1969 until now, you would have given up sixty-eight dollars in purchasing power today. That is $68 in purchasing power taken from you and given to others.

Who got your sixty-eight dollars? We will answer this question with other pieces of the puzzle.

In the preceding example we see that the paper dollar lost value while the silver dollar retained value. In other words we can see that the paper dollar is not a store of value and the silver dollar is a store of value. And to be more precise and correct, what we see is that the money system unit called a dollar is not a store of value and the silver metal is a store of value. Any ounce of silver today is worth the same as the silver ounce in a silver dollar.

A Dollar No Longer Equals A Dollar

A 2011 $1 silver coin made by the US government cannot be exchanged for a 2011 $1 bill made by the US government. How much more irrational and arbitrary can a money system be? The definition of the dollar is so corrupt that a dollar doesn't even equal a dollar. This is a total violation of the laws of logic. It would be like saying that you are not you.

The three Laws of Logic are:

The law of identity: A is A.
The law of non-contradiction: A is not non-A.
The law of the excluded middle: Either A or non-A

A silver coin is stamped $1 and a paper note is printed $1, but they are not equal to each other. Therefore, we cannot say a dollar is a dollar. The dollar violates the law of identity.

We can say a dollar is *not* a dollar, which violates the law of non-contradiction.

Since a US dollar is not itself, it must be something else.

The dollar quickly became a label for a specific collection of lies and fallacies.

Spanish Milled Dollar

One of the first things we should understand is that the original US dollar was *not* created by the US government. When the US Constitution was written the dollar was already in existence. Our founders simply recognized a particular commonly circulated coin as a standard. The coin was the Spanish milled Dollar which in 1792 was determined on average to be 371.25 grains of fine silver.

Three Examples

Following are three examples we can study in history and law to understand that some of the founders never intended for this definition of the dollar to change. Others just waited patiently for an opportunity to get the system of plunder rolling.

Continental Notes

During the Revolutionary war the Continental Congress established a money system and began printing paper money tokens called

Continental Notes. This is the practice referred to as *"emitting bills of credit"* in the Constitution.

As the war expenses grew, the Continental Congress printed more Continental Notes to pay the bills. In a few short years these paper money tokens became worthless and the farmers and merchants refused to accept any more Continental Notes in payment for goods or services.

The Continental Notes began circulation June 23, 1775 with an exchange rate of one Continental Note to one Spanish Silver Dollar. By March of 1780 the market value of these paper money tokens had fallen to forty to one. By 1783 the exchange rate was 1000 to one and soon after the paper money tokens depreciated to the point that 5000 Continental Notes were required in exchange for one Spanish Silver Dollar.

The Continental Congress was forced to exchange certificates of debt, payable in gold or silver, for the resources that were necessary to sustain the army and the government. George Washington is quoted as saying "one can scarcely buy a wagon load of goods with a wagon load of Continental Notes."

The Continental Notes created chaos and loss in the marketplace. This bad experience led the founders to constitutionally prohibit establishment of a paper based money system for both the federal government and the states. The federal government is permitted only to coin money. The states are not permitted to coin money, emit bills of credit, or make *"any Thing but gold and silver Coin a Tender in Payment of Debts."*[33] Of course coining money is the establishment of a debt based money system, which was sufficient to destroy the Roman Empire. Coin based money systems are just slower to destroy wealth and liberty than paper or electronic money systems.

7th Amendment, US Constitution

Now let's see what we can learn about the founders view on money from the seventh amendment.

Amendment 7 - Trial by Jury in Civil Cases Ratified 12/15/1791.

In Suits at common law, where the value in controversy shall exceed twenty dollars, the right of trial by jury shall be preserved, and no fact tried by a jury, shall be otherwise re-examined in any Court of the United States, than according to the rules of the common law.

---

33 Writings of Thomas Jefferson

This amendment provides a lawful standard regarding the right of a citizen to a jury trial. It is clear that the purpose of this amendment is to guarantee a jury trial under certain conditions. One of the necessary conditions before a person has the right to call on his fellow citizens to hear his case is that the value in controversy must be high enough to make a jury trial sensible.

If the founders expected the definition (and therefore the value) of a dollar to change, then the value requirement for a jury trial would not have been stated in dollars. Otherwise, in order to know whether a person should have the right to a jury trial, we would have to amend the US Constitution each time the definition (and therefore the value) of the dollar changes.

Today, holding a jury trial for an amount in controversy of twenty dollars is foolish. However, holding a jury trial for an amount in controversy equal to fifteen ounces of silver makes sense. Today fifteen ounces of silver is equal to at least $500 in purchasing power.

Did the founders propose, and the states ratify, a Constitutional amendment that has to be amended every time the definition of the dollar changes? Of course not. However, since the true meaning was twenty coins containing a weight of 371.25 grains of fine silver, then the amendment serves its purpose well, even today.

Coinage Act of 1792

Now to make the point perfectly clear consider the Coinage Act of 1792. Following are two sections from this act.

April 2, 1792 Chapter XVI

An Act establishing a Mint, and regulating the coins of the United States.

Dollars or Units

DOLLARS OR UNITS—each to be of the value of a Spanish milled dollar as the same is now current, and to contain three hundred and seventy-one grains and four sixteenth parts of a grain of pure, or four hundred and sixteen grains of standard silver.

In the preceding section of the *Coinage Act of 1792* we see that the Spanish milled dollar was the basis for the US dollar and we see that it was defined as being 371.25 grains of pure silver. The dollar was *not* created by government. The Spanish milled dollar was accepted in the market based on its consistent silver content. For that reason the government recognized the dollar as a standard. The dollar had value because of the silver content not because of anything government did or decreed.

Now let's see what penalties were put in place by the federal government to deal with anyone who changed the precious metal content of our coins.

Penalty on debasing the coins

Section 19. And be it further enacted, That if any of the gold or silver coins which shall be struck or coined at the said mint shall be debased or made worse as to the proportion of the fine gold or fine silver therein contained, or shall be of less weight or value than the same ought to be pursuant to the directions of this act, through the default or with the connivance of any of the officers or persons who shall be employed at the said mint, for the purpose of profit or gain, or otherwise with a fraudulent intent, and if any of the said officers or persons shall embezzle any of the metals which shall at any time be committed to their charge for the purpose of being coined, or any of the coins which shall be struck or coined at the said mint, every such officer or person who shall commit any or either of the said offenses, shall be deemed guilty of felony, **and shall suffer death**.

The Coinage Act of 1792 established that anyone who reduced the precious metal content of any of the coins or anyone who embezzled any of the metals was guilty of a felony and would suffer the penalty of death. The Coinage Act calls the list of actions related to debasing the coins *fraud.*

The death penalty for debasing the currency makes us certain that the founders were serious about the precise definition of the dollar.

In Review of Three Examples

Therefore we can see that the Continental Congress had such a bad experience from creating Continental Notes that the men who framed the Constitution prohibited the federal government and the states from creating paper money.

We can see in the seventh amendment to the Constitution that the value standard for the right to trial by jury was set in terms of dollars, which can only make sense if the dollar maintains its value over time.

We can understand from the discussions leading up to the

Constitutional convention and from the Coinage Act of 1792 that a dollar was recognized and explicitly defined as 371.25 grains of fine silver based on the Spanish milled dollar. We can also see in the Coinage Act of 1792 that changing the amount of silver or gold or copper in any of the coins was a felony punishable by death.

February 21, 1853 - Coin Debasement

We are told that the reason the government must create our money is to protect us from fraud. In other words, private coins, like the Spanish milled dollar that was good enough for the government to use as a standard, are unsafe for the poor defenseless people to use. Private coinage in the free market produced the coin and standard the US government adopted.

Does the government really need to be in control of exchange? Thread-count on a bolt from the hardware store is another good example of private manufacturing in the free market setting the standard and maintaining it without government intervention. If a person goes to the hardware store and buys a bolt that is represented as having 20 threads per inch, but it turns out to be 18 threads per inch, the buyer will not trust that brand of bolts anymore. But when government is setting the standard and supplying the bolts, things are different. We would be forced to use the 18 threads per inch bolt.

The difference between honest bolts and honest money is that you know you have the wrong bolt immediately when you try to use it. The only way to understand that your money token is bad is to understand how money is deceptively used to take your property, a little at a time.

Remember the Coinage Act of 1792? That was a law passed by Congress carrying the death penalty for anyone who debased the coins. Since it is possible for a government to enact unjust law, the Congress simply took the Coinage Act of 1792 off the books. For example, in 1853 Congress passed a law that prohibited free coinage of silver, reduced the silver content in several US coins, and declared that the profit of this operation would be transferred to the account of the treasury of the United States. In other words they did exactly what would have resulted in the death penalty based on the Coinage Act of 1792.

'On February 21, 1853, fractional silver coins were made subsidiary resulting from the fact that the weight of all silver pieces, excepting the dollar, was reduced. As the coins were now worth less than their face value free coinage of silver was prohibited, and the mint was authorized to

purchase its silver requirements on its own account using the bullion fund of the mint, and, according to law, "the profit of said coinage shall be,... transferred to the account of the treasury of the United States."'[34]

By the way, the government mint provided free coinage by striking private silver into coins at no direct cost to the silver owner. This was stopped when the coins began being debased by the government because then the citizens would be able to profit from the fraud just like the government did.

Templeton Reid, Georgia 1830

What would happen if a manufacturer of private coins did the same thing as the government?

'The first private gold coinage under the Constitution was struck by Templeton Reid, a jeweler and gunsmith, in Milledgeville, Georgia in July, 1830. To be closer to the mines, he moved to Gainesville where most of his coins were made. Although weights were accurate, Reid's assays were not and his coins were slightly short of claimed value. Accordingly, he was severely attacked in the newspapers and soon lost the public's confidence. He closed his mint before the end of October, 1830, and his output amounted only to about 1,600 coins. Denominations struck were $2.50, $5.00 and $10.00.'[35]

When a private manufacturer of coins doesn't abide by the standard of weights and measures, he is quickly put out of business. Problem solved.

When government manufactures coins, the laws are changed, standards are ignored, people are robbed and central power increases.

Defining Money

Earlier I wrote that the current US dollar has two of the three criteria necessary to be defined as (the mythical creature) honest money. While that is true today, we can see that the original US dollar was a definite and consistent quantity of silver whose value was retained over time. In other words the definite weights and measures of gold, silver and copper in the original US dollar functioned as honest money according to the three-part definition above. The original US dollar, which was 371.25 grains of silver, was a medium of exchange, a unit of

34 A Guide Book of United States Coins, 38th Edition, 1985, By R.S. Yeoman p. 9

35 Ibid. p. 220

account, and a store of value, *because of the silver content, not the label.*

However, since the dollar was also called money, this exposed the commodities to a government-controlled system. The system took over in due time and began changing definitions.

Once the (mythical creature) *honest money* leaves the pages of the dictionary, it doesn't last but a moment before being corrupted. It is like a con-artist doing everything right just long enough to set up his victim. We would not call his actions honest. We would call them deceptive because of the intent.

When honest money is defined in the dictionary, it is based on three properties or attributes.

Honest Money (mythical creature)
A medium of exchange
A unit of account
A store of value

Since the purchasing power of the dollar is disappearing, we can see that the current US dollar is not a store of value. Therefore, the US dollar is dishonest money, not honest money. But it is simply referred to as *money*. This is a serious problem. We have two things that are nearly exact opposites of one another, yet are supposedly used the same way and are given the same name with the same definition.

The only reason the US dollar ever had any intrinsic value was because it was originally a weight of silver, copper or gold. It was the silver, copper or gold that was valued, not the label on the coin. In the chapter titled *The Five Guys Analogy* we will see how creating paper money that cannot be redeemed for something of value causes theft and transfers power.

Following is an analogy to restate the difference between the current US dollar and the original 371.25 grains of fine silver US dollar.

Let's say that the current US dollar is like a cattle thief and the original silver US dollar is like a cattle producer. Saying the paper dollar and the silver dollar are both money, is like saying the thief and the producer are both cattlemen. This obvious conflict has caused people to divide money into four different categories, which are described on the following page.

Money – Types

Four Types of Money

1. Commodity
   Good, Honest
   Gold, Silver, Salt, Butter

2. Receipt
   Bad, Usually Dishonest
   Silver Certificate

3. Fractional
   Bad, Dishonest, Theft
   Checkbook Tokens

4. Fiat
   Bad, Dishonest, Theft
   US Dollars

Commodity Money

As you can see in the list above, commodity money would include things like gold, silver, salt or butter. Each of these items has their own intrinsic value and has properties that make them useful in indirect exchange. In the chapter titled *Benefits of Natural Money* we will review various things that make something useful as money in indirect exchange. Since money is a system, a commodity is not money. If the commodity is made a part of a money system, it is simply being used as an element in a confidence game.[36]

Certain commodities can be used as:
A medium of exchange
A unit of account
Because the commodity is:
A store of value

36 "Any elaborate swindling operation in which advantage is taken of the confidence the victim reposes in the swindler...," Encyclopedia Britannica, http://www.britannica.com/EBchecked/topic/132009/confidence-game

Receipt Money

An example of receipt money would be the 1968 one dollar bill which was a silver certificate that could be redeemed for a one ounce silver coin. Receipt money can be beneficial if there is one unit of a commodity for every one unit of the receipt money. In other words if I have 1000 ounces of silver stored with my banker and he gives me a receipt for the 1000 ounces of silver, then each receipt unit represents one silver unit. However, the money system will always assert itself and the swindle will eventually begin.

The problem is that history shows the banker will eventually issue two or more receipts for each ounce of silver stored in his vault. When this is discovered, not everyone who has a receipt will be able to redeem the receipt for silver. When these receipts are recognized as worthless the receipt will lose all of its purchasing power.

When there is one unit of receipt money for each one unit of the commodity, then receipt money is essentially the same as a commodity money system. Theft will follow close behind.

When there is more than one unit of receipt money for each one unit of the commodity, then the receipt money is essentially the same as fractional money, which is designed and engineered to steal quickly.

Fractional Money

Fractional money is also known as *checkbook money* because the banks create the fractional money from nothing and add this "new money" to the borrower's account in the bank. Only when the borrower "cashes" a check is the fractional money converted to US dollars. Fractional money is a key element in the more aggressive money system.

Imagine that you and I are partners and we own a bank that we started with one million tokens called dollars. The next statement will seem erroneous, but this is how the system works. We can immediately loan nine million tokens called dollars to our customers. In other words, we can immediately loan out our one million dollars nine times.

Suppose we loan one million dollars at 10% interest nine times. Each year we will earn $900,000 in interest from our one million dollars of "capital."[37] The reason is because we are allowed by unjust banking law to loan out the one million dollars nine times. This is called fractional reserve banking and this is the way your local bank works. The effect is that we are able to earn *ninety percent* interest on our

37 Paper money is not really capital.

"capital." Sounds crazy doesn't it? But it is true. How else could banks offer free checking?

Under normal circumstances, when the bank makes a loan to a customer, the bank never loans more than eighty percent of the value of the collateral that is pledged against the loan. This protects the bank from losses in the event that the borrower is unable to pay the debt. Because the bank has only loaned eighty dollars against something that is worth one hundred dollars, in the event of a default the bank can easily sell the property at a discount in order to recover the created-from-thin-air checkbook money that was loaned out. In other words, the bank is never at risk of loss unless the banker makes poor decisions in assessing the value of the collateral that is pledged against the loan.

To illustrate the point another way, if the bank only had one million dollars in capital and the bank made a one million dollar loan without collateral, and the borrower defaulted on the one million dollar loan, then the bank capital would be wiped out. The bank cannot use self-generated fractional money tokens to cover losses inside the bank. In this case the bank would be closed, but under early stage circumstances that is a highly unlikely outcome.

There are two ways for a bank to be closed. Both have to do with the paper value of assets. The first way is for the bank to have a high default rate on loans that are one hundred percent or more of the value of the collateral. The second way is for the value of the collateral to change dramatically and unexpectedly. Both of these things are happening now and are key ingredients in the cause of the bank failures that have been occurring in recent years.

The Community Reinvestment Act forced banks to make home loans to borrowers with no down payment. In other words, government forced private banks to make bad lending decisions. The pillaging was done with the help of Government-sponsored enterprises (GSE) like Fannie Mae and Freddie Mac. This practice along with the practice of creating ever more US dollars from nothing led to the housing bubble. To say that the housing bubble popped, is to say that all at once the market for homes declined and the prices for homes also declined. Almost overnight these two things together, caused by government intervention and paper money, changed the book value of real estate assets held as collateral by the banks. Because the paper value of the collateral changed, there are artificially induced bank failures all across the nation.

Our base money supply is multiplied nine times by our banking system. From every one dollar created by the government (actually the Federal Reserve System) the banks can create nine dollars in checkbook tokens or checkbook money.

Now here is the really important point about fractional money. Because fractional money is created from nothing, it is essentially the same as Fiat money.

Fiat Money

Fiat money is created from nothing by the decree of government. In order to bring new commodity money to market, the commodity has to be mined, refined or otherwise produced. In order to bring Fiat money to market, the most difficult thing government has to do is print a piece of paper that costs a couple of pennies, which then has a stated value of one, five, ten, twenty, fifty, one hundred or more dollars. This is why Fiat money is also called *costless money*, because it is essentially costless to make.

How would you like to spend two pennies to make hundred dollar bills by the thousands each day? Better yet, how would you like to create a trillion dollars by typing a number in a computer?

When the government creates new money tokens from nothing, it makes the value of every other unit of money people have already earned worth less. In other words, when new money is created from nothing, the people always pay directly with taxes or indirectly with loss of purchasing power.

Review of Four Money Types

Commodity

A commodity is something that is valuable because of itself, like gold, silver, salt or butter. The value has nothing to do with a decree of government. Government is powerless to change the value of commodity. Commodity money is an element in the confidence game called money, which is a system of plunder. The pillaging takes longer, but as in the case of Rome, it always leads to destruction and collapse of society.

Receipt

Receipt money is actually commodity money if it is one-to-one relative to the commodity and receipt money is actually fractional money if it is greater than one-to-one relative to the commodity.

Fractional

Fractional money is money created from nothing by the banks, which means that it is really like fiat money that is created from nothing by government. Therefore there really are only two types of money systems: commodity and fiat. Otherwise well labeled *slow money* and *fast money*.

Fiat

Fiat money is created by government decree and the purchasing power of those new units of money come from the purchasing power of existing money, along with the labor and property of the people.

Property Rights

Commodities are a protector of property rights which help maintain a healthy balance of power and authority in society. Commodities used in exchange limit the scale and sustainability of tyranny and oppression.

Tyranny

Fiat money is the engine that drives unlimited tyranny and unlimited oppression because it rapidly transfers wealth from those who labor and produce to those who steal and oppress.

Not Money

With no government involvement and no money system, commodities like silver and gold match the vain definition of honest money that says that honest money is a medium of exchange, a unit of account and store of value.

Plunder

Fiat money like the current US dollar does not match the definition of honest money because the US dollar is not a store of value. Fiat money, like the current US dollar, is used to transfer purchasing power by theft from those who have previously existing dollars, or dollar denominated assets, to those who create new money from nothing. Following is my definition for the purpose of inflation:

When inflating with costless money, the purpose of inflation is to use NEW MONEY to purchase REAL ASSETS at OLD PRICES, thereby causing a wealth transfer from the people who get the new money last, toward the people who get the new money first.

To draw on our analogy again, to say that a commodity and fiat money are both money is like saying a cattle producer and a cattle thief are both cattlemen. Commodities protect property and fiat money steals property. Using one term to describe two opposite things leads to confusion, which is then used to deceive and pillage a society of hard-working property owners.

To go one step farther, money is a system that always leads to theft. Commodities used in honest exchange based on reliable weights and measures are necessary for prosperity and abundance.

A Few Quotes

Alan Greenspan's views were once in direct opposition to the purpose of the Federal Reserve System that he later led as Chairman.

"[The] abandonment of the gold standard made it possible for the welfare statists to use the banking system as a means to an unlimited expansion of credit.... In the absence of the gold standard, there is no way to protect savings from confiscation through inflation. There is no safe store of value. If there were, the government would have to make its holdings illegal, as was done in the case of gold.... The financial policy of the welfare state requires that there be no way for the owners of wealth to protect themselves.... [This] is the shabby secret of the welfare statist's tirades against gold. Deficit spending is simply a scheme for the 'hidden' confiscation of wealth. Gold stands in the way of this insidious process. It stands as a protector of property rights." ~ Alan Greenspan, circa 1965

Ben Bernanke became the Chairman of the Federal Reserve in 2006. Here he talks about *Costless Money*. Remember that creating money from nothing plunders the producers and savers.

"Like gold, US dollars have value only to the extent that they are strictly limited in supply. But the US government has a technology, called a printing press (or, today, its electronic equivalent) that allows it to produce as many US dollars as it wishes at essentially no cost. By increasing the number of US dollars in circulation, or even by credibly threatening to do so, the US government can also reduce the value of a dollar in terms of goods and services, which is equivalent to raising the prices in dollars of those goods and services. We conclude that, under a paper-money system, a determined government can always generate higher spending and hence positive inflation." ~ (Ben Bernanke, "Deflation: Making Sure 'It' Doesn't Happen Here" [Remarks before the National Economists Club, Washington, D.C., 21 November 2002])

Our monetary system is Keynesian (Cane-z-in) and Keynes (Canes) wrote about the destructive effect of inflation at least as early as 1919. He explains that Soviet leader Vladimir Lenin knew currency debasement and inflation are the best way to destroy the capitalist system. Keynes approves.

"Lenin is said to have declared that the best way to destroy the capitalist system was to debauch the currency. By a continuing process of inflation, governments can confiscate, secretly and unobserved, an important part of the wealth of their citizens. By this method they not only confiscate, but they confiscate arbitrarily; and, while the process impoverishes many, it actually enriches some... Lenin was certainly right. There is no subtler, no surer means of overturning the existing basis of society than to debauch the currency. The process engages all the hidden forces of economic law on the side of destruction, and does it in a manner which not one man in a million is able to diagnose."

The Economic Consequences of the Peace, John Maynard Keynes, 1919

The last sentence from the preceding quote is worth our careful consideration:

"The process engages all the hidden forces of economic law on the side of destruction, and does it in a manner which not one man in a million is able to diagnose."

"The few who understand the system, will either be so interested in its profits, or so dependent on its favors that there will be no opposition from that class. The great body of people, mentally incapable of comprehending the tremendous advantages will bear its burden without complaint."

~ Rothschild Brothers of London in a private letter

Summary

To increase the supply of commodities used in exchange, the commodity must exist and be gathered (silver) or be produced (butter). This is an act of labor and production, not creation.

Receipt money that is honest is commodity money, but money in all forms is dangerous to liberty. Receipt money that is dishonest is fractional money.

Fractional money is created instantly from nothing, and is a direct claim to create or decree a quantity of something of value. Creating fractional money is to decree, or claim to create, an equivalent quantity of gold, silver, land, labor, etc. Science, history and experience prove that only God can create ex nihilo, which means *out of nothing*. Fractional money is limited only by the reserve requirements which are dictated by the Federal Reserve System.

Fiat money is the same as fractional money, except there is no limit to the quantity created ex nihilo, and therefore there is no limit to their theft or relative power. In both the case of fiat and fractional money, claiming the ability to create a commodity from nothing is a clear and precise example of government and rulers claiming a creative power which is only possessed by the Creator.

Our monetary system violates the US Constitution. Even the 7th Amendment makes this clear.

In addition, *costless money* employs differing weights or measures, which, according to the Bible, is an abomination to God. *Costless money* also violates the 8th Commandment, *you shall not steal*, as well as just secular law against theft. This matters to Christian and non-Christian alike.

Even if some of these concepts do not make sense yet, it should be obvious there are some serious problems with the idea, use and manipulation of money. Remember that this is only one piece of the puzzle. Later chapters cover some of these same things from different perspectives. As the pieces come together you will see clearly that understanding the truth about money and the truth about production is essential for building and sustaining a healthy, free and prosperous society.

3.4 Economics of Salvation

It has been my experience that when Economic Terms in Scripture are brought into focus, the typical response is amazement; perhaps even epiphany.

These concepts are important for all to know, but in order to reduce the number of qualifying statements, I will write this chapter as though speaking to Christians. Christians can be held to account for certain of their beliefs and actions based on these ideas.

An amazing condition exists in the Christian world today. The centerpiece of the Christian faith has obvious and illuminating properties that Christians barely notice. The simple observations written about here lead to incredible knowledge and understanding which can help Bible students observe new and deeper meaning in Scripture. I know this from experience and observation.

Understanding the economics of salvation is essential to understanding physical and spiritual things that words alone will not adequately describe. We live in a created world filled with color, but many Christians see creation in no more than a few shades of gray. This should not be so.

Remember that the decision to use economic concepts to describe salvation is from God.

Terms & Categories

Consider the following list of forty-two terms and think of various category names that could be used to describe the list. Also, think about the types of literature from which this list may have been collected.

Abundance	Forgive
Account	Free
Bought	Gain
Build	Gift
Buy	Give
Calculate	Inherit
Canceled	Possessions
Certificate	Price
Cost	Profit
Costly	Ransom
Credited	Redeem
Debt	Redemption
Debtor	Repay
Decree	Riches
Deposit	Sell
Due	Talents

Enough	Treasure
Entrusted	Value
Exchange	Wages
Favor	Wealth
Forfeit	Work

Other category labels could be used, but *economics* has been considered an acceptable category whenever I have chatted with others about this list. For example, *abundance* is the fruit of production and *production is the just or righteous mixture of life, liberty and property combined in a way that the output is more valuable than the input.* Since economics is in large part the study of production, abundance is an economic term.

The Source

The preceding list of economic terms was sourced from Scripture. In fact, these terms come from only *fourteen passages* and a total of *thirty verses.* Following are the Scripture references.

Matthew 16:26-27
1 Corinthians 6:20
1 Corinthians 7:23
Psalm 49:5-9
Revelation 21:6-7
Colossians 2:2
Luke 14:27-29
Matthew 13:44-46
Colossians 2:14
Matthew 6:12
Matthew 25:14-15
Romans 6:23
Romans 4:3-9
2 Timothy 1:14
2 Timothy 1:14 ESV

Think for a moment about the density of economic terms in this short passage list. *Forty-two terms* collected from *fourteen passages* which are made up of *thirty verses.* That is a significant collection of economic terms in a few verses.

All of these verses are about *something*. What are the passages about? What are the topics and subtopics?

Salvation and Relationship

The topics and/or subtopics are salvation and the relationship between God and man. Please consider the previous list of economic terms in the context of the following Bible passages. The goal is to determine if salvation and relationship between God and man is commonly described in the Bible using economic terms and concepts.

"For what will it **profit** *a man if he* **gains** *the whole world and* **forfeits** *his soul? Or what will a man* **give** *in* **exchange** *for his soul? "For the Son of Man is going to come in the glory of His Father with His angels, and WILL THEN* **REPAY** *EVERY MAN ACCORDING TO HIS DEEDS. Matthew 16:26-27 NASB95*

For you have been **bought** *with a* **price:** *therefore glorify God in your body. 1 Corinthians 6:20 NASB95*

You were **bought** *with a* **price;** *do not become slaves of men. 1 Corinthians 7:23 NASB95*

Why should I fear in days of adversity, When the iniquity of my foes surrounds me, Even those who trust in their **wealth** *And boast in the* **abundance** *of their* **riches?** *No man can by any means* **redeem** *his brother Or give to God a* **ransom** *for him— For the* **redemption** *of his soul is* **costly,** *And he should cease trying forever— That he should live on eternally, That he should not undergo decay. Psalm 49:5-9 NASB95*

Then He said to me, "It is done. I am the Alpha and the Omega, the beginning and the end. I will **give** *to the one who thirsts from the spring of the water of life without* **cost.** *"He who overcomes will* **inherit** *these things, and I will be his God and he will be My son. Revelation 21:6-7 NASB95*[38]

"that their hearts may be encouraged, having been knit together in love, and attaining to all the **wealth** *that comes from the full assurance of understanding, resulting in a true knowledge of God's mystery, that is, Christ Himself," Colossians 2:2 NASB95*

---

38 Also Isaiah 55:1 "*Ho! Every one who thirsts, come to the waters; And you who have no money come, buy and eat. Come, buy wine and milk Without money and without cost.*" (Isaiah 55:1, NASB95)

"Whoever does not carry his own cross and come after Me cannot be My disciple. "For which one of you, when he wants to **build** *a tower, does not first sit down and* **calculate** *the* **cost** *to see if he has* **enough** *to complete it? "Otherwise, when he has laid a foundation and is not able to finish, all who observe it begin to ridicule him, Luke 14:27-29 NASB95*

"The kingdom of heaven is like a **treasure** *hidden in the field, which a man found and hid again; and from joy over it he goes and* **sells** *all that he has and* **buys** *that field. "Again, the kingdom of heaven is like a merchant seeking fine pearls, and upon finding one pearl of great* **value,** *he went and* **sold** *all that he had and* **bought** *it. Matt. 13:44-46 NASB95*

having **canceled** *out the* **certificate** *of* **debt** *consisting of decrees against us, which was hostile to us; and He has taken it out of the way, having nailed it to the cross. Colossians 2:14 NASB95*

'And **forgive** *us our* **debts,** *as we also have forgiven our* **debtors.** *Matthew 6:12 NASB95*

"For it is just like a man about to go on a journey, who called his own slaves and **entrusted** *his* **possessions** *to them. "To one he* **gave** *five* **talents,** *to another, two, and to another, one, each according to his own ability; and he went on his journey. Matthew 25:14-15 NASB95*

For the **wages** *of sin is death, but the* **free gift** *of God is eternal life in Christ Jesus our Lord. Romans 6:23 NASB95*

For what does the Scripture say? "ABRAHAM BELIEVED GOD, AND IT WAS **CREDITED** *TO HIM AS RIGHTEOUSNESS." Now to the one who* **works,** *his* **wage** *is not* **credited** *as a* **favor,** *but as what is* **due.** *But to the one who does not* **work,** *but believes in Him who justifies the ungodly, his faith is* **credited** *as righteousness, just as David also speaks of the blessing on the man to whom God* **credits** *righteousness apart from* **works:** *"BLESSED ARE THOSE WHOSE LAWLESS DEEDS HAVE BEEN* **FORGIVEN,** *AND WHOSE SINS HAVE BEEN COVERED. "BLESSED IS THE MAN WHOSE SIN THE LORD WILL NOT TAKE INTO* **ACCOUNT."** *Is this blessing then on the circumcised, or on the uncircumcised also? For we say, "FAITH WAS* **CREDITED** *TO ABRAHAM AS RIGHTEOUSNESS." Romans 4:3-9 NASB95*

Guard, through the Holy Spirit who dwells in us, the **treasure** *which has been* **entrusted** *to you. 2 Timothy 1:14 NASB95*

By the Holy Spirit who dwells within us, guard the good **deposit entrusted** *to you. 2 Timothy 1:14 ESV*

What Can We Learn?

Scripture uses economic terms to describe the free gift of salvation resulting from "*the Lamb slain from the foundation of the world.*"[39]

Scripture uses economic terms to describe the reconciliation[40] between God and Man.

Economics is used to explain the *most important relationship*, the *greatest gift* and the *eternal plan* of the Creator of the universe. Economics must be important.

Not only is economics intrinsically important, economics is important for each individual to understand, since the story of salvation is communicated in those terms.

Think about it. Because economics is used to tell the story of God's greatest gift to mankind, it is essential for the person hearing the story to understand economics. How can a person understand a story told based on terms and concepts that are unknown or misunderstood?

Of course, we have been *told* by the *experts* that *modern* economics is a *complex* and *sophisticated* science. These are the same experts who didn't see the housing bubble.

Universities, professors, government, media, banks and Wall Street all tell us that economics is beyond the comprehension of the average person. The claim is that understanding economics only comes through years of dedicated study and much hard work.

Is There A Pattern?

The people and institutions *whose wealth depends on these systems of theft* say that economics is beyond our reach.

The Creator of the universe, whose whole creation operates within a framework of economic principles, chooses to tell us about the *free gift* of salvation in economic terms.

Those who ***take** life, liberty and property* say economics is complicated and beyond our understanding.

The One who ***gives** life, liberty and property* tells us how to obtain the free gift of salvation in economic terms.

Those who *twist economics* for gain tell us we cannot understand.

---

39 Revelation 13:8

40 Romans 5:10; 2 Corinthians 5:18-21

The One who *created economics* to provide and teach tells us we can understand.

If modern economics is too complicated for us to understand, then either God expects too much from us or modern economics is a false system built on theft and lies. People naturally understand the economic concept of a gift, but seeing and receiving the gift is just the first small step. Our initial understanding of the gift is milk, but growing children need solid food.

Pseudo-economics

Perhaps you are thinking to yourself "But children or uneducated people in poverty stricken places cannot understand economics." If your thoughts are along those lines, I understand. In fact, without a correct understanding of economics, that conclusion is reasonable and expected. I am reminded of something I wrote a few years ago:

"Economics in an unregulated, sound money economy is dirt simple.

Complex formulas and sophisticated knowledge are not required for study and apprehension of economics, but rather these absurd complexities reside only in the domain of policy, regulatory and legal frameworks, which are superimposed by monopoly government on the productive labor of people, resulting precisely in literal theft from productive citizens, for the explicit purpose of siphoning and aggregating resources into the hands of a few, which weakens the people and grants power to the thieves, their private systems and their minions.

No productive labor is exempt and no one can opt out of working specifically for the destruction of what they hold dear, unless they are among the few whose goals are in alignment with the actual and intentional product of our present monetary system. To promote this system is to promote systemic theft and scheduled destruction of nations."

Economics should be *observations* of production and exchange, not a complex justification for market manipulation and legal plunder. Interestingly, the earliest definition of economics was in relation to a household or its management. Children understand the requirement to clean their room before they go play. They know to finish their meal before dessert is an option. Some even have to do a little work and save a little money to buy something they want. People in poverty stricken nations know the importance of sun, rain and seed. When laziness is not subsidized, people understand that they need to work to produce what they consume or exchange. Economics is ingrained in the natural order of life. Economics only becomes confusing when lies are taught and accepted as truth. Truth is consistent and unchanging. Lies by their nature must be in conflict with things that are true.

Complex pseudo-economics are based on deceptive things like money, central banking, aggregate demand and velocity equations. Money and central banking are based on differing weights and measures that are deceptive forms of theft. Stealing is a violation of the Eighth Commandment, which says *you shall not steal.* All of the complexities of economics are organized to justify theft through deception in order to increase power for the thieves.

It *is* impossible for children and uneducated people to understand the irrational systems of theft that are currently mislabeled *economics.* But it turns out that the same is true for educated people and economists. The institutionally approved economists don't understand either.

I learned long ago that trying to make sense out of irrational thought is not possible. Irrational things are by definition, *not rational.* Therefore, when an economist claims that he understands theft-based systems of economics, either he cannot see the internal conflict in the model, or he knows his pseudo-economics is a system of plunder built on lies.

To be clear, we citizen-worker-bees are supposed to believe that economics is a *very* complex science that only the experts can understand. A major confusion is that *pseudo-economics* are presented every day as *real economics.* Consequently, when we are confused by *pseudo-economics*, we think that *real economics* is beyond our ability to comprehend. This feeling is compounded because the experts *falsely* claim that they do understand these very complex pseudo-economic systems. The bottom line is that the so-called experts are fooling themselves, fooling us, or both.

Did God make a mistake?

If we really believe that Godly economics is unimportant or too difficult for the common man or children to understand, we are in effect stating that God made a mistake using economics to teach us many things, including the value of salvation and the high cost of sin. In fact, not only would the claim be that God make a mistake in using economics as a teaching tool in Scripture, He messed up and caused the whole of creation to operate according to confusing economic principles. Even if I didn't understand the importance of economics I would never make such an accusation. However, since I have gained much understanding through economics, I can say without reservation that terms like *brilliant*, *consistent* and *productive* are good terms to *begin* describing the economic teaching tools that are woven into the fabric of creation.

Stealing our way to prosperity

When the discussion of economics gets around to honest money, the inevitable claim from many people is "*Well that simple-minded system will not work.*" People irrationally argue that money, banks and other systems, which at their base are empowered by theft, are *good*. When they finally see that theft is the foundation of the system, the argument changes to "*Well, honest money won't work because business depends on cash and loans and complex financial networks.*" They don't bother trying to directly argue that theft is acceptable. Some people try to explain how these systems of legal plunder are marvelous. Others attempt to sound sophisticated by explaining their pragmatism and business experience, as though this is somehow justification for the theft they don't want to talk about. Some argue that all the progress they have seen in their lifetime came about because of these financial systems. That is a ridiculous claim.

First of all, no one ever ate, planted, operated, or built anything with a paper dollar. If a nation had no paper dollars and then all at once they created a billion paper dollars for each person, the nation would be poorer. Think of all the paper, ink, energy and labor wasted on worthless paper. If paper money makes a nation wealthy, why is Zimbabwe poor? They have flooded their own nation with Zimbabwe dollars.

Second, the claim, in effect, is that individuals and business people are *more prosperous when they are robbed* of their life, liberty and property and when their scarce resources are wasted.

Here is the effective result of these irrational claims: "God's plan for a just, prosperous and free society will not work. That whole thing about no stealing will make us poor."

Sounds dumb when we put it in that context, but truly that is what people are claiming. We cannot prosper unless we steal from each other.

"He who steals must steal no longer; but rather he must labor, performing with his own hands what is good, so that he will have something to share with one who has need." (Ephesians 4:28, NASB95)

Economics of Theft

We are told that Satan is associated with *false* wonders. Sometimes these are referred to as *counterfeit* miracles. That would remind me of counterfeit money, except money is always counterfeit in the end. So perhaps it would be better to be reminded of counterfeit silver certificates.

"The coming of the lawless one is by the activity of Satan with all power and false signs and wonders," 2 Thessalonians 2:9 ESV

We find that Satan is like the thief who comes to steal, kill and destroy. Consider the book of Job where Job lost his children, property and health and also consider the following passage.

"The thief comes only to steal and kill and destroy; I came that they may have life, and have it abundantly." (John 10:10, NASB95)

Think about all the things we are promised by the world.

You deserve it.
You can and should have it now.
It won't really cost that much.
You can pay for it later.
There is not really a price to pay for your actions.
You can deal with the problem later.

Why do we *deserve it*? On what basis should we *have it now*? Shouldn't we *calculate the cost* before beginning? What if we can't *pay for it later*? We are told, go ahead; lie, cheat, steal. *You won't get caught.* Well maybe this is not a good idea, but I can *deal with it later*.

Every item above has a few things in common. Promises of work in the future. Paper credit. Debt. Untested standards. Untested value. Unprepared.

These are the kinds of things being said:

I promise with words I will have a job in the future and will work in the future to pay for something I want now that, based on how I feel, I subjectively believe I am capable of paying for in the future with my life, liberty and property, or someone will just give me what I want and I will do nothing.

Or in relationship:

To get what I want from you in this relationship, I made promises about things in the future that I will keep if I don't change my mind.

What would a responsible list look like?

Produce something to exchange.
Work and save, then buy.
Calculate carefully.
Save to purchase.
Understand sowing and reaping.
Resolve problems when they arise.

Every item above has a few things in common. Work completed in the Past. Real property. Savings. Tested and verified standards. Tested and verified value. Prepared.

These are the kinds of things being said:
I found work in the past and completed it, to pay for something that I have proven, by working, that I am capable of paying for with my life, liberty and property, provided I have calculated all the costs correctly.

Or in relationship:
To build our relationship, I found ways to work in the past and completed them to earn your trust, so that I have proven by actions that I am capable and willing to invest in you with my life, liberty and property.

It is interesting that much of the language in this category is interchangeable between spiritual things and economics. The terms and concepts apply in both places.

Having immediate access to credit and supposedly free gifts at every turn devalues labor, property, stewardship, gifts and planning for the future. Often the *free gift* we are exposed to daily is promotional to get people to buy things. The price of the *free gift* is rolled into the price of the products. In other words we are given a gift that we paid for, which means it was not a gift, but a lie.

Other times in our society the free gift is free to the receiver, but costly to the person who lost property by force and deception. My godfather, Jim Odom, was a very productive farmer whose production ratios far exceeded the norm in his day. He was known to say that "*whenever someone got something he didn't work for, someone else worked for something he didn't get.*" He was right. When a person's free gift is from stolen property, the thief claims credit for giving away something he didn't produce, own or have the right to give.

Understanding that purchases are made with real earnings leads to understanding and appreciating the free gift of salvation, which is the payment of a debt that cannot otherwise be paid. The *value* of the free gift is more clearly understood when each person learns that he can only give what he owns and has to work for. The gift is free to the receiver, and *costly* to the giver.

When we have a distorted understanding of economics, we have a distorted understanding of God's spiritual and eternal economy. We miss important aspects of truth.

Free Costs the Giver

If people didn't believe that getting something *free* is a normal everyday occurrence, they would place greater value on the free gift of salvation. Instead, we have a deceptive monetary system that secretly takes productivity out of our labor and then uses it to claim we have received something for free from the thief.

The government or a foundation *gives* to people things that were stolen through the covert confiscation of productivity, thereby enabling the thief to appear to be the *good guy*, when they are actually only a parasite on the healthy and wholesome productivity of the producers. The thief tries to stand in the place of the producer and claim the glory and honor of the producer. This process is further discussed in another chapter and better understood in the context of Good and Evil.

3.5 Theft by Translation

Simple truth reveals absurdity.

Next we turn to the term *money* in the Bible. This chapter is a little longer than most others and contains a good bit of information. It is probably the most tedious chapter in the book, but it is important. I hope you will agree that the serious nature of the following claims warrants the information presented here, as a bare minimum. I have tried to balance readability with a thorough foundation of reasoning. Even so, this chapter just scratches the surface of ideas that one could spend years thoroughly researching and studying. When the ideas begin to click, you will see that what is presented here unlocks history, knowledge, wisdom and understanding which have a staggering potential for good.

Please don't misunderstand what I am saying in this next paragraph. I support production, capital and wealth. I am in favor of sophisticated systems of honest exchange.

Money is one of the most dangerous and destructive concepts ever conceived by man because it is the most efficient system of plunder ever devised. Money, which is a system, plunders producers, eliminates the middle class, enables and encourages war, and fuels ever-increasing centralization of power. Note the reference to *profit* for moneychangers and the city treasury and *harm* to the public in the following excerpt from *Ancient Numismatics*:

...local copper coins [..., were] a constant source of profit for the money changer or for the city treasury (via the city bank), but [were] a constant source of harm and annoyance to the public. Things were particularly difficult in Egypt where the texts saved on papyri are the main sources of our knowledge of the relationships between value and exchange rates.

Investigating the buying power of money in the previous periods and places, [...] is not a problem for numismatists, but for political economists."[41]

The profit and changes in value were caused by the fraudulent activities of officially sanctioned minters of coins. Counterfeiting arose alongside coinage and counterfeiters were punished with fire, mutilation, torture and death. The profits for the rulers were in *debasement*, not in the *metal work*, as in the honest labor of making plows or horseshoes. Otherwise these rulers would have also outlawed the making of plows and horseshoes.

Using differing weights and measures is a case-by-case action, which causes theft. Money systematically uses differing weights and measures to steal, even as the idea began taking shape in the form of coins.

My Perspective

This chapter is an explanation of how we have been deceived through specific cases of poorly translated Scripture. For this reason, I will share my personal view of Scripture.

My view is that the Holy Bible in its original languages is inspired,

---

41 Regling, Kurt, Ancient Numismatics - The Coinage of Ancient Greece and Rome, Argonaut Inc. Publishers, Chicago, 1969. A Translation of "Munzkunde" first published in 1930 in Leipzig and Berlin. p. 64

inerrant, infallible and sufficient. This view is not required to appreciate the precise argument presented in this chapter from a literary and historical perspective, but it proved useful to me in uncovering what is arguably a 1600-year old translation error in English Bible translations. Because I believe the Scripture to be sufficient and true, when I saw a conflict between the written laws of God and the characteristics of money, I kept digging until I found the source of the conflict.

I am not a trained Bible scholar. I am a diligent student who knows how to use software tools, which enable me to ask and answer questions that would otherwise require a lifetime of study. Theological education trains people to misunderstand ideas, which would otherwise lead to unlocking these man-made riddles. I am a systems thinker who loves God and has searched for truth as long as I can remember. I have access to volumes of information, sophisticated analysis tools and I prayerfully seek understanding. Following is part of what I have learned to date.

"Teach me good discernment and knowledge, For I believe in Your commandments." (Psalm 119:66, NASB95)

The Claim

After much research, I find no basis for the English term *money* to be used as a translated term for original language terms found in the ancient copies of Scripture. In fact, the use of the term money as a translated term is an error.

This claim is based on the actual meaning of the original language terms, occasional clues in commentaries and other language resources, and the fact that *money* came 5,061 years after silver.

Call me crazy, but I don't expect to see the concept or term *refrigerator*, *automobile*, *airplane* or *computer* in the Bible book of Genesis. The *computer* didn't exist until about 5,697 years after the original term for silver.

It is also worth noting that since money is a system of tokens and ledger entries engineered to steal, without readily available and cost effective record keeping systems, the money system would not be imagined and could not be used.

Johannes Gutenberg made his first printing press in 1440 AD, about the same time money systems were in their infancy in the West. China was far ahead of the West in developing paper, which they used as tokens of exchange beginning about 800 AD. By 1455 AD China had abandoned paper tokens of exchange because of destructive hyperinflation.

There is no need to understand the ancient languages to know that it is logically impossible for the 700 year old English term *money* to be a translated term for the original language terms found in the ancient copies of Scripture, which were written before the *money system* was conceived. But with a little research, the argument is far more powerful than that.

The Implications

It seems everyone knows that the Bible says *do not judge*. Many people misunderstand and misapply the meaning from this passage, but the knowledge that the Bible says *do not judge* is widespread.

Imagine if everyone knew that Bible translations never had the word *money* printed as a translated term. Many people accept money as a necessary starting point because it is in the Bible. *If money was around in Genesis, then surely it is just part of the way things are, right?* This is a reasonable conclusion if money is written about in Genesis, but it is not written about in Genesis or anywhere else in Scripture.

If money is not present in the original text and translations didn't add the word where it doesn't belong, people would question money's place in society because of its absence from the Bible.

For a Christian, even a brief analysis of money proves it is a problem. The purpose of money is the systematic application of differing weights and measures, which is an abomination to God when it happens once, let alone when it is preplanned, built into a system and done billions of times a day.

This knowledge has the potential to reshape the current course of history.

The Explanation

This argument can be made in various ways. We will begin by looking at a verse, which contains an example phrase and the helpful added term *weight*.

Genesis 43:21 is from a passage in the story of Joseph where his brothers are returning to buy grain a second time. In this verse we will review a phrase in three translations and from there draw some conclusions.

"and it came about when we came to the lodging place, that we opened our sacks, and behold, each man's money was in the mouth of his sack, our money in full. So we have brought it back in our hand. "We

have also brought down other money in our hand to buy food; we do not know who put our money in our sacks." (Genesis 43:21–22, NASB95)

"And it came to pass, when we came to the inn, that we opened our sacks, and, behold, every man's money was in the mouth of his sack, our money in full weight: and we have brought it again in our hand. And other money have we brought down in our hands to buy food: we cannot tell who put our money in our sacks." (Genesis 43:21–22, KJV 1900)

"But at the place where we stopped for the night we opened our sacks and each of us found his silver—the exact weight—in the mouth of his sack. So we have brought it back with us. We have also brought additional silver with us to buy food. We don't know who put our silver in our sacks." (Genesis 43:21–22, NIV)

Consider the following phrases from these translations of Genesis 43:21:

our money in full	NASB
our money in full weight:	KJV
his silver—the exact weight	NIV

Looking For Clues

Weight demands Identity

The first observation we might make is that one would never refer to a substitute by weight. In logic this is called the law of identity. A is A.

For example, you would *not* refer to the weight of a picture of a truck, you would refer to the weight of the truck. If you referred to the weight of the picture, you would be talking about the picture, not the truck.

Money is a system of tokens and ledger entries which begin as a stamped commodity and are subject to constant change. A system cannot be weighed and the weight of tokens is meaningless. In the early stages, a money system uses law to *prevent* the tokens from being exchanged by weight and measure. Otherwise, people are focused on the underlying commodity or thing of intrinsic value and will perceive immediately that the officially certified object (like a stamped silver coin) is being converted to a token in a system. By focusing on the token rather than the weight and measure of the commodity, the fraud and theft develops slowly and is not recognized until much later.

Money, Money, Silver

The second observation is that across these three translations we see Hebrew translated to *money, money* and then *silver.* The underlying Hebrew term, transliterated into English, is *keseph*. It is written various ways from the three consonants *KSP* and refers back to Strong's Hebrew #3701. Why would *keseph* be translated both *money* and *silver* by these different translation teams, translating a few hundred years apart?

Keseph means Silver

The third observation is that *keseph* means the *commodity silver*. Even though *keseph* is loosely handled and loosely defined, perhaps because of economic ignorance among translators, *keseph* does not mean money, token, coin, exchange or anything else. It means *silver*.

Following are two entries from the New American Standard Hebrew-Aramaic and Greek dictionaries. The numbers 3701 and 3702 refer to the Strong's Hebrew number. After the Strong's number is the transliterated Hebrew word, followed by other cross reference numbers.

Next is the definition of the word, followed by the English words to which the Hebrew word has been translated. The number in parentheses is the count of how many times the Hebrew word is translated to that particular English word. These counts fluctuate between translations and there are sometimes errors in the totals established by computer word counts. The numbers are most often correct, but it is best to treat them as good relative guides for how many times an English word is translated from the Hebrew.

3701. כֶּסֶף keseph (494a); from 3700; silver, money:—fine(2), fine silver(2), money(100), pay(1), price(10), property(1), purchase price(1), silver(284), silver from the money(1).

3702. כְּסַף kesaph (1097c); (Ara.) corr. to 3701; silver:—money(1), silver(12).[42]

In the preceding definitions from the *New American Standard Hebrew-Aramaic and Greek dictionaries* keseph is defined as *silver, money*. This is an error, since money didn't develop for thousands of years and silver and money are not alike, as we will observe later in this chapter.

---

42 Thomas, R. L. (1998). New American Standard Hebrew-Aramaic and Greek dictionaries : Updated edition. Anaheim: Foundation Publications, Inc.

Notice that 3702 *kesaph* gives the definition *silver*, but is translated *money* at least once. I attribute this to economic ignorance and circular arguments which go back to at least 400 AD.

But What About In One Translation?

Having made this discovery, we should observe how a single translation handles the term *keseph*. Note that these word counts can vary by a small amount depending on the translation and errors in the data that software is presenting.

In the NASB, for example, *keseph* is translated *silver* 287 times and *money* 101 times. Keseph is also translated in the NASB *price* nine times, *purchase* two times, *fine silver* once, *property* once and *to pay for* once.

In the KJV, for example, *keseph* is translated *silver* 287 times and *money* 110 times. *Keseph* is also translated in the KJV *price* three times, *of the money* once, *worth* once and *silverlings* once.

The NIV translates more cases of *keseph* as *silver* than the NASB and KJV.

This is a very important fact. We have a single Hebrew word, *keseph*, which is translated to the two English words, *silver* and *money*, along with three to five other cases noted above, like *price* and *to pay for*.

Since the terms silver and money ***seem to be interchangeable***, this leads one to the conclusion that *money* and *silver* are considered by the translation teams to be ***exactly equivalent*** in their meaning, implications and use. Let's test this assertion. Are *silver* and *money* alike?

Silver

God Created

From the Judeo-Christian worldview, we would say that God created silver. From other worldviews we could agree that silver is a natural element that man does not create.

Precise

We also can see that silver is precise in its definition. It is an atom comprised of 47 protons, 61 neutrons and 47 electrons. It has been silver since creation, as noted in Genesis 1. Silver is an object with identity. Silver can be weighed and measured.

Good

Again from the Judeo-Christian worldview we can refer to Genesis

1:31 to see that "God saw all that He had made, and behold, it was very good." Therefore, as Christians, we would say silver is good.

Edifying

Additionally, when studying history we see that when used in industry, adornment or honest exchange, silver is edifying to society.

Money

Now let's consider *money*. The first step is to look at a time line.

Money Is A Recent Development

Using the following estimated time-line relationships are restated to help clarify concepts, which can be confusing. Two different methods of reckoning years are used to reference the relative times and ages of different things. The focus here is on the relative time line, not exact dates in history. This is simple math based on estimates of years since the time of Adam and Eve in the book of Genesis.

It is important to understand that *money* wasn't around in the time of Abraham and Joseph any more than you were. If you can't be named in the story of Joseph, neither can *money*.

Money is a term that seems to have come into use in the late 13th or early 14th century AD based on the Latin term *moneta*. There is some debate, so let's say money came on the scene about 700 years ago in 1300 AD.

According to the Jewish calendar, part of 2011 is in year 5772. Using that as our guide, *silver* has been around about 5,061 years longer than *money*.

Even if one goes back to 600 BC and the beginning of coinage, *silver* has been around about 3,161 years longer than *coins*. When coins are used honestly they are simply reliable shapes and purity of a commodity like silver or gold. Good coins are much like a one-inch metal bolt, a pound of butter or a yard of cloth.

Abraham lived around 2100 BC, which is 1,500 years prior to *coinage* and 3,400 years before the term *money* came on the scene.

Joseph lived around 1900 BC, which is 1,300 years prior to *coinage* and 3,200 years before the term *money* came on the scene.

Old Testament writings ended between about 500 BC and 400 BC, which was about 100 to 200 years after *coinage* began. The Old Testament writing ended about 1,700 years before the term *money* came on the scene.

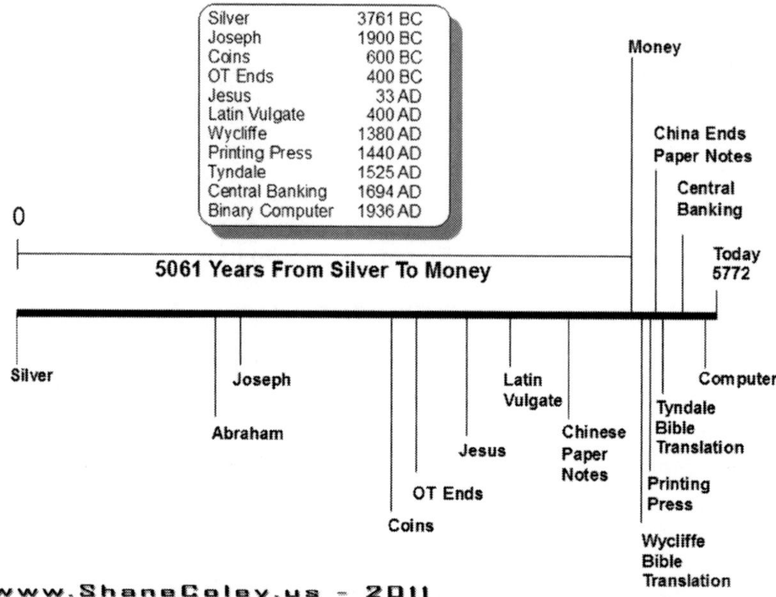

Here is a review in round numbers.

Coins came into existence about 3,000 years after silver.
Money came into existence about 5,000 years after silver.
Computers came into existence about 5,700 years after silver.

Money came into existence about 1,900 years after coins.
Computers came into existence about 2,500 years after coins.

Computers came into existence about 600 years after money.
Computers came into existence about 500 years after the printing press.

Is Money The Cause Of Prosperity?

Before continuing with the time-line, it is important to answer a common fallacy about the role of money in modern civilization.

Many people say that we *need* our sophisticated monetary system. I have often heard that our progress is the *result* of our monetary system. I disagree with this illogical claim. Even before getting into interesting debates about whether a nation of people have honored God and lived lawfully, there is a temporal comparison that makes a laughingstock of the high and glorious claims about money systems.

While ignoring other interesting factors, please consider the following question:

Which thing did more for the advancement of learning and the increase in the productive capacity of the individual? Was it the *money* that plundered his labor and capital, or the *printing press* that increased his knowledge?

Perhaps more importantly, in spite of the translation problems, while money was developing as a concept and system, the Bible was being translated into the common tongue and the printing press began being used to spread Scripture along with other knowledge. Was our access to the teachings of Scripture an important factor in the increasing standard of living in many places in the world?[43]

Again, which thing did more for the advancement of learning and the increase in the productive capacity of the individual?

Was it the *money* that plundered his labor and capital, or the *Industrial Revolution* that increased his knowledge, tools, capital and productivity?

Was it the *money* that plundered his labor and capital, or the *Energy* that powered the machines, which increased his knowledge, tools, capital and productivity?

Was it the *money* that enabled Unrestricted Global War, which wastes and destroys property and production, or these other things, which increased his knowledge, tools, capital and productivity?

What Happened To That Knowledge?

The Catholic Church tried to prevent access to knowledge by locking the Bible in Latin and not permitting anyone except those approved by the church to read it. Once common language translations and the printing press made the Holy Bible commonly available, the strategy had to change.

The same is generally true with other knowledge. If access to information cannot be restricted, then it must be confused and controlled. This is the reason for the 6th and 10th planks of the Communist Manifesto which seek to control communication, transportation and education.

By permitting production to be confiscated through money systems, teaching soon came under the control of those who control the money

43 Note: People eat food and use things. Food and things must be produced. Prosperity is the fruit of production. Production increases with increasing quantities of capital goods. With savings people expand their collection of tools and increase their production.

system. Communication tools have been used to flood people with propaganda, entertainment and confusion in order to protect systems of plunder, power and control. This is logically and objectively true.

Estimated Time Line		
Silver	3761 BC[44]	0 Years[45]
Abraham	2100 BC	1661 Years
Joseph	1900 BC	1861 Years
Coins	600 BC	3161 Years
End of OT	400 BC	3361 Years
Jesus	30-33 AD	3791 Years
Chinese Paper Notes[46]	806 AD	4567 Years
Juno Moneta - Money	1300 AD	5061 Years
Wycliffe Bible Translation	1380 AD	5141 Years
Printing Press	1440 AD	5201 Years
China Abandons Paper Notes[47]	1455 AD	5216 Years
Tyndale Bible Translation	1525 AD	5286 Years
Central Banking	1694 AD	5455 Years
Computer	1936 AD	5697 Years
Worldwide Economic Collapse Underway	2008 AD	5769 Years

Please remember that this is an estimated time line which estimates dates to give a relative sense of when these things happened in history.

44 Time of Adam and Eve based on the Jewish Calendar

45 This is a simple estimated count of years from Creation until 2008.

46 A History of Money from Ancient Times to the Present Day by Glyn Davies, rev. ed. Cardiff: University of Wales Press, 1996. 716p. ISBN 0 7083 1351 5. (Page numbers in the 3rd edition published in 2002 may be slightly different). p.180

47 Ibid. p. 183

Notice that there are only 708 years from the origin of the term money until the beginning of the current worldwide economic collapse. Even if one counts back to Chinese paper notes it has only been 1202 years since these were first used.

The first use of paper for exchange came about in China 4,600 years ***after*** silver. The term money came on the scene about 5,000 years after silver.

Joseph lived 3,200 years before *money* existed as a term and concept. Joseph lived about 3,800 years before *computer* existed as a term and concept.

Why This Matters

Debased coins cause inflation and plunder producers *slowly* and in devastating ways that destroy nations and societies.

Paper money causes inflation and plunders producers *rapidly* and in devastating ways that destroy nations and societies.

The *natural element silver* and *man-made money systems* are different in every way, including their origin and history.

Money Is Defined By Use

Sometimes people call on dictionary definitions to defend money. *I prefer to rely on the definition of the thing in practice.* History repeatedly proves that fraud is soon to follow whenever something stops being referred to as a weight and measure of a commodity and begins being called some other label like shekel, pound or thaler. Unfortunately today most dictionary definitions confuse the idea and attributes of honest money with the idea and attributes that mask deliberate systems of theft. This is a serious problem.

Remember that minting coins was profitable to minters and governments because of the fraud involved in changing the metal content of the coins. There is no other reason for a government to get in the coin making business while preventing other private businesses from doing the same. If the interest of government was the honest profit from production, then they would also be in the business of making horseshoes and plowshares.

Created By Man

Using the preceding categories regarding silver, we first see that money is a system devised by man in about 1300 AD. In 800 AD, about 500 years before money, China began using paper tokens of exchange. By 1455 China abandoned the paper token system because of hyperinflation. We can also see that coinage is developed by man about

600 BC. History is abundantly clear that coins were used as tools of plunder.

Money systems are engineered by man to plunder producers.

Imprecise Definition

We also see, to state the reality in mild terms, money is imprecise in its definition. Money is a *system* that is spoken of as though it is an *object*. Its definition and value changes constantly from day to day and between money types or currencies. Changing definitions are necessary to plunder producers. This is how our savings and retirements disappear.

Differing Weights and Measures

In addition, sooner or later anything called money employs the device known as differing weights and/or differing measures which causes theft. Secular law claims to prohibit theft, which makes this practice unacceptable, even in secular terms. The Bible commands us not to use differing weights or differing measures, even calling the practice an abomination to God.

An example of differing measure would be a grain merchant *buying* grain in a marketplace with a basket falsely marked *one bushel*, when it is *actually larger* than a bushel. The unsuspecting *seller* fills the basket with too much grain before being paid for only one bushel. The grain merchant is *stealing* part of the grain grower's production.

When the dishonest grain merchant *sells* his grain, then his basket marked *one bushel* is *actually smaller* than a bushel. The unsuspecting *buyer* leaves with less than a bushel of grain, but he pays for a whole bushel.

The US Silver Dollar which is worth one paper dollar at the bank is worth thirty or more paper dollars at the silver shop. That is a clear case of differing weights and measures.

The declining purchasing power of our dollar-denominated savings and investments is also a clear case of differing weights and measures. If our savings were in gold or silver, the purchasing power of the silver would fluctuate only slightly. In a productive society that will not tolerate theft, our purchasing power would actually increase as our production increased.

You Shall Not Steal

It is easy to see why using differing weights and measures is an abomination to God since it is a deceptive and systematic method of violating the eighth of the Ten Commandments, *You shall not steal.* This form of theft would also be illegal in a consistent secular body of law.

Money uses differing weights and measures that are always used to steal.

Economic Collapse

Finally, we find from the study of history that any nation that has devised a system to debase its coins or has used any form of dishonest exchange has eventually collapsed from within. There are reasons for this that have been written about by excellent scholars in various economic works.

Silver and Money Are Not The Same

Silver Compared to Money
Silver
Created By God / Natural
Precise definition – atom
5,061 years older than money
Good
Edifying to society
Protects Private Property
Money
A system devised by man
Imprecise definition
Uses differing weights and measures
Violates the 8th Commandment
Causes Theft
Destroys nations

Therefore, when reviewing the comparison between *silver* and *money*, we see that *silver* and *money* are ***not*** equivalent and they could not possibly be translated from a single Hebrew term which means *silver*.

"The words of the LORD are pure words; As silver tried in a furnace on the earth, refined seven times." (Psalm 12:6, NASB95)

Try refining money tokens or ledger entries in a furnace *one time* and see what is left...

"Do not trust in oppression And do not vainly hope in robbery; If riches increase, do not set your heart upon them." (Psalm 62:10, NASB95)

New Testament

In order to further reinforce the idea, we should have a look at the New Testament Greek to see if there is consistency.

Greek words translated money in the New Testament

The information about the table below is a little technical, but it is important.

The following table lists Greek terms that are translated as, include or relate to *money* in the New Testament. The table is organized into six rows for each term.

The first row is the Greek Term transliterated into English.

The second row is the Dictionary Entry from the *New American Standard Hebrew-Aramaic and Greek dictionaries.* To correctly display Greek letters and special characters, these entries are images that are clipped from the noted dictionary as displayed in *Logos Bible Software 4.*

The third row is the Dictionary Meaning, which is simply rewritten from the preceding image.

The fourth row is My View of the correct definition. This usually matches the definition given in the dictionary, but not always.

The fifth row is the Reason for any disagreement I have regarding the definition or translation of the Greek into English. In some cases, an earlier section contains another word that a later word is based on. For example, *kollubos* means *small coin* and *kollubistes* is specifically noted in the dictionary to be from *kollubos*. Therefore, *kollubistes* should be *small coin changer*, not *moneychanger*. In another case, *philos* and *arguros* are listed because they form the base for three other terms, namely *philarguros*, *aphilarguros* and *philarguria*.

The sixth row is labeled Translated To From Scripture which contains the various English words to which the Greek word is translated. There should be two striking observations as these English terms are reviewed.

First, how can anyone get *money* out of these terms? For that matter, how can anyone get *money into* some of the definitions... The base words do not mean *money*, they cannot support being translated to *money* and are from an era about 1200 years before the idea of money even came into existence.

Second, how do these *other* English words also come from the same Greek words that are twisted to mean *money*? It is true that context and time can influence the reasonable translation of an older language term into a current term in another language. However, silver is an atom that has never changed and needs no substitute word to convey its meaning. In addition, the precise term silver must not be translated to a fundamentally different imprecise term.

For example, why is *purse* translated *money belt*?

How is *money* derived from *a thing that one uses or needs* in an era when *money* was not even in existence? In a time when much exchange involved what we might call barter *things*, *property* or *wealth* are far more reasonable in translation.

A *small coin* is one of a limited number of possibilities having a limited set of attributes based on history and archeology. How does a small coin become the imprecise term *money*? The translators might as well call a donkey *transportation.*

How does *copper* or *bronze* become either a *gong* or *money*? What is the common thread that links these two terms and definitions?

How does the ***precise*** term *silver* become the ***imprecise*** term *money*?

There are several more questions of this sort which are important and worth asking. *Money* is found in unrelated words at a time when *money* didn't even exist.

Each Dictionary Entry is from: Thomas, R. L. (1998). New American Standard Hebrew-Aramaic and Greek dictionaries : Updated edition. Anaheim: Foundation Publications, Inc. The following table begins with a legend explaining the six rows in each section. The table is vertically organized to accommodate electronic readers.
1. Greek Term, 2. Dictionary Entry, 3. Dictionary Meaning, 4. My View, 5. Reason, 6. Translated From Scripture
Greek Term (Transliterated[48])
Dictionary Entry
Dictionary Meaning[49]
My View
Reason
Translated To From Scripture

48 To transliterate is to spell a word from one language using the alphabet of another.

49 Each Dictionary Entry is from: Thomas, R. L. (1998). New American Standard Hebrew-Aramaic and Greek dictionaries: Updated edition. Anaheim: Foundation Publications, Inc.

1. Greek Term, 2. Dictionary Entry, 3. Dictionary Meaning, 4. My View, 5. Reason, 6. Translated From Scripture
ballantion
905. **βαλλάντιον ballantion**; from a prim. root **βαλ- bal-**; *a purse*:—money belt(3), money belts(1).[50]
a purse
a purse
The definition is a purse. There is no basis for calling it a money belt. Notice the term is used only by Mark.
Luke 10:4; Luke 12:33; Luke 22:35,36
money belt (3) money belts (1)

1. Greek Term, 2. Dictionary Entry, 3. Dictionary Meaning, 4. My View, 5. Reason, 6. Translated From Scripture
chrema
5536. **χρῆμα chrēma**; from *5530; a thing that one uses* or *needs*:—money(4), wealthy(2).[51]
a thing that one uses or needs
a thing that one uses or needs
It means tangible property, not a system
Mark 10:23; Luke 18:24; Acts 4:37; Acts 8:18,20; Acts 24:26
money (4), wealthy (2)

1. Greek Term, 2. Dictionary Entry, 3. Dictionary Meaning, 4. My View, 5. Reason, 6. Translated From Scripture
kollubos
2855a. **κολλυβιστής kollubistēs**; from **κόλλυβος kollubos** *(a small coin); a moneychanger*:—money changers(1), moneychangers(2).[52]
a small coin
a small coin
Because it means a small coin
Not independently used - part of kollubistes

50 Thomas, R. L. (1998). New American Standard Hebrew-Aramaic and Greek dictionaries : Updated edition. Anaheim: Foundation Publications, Inc.

51 Ibid.

52 Ibid.

1. Greek Term, 2. Dictionary Entry, 3. Dictionary Meaning, 4. My View, 5. Reason, 6. Translated From Scripture
kollubistes
2855a. **κολλυβιστής kollubistēs**; from **κόλλυβος kollubos** *(a small coin); a moneychanger:*—money changers(1), moneychangers(2).[53]
money changer
small coin changer
kollubos means small coin and "istes" is similar to "er" as in reaper or "ist" as in evangelist. So small coiner or small coin changer makes sense.
Matthew 21:12; Mark 11:15; John 2:15
moneychangers (1) moneychanger (2)

1. Greek Term, 2. Dictionary Entry, 3. Dictionary Meaning, 4. My View, 5. Reason, 6. Translated From Scripture
chalkos
5475. **χαλκός chalkos**; a prim. word; *copper* or *bronze:*—bronze(1), copper(1), gong(1), money(2).[54]
copper or bronze
copper or bronze
It means copper or bronze, not money. Noisy gong in 1 Corinthians 13:1 should be loud copper or loud bronze, with a footnote that indicates what is being described is like a gong.
Matthew 10:9; Mark 6:8; Mark 12:41; 1 Corinthians 13:1; Revelation 18:12
bronze (1), copper (1), gong (1), money (2)

1. Greek Term, 2. Dictionary Entry, 3. Dictionary Meaning, 4. My View, 5. Reason, 6. Translated From Scripture
philos
5384. **φίλος philos**; a prim. word; *beloved, dear, friendly:*—friend(12), friends(17).[55]
beloved, dear, friendly
beloved, dear, friendly
brotherly love
friend (12), friends (17)

53 Ibid.
54 Ibid.
55 Ibid.

1. Greek Term, 2. Dictionary Entry, 3. Dictionary Meaning, 4. My View, 5. Reason, 6. Translated From Scripture
arguros
696. **ἄργυρος arguros**; from **ἀργός argos** *(shining); silver:*—silver(4).[56]
silver
silver
Arguros means silver.
Matthew 10:9; Acts 17:29; 1 Corinthians 13:12; James 5:3; Revelation 18:12
silver (4)

1. Greek Term, 2. Dictionary Entry, 3. Dictionary Meaning, 4. My View, 5. Reason, 6. Translated From Scripture
philarguros
5365. **φιλαργυρία philarguria**; from *5366; love of money, avarice:*—love of money(1). 5366. **φιλάργυρος philarguros;** from 5384 and 696; loving money:—lovers of money(2).
loving money
love of silver
philos can mean beloved and arguros means silver. In addition, silver is an atom God created and called good, but money is a system which always uses differing weights and measures which God calls an abomination. The term means love of silver. 5366 points back to 5384 and 696 which mean beloved and silver.
Luke 16:14; 2 Timothy 3:2
lovers of money (2)

1. Greek Term, 2. Dictionary Entry, 3. Dictionary Meaning, 4. My View, 5. Reason, 6. Translated From Scripture
glossokomon
1101. **γλωσσόκομον glōssokomon**; from *1100* and the same as *2865; a case, a box:*—money box(2).[57]
a case, a box
a case, a box
It means a case or a box. Since there is no basis for the term money, which came 1200 years after these writings, it cannot mean money box. When reading the text, neither money nor coins are stated, although coins are implied through the term denarii. Even so, since John, the author, did not go beyond calling it a case or box, there is no reason to qualify the case or box as a money box or coin box. Apparently John assumed that its general use would be gleaned from context.
John 12:6; John 13:29
money box (2)

56 Ibid.
57 Ibid.

1. Greek Term, 2. Dictionary Entry, 3. Dictionary Meaning, 4. My View, 5. Reason, 6. Translated From Scripture
aphilarguros
866. **ἀφιλάργυρος aphilarguros**; from *1* (as a neg. pref.) and *5366; without love of money*:—free from the love of money(1), free from the love(1).[58]
without love of money
not silver lover or not loving silver
In the Greek, a means not. Philos means beloved and arguros means silver. Money and silver are fundamentally different, as noted elsewhere. 866 points to 5366, which points to 5384 and 696.
1 Timothy 3:3; Hebrews 13:5
free from the love of money (2)

1. Greek Term, 2. Dictionary Entry, 3. Dictionary Meaning, 4. My View, 5. Reason, 6. Translated From Scripture
zone
2223. **ζώνη zōnē**; from *2224; a belt*:—belt(5), belts(1), money belts(1), sash(1), sashes(1).[59]
a belt
a belt
Zone means a belt. It is translated as such in other places. This was the belt which people often wore folded to carry copper, silver, gold or coins or other things. The text does not say money belt, it says the belt. Adding the term money is completely illogical, since money did not exist as a term and the items which the disciples are told not to acquire in Matthew 10:9 are gold, silver and copper.
belt (5), belts (1), money belts (1), sash (1), sashes (1)

58 Ibid.
59 Ibid.

<table>
<tr><td>1. Greek Term, 2. Dictionary Entry, 3. Dictionary Meaning, 4. My View, 5. Reason, 6. Translated From Scripture</td></tr>
<tr><td>autos</td></tr>
<tr><td>846. αὐτός autos; an intensive pron., a prim. word; (1) self (emphatic) (2) he, she, it (used for the third pers. pron.) (3) the same:—accompanied*(2), agree*(1), anyone(1), both*(1), city(2), even(1), here*(1), herself(5), himself(83), itself(7), just(1), lies(1), like(1), like-minded(1), money(1), myself(10), number(1), one(1), one's(2), other(1), ourselves(8), own(2), part(1), people(1), person(1), personally(1), righteousness(1), same(59), same things(4), same way(1), selves(1), sight(1), temple(1), theirs(3), themselves(23), there*(2), these(1), these things(2), this(1), those(2), together*(8), very(17), very one(1), very thing(4), well(1), who(3), whose(2), whose*(1), women(1), yourself(3), yourselves(14), yourselves*(3).[60]</td></tr>
<tr><td>self; he, she, it; the same</td></tr>
<tr><td>self; he, she, it; the same</td></tr>
<tr><td>"Then when Judas, who had betrayed Him, saw that He had been condemned, he felt remorse and returned the thirty pieces of silver to the chief priests and elders, saying, "I have sinned by betraying innocent blood." But they said, "What is that to us? See to that yourself!" And he threw the pieces of silver into the temple sanctuary and departed; and he went away and hanged himself. The chief priests took the pieces of silver and said, "It is not lawful to put them into the temple treasury, since it is the price of blood." And they conferred together and with the money bought the Potter's Field as a burial place for strangers. For this reason that field has been called the Field of Blood to this day. Then that which was spoken through Jeremiah the prophet was fulfilled: "AND THEY TOOK THE THIRTY PIECES OF SILVER, THE PRICE OF THE ONE WHOSE PRICE HAD BEEN SET by the sons of Israel; AND THEY GAVE THEM FOR THE POTTER'S FIELD, AS THE LORD DIRECTED ME." (Matthew 27:3–10, NASB95)
Matthew 27:3,5,6 refer to silver three times and then Matthew 27:7 all at once translates autos as the money which should be translated the same. This is a passage which talks about the 30 pieces of silver which was the price paid to Judas to betray Jesus. Matthew 27:9 refers to Zechariah 11:13 which is the prophecy of thirty pieces of silver – which in Hebrew is keseph.
"And they conferred together and with the [same] bought..."
The term autos is clearly referring to silver.</td></tr>
<tr><td>[many other things as noted above plus] money (1)
Incorrectly translated the money in reference to thirty pieces of silver</td></tr>
</table>

60 Ibid.

1. Greek Term, 2. Dictionary Entry, 3. Dictionary Meaning, 4. My View, 5. Reason, 6. Translated From Scripture
diaseio
1286. **διασείω diaseiō**; from *1223* and *4579; to shake violently, to intimidate*:—take money … by force(1).[61]
to shake violently, to intimidate
to shake violently, to intimidate
This passage should be translated intimidate no one. Instead the translators have somehow discovered in the text the term money and the specific idea of taking money from people. This is not what the passage says. The translators have taken two Greek words which mean intimidate no one and turned them into eight English words, including money which didn't even exist at the time. The definitions given are circular arguments, meaning the translators translate to English, then refer to the translation as part of the definition. Look closely: The definition is to shake violently, to intimidate, and then immediately we see take money... by force as somehow being a valid translation. This translation then shows up in commentaries as a definition.
Luke 3:14
do not take money from anyone by force (1)

1. Greek Term, 2. Dictionary Entry, 3. Dictionary Meaning, 4. My View, 5. Reason, 6. Translated From Scripture
kerma
2772. **κέρμα kerma**; from *2751; a slice,* hence *a small coin*:—coins(1).[62]
a slice
a slice
"And He made a scourge of cords, and drove them all out of the temple, with the sheep and the oxen; and He poured out the coins of the money changers and overturned their tables;" (John 2:15, NASB95)
I agree that this is referring to coins because of the context. However, that also means that the next two words in John 2:15, kollubistes, should be the small coin changers, not the money changers.
coins (1)

61 Ibid.
62 Ibid.

1. Greek Term, 2. Dictionary Entry, 3. Dictionary Meaning, 4. My View, 5. Reason, 6. Translated From Scripture
kermatistes
2773. **κερματιστής kermatistēs**; from a der. of *2772; a moneychanger*:—money changers(1).[63]
a moneychanger
a small slice changer
"And He found in the temple those who were selling oxen and sheep and doves, and the money changers seated at their tables." (John 2:14, NASB95)
kerma means a slice, which in context can easily refer to a coin. However, a coin is far more precise than money. As noted already, money didn't exist as a concept until 1200 years later and coins were clearly present at the time of the writing. A coin is far more definite than money. There is no basis for calling these people money changers. Small coin changers is a correct translation.
moneychangers (1)

1. Greek Term, 2. Dictionary Entry, 3. Dictionary Meaning, 4. My View, 5. Reason, 6. Translated From Scripture
kephalaion
2774. **κεφάλαιον kephalaion**; from *2776; of the head, the main point*:—main point(1), sum of money(1).[64]
of the head, the main point
of the head, the main point
"The commander answered, "I acquired this citizenship with a large sum of money." And Paul said, "But I was actually born a citizen." (Acts 22:28, NASB95)
This example is one I have not studied in depth, but it is still quite a reach, which makes it worth noting. I am under the impression kephalaion is the word from which we get the idea of capital, which would refer to some sort of real wealth. In any case, it makes no sense to translate of the head or the main point into a large sum of money. Based on research regarding uses of the term, I am of the early opinion it could be translated "I acquired this citizenship with much capital." It could possibly be translated "I acquired this citizenship as a great main point," which makes sense given that being a soldier was a way to earn citizenship. Certain military duties could fast track citizenship. In any case, the translation large sum of money is not correct. The other verse which contains kephalaion is Hebrews 8:1. The idea of the head or the main point makes sense here. "Now the main point in what has been said is this: we have such a high priest, who has taken His seat at the right hand of the throne of the Majesty in the heavens, a minister in the sanctuary and in the true tabernacle, which the Lord pitched, not man." (Hebrews 8:1–2, NASB95)
main point (1), large sum of money (1)

63 Ibid.
64 Ibid.

1. Greek Term, 2. Dictionary Entry, 3. Dictionary Meaning, 4. My View, 5. Reason, 6. Translated From Scripture
philarguria
5365. **φιλαργυρία philarguria**; from *5366; love of money, avarice*:—love of money(1).[65]
love of money, avarice
love of silver
philos means beloved and arguros means silver. The translation of philarguria as love of silver will stand logically in the context of language, consistency in translation and the time line of history. In addition, the Strong's number 5365, which is philarguria, points to 5366, which is philarguros, which points to 5384 and 696, which are philos and arguros, respectively.
1 Timothy 6:10
love of money (1)

A Brief Review

"And He found in the temple those who were selling oxen and sheep and doves, and the money changers seated at their tables. And He made a scourge of cords, and drove them all out of the temple, with the sheep and the oxen; and He poured out the coins of the money changers and overturned their tables; and to those who were selling the doves He said, "Take these things away; stop making My Father's house a place of business." His disciples remembered that it was written, "ZEAL FOR YOUR HOUSE WILL CONSUME ME." (John 2:14–17, NASB95)

Kermatistes means "small slice changer" and *kollubistes* means "small coin changer" and *kerma* means "small slice." I find *kerma* and *kermatistes* <u>one</u> <u>time</u> each in the New Testament in John 2:14-15, describing the time when Jesus overturned the tables of the *moneychangers* in the temple. I find *kollubistes* <u>three</u> <u>times</u> in the New Testament, in Matthew 21:12, Mark 11:15 and John 2:15, with each passage being about this same event. In this case the translators incorrectly translate *coin* as *money*. Think about the synonyms for *money*. When one reads *money*, one could think of any number of possibilities as to what was meant in the original text. When one reads *coin*, the possibilities are narrowed greatly, as any good archeological reference work will make clear.

The Greek term *kerma* which means "a slice" is translated *coin* in John 2:15. Consistency in translation requires that the term *kermatistes* in John 2:14 refer to *coins*, not *money*.

---

65 Ibid.

It turns out that a primary reason the *small coin changers* were in the temple was to exchange debased Antiochene coins for other coins from Tyre which were more trusted. The Temple law forbade the use of these Roman coins because they did not contain enough silver.[66] The *small coin changers* were making a profit for the service of exchanging debased coins for quality coins.

Since a coin may be full weight or less than full weight, a coin may be honest or dishonest, but the object whose quality is in question is in hand. With money, especially today, the thing of questionable value may be no more than an electronic bit. *Money* is far too abstract and varied in meaning to be used as a translated term which means *coin.* Besides, money didn't even exist as a concept for another 1200 years. Using the term *money* in that era would be like using the term *television, computer* or *car* in the same text.

"But those who want to get rich fall into temptation and a snare and many foolish and harmful desires which plunge men into ruin and destruction. For the love of money is a root of all sorts of evil, and some by longing for it have wandered away from the faith and pierced themselves with many griefs." (1 Timothy 6:9–10, NASB95)

The term from which "love of money" is derived is *philarguria* or *philargyria* which comes from the two root words *philos* and *arguros. Philos* means *beloved* and *arguros* means *silver.* This is clearly denoted based on the Strong's references, which are noted above.

The correct translations is "loving silver is a root of all sorts of evil."

In 1 Timothy 3:3, free from the love of money is translated from *aphilargyron* which means not-silver-lover.

"not addicted to wine or pugnacious, but gentle, peaceable, free from the love of money." (1 Timothy 3:3, NASB95)

66 Tyndale New Bible Dictionary, Second Edition, 1982 Money, II, b, p.792

In Hebrews 13:5 free from the love of money is translated from *aphilargyros* which means not-silver-lover.

"Make sure that your character is free from the love of money, being content with what you have; for He Himself has said, "I WILL NEVER DESERT YOU, NOR WILL I EVER FORSAKE YOU," (Hebrews 13:5, NASB95)

Chrema is a bit more of a challenge to get clear in one's thinking. In Acts 8:20 *silver* is translated from *argyrion* which means *silver*. But then *money* is translated from *chrematon*, which is from *chrema*.

Chrema means a thing that one uses or needs.

Chremata is translated *wealth* twice and *money* four times. However, since *chrema* is *something one uses or needs*, it easily represents anything of value that might be exchanged, including *silver*. The silver could be in the form of a coin, but that is simply a shape and weight of a commodity, unless it is being debased. Remember coins were not minted until 700 BC at the earliest and many argue that the earliest minting of coins was closer to 600 BC.[67] Prior to that time the commodities were simply traded by weight, whether precious metal, cattle, tools or timber. Coins are simply a readily recognizable weight and shape of a commodity. Coins may be debased, but if so, the proof is in hand, which at least slows the process of plunder.

This should be translated either:

"because you thought you could obtain the gift of God with things!"

Or:

"because you thought you could obtain the gift of God with wealth!"

"But Peter said to him, "May your silver perish with you, because you thought you could obtain the gift of God with money!" (Acts 8:20, NASB95)

67 The following quote from a book in my possession published in 1840 sets the time closer to 600 BC, which is the 7th Century BC. "The earliest coinage, from the time of Phidon to the reign of Alexander I. Of Macedon, who died about the year 454 B.C., a period of two hundred years, the invention of coinage being assigned to the seventh century B.C." *Akderman, John Yonge, F.S.A., A Numismatic Manual, Taylor & Walton, 28, Upper Gower Street, London, 1840* p. 4

Consider Luke 18:24 for another perspective on *chrema*. To say that *chrema* should be translated *money* makes no sense if it can also be translated *wealth*. *Wealth* and *money* are not the same thing.

Clearly, this next passage demands that the meaning go beyond *money*, since we know that debased *money* is not *wealth*. Paper money tokens can become worthless overnight, as happened with Continental notes during the American Revolutionary War. Worthless money provides no security, yet the point of the passage is that the security of *wealth*, or having plenty of *things one uses or needs*, makes it difficult to enter the kingdom of heaven.

"And Jesus looked at him and said, "How hard it is for those who are wealthy to enter the kingdom of God!" (Luke 18:24, NASB95)

Another passage that is helpful to review is Matthew 6:24. In different Bible translations, the Greek term *mamona* is translated *wealth*, *mammon* and *money*. It means wealth, not money.

"No one can serve two masters; for either he will hate the one and love the other, or he will be devoted to one and despise the other. You cannot serve God and wealth." (Matthew 6:24, NASB95)

Therefore, after much research, I find no basis for the English term money to be used as a translated term for original language terms found in the ancient copies of Scripture.

Origin of the Translation Error

The following comments on Latin terms and bits of history are intended only to share a starting point for more research on the subject. I plan to do more work in this area in the future.

Pecunia

In the Latin Vulgate, which was translated around 400 AD by Jerome, we find that variations of the Latin term *pecunia* were sometimes used when some variation of *argentum* was the correct Latin term.

Pecunia is a Latin word for *wealth* which is based on *pecus*, the Latin word for *cattle*. Cattle have remained valuable property over the centuries. Consider these excerpts from *Ancient Numismatics*:

."..the simplest necessities were the most common media of exchange in the beginning, and consequently these became the measure of value. Foremost among these were cattle, since they provided food as well as the most important raw material for clothing, ornaments and tools with their hides, bones and horns. Proof of the use of cattle as money among the Greeks is in the existence of verbal formations and expressions [...], impositions of fines and rewards measured in head of cattle as are mentioned in the laws of Drakon and in the festival of Delia. As for the Romans, we may cite the evidence of the etymology of pecunia, peculatus, etc., and the legal fines involving head of cattle. These fines were changed into quantities of metal only in the second half of the Fifth Century B.C."[68]

"The epics of Homer depict the Greeks in an intermediary stage: cattle as monetary units were still the measure of value - a piece of merchandise was worth 4, 9, 12, 20 or 100 head of cattle. On the other hand, metal tools as monetary units already served as a medium of payment; the brass bowls and tripods appearing as gifts and prizes, as well as axes, were no longer mere utensils, but objects of treasure, as their large numbers show."[69]

Notice that the author, Kurt Regling, calls cattle and metal tools money. His thinking is correct if money is considered to be a medium of exchange, unit of account and store of value. However, in practice nothing called money has ever been used that way. Money is never a store of value. Money is always a system of plunder. Cattle were used in honest exchange, but they could not be debased. They were not a system, they were and are precise objects with identity. Cattle are living things precisely defined by genetics. His implied definition of money may as well be defining a unicorn.

---

68 Regling, Kurt, Ancient Numismatics – The Coinage of Ancient Greece and Rome, Argonaut Inc. Publishers, Chicago, 1969. A Translation of "Munzkunde" first published in 1930 in Leipzig and Berlin. p. 7

69 Ibid.

In any case, *Pecuniam* began as *wealth*, but over the years it has come to mean *money*. There is no way for *pecunia* to have been a word for *money* before *money* became a word. *Pecunia* referred to objects of wealth, not systems of plunder.

The actual term *money* is derived from the coin making activity in the temple of a Roman goddess called Juno. The phrase Juno Moneta in the late 13th or early 14th century lead to the development and use of the term *moneta* for *money*. Therefore, *pecunia* in 400 AD could not have been a Latin word for *money*, when the *money* was derived from words associated with a Roman temple 900 years later. The time-line just doesn't work.

Pecuniam is now inappropriately associated with *money*, but it gets worse. *Argentum* is also now sometimes defined as *silver* and *money*.

I have a Latin reader and dictionary from 1860 which defines *argentum* as *silver; silver money; money.*[70] On one hand, this seems to be a credible definition being that it is "so old."

But is the book really that old? The translation error began at least in 400 AD, which was 1,460 years before this 1860 Latin dictionary was published. The change in the meaning of *pecuniam* and *argentum* is subtle and dangerous.

At the start, *pecus* is *cattle* and *pecuniam* is *wealth*. But then later *pecuniam* becomes *money*. This is how we arrive at the definition of the English term *pecuniary* being all about *money*. Money is a vapor which cannot be precisely or consistently defined, except as a system of plunder.

With the passing of time *pecuniam* supposedly comes to mean *money*. Along the way, the translators notice that the Hebrew term *keseph* is translated *pecuniam* and *argentum*. Therefore they falsely argue that *argentum* must mean both *silver* and *money*. These are two things which are fundamentally different and have totally different origins and effects in society.

In other words, equating *argentum*, *silver* and *money* is accomplished with circular arguments that have no logical foundation. This supposed equality is a fallacy.

The symbol for *silver* in the Periodic Table of Elements is *Ag*, which is from the Latin *argentum*. *Money* is not an element. *Money* is a system.

---

70 Andrews, E. A., Sallust's History of the War Against Jugurtha, and of the Conspiracy of Catiline: with a Dictionary and Notes, Crocker and Brewster, 47 Washington Street, Boston, 1860. p. 149

In the Old Testament the term *keseph* means the commodity *silver*. *Keseph* cannot mean *coin* or *money*, since *coins* came hundreds of years later and *money* came thousands of years later.

Role of the Latin Vulgate

The term money began its entry into Bible translations in at least 400 AD, through the Latin Vulgate, under the pen of Jerome of Bethlehem, and perhaps through the earlier work of other Latin translations on which Jerome relied. For about one thousand years the Catholic Church trained the priests, and only the priests had access to the Scripture, since the common man neither read nor spoke Latin. By 1209 AD Bible reading was outlawed and violators came under the harsh punishments of the Inquisition.

After 980 years, Wycliffe (1380 AD) and later Tyndale (1525 AD) translated copies of Scripture into the common language because they believed that everyone, including the plow-boy, should have access to the Scripture.

Wycliffe was forced to hide from church and state, his books were burned during his life and his bones were dug up and scattered 45 years after his death. Tyndale was labeled a heretic, then strangled and burned at the stake.

Wycliffe's followers, derisively called Lollards, preached directly from the Bible wherever they could. When caught, these people were commonly executed, sometimes by being burned at the stake with their Bible chained to their neck. The Catholic Church burned Bibles, translators and Protestants, otherwise known as heretics[71]. The Catholic Church as an institution did everything in its power to prevent the common man from directly reading the Scriptures.

Perhaps because the Catholic Church was seeking wealth and holding kings to account to gain greater power, the institution had an interest in shrouding some of their activities in secrecy. Whatever the original reason, as time has passed, replacing the term *keseph* with *pecuniam* in the Latin Vulgate has turned *silver* into *money*, first in Scripture and eventually in the broader culture.

"Give me control of a nation's money and I care not who makes the laws." — Mayer Rothschild (1744-1812)

---

71 Times were different and burning at the stake was not rejected outright, as it should have been. Protestants also burned "witches" and probably a few Catholics. The focus here is on the reason the Catholic Church was burning people, namely for placing direct reading of Scripture above Catholic teaching.

Result Restated

Pecuniam began as *wealth* and over time the definition has changed to mean *money*. With *money* thereby introduced into the reading of the Bible, over the course of time, an intellectual and doctrinal wall of separation was erected between rational, Godly economics and theology. We have been paying an increasingly high price ever since.

Becoming Expert Economists

"My people are destroyed for lack of knowledge. Because you have rejected knowledge, I also will reject you from being My priest. Since you have forgotten the law of your God, I also will forget your children." (Hosea 4:6, NASB95)

Economic terms in Scripture, which are used extensively to explain salvation, mean that every Christian should correctly understand economics. The entire Christian community must advance the study and understanding of economics in the church. Economic terms in Scripture illustrate the importance of economics temporally and spiritually. The precise meaning and translation history of *keseph* and *arguros* bring us face to face with the evil and fraudulent nature of our monetary system. For those who are not Christian, the literary position of the Bible may pique your interest and draw you into the same understanding through the lens of math, reason, logic, history and current events.

Society will never prosper without the producer understanding economics and the methods by which his labor and property are used to oppress him. A producer must not only learn to produce, but he also must learn to protect his life, liberty and property. Being ignorant of economics eventually leads to hardworking people funding their own oppression and poverty. Consider these quotes from Thomas Jefferson.

"If a nation expects to be ignorant and free in a state of civilization, it expects what never was and never will be." —Thomas Jefferson to Charles Yancey, 1816.

"I, however, place economy among the first and most important virtues, and public debt as the greatest of dangers to be feared. To preserve our independence, we must not let our rulers load us with perpetual debt. If we run into such debts, we must be taxed in our meat and drink, in our necessities and in our comforts, in our labor and in our amusements. If we can prevent the government from wasting the

labor of the people, under the pretense of caring for them, they will be happy." —Thomas Jefferson, Letter to William Plumer, 1816

"I am not among those who fear the people. They, and not the rich, are our dependence for continued freedom. And to preserve their independence, we must not let our rulers load us with perpetual debt. We must make our election between economy and liberty, or profusion and servitude. If we run into such debts, as that we must be taxed in our meat and in our drink, in our necessaries and our comforts, in our labors and our amusements, for our callings and our creeds, as the people of England are, our people, like them, must come to labor sixteen hours in the twenty-four, give the earnings of fifteen of these to the government for their debts and daily expenses; and the sixteenth being insufficient to afford us bread, we must live, as they now do, on oatmeal and potatoes; have no time to think, no means of calling the mismanagers to account; but be glad to obtain subsistence by hiring ourselves to rivet their chains on the necks of our fellow-sufferers."

— Thomas Jefferson, excerpt from his letter to Samuel Kercheval, July 12, 1816

Conclusion

This chapter covers a lot of ground in order to show that original language terms in Scripture cannot justifiably be translated to the English term *money*. It reviews the meaning of Greek and Hebrew words, shows them in context, reviews definitions and concordance entries and presents all these things in the context of history and time. The relative time line makes it clear that silver has always been here and coins and money are very recent developments.

We see that the translation error was introduced in at least 400 AD, and for one thousand years the Catholic Church was able to suppress the knowledge of Scripture to a great degree, even to the point of having governments outlaw the reading of the Bible. By the time Wycliffe and others began translating to the common language, the idea of *wealth and money* regularly taking the place of *silver* in translation was well developed in conventional thought.

Because currency debasement in those days was a long and slow process, the danger and effects were easier to miss. At the same time, the good fruit of other truth in Scripture began reshaping the culture in excellent ways. Over the course of time, the Christian work ethic lead to increased production. This increased production was confiscated through money systems and used to undermine the very teaching that was responsible for the increased production and knowledge. Because translation errors have caused us to misunderstand money, we actually fund our own oppression. We pay for the propaganda that leads us astray.

If people knew that the term money didn't exist in the original languages of Scripture, then they would question money, which they would learn is a system of plunder. By questioning money, the systems of plunder would be severely limited, perhaps eliminated, and the producers would control how they and their children were educated. By pursuing truth, which is necessary to be productive, the ideas which defend individual life, liberty and property and enhance production would be taught.

3.6 Watching The Changes

This chapter needs an introduction of sorts to ensure that my intended meaning is clearly conveyed to the reader.

The first thing I want to make clear is my high regard for Bible software study tools in general and Logos Bible Software specifically. I have three Bible software applications on my computer and I use online tools as well.

I also have old books, Bible commentaries, writing from authors on topics including Christian life, apologetics, literature, history, science, government, economics and more than twenty physical copies of the Bible. It is important in our time to have hard copy that is slow to change and soft copy that is quick to search.

Hard copy is slow to search, but has a certain reliability because *your copy* will not change. Changes do occur in books, but the changes take decades and centuries and require multiple reprints.

Soft copy is amazing because the student can ask questions and get answers – in seconds. The great danger in soft copy is that same content can change in seconds.

When reading hard copy, meaning a physical book, people often have a tendency to consider it to be true and correct, especially if it is old to the reader. However, that may not be a good assessment. We have to learn to see the sweep of history in terms of all known history, viewed at least through the lens of principle and economics. That old book was new once. The printer and powers which surrounded the making of the book may have had bad motives, which negatively influenced its contents.

There are true and reliable things in the world which can be used to test the validity of certain ideas. None of these true and reliable things are men or man made institutions. But math, reason, logic, some history and, in my view, Scripture in the original languages have served us well in this regard. In other words, those things that a person can use to understand what is true and correct, that no man or institution can change, are most reliable.

Granted, even when using correct information the student can misunderstand and reach wrong conclusions, but the error tends to be on one side of the process, not both. Even a smart and diligent student who is trying to master material that someone has deceptively changed is prevented from getting the right answers. The cycle of learning is thrown off course and there is no hope of setting things right unless the student begins to question the material he is learning. That process can only work by finding reliable standards against which to measure the deceptive teaching.

In addition, a student must learn to look past his teacher, who was also once a student at the feet of a teacher.

An Example

In the following text I am using a particular electronic document that resides in a particular software program as an EXAMPLE of the problems we face in searching for the truth about things in history and Scripture. Did I mention this is an example?

This example is used because it is current and illustrates the problem, the process and the confusion that is doing damage in society today. It is a great example because thousands of other people can test these exact claims. It is an example of literal translation starting out correctly, then being corrupted by tradition and error. It is a warning of the dangers and high responsibility associated with electronic publication. It is an example of how easily error can be corrected with electronic publication.

The example presented in the following text includes some detailed names and exact file details which are intended to clearly identify the electronic copy of the document in question, as well as my method of accessing the document. This detailed information is NOT intended to draw unwarranted attention to the software or the work in question. The detailed information is intended to enable others to duplicate my findings.

To be perfectly clear, I would encourage everyone to consider purchasing a Bible software study application. My preference is Logos Bible Software 4. I also caution and encourage everyone to help hold these tools and documents to a high standard by comparing sources and learning. The wonderful opportunity we have is this: It is true that error can be introduced in seconds, but the correction of error that has harmed individuals and society for centuries can also be introduced the same way.

The Details

One of the ways that I discovered the truth about money in Scripture was by studying the OpenText.org sentence diagrams[72] in my Libronix Digital Library System[73] version 3.0d Bible software, which is a product of Logos Research Systems, Inc.

Because I believe Scripture is *sufficient*, I believe that anything we *need* to know will be written there. Because I spent fifteen years learning the truth about money and production, I was able to recognize something was not adding up with regard to money as I read and studied the Bible. Studying various translations and reading commentaries did not provide a logically consistent explanation. Dictionary entries held some clues, but clues were difficult to see during the learning phase, especially since the clues were mixed with error.

Fortunately, I knew enough about economics to know something was wrong. Because my belief about Scripture told me that if there was a conflict, it had to be the interpretation and not the text, I kept searching.

One day while working in Logos 3 I came across a real treasure: The OpenText.org Syntactically Analyzed Greek New Testament: Clause Analysis.

These sentence diagrams have played two important roles regarding my research into these 1600 year old translation errors. One role is good, the other is a mixture of good and bad.

The Good

First, the July, 27 2007 diagrams in Logos 3 give a true and accurate literal translation of the terms in question. I have concluded the reason for this is as follows:

---

72 Porter, S. E., O'Donnell, M. B., Reed, J. T., Tan, R., & OpenText.org. (2006). *The OpenText.org Syntactically Analyzed Greek New Testament: Clause Analysis; OpenText.org Clause Analysis.* Logos Research Systems, Inc.

73 http://www.libronix.com/

When working in Logos as a user, the setting to display the English word in the clause analysis is titled *Literal Translation*. This is an excellent label because the Greek words are being translated literally, even though they are a bit difficult to read that way. The purpose of literal translation is to be literal, not to present the terms for readability.

I suspect the work that went into this clause analysis was properly myopic and quite literal, since the work was not intended to produce readable text. The purpose was to analyze clause and sentence structure and also to present literal translations of the Greek terms. This becomes a tool for translators, Pastors and Bible students to use in better understanding the original text.

It is worth noting that this sort of work would not rely on commentaries and translations in the same way that other kinds of translation work would. Because the commentaries and definitions would be of little use in this process and the resulting text was not being judged for readability, the Greek terms didn't have the 1600 years of baggage to carry.

The result? The terms were translated literally and correctly.

The Mixed

Second, I was shocked and amazed to find that the *correct literal translations* in the sentence diagrams *changed to incorrect literal translations* sometime between my copies of Logos 3 and Logos Bible Software 4. The translators had these terms and translations right and then changed them!

The bad thing about this is the change that introduced error. If I started after October 27, 2009 with my Logos software, chances are this would not have been a clue to the answer I was seeking.

The example of how these kinds of things can change over time is a good warning. A second good thing here is that *two* translation teams validated the claims that I am making, before someone reintroduced error in their work. Even if one wanted to illogically argue that the readable translation should be different, arguing the literal translation should be fluffed up for readability is absurd and contrary to the correct development and purpose of the clause analysis.

To be clear, I hold the Logos company and software in high regard and greatly enjoy and appreciate the work that has gone into these resources. I respect and appreciate the work of the OpenText.org team. However, the Logos software has a *Report typo* feature for a reason. People make mistakes. For example, I hope any errors in *Know Stealing* will be pointed out so that I can correct them.

Presenting The Case

In the following images, you will see clearly that a correct set of translations was replaced with an incorrect set of translations in these sentence diagrams. I do not think this was done maliciously.

Instead I believe that the people doing the work are uninformed about economics and do not realize the serious problems we have regarding *money* in our Bible translations. I hope to have the opportunity to work together with any and all who are interested in getting this straightened out.

The following pages of our example begin with a partial Logos 3 screen-shot, followed by a partial Logos Bible Software 4 screen-shot. These two images will enable the reader to visualize the context from which the next set of images is collected.

The next set of images is grouped by verse and display between one and four lines from the OpenText.org sentence diagrams, as presented in these two versions (Logos 3 and Logos 4) of the Logos software[74]. For readability, the OpenText.org image from Logos 3 contains a smaller font and the OpenText.org image from Logos Bible Software 4 contains a larger font.

These images show a real-life, present day example of changes in the literal translation of terms in Bible study resources. An example of the gradual errors that have been introduced over the course of 1600 years has played out right here, sometime between July, 27 2007 and October 27, 2009.

Technical Details

Within both versions of the software, the file that contains this information is:

OpenTextGraph.lbxclv

In my copy of Logos 3 the file is dated: *2007-07-27T00:30:44Z*
In Logos Bible Software 4 the file is dated: *2009-10-27T19:04:54Z*

Following is an image of the file information in Logos 4.

---

74 I expect that a resource update in Logos 3 will update the OpenText.org file to the October 27, 2009 version. In that case the Logos 3 diagrams will match the Logos 4 diagrams.

Support Info	OPENTEXTGRAPH 2009-10-27T19:04:54Z OpenTextGraph.lbxclv

Again, please note that in these images the font is smaller in Logos 3 and larger in Logos 4. This will be the same in the following comparison images.

Logos 3.0d

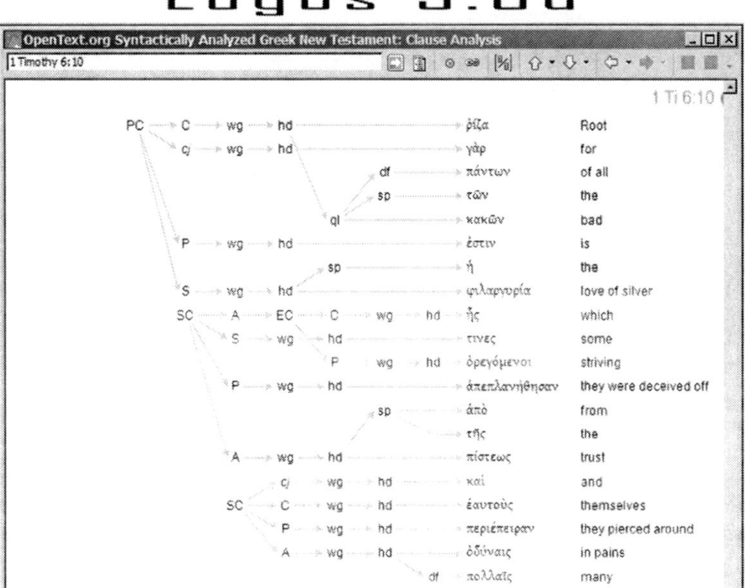

In the following images, within each rectangle, a verse is noted at the top and then one or more terms from that verse are listed from the *OpenText.org* sentence diagrams and clause analysis.

The first terms in smaller font are from the *OpenTextGraph.lbxclv* file dated *2007-07-27T00:30:44Z* in Logos 3.

The second terms in a larger font are from the *OpenTextGraph.lbxclv* file dated *2009-10-27T19:04:54Z* in Logos 4.

Logos 4

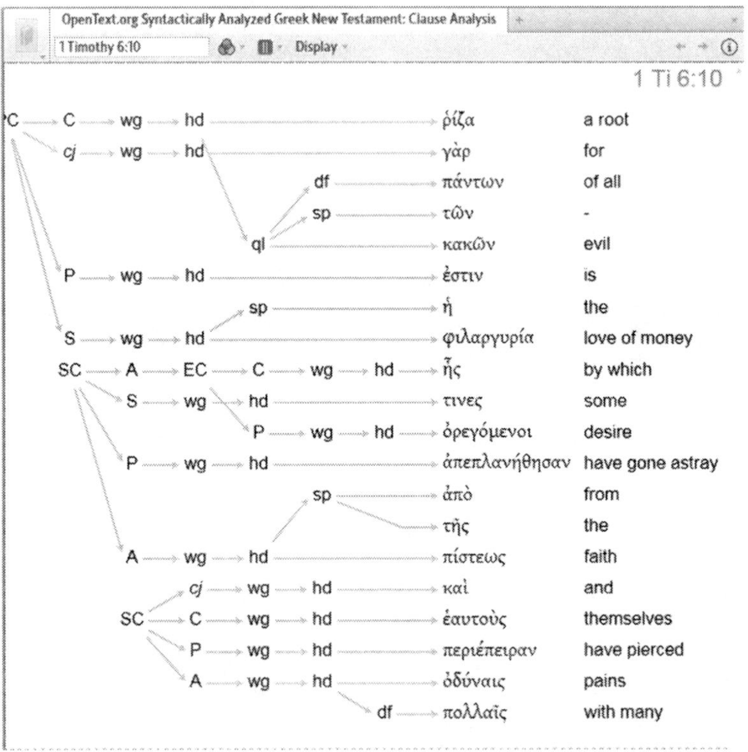

Many of these verses and terms have been covered already in previous chapters. The goal in this chapter is not to discuss the terms, but simply to show that they have been changed.

In the first image the verse is labeled and the two versions of the file are noted as 2007 and 2009. This is the same pattern in every rectangle in the next five images.

The Issue Summarized

I suspect that when this diagramming work was going on, the team was focused intently on the exact words being diagrammed, and not so much on the way the Greek would be translated into English for the typical Bible reader. After all, the label for these English words is *Literal Translation*. For this reason their work was not influenced by commentaries and Bible translations to the degree that other kinds of work would be. Consequently, they correctly translated these terms in the 2007 file. For some reason they came back later and changed the Greek terms to the wrong English terms in the 2009 file.

A Picture = A Thousand Words

So here are twenty pictures...

At the end of these five images, which contain twenty examples of these errors, a second example is presented where a separate team has done a similar thing.

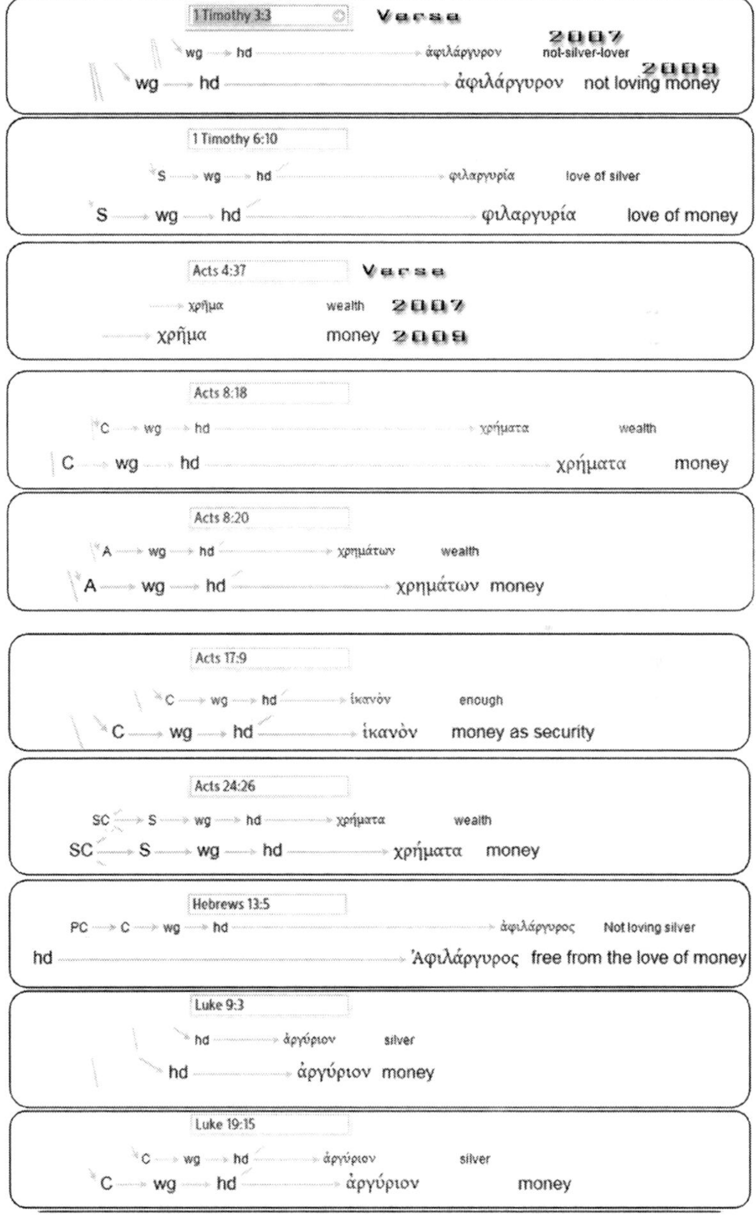

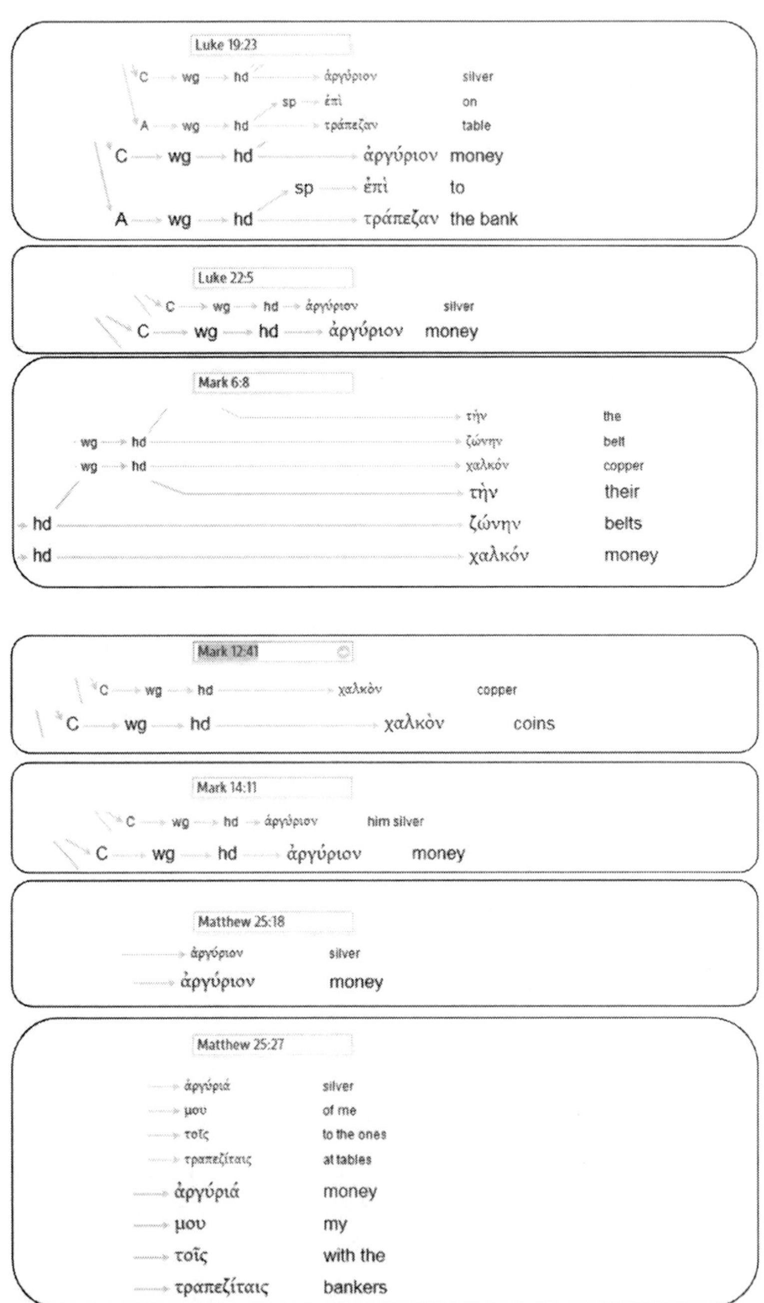
Luke 19:23
C wg hd ἀργύριον silver
sp ἐπὶ on
A wg hd τράπεζαν table
C wg hd ἀργύριον money
sp ἐπὶ to
A wg hd τράπεζαν the bank
Luke 22:5
C wg hd ἀργύριον silver
C wg hd ἀργύριον money
Mark 6:8
τὴν the
wg hd ζώνην belt
wg hd χαλκόν copper
τὴν their
hd ζώνην belts
hd χαλκόν money
Mark 12:41
C wg hd χαλκὸν copper
C wg hd χαλκὸν coins
Mark 14:11
C wg hd ἀργύριον him silver
C wg hd ἀργύριον money
Matthew 25:18
ἀργύριον silver
ἀργύριον money
Matthew 25:27
ἀργύριά silver
μου of me
τοῖς to the ones
τραπεζίταις at tables
ἀργύριά money
μου my
τοῖς with the
τραπεζίταις bankers

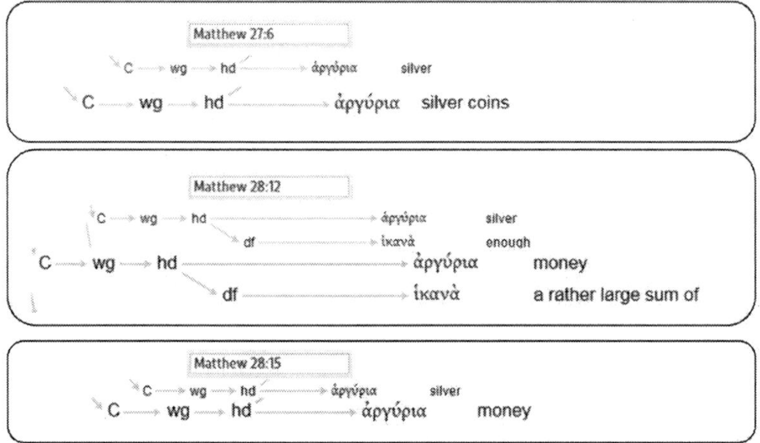

Matthew 27:6 partly survives the update because of the three other references to silver in Matthew 27:3-9 and the fact that it is commonly known that Jesus was betrayed by Judas for thirty pieces of silver. Notice that *coins* is added, but there is no basis for the addition.

Another good example that has not been covered is *bank*[75]. The English word *bank* is from the Greek word *trapeza*. *Trapeza* means *a table* or *a dining table*.

First, there is one place in Scripture, Matthew 25:27, where the specific term *trapezites* is used and it is translated *bankers*. Having "*ites*" on the end of *trapeza* could lead to the translation *tabler*, meaning something like *one who is at the table*.

Then there are fifteen other cases where the term *trapeza* is used. This Greek term *trapeza* is translated *table* or *tables* thirteen times, *set food before them* once and *bank* once.

In Acts 16:34 when *trapeza* is translated *set food before them* it should simply be *table*. Therefore, out of fifteen times that *trapeza* is used, 14 are explicitly or clearly *table*.

What about the one time *trapeza* is translated *bank*? How does a *table* become a *bank*?

In Matthew 21:12, Mark 11:15 and John 2:15 *trapeza* refers to the *tables* of the moneychangers, which is the same object translated a *bank* in two other places.

75 In the Old Testament *bank* refers to a river bank 16 times and once to a bank or tower of herbs in Song of Solomon 5:13. There are no other references to *bank* in the OT.

This is another troubling translation error. We accept the idea of a *bank*, in part, because it is a term present in Scripture – only twice. In addition, *bank* is translated from a term that means *table* everywhere else it is used.

The term *trapeza* is also used in the following verses: Matthew 15:27, Mark 7:28, Luke 16:21, Luke 22:21, Luke 22:30, Acts 6:2, Romans 11:9, 1 Corinthians 10:29 and Hebrews 9:2.

In my opinion, the content of these verses make the translation of *trapeza* to *bank* a disgrace.

Another Example

I mentioned earlier that a second team had done a similar thing by starting out with a correct translation and then later changing to an incorrect translation. In the second team's work, there was only one matching case from the preceding examples, because their work was in progress. *The Lexham Syntactic Greek New Testament: Sentence Analysis* from November 10, 2008 included the following New Testament books:

Romans, 1 & 2 Corinthians, Galatians, Ephesians, Philippians, Colossians, Hebrews, James, 1 & 2 Peter, 1, 2 & 3 John, Jude and Revelation.

In this collection of books, only Hebrews contains a verse from the preceding list of examples.

From the *November 10, 2008* file, *aphilarguros* in Hebrews 13:5 is translated "*not loving silver.*"

From the July 23, 2010 file *aphilarguros* in Hebrews 13:5 is translated "free from the love of money."

Following are the file details, which can be used for comparison by anyone with access to the two versions of the files in Logos software.

Lukaszewski, A. L. (2007). The Lexham Syntactic Greek New Testament: Sentence Analysis. Logos Research Systems, Inc.

Logos 3: LexhamSGNTGraph.lbxclv 2008-11-10T22:07:58Z

Lukaszewski, A. L., & Dubis, M. (2009). *The Lexham Syntactic Greek New Testament: Sentence Analysis.* Logos Research Systems, Inc.

Logos 4: LexhamSGNTGraph.lbxclv 2010-07-23T17:23:05Z

Conclusion

Two teams of Bible scholars working myopically on clause analysis provided a correct literal translation of a series of terms related to silver, copper, belts and tables. There may be other examples as well.

When using the Logos 3 or Logos 4 software, the way to cause the English words to be displayed on the screen is to check the box titled *Literal Translation*. These literal translations agree with a logically coherent analysis of silver, money, banks, tables, history and time.

Sometime later someone came back and changed these correct translations to incorrect translations. The reason is unknown to me, but it is probably rooted in the same confusion that has been causing us problems since at least 400 AD when *pecuniam* was inserted into the Latin Vulgate.

I have spoken to two Logos representatives about some of this and also posted a brief note about these findings on my blog in February 2009. Otherwise, I have not yet had an in depth discussion with Logos or the teams who have done this work, because my complaint is not about this single case. Resolving this particular error does not solve the greater problem we have regarding incorrect translations of money in Scripture. This is only one example of a centuries old pervasive problem.

In the Chapter titled *What Can I Do?* there is a list of actions that Logos Bible Software users can take to participate in resolving this error in the clause analysis. There are also some easy steps we can take with regard to Bible translations using the wonderful Logos Bible Software. Individuals who use other Bible software or no Bible software also have ways to participate in solving this narrow but important collection of Bible translation errors. The important thing is for the knowledge to spread and the change to come about because the truth is known. It does no good for a single error to be corrected if the same underlying problem remains.

The Bible is God's Holy word and I treasure it enough to speak up if we have misinterpreted or misrepresented what was originally written by anyone at any time in history. I hope those who see Scripture the same will join me. I also hope those interested in correctly preserving and translating important ancient literature will do the same.

3.7 A Simple Test

The person reading performs the Simple Test by inserting the word silver in place of the word money in the following Bible verses to see if the verse, passage and context still make sense.

This chapter is included in its present form as a resource to the reader. It is not intended to be read word by word, but rather to be scanned and observed. Of course reading word by word is a perfectly good thing to do, but it is not necessary for the purpose here.

The contents include Bible verses and commentary.

The reader will find commentary before the section containing verses about *money*, which follows the section containing verses about *silver*. Depending on your electronic reader, this could be 20 to 40 screens from the start of the section on *silver*.

The Text

The following pages include the verses from the King James Translation of the Bible which contain the 403 occurrences of KSP (keseph) in the original language. Keseph is translated *silver* 287 times, *money* 110 times and a few other things as well.

This list of verses permits a quick scan to get a feel for how the term KSP is translated from the original Hebrew and enables a simple test to see if the various translations of KSP make sense. In addition, the reader can easily compare these passages to his or her Bible.

Keseph

The following verses include English terms which are translated from a Hebrew word written with three Hebrew letters. Transliterated into English, these three letters are KSP, which is Strong's Hebrew #3701.

3701. כֶּסֶף keseph (494a); from 3700; silver, money:—fine(2), fine silver(2), money(100), pay(1), price(10), property(1), purchase price(1), silver(284), silver from the money(1).[76]

Take a look at the *dots* in and around the Hebrew letters above. I understand these dots or markings to be variations of the word.

There are a few combinations of markings on these letters, which

76 Thomas, R. L. (1998). New American Standard Hebrew-Aramaic and Greek dictionaries: Updated edition. Anaheim: Foundation Publications, Inc.

are then considered to be some particular word in translation. However, the translation of KSP written a certain way is handled ***inconsistently***.

Depending on the translation team, a certain set of markings may be translated *silver* one time and *money* another. In other words, even without being an ancient Hebrew scholar, anyone can see by way of *logic* that this sort of translation is not correct.

In addition to "dot pattern" contradiction, logically speaking, no combination of markings associated with KSP can mean an English word or concept that didn't exist at the time.

It is also logically impossible for a single Hebrew word written and used the same way to mean two English words which are fundamentally opposite in nature and meaning.

Following are all the English words in the KJV translated from Strong's number 3701.

silver	287
money	110
price	3
of the money	1
worth	1
silverlings	1

The following verses are divided into groups following each of the English words which are translated from the Hebrew KSP. The section heading includes the English word, followed by the number of times it is translated from Strong's #3701, KSP. Transliterated into English with vowels, KSP is *keseph* or *keceph*.

The Simple Test is done with verses in the section where *keseph* is translated *money*.

The Simple Test is this: In every case where you see the term *money*, insert the term *silver* and see if the passage makes sense. (Hint: Inserting *silver* in place of *money* when translated from KSP always works.)

silver 287 of 403

Genesis 13:2 And Abram was very rich in cattle, in ***silver***, and in gold.

Genesis 20:16 And unto Sarah he said, Behold, I have given thy brother a thousand pieces of ***silver***: behold, he is to thee a covering of the eyes, unto all that are with thee, and with all other: thus she was reproved.

Genesis 23:15 My lord, hearken unto me: the land is worth four hundred shekels of ***silver***; what is that betwixt me and thee? bury therefore thy dead.

Genesis 23:16 And Abraham hearkened unto Ephron; and Abraham weighed to Ephron the ***silver***, which he had named in the audience of the sons of Heth, four hundred shekels of ***silver***, current money with the merchant.

Genesis 24:35 And the Lord hath blessed my master greatly; and he is become great: and he hath given him flocks, and herds, and ***silver***, and gold, and menservants, and maidservants, and camels, and asses.

Genesis 24:53 And the servant brought forth jewels of ***silver***, and jewels of gold, and raiment, and gave them to Rebekah: he gave also to her brother and to her mother precious things.

Genesis 37:28 Then there passed by Midianites merchantmen; and they drew and lifted up Joseph out of the pit, and sold Joseph to the Ishmeelites for twenty pieces of ***silver***: and they brought Joseph into Egypt.

Genesis 44:2 And put my cup, the ***silver*** cup, in the sack's mouth of the youngest, and his corn money. And he did according to the word that Joseph had spoken.

Genesis 44:8 behold, the money, which we found in our sacks' mouths, we brought again unto thee out of the land of Canaan: how then should we steal out of thy lord's house ***silver*** or gold?

Genesis 45:22 To all of them he gave each man changes of raiment; but to Benjamin he gave three hundred pieces of ***silver***, and five changes of raiment.

Exodus 3:22 but every woman shall borrow of her neighbour, and of her that sojourneth in her house, jewels of ***silver***, and jewels of gold, and raiment: and ye shall put them upon your sons, and upon your daughters; and ye shall spoil the Egyptians.

Exodus 11:2 Speak now in the ears of the people, and let every man borrow of his neighbour, and every woman of her neighbour, jewels of ***silver***, and jewels of gold.

Exodus 12:35 And the children of Israel did according to the word of Moses; and they borrowed of the Egyptians jewels of ***silver***, and jewels of gold, and raiment:

Exodus 20:23 Ye shall not make with me gods of ***silver***, neither shall ye make unto you gods of gold.

Exodus 21:32 If the ox shall push a manservant or a maidservant; he shall give unto their master thirty shekels of ***silver***, and the ox shall be stoned.

Exodus 25:3 And this is the offering which ye shall take of them; gold, and ***silver***, and brass,

Exodus 26:19 And thou shalt make forty sockets of ***silver*** under the twenty boards; two sockets under one board for his two tenons, and two sockets under another board for his two tenons.

Exodus 26:21 and their forty sockets of ***silver***; two sockets under one board, and two sockets under another board.

Exodus 26:25 And they shall be eight boards, and their sockets of ***silver***, sixteen sockets; two sockets under one board, and two sockets under another board.

Exodus 26:32 and thou shalt hang it upon four pillars of shittim wood overlaid with gold: their hooks shall be of gold, upon the four sockets of ***silver***.

Exodus 27:10 and the twenty pillars thereof and their twenty sockets shall be of brass; the hooks of the pillars and their fillets shall be of ***silver***.

Exodus 27:11 And likewise for the north side in length there shall be hangings of an hundred cubits long, and his twenty pillars and their twenty sockets of brass; the hooks of the pillars and their fillets of ***silver***.

Exodus 27:17 All the pillars round about the court shall be filleted with ***silver***; their hooks shall be of ***silver***, and their sockets of brass.

Exodus 31:4 to devise cunning works, to work in gold, and in ***silver***, and in brass,

Exodus 35:5 Take ye from among you an offering unto the Lord: whosoever is of a willing heart, let him bring it, an offering of the Lord; gold, and ***silver***, and brass,

Exodus 35:24 Every one that did offer an offering of ***silver*** and brass brought the Lord's offering: and every man, with whom was found shittim wood for any work of the service, brought it.

Exodus 35:32 and to devise curious works, to work in gold, and in ***silver***, and in brass,

Exodus 36:24 and forty sockets of ***silver*** he made under the twenty boards; two sockets under one board for his two tenons, and two sockets under another board for his two tenons.

Exodus 36:26 and their forty sockets of ***silver***; two sockets under one board, and two sockets under another board.

Exodus 36:30 And there were eight boards; and their sockets were sixteen sockets of ***silver***, under every board two sockets.

Exodus 36:36 And he made thereunto four pillars of shittim wood, and overlaid them with gold: their hooks were of gold; and he cast for them four sockets of ***silver***.

Exodus 38:10 their pillars were twenty, and their brasen sockets twenty; the hooks of the pillars and their fillets were of ***silver***.

Exodus 38:11 And for the north side the hangings were an hundred cubits, their pillars were twenty, and their sockets of brass twenty; the hooks of the pillars and their fillets of ***silver***.

Exodus 38:12 And for the west side were hangings of fifty cubits, their pillars ten, and their sockets ten; the hooks of the pillars and their fillets of ***silver***.

Exodus 38:17 And the sockets for the pillars were of brass; the hooks of the pillars and their fillets of ***silver***; and the overlaying of their chapiters of ***silver***; and all the pillars of the court were filleted with ***silver***.

Exodus 38:19 And their pillars were four, and their sockets of brass four; their hooks of ***silver***, and the overlaying of their chapiters and their fillets of ***silver***.

Exodus 38:25 And the ***silver*** of them that were numbered of the congregation was an hundred talents, and a thousand seven hundred and threescore and fifteen shekels, after the shekel of the sanctuary:

Exodus 38:27 And of the hundred talents of ***silver*** were cast the sockets of the sanctuary, and the sockets of the vail; an hundred sockets of the hundred talents, a talent for a socket.

Leviticus 5:15 If a soul commit a trespass, and sin through ignorance, in the holy things of the Lord; then he shall bring for his trespass unto the Lord a ram without blemish out of the flocks, with thy estimation by shekels of ***silver***, after the shekel of the sanctuary, for a trespass offering:

Leviticus 27:3 And thy estimation shall be of the male from twenty years old even unto sixty years old, even thy estimation shall be fifty shekels of ***silver***, after the shekel of the sanctuary.

Leviticus 27:6 And if it be from a month old even unto five years old, then thy estimation shall be of the male five shekels of ***silver***, and for the female thy estimation shall be three shekels of ***silver***.

Leviticus 27:16 And if a man shall sanctify unto the Lord some part of a field of his possession, then thy estimation shall be according to the seed thereof: an homer of barley seed shall be valued at fifty shekels of ***silver***.

Numbers 7:13 and his offering was one ***silver*** charger, the weight thereof was an hundred and thirty shekels, one ***silver*** bowl of seventy shekels, after the shekel of the sanctuary; both of them were full of fine flour mingled with oil for a meat offering:

Numbers 7:19 he offered for his offering one ***silver*** charger, the weight whereof was an hundred and thirty shekels, one ***silver*** bowl of seventy shekels, after the shekel of the sanctuary; both of them full of fine flour mingled with oil for a meat offering:

Numbers 7:25 his offering was one ***silver*** charger, the weight whereof was an hundred and thirty shekels, one ***silver*** bowl of seventy shekels, after the shekel of the sanctuary; both of them full of fine flour mingled with oil for a meat offering:

Numbers 7:31 his offering was one ***silver*** charger of the weight of an hundred and thirty shekels, one ***silver*** bowl of seventy shekels, after the shekel of the sanctuary; both of them full of fine flour mingled with oil for a meat offering:

Numbers 7:37 his offering was one ***silver*** charger, the weight whereof was an hundred and thirty shekels, one ***silver*** bowl of seventy shekels, after the shekel of the sanctuary; both of them full of fine flour mingled with oil for a meat offering:

Numbers 7:43 his offering was one ***silver*** charger of the weight of an hundred and thirty shekels, a ***silver*** bowl of seventy shekels, after the shekel of the sanctuary; both of them full of fine flour mingled with oil for a meat offering:

Numbers 7:49 his offering was one ***silver*** charger, the weight whereof was an hundred and thirty shekels, one ***silver*** bowl of seventy shekels, after the shekel of the sanctuary; both of them full of fine flour mingled with oil for a meat offering:

Numbers 7:55 his offering was one ***silver*** charger of the weight of an hundred and thirty shekels, one ***silver*** bowl of seventy shekels, after the shekel of the sanctuary; both of them full of fine flour mingled with oil for a meat offering:

Numbers 7:61 his offering was one ***silver*** charger, the weight whereof was an hundred and thirty shekels, one ***silver*** bowl of seventy shekels, after the shekel of the sanctuary; both of them full of fine flour mingled with oil for a meat offering:

Numbers 7:67 his offering was one ***silver*** charger, the weight whereof was an hundred and thirty shekels, one ***silver*** bowl of seventy shekels, after the shekel of the sanctuary; both of them full of fine flour mingled with oil for a meat offering:

Numbers 7:73 his offering was one ***silver*** charger, the weight whereof was an hundred and thirty shekels, one ***silver*** bowl of seventy shekels, after the shekel of the sanctuary; both of them full of fine flour mingled with oil for a meat offering:

Numbers 7:79 his offering was one ***silver*** charger, the weight whereof was an hundred and thirty shekels, one ***silver*** bowl of seventy shekels, after the shekel of the sanctuary; both of them full of fine flour mingled with oil for a meat offering:

Numbers 7:84 This was the dedication of the altar, in the day when it was anointed, by the princes of Israel: twelve chargers of ***silver***, twelve ***silver*** bowls, twelve spoons of gold:

Numbers 7:85 each charger of ***silver*** weighing an hundred and thirty shekels, each bowl seventy: all the ***silver*** vessels weighed two thousand and four hundred shekels, after the shekel of the sanctuary:

Numbers 10:2 Make thee two trumpets of ***silver***; of a whole piece shalt thou make them: that thou mayest use them for the calling of the assembly, and for the journeying of the camps.

Numbers 22:18 And Balaam answered and said unto the servants of Balak, If Balak would give me his house full of ***silver*** and gold, I cannot go beyond the word of the Lord my God, to do less or more.

Numbers 24:13 If Balak would give me his house full of ***silver*** and gold, I cannot go beyond the commandment of the Lord, to do either good or bad of mine own mind; but what the Lord saith, that will I speak?

Numbers 31:22 only the gold, and the ***silver***, the brass, the iron, the tin, and the lead,

Deuteronomy 7:25 The graven images of their gods shall ye burn with fire: thou shalt not desire the ***silver*** or gold that is on them, nor take it unto thee, lest thou be snared therein: for it is an abomination to the Lord thy God.

Deuteronomy 8:13 and when thy herds and thy flocks multiply, and thy ***silver*** and thy gold is multiplied, and all that thou hast is multiplied;

Deuteronomy 17:17 Neither shall he multiply wives to himself, that his heart turn not away: neither shall he greatly multiply to himself ***silver*** and gold.

Deuteronomy 22:19 and they shall amerce him in an hundred shekels of ***silver***, and give them unto the father of the damsel, because he hath brought up an evil name upon a virgin of Israel: and she shall be his wife; he may not put her away all his days.

Deuteronomy 22:29 then the man that lay with her shall give unto the damsel's father fifty shekels of ***silver***, and she shall be his wife; because he hath humbled her, he may not put her away all his days.

Deuteronomy 29:17 and ye have seen their abominations, and their idols, wood and stone, ***silver*** and gold, which were among them:)

Joshua 6:19 But all the ***silver***, and gold, and vessels of brass and iron, are consecrated unto the Lord: they shall come into the treasury of the Lord.

Joshua 6:24 And they burnt the city with fire, and all that was therein: only the ***silver***, and the gold, and the vessels of brass and of iron, they put into the treasury of the house of the Lord.

Joshua 7:21 when I saw among the spoils a goodly Babylonish garment, and two hundred shekels of ***silver***, and a wedge of gold of fifty shekels weight, then I coveted them, and took them; and, behold, they are hid in the earth in the midst of my tent, and the ***silver*** under it.

Joshua 7:22 So Joshua sent messengers, and they ran unto the tent; and, behold, it was hid in his tent, and the ***silver*** under it.

Joshua 7:24 And Joshua, and all Israel with him, took Achan the son of Zerah, and the ***silver***, and the garment, and the wedge of gold, and his sons, and his daughters, and his oxen, and his asses, and his sheep, and his tent, and all that he had: and they brought them unto the valley of Achor.

Joshua 22:8 and he spake unto them, saying, Return with much riches unto your tents, and with very much cattle, with ***silver***, and with gold, and with brass, and with iron, and with very much raiment: divide the spoil of your enemies with your brethren.

Judges 9:4 And they gave him threescore and ten pieces of ***silver*** out of the house of Baal-berith, wherewith Abimelech hired vain and light persons, which followed him.

Judges 16:5 And the lords of the Philistines came up unto her, and said unto her, Entice him, and see wherein his great strength lieth, and by what means we may prevail against him, that we may bind him to afflict him: and we will give thee every one of us eleven hundred pieces of ***silver***.

Judges 17:2 And he said unto his mother, The eleven hundred shekels of ***silver*** that were taken from thee, about which thou cursedst, and spakest of also in mine ears, behold, the ***silver*** is with me; I took it. And his mother said, Blessed be thou of the LORD, my son.

Judges 17:3 And when he had restored the eleven hundred shekels of ***silver*** to his mother, his mother said, I had wholly dedicated the ***silver*** unto the Lord from my hand for my son, to make a graven image and a molten image: now therefore I will restore it unto thee.

Judges 17:4 Yet he restored the money unto his mother; and his mother took two hundred shekels of ***silver***, and gave them to the founder, who made thereof a graven image and a molten image: and they were in the house of Micah.

Judges 17:10 And Micah said unto him, Dwell with me, and be unto me a father and a priest, and I will give thee ten shekels of ***silver*** by the year, and a suit of apparel, and thy victuals. So the Levite went in.

1 Samuel 2:36 And it shall come to pass, that every one that is left in thine house shall come and crouch to him for a piece of ***silver*** and a morsel of bread, and shall say, Put me, I pray thee, into one of the priests' offices, that I may eat a piece of bread.

1 Samuel 9:8 And the servant answered Saul again, and said, Behold, I have here at hand the fourth part of a shekel of ***silver***: that will I give to the man of God, to tell us our way.

2 Samuel 8:10 then Toi sent Joram his son unto king David, to salute him, and to bless him, because he had fought against Hadadezer, and smitten him: for Hadadezer had wars with Toi. And Joram brought with him vessels of ***silver***, and vessels of gold, and vessels of brass:

2 Samuel 8:11 which also king David did dedicate unto the Lord, with the ***silver*** and gold that he had dedicated of all nations which he subdued;

2 Samuel 18:11 And Joab said unto the man that told him, And, behold, thou sawest him, and why didst thou not smite him there to the ground? and I would have given thee ten shekels of ***silver***, and a girdle.

2 Samuel 18:12 And the man said unto Joab, Though I should receive a thousand shekels of ***silver*** in mine hand, yet would I not put forth mine hand against the king's son: for in our

hearing the king charged thee and Abishai and Ittai, saying, Beware that none touch the young man Absalom.

2 Samuel 21:4 And the Gibeonites said unto him, We will have no ***silver*** nor gold of Saul, nor of his house; neither for us shalt thou kill any man in Israel. And he said, What ye shall say, that will I do for you.

2 Samuel 24:24 And the king said unto Araunah, Nay; but I will surely buy it of thee at a price: neither will I offer burnt offerings unto the Lord my God of that which doth cost me nothing. So David bought the threshingfloor and the oxen for fifty shekels of ***silver***.

1 Kings 7:51 So was ended all the work that king Solomon made for the house of the Lord. And Solomon brought in the things which David his father had dedicated; even the ***silver***, and the gold, and the vessels, did he put among the treasures of the house of the Lord.

1 Kings 10:21 And all king Solomon's drinking vessels were of gold, and all the vessels of the house of the forest of Lebanon were of pure gold; none were of ***silver***: it was nothing accounted of in the days of Solomon.

1 Kings 10:22 For the king had at sea a navy of Tharshish with the navy of Hiram: once in three years came the navy of Tharshish, bringing gold, and ***silver***, ivory, and apes, and peacocks.

1 Kings 10:25 And they brought every man his present, vessels of ***silver***, and vessels of gold, and garments, and armour, and spices, horses, and mules, a rate year by year.

1 Kings 10:27 And the king made ***silver*** to be in Jerusalem as stones, and cedars made he to be as the sycomore trees that are in the vale, for abundance.

1 Kings 10:29 And a chariot came up and went out of Egypt for six hundred shekels of ***silver***, and an horse for an hundred and fifty: and so for all the kings of the Hittites, and for the kings of Syria, did they bring them out by their means.

1 Kings 15:15 And he brought in the things which his father had dedicated, and the things which himself had dedicated, into the house of the Lord, ***silver***, and gold, and vessels.

1 Kings 15:18 Then Asa took all the ***silver*** and the gold that were left in the treasures of the house of the Lord, and the treasures of the king's house, and delivered them into the hand of his servants: and king Asa sent them to Ben-hadad, the son of Tabrimon, the son of Hezion, king of Syria, that dwelt at Damascus, saying,

1 Kings 15:19 There is a league between me and thee, and between my father and thy father: behold, I have sent unto thee a present of ***silver*** and gold; come and break thy league with Baasha king of Israel, that he may depart from me.

1 Kings 16:24 And he bought the hill Samaria of Shemer for two talents of ***silver***, and built on the hill, and called the name of the city which he built, after the name of Shemer, owner of the hill, Samaria.

1 Kings 20:3 Thy ***silver*** and thy gold is mine; thy wives also and thy children, even the goodliest, are mine.

1 Kings 20:5 And the messengers came again, and said, Thus speaketh Ben-hadad, saying, Although I have sent unto thee, saying, Thou shalt deliver me thy ***silver***, and thy gold, and thy wives, and thy children;

1 Kings 20:7 Then the king of Israel called all the elders of the land, and said, Mark, I pray you, and see how this man seeketh mischief: for he sent unto me for my wives, and for my children, and for my ***silver***, and for my gold; and I denied him not.

1 Kings 20:39 And as the king passed by, he cried unto the king: and he said, Thy servant went out into the midst of the battle; and, behold, a man turned aside, and brought a man unto me, and said, Keep this man: if by any means he be missing, then shall thy life be for his life, or else thou shalt pay a talent of ***silver***.

Preface to the verses containing money

In the following section, one hundred percent of the cases where *keseph* is translated *money* make more sense when translated *silver*. Even with no knowledge of the error, the passages make at least as much sense with *keseph* translated *silver*.

Pay close attention to 2 Kings 12:9-13, 2 Chronicles 24:14, and Jeremiah 32:9-10.

In 2 Kings 12:9-13 *keseph* is repeatedly translated *money*, but in verse 13 it suddenly says that *silver* objects were not made of the *money* which had been collected. It is not possible to make *silver* objects from anything but *silver*. If the thing being translated *money* could have been made into a *silver* object, the thing being called *money* has to be *silver*. Since *keseph* means *silver*, this passage makes perfect sense if *keseph* were consistently translated *silver*.

In 2 Chronicles 24:14, the thing incorrectly called *money* is made into utensils and other things of gold[77] and *silver*. Again, the supposed *money* is being used to make utensils of *silver*, which means the *money* ***is*** *silver*. This further supports the claim that *keseph* means *silver* because the term KSP is being translated *money* and *silver* in the same passage talking about the same object.

In Jeremiah 32:9-10, the meaning is explicit. *"[I] weighed him the money, even seventeen shekels of silver"* which means the money *was* seventeen shekels of silver. That is an example of a commodity by weight. Then KSP is incorrectly translated *money* again, stating *"[I] weighed him the money in the balances."* We already know that what is being called *money* is *silver* because it is explicitly stated in the preceding sentence. We also know that *keseph* means *silver* and that *money* cannot be referred to by *weight*.

> *"And I bought the field of Hanameel my uncle's son, that was in Anathoth, and weighed him the money, even seventeen shekels of silver. And I subscribed the evidence, and sealed it, and took witnesses, and weighed him the money in the balances."* (Jeremiah 32:9–10, KJV 1900)

Contradictions like these help make it obvious that *keseph* is being incorrectly translated when it is replaced by Latin *pecuniam* or English *money*. There are other similar examples, which can be found as well. For a challenging example, Isaiah 55:1 is confusing with the term *money*, and is clear with the term *silver*. *Money* by its nature may be created and possessed by bankers without cost. *Money* is always partly or completely debt. The debt portion of *money* is *costless* to create. Therefore, *money* is illogical as a term in the end of Isaiah 55:1.

---

77 My interpretation is that the meaning here is something like gold articles inlaid with silver.

money | 110 of 403

Genesis 17:12 And he that is eight days old shall be circumcised among you, every man child in your generations, he that is born in the house, or bought with ***money*** of any stranger, which is not of thy seed.

Genesis 17:13 He that is born in thy house, and he that is bought with thy ***money***, must needs be circumcised: and my covenant shall be in your flesh for an everlasting covenant.

Genesis 17:23 And Abraham took Ishmael his son, and all that were born in his house, and all that were bought with his ***money***, every male among the men of Abraham's house; and circumcised the flesh of their foreskin in the selfsame day, as God had said unto him.

Genesis 17:27 And all the men of his house, born in the house, and bought with ***money*** of the stranger, were circumcised with him.

Genesis 23:9 that he may give me the cave of Machpelah, which he hath, which is in the end of his field; for as much ***money*** as it is worth he shall give it me for a possession of a buryingplace amongst you.

Genesis 23:13 And he spake unto Ephron in the audience of the people of the land, saying, But if thou wilt give it, I pray thee, hear me: I will give thee ***money*** for the field; take it of me, and I will bury my dead there.

Genesis 31:15 Are we not counted of him strangers? for he hath sold us, and hath quite devoured also our ***money***.

Genesis 42:25 Then Joseph commanded to fill their sacks with corn, and to restore every man's ***money*** into his sack, and to give them provision for the way: and thus did he unto them.

Genesis 42:27 And as one of them opened his sack to give his ass provender in the inn, he espied his ***money***; for, behold, it was in his sack's mouth.

Genesis 42:28 And he said unto his brethren, My ***money*** is restored; and, lo, it is even in my sack: and their heart failed them, and they were afraid, saying one to another, What is this that God hath done unto us?

Genesis 42:35 And it came to pass as they emptied their sacks, that, behold, every man's bundle of ***money*** was in his sack: and when both they and their father saw the bundles of ***money***, they were afraid.

Genesis 43:12 and take double ***money*** in your hand; and the ***money*** that was brought again in the mouth of your sacks, carry it again in your hand; peradventure it was an oversight:

Genesis 43:15 And the men took that present, and they took double ***money*** in their hand, and Benjamin; and rose up, and went down to Egypt, and stood before Joseph.

Genesis 43:21 and it came to pass, when we came to the inn, that we opened our sacks, and, behold, every man's ***money*** was in the mouth of his sack, our ***money*** in full weight: and we have brought it again in our hand.

Genesis 43:22 And other ***money*** have we brought down in our hands to buy food: we cannot tell who put our ***money*** in our sacks.

Genesis 43:23 And he said, Peace be to you, fear not: your God, and the God of your father, hath given you treasure in your sacks: I had your ***money***. And he brought Simeon out unto them.

Genesis 44:1 And he commanded the steward of his house, saying, Fill the men's sacks with food, as much as they can carry, and put every man's ***money*** in his sack's mouth.

Genesis 44:2 And put my cup, the silver cup, in the sack's mouth of the youngest, and his corn ***money***. And he did according to the word that Joseph had spoken.

Genesis 44:8 behold, the ***money***, which we found in our sacks' mouths, we brought again unto thee out of the land of Canaan: how then should we steal out of thy lord's house silver or gold?

Genesis 47:14 And Joseph gathered up all the ***money*** that was found in the land of Egypt, and in the land of Canaan, for the corn which they bought: and Joseph brought the ***money*** into Pharaoh's house.

Genesis 47:15 And when ***money*** failed in the land of Egypt, and in the land of Canaan, all the Egyptians came unto Joseph, and said, Give us bread: for why should we die in thy presence? for the ***money*** faileth.

Genesis 47:16 And Joseph said, Give your cattle; and I will give you for your cattle, if ***money*** fail.

Genesis 47:18 When that year was ended, they came unto him the second year, and said unto him, We will not hide it from my lord, how that our ***money*** is spent; my lord also hath our herds of cattle; there is not ought left in the sight of my lord, but our bodies, and our lands:

Exodus 12:44 but every man's servant that is bought for ***money***, when thou hast circumcised him, then shall he eat thereof.

Exodus 21:11 And if he do not these three unto her, then shall she go out free without ***money***.

Exodus 21:21 Notwithstanding, if he continue a day or two, he shall not be punished: for he is his ***money***.

Exodus 21:34 the owner of the pit shall make it good, and give ***money*** unto the owner of them; and the dead beast shall be his.

Exodus 21:35 And if one man's ox hurt another's, that he die; then they shall sell the live ox, and divide the ***money*** of it; and the dead ox also they shall divide.

Exodus 22:7 If a man shall deliver unto his neighbour ***money*** or stuff to keep, and it be stolen out of the man's house; if the thief be found, let him pay double.

Exodus 22:17 If her father utterly refuse to give her unto him, he shall pay ***money*** according to the dowry of virgins.

Exodus 22:25 If thou lend ***money*** to any of my people that is poor by thee, thou shalt not be to him as an usurer, neither shalt thou lay upon him usury.

Exodus 30:16 And thou shalt take the atonement ***money*** of the children of Israel, and shalt appoint it for the service of the tabernacle of the congregation; that it may be a memorial unto the children of Israel before the Lord, to make an atonement for your souls.

Leviticus 22:11 But if the priest buy any soul with his ***money***, he shall eat of it, and he that is born in his house: they shall eat of his meat.

Leviticus 25:37 Thou shalt not give him thy ***money*** upon usury, nor lend him thy victuals for increase.

Leviticus 25:51 If there be yet many years behind, according unto them he shall give again the price of his redemption out of the ***money*** that he was bought for.

Leviticus 27:15 And if he that sanctified it will redeem his house, then he shall add the fifth part of the ***money*** of thy estimation unto it, and it shall be his.

Leviticus 27:18 But if he sanctify his field after the jubile, then the priest shall reckon unto him the ***money*** according to the years that remain, even unto the year of the jubile, and it shall be abated from thy estimation.

Leviticus 27:19 And if he that sanctified the field will in any wise redeem it, then he shall add the fifth part of the ***money*** of thy estimation unto it, and it shall be assured to him.

Numbers 3:48 And thou shalt give the ***money***, wherewith the odd number of them is to be redeemed, unto Aaron and to his sons.

Numbers 3:49 And Moses took the redemption ***money*** of them that were over and above them that were redeemed by the Levites:

Numbers 3:50 Of the firstborn of the children of Israel took he the ***money***; a thousand three hundred and threescore and five shekels, after the shekel of the sanctuary:

Numbers 3:51 and Moses gave the ***money*** of them that were redeemed unto Aaron and to his sons, according to the word of the Lord, as the Lord commanded Moses.

Numbers 18:16 And those that are to be redeemed from a month old shalt thou redeem, according to thine estimation, for the ***money*** of five shekels, after the shekel of the sanctuary, which is twenty gerahs.

Deuteronomy 2:6 Ye shall buy meat of them for ***money***, that ye may eat; and ye shall also buy water of them for ***money***, that ye may drink.

Deuteronomy 2:28 Thou shalt sell me meat for ***money***, that I may eat; and give me water for ***money***, that I may drink: only I will pass through on my feet;

Deuteronomy 14:25 then shalt thou turn it into ***money***, and bind up the ***money*** in thine hand, and shalt go unto the place which the Lord thy God shall choose:

Deuteronomy 14:26 and thou shalt bestow that ***money*** for whatsoever thy soul lusteth after, for oxen, or for sheep, or for wine, or for strong drink, or for whatsoever thy soul desireth: and thou shalt eat there before the Lord thy God, and thou shalt rejoice, thou, and thine household,

Deuteronomy 21:14 And it shall be, if thou have no delight in her, then thou shalt let her go whither she will; but thou shalt not sell her at all for ***money***, thou shalt not make merchandise of her, because thou hast humbled her.

Deuteronomy 23:19 Thou shalt not lend upon usury to thy brother; usury of ***money***, usury of victuals, usury of any thing that is lent upon usury:

Judges 5:19 The kings came and fought, Then fought the kings of Canaan In Taanach by the waters of Megiddo; They took no gain of ***money***.

Judges 16:18 And when Delilah saw that he had told her all his heart, she sent and called for the lords of the Philistines, saying, Come up this once, for he hath shewed me all his heart. Then the lords of the Philistines came up unto her, and brought ***money*** in their hand.

Judges 17:4 Yet he restored the ***money*** unto his mother; and his mother took two hundred shekels of silver, and gave them to the founder, who made thereof a graven image and a molten image: and they were in the house of Micah.

1 Kings 21:6 And he said unto her, Because I spake unto Naboth the Jezreelite, and said unto him, Give me thy vineyard for ***money***; or else, if it please thee, I will give thee another vineyard for it: and he answered, I will not give thee my vineyard.

1 Kings 21:15 And it came to pass, when Jezebel heard that Naboth was stoned, and was dead, that Jezebel said to Ahab, Arise, take possession of the vineyard of Naboth the Jezreelite, which he refused to give thee for ***money***: for Naboth is not alive, but dead.

2 Kings 5:26 And he said unto him, Went not mine heart with thee, when the man turned again from his chariot to meet thee? Is it a time to receive ***money***, and to receive garments, and oliveyards, and vineyards, and sheep, and oxen, and menservants, and maidservants?

2 Kings 12:4 And Jehoash said to the priests, All the ***money*** of the dedicated things that is brought into the house of the Lord, even the ***money*** of every one that passeth the account, the ***money*** that every man is set at, and all the ***money*** that cometh into any man's heart to bring into the house of the Lord,

2 Kings 12:7 Then king Jehoash called for Jehoiada the priest, and the other priests, and said unto them, Why repair ye not the breaches of the house? now therefore receive no more ***money*** of your acquaintance, but deliver it for the breaches of the house.

2 Kings 12:8 And the priests consented to receive no more ***money*** of the people, neither to repair the breaches of the house.

2 Kings 12:9 But Jehoiada the priest took a

chest, and bored a hole in the lid of it, and set it beside the altar, on the right side as one cometh into the house of the Lord: and the priests that kept the door put therein all the ***money*** that was brought into the house of the Lord.

2 Kings 12:10 And it was so, when they saw that there was much ***money*** in the chest, that the king's scribe and the high priest came up, and they put up in bags, and told the ***money*** that was found in the house of the Lord.

2 Kings 12:11 And they gave the ***money***, being told, into the hands of them that did the work, that had the oversight of the house of the Lord: and they laid it out to the carpenters and builders, that wrought upon the house of the Lord,

2 Kings 12:13 Howbeit there were not made for the house of the Lord bowls of silver, snuffers, basons, trumpets, any vessels of gold, or vessels of silver, of the ***money*** that was brought into the house of the Lord:

2 Kings 12:15 Moreover they reckoned not with the men, into whose hand they delivered the ***money*** to be bestowed on workmen: for they dealt faithfully.

2 Kings 12:16 The trespass ***money*** and sin ***money*** was not brought into the house of the Lord: it was the priests'.

2 Kings 15:20 And Menahem exacted the ***money*** of Israel, even of all the mighty men of wealth, of each man fifty shekels of silver, to give to the king of Assyria. So the king of Assyria turned back, and stayed not there in the land.

2 Kings 22:7 Howbeit there was no reckoning made with them of the ***money*** that was delivered into their hand, because they dealt faithfully.

2 Kings 22:9 And Shaphan the scribe came to the king, and brought the king word again, and said, Thy servants have gathered the ***money*** that was found in the house, and have delivered it into the hand of them that do the work, that have the oversight of the house of the Lord.

2 Kings 23:35 And Jehoiakim gave the silver and the gold to Pharaoh; but he taxed the land to give the ***money*** according to the commandment of Pharaoh: he exacted the silver and the gold of the people of the land, of every one according to his taxation, to give it unto Pharaoh-nechoh.

2 Chronicles 24:5 And he gathered together the priests and the Levites, and said to them, Go out unto the cities of Judah, and gather of all Israel ***money*** to repair the house of your God from year to year, and see that ye hasten the matter. Howbeit the Levites hastened it not.

2 Chronicles 24:11 Now it came to pass, that at what time the chest was brought unto the king's office by the hand of the Levites, and when they saw that there was much ***money***, the king's scribe and the high priest's officer came and emptied the chest, and took it, and carried it to his place again. Thus they did day by day, and gathered ***money*** in abundance.

2 Chronicles 24:14 And when they had finished it, they brought the rest of the ***money*** before the king and Jehoiada, whereof were made vessels for the house of the Lord, even vessels to minister, and to offer withal, and spoons, and vessels of gold and silver. And they offered burnt offerings in the house of the Lord continually all the days of Jehoiada.

2 Chronicles 34:9 And when they came to Hilkiah the high priest, they delivered the ***money*** that was brought into the house of God, which the Levites that kept the doors had gathered of the hand of Manasseh and Ephraim, and of all the remnant of Israel, and of all Judah and Benjamin; and they returned to Jerusalem.

2 Chronicles 34:14 And when they brought out the ***money*** that was brought into the house of the Lord, Hilkiah the priest found a book of the law of the Lord given by Moses.

2 Chronicles 34:17 And they have gathered together the ***money*** that was found in the house of the Lord, and have delivered it into the hand of the overseers, and to the hand of the workmen.

Ezra 3:7 They gave ***money*** also unto the masons, and to the carpenters; and meat, and drink, and oil, unto them of Zidon, and to them of Tyre, to bring cedar trees from Lebanon to the sea of Joppa, according to the grant that they had of Cyrus king of Persia.

Nehemiah 5:4 There were also that said, We have borrowed ***money*** for the king's tribute, and that upon our lands and vineyards.

Nehemiah 5:10 I likewise, and my brethren, and my servants, might exact of them ***money*** and corn: I pray you, let us leave off this usury.

Nehemiah 5:11 Restore, I pray you, to them, even this day, their lands, their vineyards, their oliveyards, and their houses, also the hundredth part of the ***money***, and of the corn, the wine, and the oil, that ye exact of them.

Esther 4:7 And Mordecai told him of all that had happened unto him, and of the sum of the ***money*** that Haman had promised to pay to the king's treasuries for the Jews, to destroy them.

Job 31:39 If I have eaten the fruits thereof without ***money***, Or have caused the owners thereof to lose their life:

Psalms 15:5 He that putteth not out his ***money*** to usury, Nor taketh reward against the innocent. He that doeth these things shall never be moved.

Proverbs 7:20 He hath taken a bag of ***money*** with him, And will come home at the day appointed.

Ecclesiastes 7:12 For wisdom is a defence, and ***money*** is a defence: but the excellency of knowledge is, that wisdom giveth life to them that have it.

Ecclesiastes 10:19 A feast is made for laughter, and wine maketh merry: but ***money*** answereth all things.

Isaiah 43:24 Thou hast bought me no sweet cane with ***money***, Neither hast thou filled me with the fat of thy sacrifices: But thou hast made me to serve with thy sins, Thou hast wearied me with thine iniquities.

Isaiah 52:3 For thus saith the Lord, Ye have sold yourselves for nought; And ye shall be redeemed without ***money***.

Isaiah 55:1 Ho, every one that thirsteth, come ye to the waters, And he that hath no ***money***; Come ye, buy, and eat; Yea, come, buy wine and milk without ***money*** and without price.

Isaiah 55:2 Wherefore do ye spend ***money*** for that which is not bread? And your labour for that which satisfieth not? Hearken diligently unto me, and eat ye that which is good, And let your soul delight itself in fatness.

Jeremiah 32:9 And I bought the field of Hanameel my uncle's son, that was in Anathoth, and weighed him the ***money***, even seventeen shekels of silver.

Jeremiah 32:10 And I subscribed the evidence, and sealed it, and took witnesses, and weighed him the ***money*** in the balances.

Jeremiah 32:25 And thou hast said unto me, O Lord God, Buy thee the field for ***money***, and take witnesses; for the city is given into the hand of the Chaldeans.

Jeremiah 32:44 Men shall buy fields for ***money***, and subscribe evidences, and seal them, and take witnesses in the land of Benjamin, and in the places about Jerusalem, and in the cities of Judah, and in the cities of the mountains, and in the cities of the valley, and in the cities of the south: for I will cause their captivity to return, saith the Lord.

Lamentations 5:4 We have drunken our water for ***money***; Our wood is sold unto us.

Micah 3:11 The heads thereof judge for reward, And the priests thereof teach for hire, And the prophets thereof divine for ***money***: Yet will they lean upon the Lord, and say, Is not the Lord among us? None evil can come upon us.

The next six instances should also be translated *silver*.

price | 3 of 403

Leviticus 25:50 And he shall reckon with him that bought him from the year that he was sold to him unto the year of jubile: and the ***price*** of his sale shall be according unto the number of years, according to the time of an hired servant shall it be with him.

1 Chronicles 21:22 Then David said to Ornan, Grant me the place of this threshingfloor, that I may build an altar therein unto the Lord: thou shalt grant it me for the full ***price:*** that the plague may be stayed from the people.

1 Chronicles 21:24 And king David said to Ornan, Nay; but I will verily buy it for the full ***price***: for I will not take that which is thine for the Lord, nor offer burnt offerings without cost.

silverlings | 1 of 403

Isaiah 7:23 And it shall come to pass in that day, That every place shall be, Where there were a thousand vines at a thousand ***silverlings***, It shall even be for briers and thorns.

of the money | 1 of 403

Genesis 43:18 And the men were afraid, because they were brought into Joseph's house; and they said, Because ***of the money*** that was returned in our sacks at the first time are we brought in; that he may seek occasion against us, and fall upon us, and take us for bondmen, and our asses.

worth | 1 of 403

1 Kings 21:2 And Ahab spake unto Naboth, saying, Give me thy vineyard, that I may have it for a garden of herbs, because it is near unto my house: and I will give thee for it a better vineyard than it; or, if it seem good to thee, I will give thee the ***worth*** of it in money.

In 1 Kings 21:2, the term money is translated from a Hebrew term transliterated *mechir* that means *price*, and *worth* is translated from *keseph*. In other translations the idea is turned to *price in money*, which should be *price in silver*.

3.8 Hamilton's Scheme

In government, we need an impenetrable wall of separation between motive and means. It is one thing to desire an outcome. It is another thing entirely to have unlimited access to the means to bring it about.

Losing Liberty in America

Those who study our US history know that Thomas Jefferson and Alexander Hamilton represented opposing views in the early years of our Republic. Jefferson stood for Liberty and Republican government, while Hamilton stood for Subjection and Monarchial government.

Following are excerpts from the preface of Jefferson's writing during the time he was Secretary of State under our first president, George Washington. Jefferson begins explaining how he was reintroduced after being away as Ambassador to France.

Jefferson then explains that Hamilton sought to confuse the people and corrupt the legislature through a financial system, which succeeded. Then Jefferson explains that paper money and debt certificates were used to plunder the poor and amass fortunes for the previously poor.

There are other sections that follow. I would highlight the important parts, but the whole of the text is extremely enlightening and valuable. Please read carefully and prepare to be amazed and angered.

Hamilton's Financial System

From a preface written February 4th, 1818 regarding Jefferson's work as Secretary of State under George Washington ~

"The courtesies of dinner parties given me, as a stranger newly arrived among them, placed me at once in their familiar society. But I cannot describe the wonder and mortification with which the table conversations filled me. Politics were the chief topic, and a preference of kingly over republican government was evidently the favorite sentiment. An apostate I could not be, nor yet a hypocrite; and I found myself, for the most part, the only advocate on the republican side of the question, unless among the

guests there chanced to be some member of that party from the legislative Houses.

Hamilton's financial system had then passed. It had two objects; 1st, as a puzzle, to exclude popular understanding and inquiry; 2d, as a machine for the corruption of the legislature; for he avowed the opinion, that man could be governed by one of two motives only, force or interest; force, he observed, in this country was out of the question, and the interests, therefore, of the members must be laid hold of, to keep the legislative in unison with the executive.

And with grief and shame it must be acknowledged that his machine was not without effect; that even in this, the birth of our government, some members were found sordid enough to bend their duty to their interests, and to look after personal rather than public good.

It is well known that, during the war, the greatest difficulty we encountered was the want of money or means, to pay our soldiers who fought, or our farmers, manufacturers & merchants who furnished the necessary supplies of food & clothing for them.

After the expedient of paper money had exhausted itself, certificates of debt were given to the individual creditors, with assurance of payment, so soon as the U. S. should be able.

But the distresses of these people often obliged them to part with these for the half, the fifth, and even a tenth of their value; and Speculators had made a trade of cozening them from the holders, by the most fraudulent practices and persuasions that they would never be paid. In the bill for funding & paying these, Hamilton made no difference between the original holders, & the fraudulent purchasers of this paper. Great & just repugnance arose at putting these two classes of creditors on the same footing, and great exertions were used to pay to the former the full value, and to the latter the price only which he had paid, with interest. But this would have prevented the game, which was to be played, & for which the minds of greedy members were already tutored and prepared.

When the trial of strength on these several efforts had indicated the form in which the bill would finally pass, this being known within doors sooner than without, and especially than to those who were in distant parts of the Union, the base scramble began. Couriers & relay horses by land, and swift sailing pilot boats by sea, were flying in all directions. Active part[n]ers & agents were associated & employed in every state, town and country neighborhood, and this paper was bought up at 5 shillings and even as low as 2 shillings in the pound, before the holder knew that Congress had already provided for it's redemption at par.

Immense sums were thus filched from the poor & ignorant, and fortunes accumulated by those who had themselves been poor enough before. Men thus enriched by the dexterity of a leader, would follow of course the chief who was leading them to fortune, and become the zealous instruments of all his enterprises."

Assumption of State Debts

This game was over, and another was on the carpet at the moment of my arrival; and to this I was most ignorantly & innocently made to hold the candle. This fiscal maneuver is well known by the name of the Assumption. Independently of the debts of Congress, the states had, during the war, contracted separate and heavy debts; and Massachusetts particularly in an absurd attempt, absurdly conducted, on the British post of Penobscot: and the more debt Hamilton could rake up, the more plunder for his mercenaries. This money, whether wisely or foolishly spent, was pretended to have been spent for general purposes, and ought therefore to be paid from the general purse.

But it was objected that nobody knew what these debts were, what their amount, or what their proofs. No matter; we will guess them to be 20 millions. But of these 20 millions we do not know how much should be reimbursed to one state, nor how much to another. No matter; we will guess.

And so another scramble was set on foot among the several states, and some got much, some little, some nothing. But the main object was obtained, the phalanx of the treasury was reinforced by additional recruits. This measure produced the most bitter & angry contests ever known in Congress, before or since the union of the states. I arrived in the midst of it. But a stranger to the ground, a stranger to the actors on it, so long absent as to have lost all familiarity with the subject, and as yet unaware of it's object, I took no concern in it.

The great and trying question however was lost in the H. of Representatives. So high were the feuds excited by this subject, that on it's rejection, business was suspended. Congress met and adjourned from day to day without doing any thing, the parties being too much out of temper to do business together. The Eastern members particularly, who, with Smith from South Carolina, were the principal gamblers in these scenes, threatened a secession and dissolution.

Hamilton was in despair. As I was going to the President's one day, I met him in the street. He walked me backwards & forwards before the President's door for half an hour. He painted pathetically the temper into which the legislature had been wrought, the disgust of those who were called the Creditor states, the danger of the secession of their members, and the separation of the states. He observed that the members of the administration ought to act in concert, that tho' this question was not of my department, yet a common duty should make it a common concern; that the President was the center on which all administrative questions ultimately rested, and that all of us should rally around him, and support with joint efforts measures approved by him; and that the question having been lost by a small majority only, it was probable that an appeal from me to the judgment and discretion of some of my friends might effect a change in the vote, and the machine of government, now suspended, might be again set into motion. I told him that I was really a stranger to the whole subject; not having yet informed myself of the system of finances adopted, I knew not how far this was a necessary sequence; that undoubtedly if it's rejection endangered a dissolution of our union at this incipient stage, I should deem that the most unfortunate of all consequences, to avert which all partial and temporary evils should be yielded. I proposed to him however to dine with me the next day, and I would invite another friend or two, bring them into conference together, and I thought it impossible that reasonable men, consulting together coolly, could fail, by some mutual sacrifices of opinion, to form a compromise which was to save the union. The discussion took place. I could take no part in it, but an exhortatory one, because I was a stranger to the circumstances, which should govern it.

But it was finally agreed that, whatever importance had been attached to the rejection of this proposition, the preservation of the union, & and of concord among the states was more important, and that therefore it would be better that the vote of rejection should be rescinded, to effect which some members should change their votes. But it was observed that this pill would be peculiarly bitter to the Southern States, and that some concomitant measure should be adopted to sweeten it a little to them. There had before been propositions to fix the seat of government either at Philadelphia, or at Georgetown on the Potomac; and it was thought that by giving it to Philadelphia for ten years, and to Georgetown permanently afterwards, this might, as an anodyne, calm in some degree the ferment which might be excited by the other measure alone. So two of the Potomac members (White & Lee, but White with a revulsion of stomach almost convulsive) agreed to change their votes, & Hamilton undertook to carry the other point. In doing this the influence he had established over the Eastern members, with the agency of Robert Morris with those of the middle states, effected his side of the engagement, and so the assumption was passed, and 20 millions of stock divided among favored states, and thrown in as pabulum to the stock-jobbing herd.

This added to the number of votaries to the treasury and made its Chief the master of every vote in the legislature, which might give to the government, the direction suited to his political views. I know well, and so must be understood, that nothing like a majority in Congress had yielded to this corruption. Far from it. But a division, not very unequal, had already taken place in the honest part of that body, between the parties styled republican and federal. The latter being monarchists in principle, adhered to Hamilton of course, as their leader in that principle, and this mercenary phalanx added to them ensured him always a majority in both houses: so that the whole action of the legislature was now under the direction of the treasury.

Hamilton's Financial System, 3: The Bank of the United States

Still the machine was not compleat. The effect of the funding system, & of the assumption, would be temporary. It would be lost with the loss of the individual members whom it had enriched, and some engine of influence more permanent must be contrived, while these myrmidons were yet in place to carry it thro' all opposition. This engine was the Bank of the US All that history is known; so I shall say nothing about it. While the government remained at Philadelphia, a selection of members of both houses were constantly kept as Directors, who, on every question interesting to that institution, or to the views of the federal head, voted at the will of that head; and, together with the stockholding members, could always make the federal vote that of the majority. By this combination, legislative expositions were given to the constitution, and all the administrative laws were shaped on the model of England, & so passed. And from this influence we were not relieved until the removal from the precincts of the bank, to Washington.

"The Real Ground of Opposition": Hamilton as Monarchist Conspirator

Here then was the real ground of the opposition which was made to the course of administration. It's object was to preserve the legislature pure and independent of the Executive, to restrain the administration to republican forms and principles, and not permit the constitution to be construed into a monarchy, and to be warped in practice into all the principles and pollutions of their favorite English model. Nor was this an opposition to Genl. Washington. He was true to the republican charge confided to him; & has solemnly and repeatedly protested to me, in our private conversations, that he would lose the last drop of his blood in support of it, and he did this the oftener, and with the more earnestness, because he knew my suspicions of Hamilton's designs against it; & wished to quiet them. For he was not aware of the drift, or of the effect of Hamilton's schemes. Unversed in financial projects & calculations, & budgets, his approbation of them was bottomed on his confidence in the man. But Hamilton was not only a monarchist, but for a monarchy bottomed on corruption. In proof of this I will relate an anecdote, for the truth of which I attest the God who made me. Before the President set out on his Southern tour in April 1791. he addressed a letter of the 4th. of that month, from Mt. Vernon to the Secretaries of State, Treasury & War, desiring that, if any serious and important cases should arise during his absence, they would consult & act on them, and he requested that the Vice-president should also be consulted. This was the only occasion on which that officer was ever requested to take part in a Cabinet question. Some occasion for consultation arising, I invited those gentlemen (and the Attorney genl. as well as I remember) to dine with me in order to confer on the subject. After the cloth was removed, and our question agreed & dismissed, conversation began on other matters and, by some circumstance, was led to the British constitution, on which Mr. Adams observed "purge that constitution of it's corruption, and give to it's popular branch equality of representation, and it would be the most perfect constitution ever devised by the wit of man." Hamilton paused and said, "purge it of it's corruption, and give to it's popular branch equality of representation, & it would become an impracticable government: as it stands at present, with all it's supposed defects, it is the most perfect government which ever existed." And this was assuredly the exact line which separated the political creeds of these two gentlemen. The one was for two hereditary branches and an honest elective one: the other for a hereditary king with a house of lords & commons, corrupted to his will, and standing between him and the people. Hamilton was indeed a singular character. Of acute understanding, disinterested, honest, and honorable in all private transactions, amiable in society, and duly valuing virtue in private life, yet so bewitched & perverted by the British example, as to be under thorough' conviction that corruption was essential to the government of a nation."

Summary

The preceding text illustrates the intent of Jefferson and Hamilton. It explains the tools that Hamilton used to rob large groups of men for the benefit of smaller groups of men.

Notice that Jefferson said of Washington: "For he was not aware of the drift, or of the effect of Hamilton's schemes. Unversed in financial projects & calculations, & budgets, his approbation of them was bottomed on his confidence in the man."

Given George Washington's view of the Bible, I suspect that if he had known that the Bible contained no original language terms which could be translated money, Hamilton would have been unable to confuse and deceive Washington or the people of the country.

If Hamilton had been denied the use of differing weights and measures, he would have had no power over the congress and we would have had a far better chance of living in peace, freedom and prosperity for the past two hundred twenty years.

Conclusion

Hamilton believed that the legislature must be corrupted to achieve his goals.

Hamilton repeatedly used differing weights and differing measures to corrupt the legislature.

If Washington knew the Bible never mentions money, he would have understood and rejected Hamilton's schemes.

3.9 Savings Vs Credit

This chapter will compare two schools of economic thought. The first is named for John Maynard Keynes and is called Keynesianism. Keynesian Economics is what you hear about every day on the news. Keynesianism tries to control markets, creates money from nothing, bails out banks and favored businesses, destroys the savings and retirement of the middle class, and believes government makes us wealthy.

The second is the Austrian School of Economics which is based on capital, production and human action.

Following is a simple but powerful chart that explains a few key differences between the Austrian School of Economics and the Keynesian School of Economics. I use the phrase "Keynesian School of Economics" loosely, since Keynesianism is actually a political ideology with no basis in economics, except in terms of plunder, control and destruction.

Following is an illustration of the way that each system views Private Property and Time.

Note: To be brief and direct, I will ascribe positions to the Austrian School based on my own perspective. To get a full spectrum of Austrian views, refer to the vast library of materials on the subject, which may be found at http://mises.org.

Austrian School Based On Real Private Property Work in the Past	***Keynesian School*** Based On Illusion Of Private Property Work in the Future
Past	**Present** / **Future**
Past Production Work Completed	Future Production Work Promised
Wealth Savings Natural Money	Debt Credit Costless Money
Honest Healthy Sustainable	Dishonest Destructive Unsustainable
Bible Supports	Bible Condemns
Failed Investment Isolated to Lender and Borrower	Failed Investment Costs All Producers Protects Banks
Strengthens Nations	Destroys Nations

www.shanecoley.us - 2009

Private Property

Austrian View

The Austrian School holds that Private Property is inseparable from Liberty. How can a person experience liberty without owning the means of production which sustain his life?

A just economic system will not include any scheme that forces a person to work in order to retain his private property. Property tax, income tax and money created from nothing (i.e. costless money) all force people to work to retain property that is rightfully their own. Real private property that is paid for in full should not be subject to loss because of taxation or valuations on paper.

Keynesian View

In the Keynesian system, property tax essentially makes a person a tenant on government property. If the present owner does not produce enough to pay the tax, the government takes the property away and assigns it to a serf, um... I mean citizen, who will produce enough to pay the tax.

The Keynesian system is designed to allocate property based on production. The state and favored business are to be the beneficiary of the productivity of the property manager.

We sometimes think of the Keynesian property manager as an "owner," but a true Keynesian never does. A Keynesian knows a serf when he sees one.

Work Completed or Promised?

Austrian View

The Austrian School recognizes that people are more prosperous based on quantity, quality and efficiency of production. The more people produce, the more prosperous the society becomes.

It really is a simple idea. Produce more, have more.

In simple terms, to be more productive, we use machines.

Machines enter the production system through innovation, engineering, testing, manufacturing and deployment.

In order to bring a more efficient machine into the production process, one will need to use capital. The capital will come from real savings of real property that has been produced and collected in the past.

In simple terms, if a new machine makes everyone more efficient, then the machine will cause our purchasing power to increase. We will all benefit from the extra production.

Think of a new business venture where the start-up cost is one thousand ounces of silver. With regard to capital, if the business venture fails, the producer will lose his capital or collateral.

If the capital was borrowed, the lender will gain or lose based on the value of the pledged collateral. If the collateral is worth more than the amount borrowed, the lender comes out ahead. If the collateral is worth less, the lender will lose the difference in value between the loan and the collateral.

Since everything spent in the venture was real property resulting from actual production in the past, every vendor was fully paid with that real property. Accounts are current and the effect on society is healthy.

Keynesian View

On the other hand, the Keynesian approach is based on *consumption*. The claim is that increased spending makes the economy prosper. A sophisticated argument can be made, but I will keep the explanation very simple by noting three things.

First, the Keynesians explicitly state that the purpose of their system, which we have used for over 100 years, is to destroy capitalism and therefore to destroy individual liberty and the right of private property. In other words, since Keynesians promote a consumption model, and the Keynesian objective is to undermine our society, the consumption model is necessarily bad.

Secondly, Keynesians claim the way the "economy is stimulated" is to borrow against future productivity by creating costless money. This approach is like an individual attempting to borrow his way out of debt. It doesn't work.

Thirdly, producers exchange with producers. A system where people buy things before producing something to exchange is unsustainable. People depend on production. Production is undermined when producers are pillaged and robbed of their capital and when the rewards for hard work are plundered by unjust law and inflation over the course of their working life.

Savings Vs Credit

When property is purchased based on savings from work in the past, the buyer and seller are secure in the transaction. Since there is no inflation, purchasing power increases as the society increases in productive capacity.

When property is purchased based on credit and the promises of work in the future, the seller is paid with dollars that decrease the seller's purchasing power. The borrower pledges to make payments based on work in the future, but his job may be lost, in which case he will lose his property. While he is paying the loan, prices rise faster than wages due to inflation caused by bank loans, which makes it difficult to make his payments. In the process, the bank is making interest at a rate of 50 to 90 percent per year, since the banker only needs ten cents on hand for every dollar you borrow.

If you are unable to pay the loan, since you made a down payment of 20 percent, the bank can sell the property at a discount and recover all their money tokens, in addition to the interest, which has been collected from you. If, for example, the government has stepped in and forced the bank to loan one hundred percent of the value of the home, then all producers will be forced to pay for the bank's losses through bailouts from the government, which again decrease our purchasing power. The small banks which have been agents in this scheme for decades, will be consumed by the large banks, exactly according to plan.

Natural Money Vs Costless Money

The easiest way to identify natural money is to ask the following question: If this thing that claims to be natural money stopped being used as money immediately without warning, would it still have other useful purposes?

For example, gold, silver, salt, butter or cattle all have other useful purposes beyond exchange.

On the other hand, *costless money* is something that is essentially costless to produce. For example, a paper US dollar note costs no more than a couple of pennies to produce, regardless of the denomination. A one-dollar bill and one hundred dollar bill both cost essentially the same thing to produce. An electronic dollar in a computer costs even less.

The benefit of *natural money* is that someone has to work in order to produce even one new unit. *Costless money* is destructive because no work is required to produce immense quantities of new money in seconds.

Think of all the time, energy and work that go into mining and refining a single ounce of silver.

On the other hand, when the Federal Reserve System or your local banker creates new money from nothing, the new money is created in a flash with the stroke of a pen.

Natural money protects property. Costless money steals property.

Keynesian Purpose

"Lenin is said to have declared that the best way to destroy the capitalist system was to debauch the currency. By a continuing process of inflation, governments can confiscate, secretly and unobserved, an important part of the wealth of their citizens. By this method they not only confiscate, but they confiscate arbitrarily; and, while the process impoverishes many, it actually enriches some... Lenin was certainly right. There is no subtler, no surer means of overturning the existing basis of society than to debauch the currency. The process engages all the hidden forces of economic law on the side of destruction, and does it in a manner which not one man in a million is able to diagnose."

The Economic Consequences of the Peace, John Maynard Keynes, 1919

Summary

The Keynesian model is anti-liberty, anti-capitalism, anti-prosperity and leads to destruction. Keynesianism is about gaining control by promising instant gratification for today and assuring us the bill will be paid with someone else's future (read "kids and grand kids") production.

The Austrian model is significantly in agreement with Biblical principle and leads to liberty, justice, prosperity, and personal accountability. The Austrian School is about the good stewardship of work that has been completed in the past.

Keynesians advocate for costless money that *steals* property.

Austrians advocate for natural money that *protects* property.

4. Illustrations

Highlighting truth with word pictures.
Propaganda depends on confusion and control.
Truth is freely available, but it must be sought out.

4.1 Five Guys Analogy

Because the intent here is to illustrate principles and specific points, very simple analogies will be used, studied in extremes. More complex models with more variables will confirm the process, given that one has sufficient time and the patience to work through the details.

The ideas are presented in two separate cases of one illustration. The first case will illustrate what the purpose of inflation is NOT and the second case will illustrate what the purpose of inflation IS.

Imagine a country with a currency called a dollar. This country defines their dollar[78] as one-tenth of an ounce of gold. Therefore, each gold ounce is worth ten of this country's dollars.

Quantity	Object	Defined Value
0.1	Ounce of Gold	$1.00
0.5	Ounce of Gold	$5.00
1	Ounce of Gold	$10.00
5	Ounce of Gold	$50.00
10	Ounce of Gold	$100.00

In this country there are exactly five guys who each have ten ounces of gold. These five guys are the entire population of the country.

Quantity	Object	Total Value
10	Ounce of Gold	$100.00
10	Ounce of Gold	$100.00
10	Ounce of Gold	$100.00
10	Ounce of Gold	$100.00
10	Ounce of Gold	$100.00
50	Ounces of Gold	$500.00

78 The original definition for the US Dollar was established in the Coinage Act of 1792 as 371.25 grains of fine silver.

Imagine that they like using receipt money, so their coins are in a vault.

Quantity	Object	Total Value
10	Receipt	$100.00
10	Receipt	$100.00
10	Receipt	$100.00
10	Receipt	$100.00
10	Receipt	$100.00
50	Receipts For 50 Gold Ounces	$500.00

Let's keep this simple. Imagine that they each grow different varieties of corn and that all corn is priced at $1 per bushel. These gentlemen grow flint corn, dent corn, sweet corn, popcorn and flour corn. Each type of corn is used for different purposes.

Illustrating what the purpose of inflation is NOT...

Here we begin our illustration for the first case. It involves two years.

In this imaginary world, the five guys have an annual economic summit on January 1st. In *year one*, they meet and then go about their business. In this simple low velocity economy, each man uses his $100 in receipt money to purchase 100 bushels of corn.

In *year two* they meet and decide to *"lubricate"* their economy so they can be sophisticated like the neighboring countries. They casually ignore the definition of their dollar. They print and *immediately* distribute an extra one hundred dollars each in receipts, thereby giving each man two hundred dollars.

Quantity	Object	Total Value
20	Receipt	$200.00
20	Receipt	$200.00
20	Receipt	$200.00
20	Receipt	$200.00
20	Receipt	$200.00
100	Receipts For 50 Gold Ounces	$1,000.00

Has the wealth of their nation increased?

The answer is no. The paper receipt is costless to produce and therefore valueless in its own right. The paper references the *same 50 ounces of gold* in the vault. Therefore, with double the receipts and no more gold, each receipt is instantly worth half as much.

Has the value of the corn changed?

The answer is no. The corn has the same nutritional value and other value attributes as it did before someone pressed the print button to create extra receipts. Corn is real property with identity and it can be weighed and measured.

Has the price of the corn changed?

The answer is ***yes***. Since the receipts are half as valuable and the corn retains its same value, one now needs to spend two dollars (in terms of inflated receipt money) for each bushel of corn.

How many bushels of corn can each of the five guys purchase with their $200 of old and new receipt money? Corn is $2 a bushel now so they are able to purchase exactly what they could before; 100 bushels of corn. ***Nothing changed.***

Therefore, one can see that inflation serves no purpose if everyone gets the new money on the same day.

So what is the purpose of inflation?

Illustrating what the purpose of inflation is...

Let's erase the last two years and start again in year one, this time with a different twist.

This time *on January 2nd in year one*, one of the five guys decides to become a *central banker*.

He prints an extra $500 in receipt money, places it on the ledgers in the bank and then borrows it. Instead of $500, all together they now have the same 50 gold ounces, but there is $1000 in receipt money floating around.

Remember in the previous analogy when the new receipts were printed, each of our five guys received his share of the new receipts. Because everyone knew the true ratio of receipts to gold, each of the five guys could go and get his, and only his, gold ounces out of the vault.

But this time, only one farmer, who is also the *central banker*, will get *all* the new receipts. Instead of ten, he will have his ten, plus the newly printed duplicate receipts which match the original receipts of his and the other four farmers. He will have 10+50=60 receipts, having a false face value of $600.

Quantity	Object	Total Value
60	Receipt	$600.00
10	Receipt	$100.00
10	Receipt	$100.00
10	Receipt	$100.00
10	Receipt	$100.00
100	Receipts For 50 Gold Ounces	$1,000.00

Has the wealth of their nation increased?

The answer is no. The paper is costless and therefore valueless in its own right. The paper references the same gold coins and therefore each receipt is now worth half as much. They still have only 50 gold coins in the vault.

Previously, when the other four guys lost half of their purchasing power, they each received additional receipts at no cost which maintained their purchasing power at the same level.

This time, the paper in four of the guy's pockets *lost half of its value, but they received no replacement receipts.* Instead, the banker gets all the new receipts. He enjoys an increase in purchasing power at least equal to the loss in purchasing power of the other four guys.

Has the value of the corn changed?

The answer is no. The corn has the same nutritional value and other value attributes as it did before someone pressed the print button to create extra receipts. Corn is real property with identity and it can be weighed and measured.

Has the price of the corn changed?

The answer is yes according to math, but no according to knowledge. Since the receipts are half as valuable and the corn retains its same value, corn should now be priced at two dollars (in terms of inflated receipt money) per bushel. However, the other four guys don't know about the new money so they continue to trade corn at the price of $1 per bushel. Over time, the market will reflect the decrease in purchasing power, but bad things happen along the way.

Consider how this plays out. The banker *started* with $100 like everyone else, then secretly printed $500 in new receipts. Then he borrowed the extra $500.

The banker now has $600 dollars to spend.

The market will always cause price changes to occur when the money system is manipulated. However, to keep the math simple, let's stipulate that the price changes in our analogy do not occur until the January 1st economic summit a year from now.

In the meantime, the banker is *purchasing* more corn than normal with the secretly printed new receipt money. The four guys are going to be quiet, but happy, because each thinks that he is making really big money this year as he *sells* more corn than normal and his account swells from $100 to $200. The other four farmers are thinking about all the extra corn of other varieties they will be able to buy next year. And an imported fishing boat.

For the purpose of illustration, let's specify that each of the four guys winds up with $200 dollars at the end of the year. The banker has $200 from the variety of corn he grew and sold that year along with some trading of the corn he purchased.

The four guys have 100 bushels of corn at the end of the year.

The banker, on the other hand ends the year with 500 bushels of corn.

What Happened?

At the economic summit it quickly becomes clear that the banker has inflated the money supply, which halved the value of the dollar receipts already in existence. The farmers discover they should have been selling corn for $2 a bushel.

Since everyone is now aware of the true value of the inflated receipts, in the upcoming year they will only be able to buy 100 bushels of corn with their deceptively big $200 dollar bank account. After all, $200 dollars in receipts are really only worth the same 10 ounces of gold they have in the vault.

What is the Effect?

Since everyone ended up with the same amount of dollars relative to one another, one might conclude there is not really any harm done, but that conclusion would be incorrect. ***Remember that the banker now has 500 bushels of corn when he should only have 100 bushels.***

Next year, the banker will be able to sell 500 bushels of corn at $2 a bushel. With his $1,000 income he will pay off the $500 bank loan and pocket $500 in profit. In that year or the next he will also begin printing more receipts which are not tied to any gold ounces and the process will repeat.

Since no one understood the game yet and the receipts each say that they can be redeemed for one gold ounce, the banker uses his $500 in profit to redeem the gold ounces from the vault. Now the banker has all the gold.

When the other farmers finally catch on, they will come to pick up their gold, but it is already gone. The solution ***for the banker*** is to pass a law that says it is illegal to own gold and all transactions must take place using the receipt money he is creating.

Purpose of Inflation

So now we can see the purpose of inflation.

"When inflating with costless money, the purpose of inflation is to use NEW MONEY to purchase REAL ASSETS at OLD PRICES, thereby causing a wealth transfer from the people who get the new money last, toward the people who get the new money first." ~ Shane Coley

Restated:

When inflating with costless money, the purpose of inflation is to use THE BANKER'S NEW RECEIPT MONEY to purchase THE FARMER'S $2 CORN at THE OLD CORN PRICE OF $1, thereby causing a wealth transfer from the four farmers who get the new money last, toward the banker who gets the new money first. After the banker has the corn, he sells it for cash and then takes all the gold.

Observe the illustration closely. Remember when the new receipts were created in the first case and all the guys received the new money at the same time? In that case no one's purchasing power changed. Prices doubled, but everyone had twice as much money, so the purchasing power was unchanged. The new receipts were meaningless.

In the second case only the banker knew about the new money. No one else suspected prices should be doubled.

Since in *both cases* the new receipts decreased the purchasing power of the other four guys, whose money was the banker actually handing over when he made his purchases of corn?

The banker was actually giving the other four guys their own money back again **and** *taking the fruits of their labor at the same time.*

The banker was buying the farmer's corn with the farmer's own money!

What does this mean for those who are members of a society which operates under an inflationary monetary system? Whoever gets the new money first has artificially increased his purchasing power, and that increase is paid for by the people who get the new money later. This is how our savings and retirements disappear.

The new money is used to purchase real property, like the corn, from the producer, using the producer's own purchasing power. It is no different than the banker just coming and taking the farmer's corn by force, except this method gets the job done in secret using differing weights and measures.

Perhaps these illustrations help explain this popular quote attributed to a past Chairman of the Bank of England:

"Banking was conceived in iniquity and was born in sin. The bankers own the earth. Take it away from them, but leave them the power to create money, and with the flick of the pen they will create enough deposits to buy it back again. However, take it away from them, and all the great fortunes like mine will disappear and they ought to disappear, for this would be a happier and better world to live in. But, if you wish to remain the slaves of bankers and pay the cost of your own slavery, let them continue to create money." ~ Sir Josiah Stamp, Director of the Bank of England (appointed 1928).[79]

4.2 Birthing Money

Anyone else would have to own property and operate a mine in order to bring new gold to market. The government simply decrees its existence.

The Club

Suppose there was a club that required all members to be grandparents. The base membership is purchased by having one grandchild. The club is organized in a way that the more grandkids you have, the higher up you are in the organization.

Any young man who wants to become a member and rank high in the organization needs to begin planning ahead so that he can raise his own children in order to have grandkids. He will need to raise productive children who love family and are responsible at a young age, so that they will be early to marry and begin raising him some of these grand-kids. That is a lot of work at every stage!

---

79 This quote is debatable in terms of source, but the text conveys accurate and important ideas.

If there was a gentleman who wanted to join the club, but had no grandchildren, he has a problem that takes time to solve. But wait!

He cannot produce grandkids without a lot of time and investment, but he can produce *pictures* of grand-kids...

As long as no one asks to see the actual children and grandchildren, all he needs to join the club is a picture of someone's grandchild. In this modern age of computing, he can get these pictures together in one afternoon. He will be king of the club in no time!

The Point

Producing natural money is like producing grand-kids. It takes resources, time and energy. Creating costless money from nothing is like showing off pictures of someone else's grand-kids. They do the work, you get the purchasing power to rank high in the club.

Some methods of having grand-kids to get in the club are ethical, while others are not ethical.

Some methods of increasing a money supply are ethical, while others are not ethical.

For example, some people suppose that a flood of new Silver or Gold in the market will cause unhealthy inflation. Childbirth is a labor intensive process. ***There are many differences***, but ask any miner and he will tell you that bringing precious metals to market is also a labor intensive process.

Inflation

Before further addressing the error in the claim about inflation and new silver or gold, we need to define inflation.

In addition to quantity, working definitions of inflation often include reference to *money class* and *ethics of production.* Here are three definitions of inflation, beginning with the most basic definition.

The first definition addresses only the quantity attribute in defining inflation.

Definition 1: Inflation is any increase in a money supply.

The next two definitions of inflation take into account the following three attributes:

Money class
Relative money quantity between money classes
Ethics of money production and use

Definition 2: Inflation is defined as "an extension of the nominal quantity of any medium of exchange beyond the quantity that would have been produced on the free market" - The Ethics of Money Production, Jorg Guido Hulsmann

Definition 3: Inflation is defined as "the process of issuing money beyond any increase in the stock of specie" - (Man, Economy, and State, 3rd ed., 1993, p. 851, Murray Rothbard)

If we say that *inflation is any increase in the money supply*, then an increase in the quantity of silver used in exchange would be inflation. However an increase in the quantity of silver in a market is not ultimately unhealthy.

The second case essentially provides a flexible definition for the money supply in a free market system, while rejecting any extension of the money supply through intervention by force. This definition leaves room for free banking where customers are permitted to do business with a bank that uses very limited fractional reserves as an independent institution. Such a bank will fail if customers lose confidence and demand their gold and silver from the bank vaults all at once. In other words there can be no bailouts, but customers can choose to do business with whom they please.

Definition three essentially says the weight and measure of your coinage is your money supply. Increasing the supply of coins is not inflation. Any money increase beyond the coinage is inflation.

I prefer definition one, *inflation is any increase in a money supply*, because the increase or decrease of the money supply in itself is not the problem. Rather than looking at the quantity, we need to consider how the commodity or money token is produced, what the object is and how it enters or leaves the market. Please consider the following analogy.

Two Buyers

Imagine that you own a farm on which you produce 100,000 bushels of wheat each year. In order to produce this wheat you use your land, labor, equipment and knowledge. You rise early in the morning and return late at night for months on end maintaining your farm, maintaining your equipment, managing your finances, and planting and harvesting your crops. You work hard.

The Printer

Let us say that while you are doing all of that work, there is another fellow who is lying around all year long doing nothing of value. Let us say that this fellow has a printer that he uses to print receipt money that no one would ever suspect is counterfeit.

Now imagine that one day he decides he would like to have your wheat crop. He prints out enough receipt money in a few minutes to exchange for your entire year of production.

You take your new counterfeit receipt money to town and are able to purchase groceries, diesel fuel, seed, fertilizer and tractor parts. But there is more going on here.

These new receipts, like dollars, decrease the purchasing power of all other dollars that you already possess or will be paid in the future. If there is a lot of this going on, everything you purchase is going to increase in price as the flood of new receipt money bids up prices on existing goods and services.

Also, this fellow with the printer didn't do any work, didn't hire any labor, didn't purchase any fuel, didn't buy any equipment and didn't do anything productive that would create a demand for your product on the market. In other words, if he is not employing people or purchasing real property that is built and serviced by people, then the only wheat he will consume is for himself, and he won't eat much because he isn't working. This lower demand means that your wheat price will be depressed. He has contributed nothing to production, which leads to abundance, which leads to prosperity.

The Producer

Suppose there is another man with a silver mine. This man must also own land and equipment. He will employ much labor in the process of mining, refining, shaping and securing the silver that he mines. He will purchase equipment, parts, and fuel to keep his mining operation going.

Since his product is silver, much of what he produces will pay for the overhead of production. If he runs an efficient operation, then after paying his overhead he will have a profit, just like the wheat farmer. Because he has a large labor force and uses many productive resources, he will create a demand for the wheat crop produced by the farmer.

If the miner wants the farmer's wheat crop, he has to either use savings from past production or do the work to produce the silver necessary to exchange for the wheat. He can't lie around and do nothing all year and then just decide one afternoon he wants the wheat.

When the miner exchanges silver for the farmer's wheat crop, there is indeed new silver in the market that is now being used in exchange. However, many other workers and businesses benefited from the process of producing the silver. As long as there is work being done to bring the silver to market, the increase in the supply of silver is a benefit to producers and society in general.

The Limit

The other very important thing to understand is that silver is limited in supply. If anyone wanted to flood the market with silver, they would physically have to mine and refine the silver in order to bring it to market. Even if the silver ore were lying on top of the ground, the silver exists in very small percentages in chunks of ore containing other metals.

On the other hand, costless money can be created in unlimited quantities, particularly in the age of computing. The savings, retirement, homes and wealth of the productive middle-class can be wiped out in a day by costless money created from nothing. That could never happen with silver.

Silver mining creates jobs. A commodity-based system of exchange secures private property and limits unlawful government. Suggesting that an increase in the quantity of silver is in any way the same as an increase in the quantity of costless money that is created by the stroke of a pen is ignorant and absurd.

4.3 Purchasing Power and Productivity

Productivity begets prosperity.

Can you imagine an exchange that does not have productivity mixed in?

It is impossible to have an exchange without productivity mixed in. Production may be consumed in the exchange or may be increased, but there is always productivity mixed in with any exchange.

Money is not a necessary ingredient in exchange. Exchange can occur without money.

I will illustrate these points with a simple example.

Suppose you owned 100 train cars filled with gold. Let's assume that the cars are secure and that people are willing to accept gold in exchange.

Could you purchase a hamburger with some of your abundant supply of gold?

The answer is a dependent yes. There is a prerequisite of productivity.

Someone must till the ground, plant wheat and make flour. Someone must raise and slaughter a steer to have the meat. Someone must plant a tomato and make ketchup. Someone must collect these and other related ingredients and resources into a single location and prepare the hamburger. And all of this has to happen in an environment that includes the producers being better off to exchange their product rather than keep it.

In addition, your gold would not have been secured, mined, refined, and aggregated unless someone engaged in productive labor.

Additionally, it is possible to exchange the makings of a hamburger for a quantity of fresh chicken eggs, instead of money.

Thus we see that productivity is a required component in exchange while money is optional. This is a critical point.

Think of costless money as a lazy and uninvited slob who barges in to your private dinner and forcibly takes the head seat at the table, demanding your honor and obedience.

Remember, the dinner cannot even occur unless gentle, honest productivity is at the table; perhaps this is productivity generated by the dinner party or perhaps captured by force. But always productivity will be present.

To be clear, money is not required at all. In addition to money not being required, unless it is honest money, money goes even further and steals from your productivity while giving nothing back.

Money gets up from the table, well fed by your labor, with your silverware in his pocket and various other articles openly picked up on the way out the door, all to be delivered back to his masters; masters who control his very existence by the stroke of a pen.

What does this mean?

If productivity is involved in every exchange and money is never necessary in any exchange then we can draw a few simple conclusions.

Apart from Productivity, costless money will never feed even one person one meal.

Productivity alone, without money, is capable of providing food, shelter and wealth.

If a person were hungry or cold and had the choice of solving their problem by choosing one and only one of these two elements, then choosing a quantity of money without productivity would leave them in a worse condition, while choosing from a pool of productivity would enable them to be warm and well fed.

In the case of a gift, the same holds true. If we give costless money apart from productivity, the recipient has nothing. If we give productivity apart from costless money, the recipient has a gift with usefulness and value.

Costless Paper Money

We see that gold apart from other productivity cannot provide anyone with a meal.

What about costless money?

Suppose in our nation there are 1,000,000 acres of farm land and 10,000 factories which produce our food and the products we value in exchange.

Now imagine that we print one trillion dollars.

Do we now suddenly have more acres of farmland? Do we now suddenly have more factories?

Someone may say, no, but with this new money, now we can build more factories!

Why can we? Will you build the factory with paper? Will you plant paper seeds in a paper field? No…? Then what do you mean?

I can only purchase more if I produce more things for which people are willing to exchange their own production. As our production becomes increasingly efficient, there will be a need for more acres and factories to engage in production. Increasing production requires real resources; bricks and steel, acres and seed - not paper.

All that costless money does is grant the first users of the New Money the fraudulent ability to lay claim to your productivity and property which they have not worked to acquire.

I could print money today and immediately acquire your entire year of production from your factory or farm, without doing anything productive myself. I would simply take your labor and property with the stroke of a pen.

The Keynesian monetary system we labor under does this every single day.

Government Stimulus

Since only productivity applied together with real resources can feed a person or increase one's wealth, the only thing anyone can ever give in exchange for any other thing is productivity.[80]

When the government issues new costless money into the system and the banking sector multiplies it yet again, the costless money only has value to the extent that productivity is absorbed into the costless money.

If we had trillions and trillions of dollars, but no one planted crops or made things, we would be a poor nation. Consider Zimbabwe. A few decades ago 1 Zim Dollar would buy as much as 1.47 US Dollars. Today it takes 37,456,777 Zim Dollars to equal 1 US Dollar.

Do big numbers on slips of paper make a nation wealthy? No. Impossible.

Therefore when the government prints costless money, your property and productivity are necessarily used to impute value to the new dollars, but someone else gets these "valuable" new tokens. They are worthless on their own account, apart from your labor.

Conclusion

The clear and logical economic arguments against the current stimulus and our monetary system in general are somewhat involved and will not be covered in this article. However, the point that we want to convey is this:

The only thing government can give away is productivity and, since government produces nothing, government can only give away your hard earned and valuable productivity. Costless money is nothing except a tool to steal what belongs to you.

---

80 I want to mention that one of my favorite books is *Our Enemy The State* by Albert J Nock. I discovered this book about a year ago and found it to closely match my own thinking in many areas. It is worth the read, as is The Law by Frederic Bastiat. These and other great works can be found at mises.org.

Furthermore, if we produce nothing then there is nothing to take and nothing to give away, regardless of how many money tokens are created. Again, observe Zimbabwe for an example.

The more we produce, the more the government has access to, which will be used to do the things government does best; destroy liberty and enslave people.

4.4 Production & the Prodigal Son

I recently taught a series of Sunday school lessons on the parable of the Prodigal Son, which is found in Luke chapter 15. The Sunday school material I used began by observing how deeply ingrained the parable of the Prodigal Son is in our Spiritual and literary traditions. It was noted that Shakespeare used plot points from the parable of the Prodigal Son in the *Merchant of Venice* and in *Henry IV*. Country music singer Hank Williams recorded a song called the *Prodigal Son* comparing the Prodigal's homecoming to the joys of heaven. The world's great Art museums contain many works featuring scenes from the Prodigal Son's experience. Of course we recognize terms like a wayward child being referred to as a prodigal son or daughter and we hear people talk about killing the fattened calf or riotous living. So the stories and the ideas of the prodigal son are very familiar in our traditions, culture and language.

In addition one can argue that this parable is the most richly detailed and personal of all the parables of Jesus. It is safe to say that everyone can relate to at least one of the three characters in the parable at sometime in their life.

Because of the details in this parable, many people seek complex symbolism, layers of meaning or hidden lessons that bend the rules of interpretation. We want to be very careful to focus on the plain meaning of Scripture and not invent our own meaning for the parable.

Our goal then, is to read the parable and observe the details that provide the framework for the story, so that we can understand the plain meaning of the passage. As I began to prepare my Sunday school lesson, a new facet of the details of the story came into my view. I noticed that there were many terms that were directly related to production. So class began with the study of how production fits into the parable. Our first task as a class was to agree on a definition of production.

Production is the just or righteous mixture of life, liberty and property combined in a way that the output is more valuable than the input.

It was easy for us to recognize and agree that production is some form of gain or increase. Next we went through a series of questions to see if production was reasonable to consider in studying our Bible lesson.

First we asked, "Since people eat food and use things, do people depend on production?" The answer is obviously yes.

Next we asked, "Does our dependence on production influence our decisions?" Again the obvious answer is yes, with a good example being that we often go to work because we want to have food, clothing and shelter.

Next we asked, "Does our dependence on production challenge our morals?" Again the obvious answer was yes.

Then we asked, "As Christians, does our dependence on production challenge our obedience?" Again the clear answer was yes.

Finally we asked, "Who made us dependent on production?" As Christians we believe that God is our Creator, which means that God made us dependent on production.

So let's think about what we just observed. People eat food and use things, which means that people depend on production. Our dependence on production influences our decisions, challenges our morals and challenges our obedience - all because God made things that way[81]. There is no question that thinking about production while studying Scripture is a good idea.

50 Terms

There are more than 50 terms in the parable of the prodigal son that are related to production. In the passage that is on the following page you will see various terms in bold. These are terms related to production.

For example the term ***give*** is meaningless unless there is something to give. The term ***share*** is meaningless unless there is something to divide. The term ***estate*** obviously refers to the property of the father. The term ***everything*** refers to all of the property belonging to the son. ***Journey*** is a term indirectly related to production because in order to take a journey one must have the resources to do so. Think of your vacation.

Loose living is a term related to production. As we see in the parable, when his resources are gone his loose living stopped. He was

81 Until someone can explain how no one used nothing to create everything, the idea of a Creator is at least as valid as any other idea.

then focused on finding something to eat, which brings us to the term ***enough bread. Bread*** is clearly related to production and ***enough*** communicates a quantity of production.

Further down we see the terms ***music*** and ***dancing. Music*** flows from an instrument which would have been produced from profits which belonged to a producer. He was willing to use these profits to create a musical instrument because his more immediate needs of food, shelter and clothing had been met. And of course ***dancing*** is something that typically involves music and is something that occurs among people who are in good spirits with full stomachs.

We could go on and on looking at the terms, but we have sufficiently illustrated the reason that various terms are considered to be related to production.

Luke 15:11-32 - And He said, "A man had two sons. "The younger of them said to his father, 'Father, ***give*** *me the* ***share*** *of the* ***estate*** *that falls to me.' So he* ***divided*** *his* ***wealth*** *between them. "And not many days later, the younger son gathered* ***everything*** *together and went on a* ***journey*** *into a distant country, and there he* ***squandered*** *his* ***estate*** *with* ***loose living.*** *"Now when he had* ***spent everything,*** *a severe* ***famine*** *occurred in that country, and he began to be* ***impoverished.*** *"So he went and* ***hired*** *himself out to one of the citizens of that country, and he* ***sent*** *him into his* ***fields*** *to* ***feed swine.*** *"And he would have gladly* ***filled*** *his* ***stomach*** *with the* ***pods*** *that the* ***swine*** *were* ***eating,*** *and no one was* ***giving anything*** *to him. "But when he came to his senses, he said, 'How many of my father's* ***hired*** *men have more than* ***enough bread,*** *but I am* ***dying*** *here with* ***hunger!*** *'I will get up and* ***go*** *to my father, and will say to him, "Father, I have sinned against heaven, and in your sight; I am no longer worthy to be called your son; make me as one of your* ***hired*** *men."' "So he got up and came to his father. But while he was still a long way off, his father saw him and felt compassion for him, and ran and embraced him and kissed him. "And the son said to him, 'Father, I have sinned against heaven and in your sight; I am no longer worthy to be called your son.' "But the father said to his* ***slaves,*** *'Quickly bring out the* ***best robe*** *and put it on him, and put a* ***ring*** *on his hand and* ***sandals*** *on his feet; and bring the* ***fattened calf, kill it,*** *and let us* ***eat*** *and* ***celebrate;*** *for this son of mine was dead and has come to life again; he was lost and has been found.' And they began to* ***celebrate.*** *"Now his older son was in the* ***field,*** *and when he came and approached the* ***house,*** *he heard* ***music*** *and* ***dancing.*** *"And he* ***summoned*** *one of the* ***servants*** *and began inquiring what these things could be. "And he said to him, 'Your brother* *has come, and your father has **killed** the **fattened calf** because he has received him back safe and sound.' "But he became angry and was not willing to go in; and his father came out and began pleading with him. "But he answered and said to his father, 'Look! For so many **years** I have been **serving** you and I have never neglected a command of yours; and yet you have never **given** me a young **goat**, so that I might **celebrate** with my friends; but when this son of yours came, who has **devoured** your **wealth** with prostitutes, you killed the **fattened calf** for him.' "And he said to him, 'Son, you have always been with me, and **all** that is **mine** is **yours.** 'But we had to **celebrate** and rejoice, for this brother of yours was dead and has begun to live, and was lost and has been found.'" NASB95*

As I prepared to teach, I noticed that there were several terms related to production in the story of the prodigal son. After I went through the passage marking the terms that were related to production, it became clear that if these terms were removed there would be no story. So now we have this richly detailed parable which influences our traditions and culture and art, and which is meaningful to nearly every person in some way at some point in their life, and we find that if we remove terms related to production the story falls apart. To be very clear, I'm not saying that the truth of the story is lost, because truth exists apart from the story and apart from the framework used to tell the story. However, this parable relies heavily on the concepts of production to convey certain truth.

Welfare State

Our country today is sometimes called a welfare state, which means that there is a significant portion of our population that depends on welfare for food, shelter and clothing. If the story of the prodigal son were told today in our country, it would go a little bit differently. After the younger son had squandered his wealth on loose living, he would have gone to the welfare office and signed up for his welfare check and food stamps. This would have kept him from "coming to his senses," thinking about the condition of the hired help on his father's estate, recognizing the error of his ways, repenting of his bad choices and bad attitude, confessing these to his father and ultimately being received back into the family, once again becoming a productive member of the society.

The parable of the prodigal son tells us things about God the Father, about Jesus as Savior, about Christians as prodigal sons and daughters and about the religious people like the scribes and the Pharisees who approach God based on their works and confidence in themselves.

However, this parable also tells us something about how God's natural order and natural law is used to draw people to truth.

A Christian is supposed to be led by the Spirit, not by the flesh. According to the Christian worldview, an unsaved person is led by the flesh rather than by the spirit.

A person who understands spiritual truth will filter the desires of his flesh through spiritual understanding. If a person who is led by the flesh is going to learn spiritual truth, his flesh sometimes has a role in leading him there. The parable of the prodigal son is an excellent example of how a hungry belly can bring a person to his senses. Therefore whether the flesh leads the spirit or the spirit leads the flesh, it is important that the flesh and the spirit generally move in the same direction. With that thought in mind let's consider what happens if the flesh and the spirit go in different directions.

Based on my Christian worldview I believe that the God of the Bible is the creator of the universe and everything in it. I also believe that God is the ultimate producer, even going beyond production to the act of creation ex nihilo. I also believe that man is created in the image of God and, because God is a producer by nature, we also are producers by nature. However not everyone produces. So the question is, if people are by nature producers but are not always productive, how does a person feel when they are not productive?

I agree that there are many people who are lazy and unproductive and have no desire to change, but what is going on inside?

Consider the drug addict who is destroying his body. He is choosing temporary immediate pleasure over the immediate and long-term good health of his body.

Likewise, people will choose to be lazy and unproductive even at the expense of their spiritual well-being.

When a person lives in such a way that he squanders the property that he has and does not work to replace it, he faces poverty and hunger. Poverty and hunger led the prodigal son back to his senses. If some ancient welfare agency had given the prodigal son enough food, clothing and shelter to survive, chances are he would not have come to his senses, repented, confessed and been reconciled to his family. His inner man would have become corrupt and undergone increasing decay, rather than healing.

Therefore if a Christian really loves other people he will never do anything to support the physical man in a way that will ultimately harm the spiritual man. Let's consider the passages from Scripture that will guide us in best serving the physical and the spiritual man.

"For even when we were with you, we used to give you this order: if anyone is not willing to work, then he is not to eat, either." (2 Thessalonians 3:10, NASB95)

"There is a way which seems right to a man, But its end is the way of death. A worker's appetite works for him, For his hunger urges him on." (Proverbs 16:25–26, NASB95)

Use of the Fruits

I want to consider one other point in the parable. When the young son returned, his father hugged him around the neck and commanded his servants to bring a robe, a ring, and sandals for his young son. Each of these gifts has a significant meaning, but we are going to focus on the ring right now.

In those days, that ring would have been a signet ring which gave the possessor a right called usufruct. Usufruct is a Latin term that literally means *use of the fruits* and it describes the legal right to use someone else's property at no cost, while reaping the fruits as though the property were your own. The only requirement was that the property be maintained in equal or better condition during use and when it was returned to the owner.

We can see in the parable that the young son lost his right to any further inheritance, but while his father was alive he was able to use a portion of his father's property in order to produce and begin building sufficient wealth to take care of his own future family.

Scripture records that God told the children of Israel that the land was His and they were tenants. With a little thought we can see the similarity between the Garden of Eden as the father's estate and Adam and Eve being evicted, but given the right to use God's property to satisfy their needs and some of their wants. One could say we now possess the right of usufruct, meaning *use of the fruits,* but we have to work and produce in order to maintain the property and care for ourselves.

Summary

In summary, the parable of the prodigal son is heavily dependent on terms related to production. Our decisions are influenced by our dependence on production. Our morals and obedience are challenged by our dependence on production.

God made us dependent on production and God's natural order will cause a hungry man to lead his inner man toward right-thinking, restoration and productive life. An empty belly can get the attention of a stubborn man when no amount of persuasion will work. Supporting a hungry man who is unwilling to work sets in motion an internal decay that typically cannot be halted or reversed, until the physical man is once again subject to the natural order and his dependence on production.

If we subsidize bad behavior, we will get more of it. If we penalize production, we will get less of it.

4.5 Two Social Models

When we subsidize unfruitful behavior, we glorify laziness and dishonor production. People who play are honored; those who pay are mocked.

This chapter contains a chart with two sections: The top section is titled *Social Model Based on Scripture and Natural Law*. The bottom section is titled *Social Model Employed in Modern Civilization*. The sections are first separated for easier viewing and discussed. The sections are also combined in one image at the end for easier comparison.

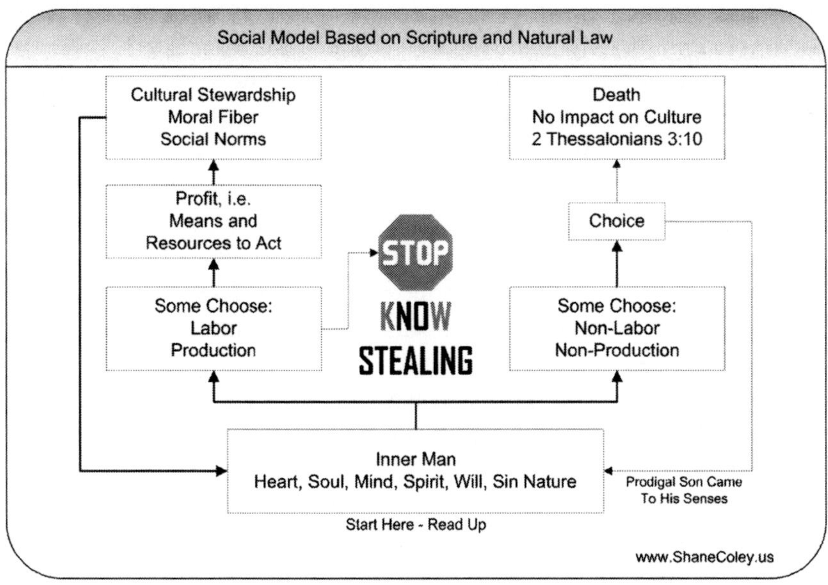

These charts are read from the bottom up. The starting box contains the text *Inner Man*, followed by terms typically associated with the inner man. The list is *Heart, Soul, Mind, Spirit, Will* and *Sin Nature*. The inner man represents an individual.

Each individual has a basic decision to make each day in life. A person can either choose to engage in labor and production, or a person can choose to *not* engage in labor and *not* engage in production. Some choose labor and production and some choose non-labor and non-production, otherwise known as being lazy.

Moving up to the right on the chart leads to a box containing the word *death*. This box is based on Scripture that says if a person is not *willing* to work, he is not to eat.

"For even when we were with you, we used to give you this order: if anyone is not willing to work, then he is not to eat, either." (2 Thessalonians 3:10, NASB95)

An able person who will not work will not be permitted to eat. He will eventually choose to work or he will die. Under these conditions, a person who does not work will have a short life, during which glory, popularity and prosperity will *not* be his. In this system, a person who doesn't work or eat is not going to be a role model.

On the left side of the chart is a box indicating that some choose labor and production, which is otherwise known as *work*. By our labor we develop *profits*, which are *the means and resources to act*. If I want to have corn to eat next year then I have to grow corn or exchange something else I produce with someone who has corn.

In order for a school to exist someone had to make the bricks and build the building and make the desks and the chalkboard and the books and paper and whatever else is involved in that teaching environment. Someone had to hire the teacher and make the clothes that the teacher wears and someone has to provide the food that the teacher will eat. A school operates using the output of producers, not the output of lazy people and central banks.

In other words, you cannot have a school system, television station, any institution or any resources to do anything at all, unless someone works to produce those resources.

The means and resources to act, come from those who labor and produce. Because those who labor and produce are able to keep their property, then they engage in cultural stewardship. Producers strengthen the moral fiber of a society.

Because the producers are not robbed, they become the ones who shape the social norms. Those people who are unwilling to work do not even survive, let alone influence society as bad role models.

People who work understand the challenges of production. Producers understand what it is to be accountable. Producers must be good stewards of property and relationships and must respect the property rights of other people in order to protect their own property rights. Producers understand what it is to work hard and keep commitments. Producers become the people who shape the moral fiber and the social norms. They engage in cultural stewardship. Their influence affects the inner man in positive ways.

The Parable of the Prodigal Son is a great example of this model. The wasteful son squandered his estate until he had nothing left. When he was finally hungry enough *he came to his senses* and went home with a humble attitude, ready to work.

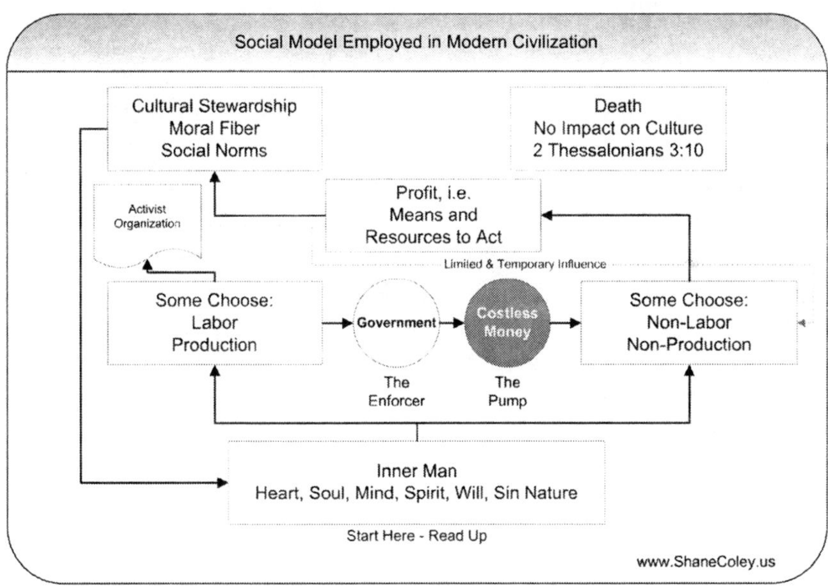

The section titled Social Model Employed in Modern Civilization is the most concise way I know of illustrating what we have done to ourselves.

The chart begins at the bottom with the inner man, meaning an individual. Again an individual can choose labor and production or non-labor and non-production.

Those who choose labor and production are exposed to government, which we will call *The Enforcer.* Consider the following quote from George Washington, the first president of the United States.

Government is not reason; it is not eloquence. It is force. Like fire, government is a dangerous servant and a fearful master. ~ George Washington

To the right of government is a red circle entitled Costless Money. Money Systems always create new money from nothing, which is a *wealth pump*. The United States has the Federal Reserve System which, along with all the member banks in the country, creates money from thin air. That includes every little local bank.

Costless Money transfers wealth from those who produce to those who do not. Producers are being taxed and regulated and their profits are being inflated away, so that their profits from production are transferred to non-producers.

Non-producers include welfare at the low end of the spectrum, meaning your typical welfare recipient that does not work. Non-Producers also include corporate welfare through bailouts and all manner of regulatory and tax loopholes. Non-producers can also be jobs or institutions where people are not producing something of value to be used by themselves or others in the society. The test for this class of non-producers is simply whether the activity will be sustained in a free market. The categories are set by votes cast through uncoerced market exchanges.

Producers are forced to support non-producers by government, The Enforcer, through rules, regulations and laws, which provide a framework for legal plunder. Costless money is the primary *Pump* for getting resources to the non-producers. Non-producers are dependent on pillaging and theft for profits and even their very survival.

The producer who is managing his property and his resources does not have time to leave his business and lobby the government, so he cannot even defend himself.

The non-producers have profits rolling in because they sway lawmakers with propaganda, perks, favors and gifts. The lawmakers bring more property under the control of the non-producers. The only possible protection that the producer has is to hire an activist organization to lobby the lawmakers, but that never works for four principle reasons.

First, the activist organization is typically populated by people with the non-producers mindset.

Second, the system functions based on theft, not production. Therefore the only favor that producers can offer is to continue producing. The natural order provides limited sustainable profits in the long term. Producers are not going to willingly be blackmailed into paying off lawmakers. They will resist when the favors being asked are clearly unlawful. Producers having nothing to offer in direct dealing with government.

Third, producers and non-producers don't speak the same language. Non-producers have no respect for property rights. Non-producers necessarily *must* violate property rights in order to have their meals, housing, retirements, vacations and profits. The decent people caught in the system spend their time justifying what they do, individually and together in groups. The only way to change their thinking is through their stomach.

Finally, a society that permits legal plunder makes people wealthy by manipulating paper, not by producing. If the people who are profiting from this system expect to continue profiting, they cannot condemn the system. They want to keep the system in place so that the paper profits keep coming. The only way for that to happen is for there to be an underlying class of producers to carry the load. If you are a producer, don't bother lobbying the government to be treated fairly. You are the backbone of the scam. The only way a producer organization can get a favor from government is to be willing to pillage other less connected producers, which is ultimately unsustainable.

So the communication by the activist organization, on behalf of the producer, with the non-producers is fruitless, but that is the way the effort is made.

Since the producers are losing their profits and digging into capital to maintain their businesses, they do not have time or the resources to influence the culture.

Instead *the non-producers* use profits from production to build the schools, hire the teachers, write the textbooks and control the media. The non-producers use the profits from production to advertise cleverly engineered propaganda. The non-producers control the government. The non-producers write the laws, rules and regulations that keep profits from production flowing into the coffers of government and favored business.

The people whose very existence is based on violating natural law manage the profits from production and use those profits to strengthen their wealth capturing position.

The non-producers control *the means and resources to act.* They shape the culture. Because their entire existence is founded on theft and lies, they cannot help but degrade social norms, which then influence the individual. How can a thief teach others to be honest? How can one who lives off of others teach a young man to be productive? This necessarily leads to a complete breakdown in the moral fiber of society.

After creating this chart I was struck by how closely it illustrated a quote written in 1919 by John Maynard Keynes in a book called the Economic Consequences of the Peace.

Keynes wrote, "*Lenin is said to have declared that the best way to destroy the capitalist system was to debauch the currency. By a continuing process of inflation, governments can confiscate, secretly and unobserved, an important part of the wealth of their citizens. By this method they not only confiscate, but they confiscate arbitrarily; and, while the process impoverishes many, it actually enriches some... Lenin was certainly right. There is no subtler, no surer means of overturning the existing basis of society than to debauch the currency. The process engages all the hidden forces of economic law on the side of destruction, and does it in a manner which not one man in a million is able to diagnose.*"

These two social charts illustrate the way that unlawful government and costless money undermine the productive capacity and moral foundations of a society.

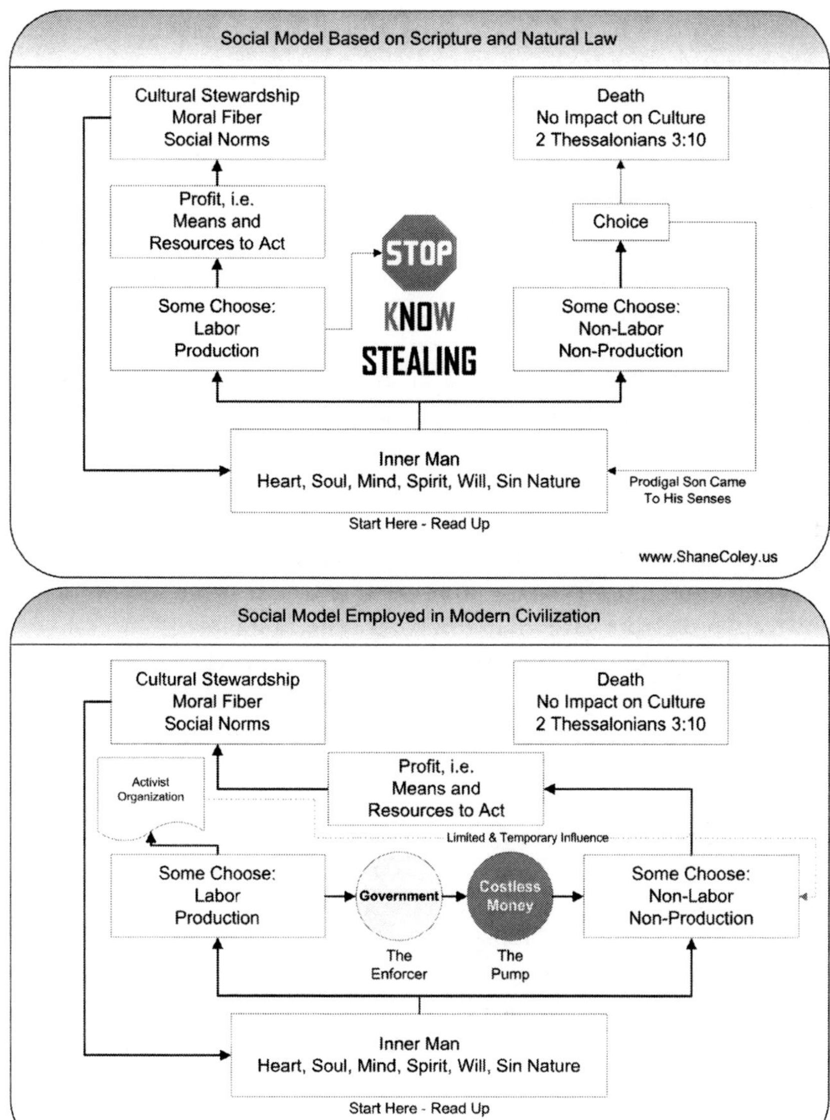

Ten Old Farmers

The following story illustrates how the profits from production are confiscated and used to shape the culture according to the intent of the non-producers.

Our higher education system in the United States teaches many things to many people. College professors are provided with salaries and places to work so that what professors believe is important can be taught to many young minds.

College professors eat food and use things. Food and things must be produced. Government hires and pays most college professors, directly or indirectly. But government produces nothing and wastes much. Therefore every resource used by college professors must be produced by a producer. There is no other source. Many of the resources professors use must be produced by a farmer. For example, food and fiber from the farm play an important role in supplying homes, offices, groceries, clothes and paper for these professors.

But not everyone is especially pleased with some college professors and the job they do. Some people think that there are college professors who don't know how to get out of the rain. Some would even say that some college professors are those who teach because they can't do. It is commonly believed by some professors that they are above the rest of the folks, and the rest of the folks acknowledge that sort of arrogance is common among professors. It may even be true that the way we select and train professors has lead to this sorry state of affairs.

Of course one of the first arguments that comes up in any conversation about education is how important education is to modern society. Education is said to be the glue and foundation and glory of modern society.

That presents us with a problem, because modern society is crumbling. Students graduate and cannot find jobs. Higher education degrees have become so commonplace that the degree no longer results in increased earning power. Diplomas are a commodity now. If education is clamoring for the *credit* as the great requirement for the success of modern civilization, then education must also accept *responsibility* for the problems of modern civilization. If education cannot take responsibility for the problems, then education cannot claim great and overriding influence in society, for good or bad.

No institution can claim great influence without accepting responsibility for the outcomes, good or bad. If education is not the chief cause of our problems, then maybe education is not as influential as educators are trained to believe. There is no question that education is important, but education has great potential for good or evil. If we mock and dishonor those who are most satisfied putting their hand to the wrench or plow, then force them to go to college, cause them to be in debt directly or indirectly, graduate them with no job and no development of their true natural talents of doing foundational productive work, then we have set them up for failure. At the same time, the food and things they depend on are no longer produced efficiently. We have taken away the people and the training, generational knowledge and skill required to make a nation strong, because people depend on production. Now our untrained natural machinist or farmer has no tools and no one to make or grow the things he and his family need to live and prosper.

Suppose the following plan was put in motion to resolve the problem. The plan involves a group of wise old farmers who are well read, well traveled and brilliant by all accounts. These men are just in their dealings, good listeners, fair-minded and appreciate useful knowledge and skill, especially when practiced at the hand of honest, hard working and productive people.

Imagine getting a group of these ten wise old farmers together to form a review board to assess the job performance of all the college professors in the United States. Let's suppose that these gentlemen could, by some miracle, do their performance review thoroughly, completely and correctly in ten days. Furthermore, whatever they decided would be done immediately for each and every position and professor they reviewed. Their judgments would be handed down in the following ten days.

At the end of the ten days of performance review, how many college professors would this group of wise old farmers keep? Stated another way, if you are a professor, would you be able to defend your position to this group of wise old farmers?

I'll be generous. For the sake of argument, let's say that for arguments sake that the farmers retain fifty percent of the professors and terminate the remaining fifty percent. The review board will have added a footnote that says some really good people were terminated for suffering from nothing more than a lack of real world experience and bad guidance from the days when those same professors were students. They will remark that these professors are like a prodigal son who never had to want for anything because someone was always there to pay the bill or do the work on which his learning opportunity depended.

Of course there will be professors who are highly offended! But that's okay. In fact, that's really the point. Producers have a different value system than non-producers. These professors were hired by non-producers in government or in government subsidized institutions. Every promise made by government has to kept by a producer, but that doesn't mean the producer is consulted before the promise is made.

If our farmers would fire a large percentage of the professors currently teaching in our public higher education system, then the farmers would not have hired these people from the start.

So here is the question: Why do the people who pay the bills not get to make the hiring decisions?

If we did a similar analysis on the few higher education institutions that get no government assistance, the percentage would be different. First of all, I suspect our review board would approve of nearly all, if not all of the professors in those institutions on merit. Secondly, these farmers are producers and they would decline on principle if asked to make a hiring or firing decision for someone else's employee. The producers would respect the property rights of the other producers who were guiding the use of their own resources in that private institution. If the institution is earning its keep by providing a valuable service that people are willing to pay for, then that would be enough to satisfy our farmers. They would even say, *well done.*

4.6 Robbing Farmers

Who subsidizes who...?

A nation can stop being concerned about its farmers just as soon as the people stop eating food and using things. As farmers go, so goes the nation.

I was raised on a farm in the cattle business and my dad was a pioneer in the field of embryo transfer. Because his business dealt with purebred cattle and expensive new technology, many of his customers were people who were successful in other businesses. After individuals made their millions in some other enterprise they often purchased land, and then either planted trees or bought cattle. Other customers were true farmers, farming land which had been in their families for generations. This environment provided me with an interesting view of some of the changes in agriculture over the past century.

Farm Subsidies

Farm subsidies are a major complaint the American consumer has about farmers. Farm subsidies or farm payments involve a complex web of plunder. The question is: Who is plundering who? I will share the answer in the form of an analogy.

Dry Pond

Imagine that you and I were taken up in an airplane and flown to an unfamiliar and remote location. Suppose that we parachuted out of the plane and landed on a dirt road far from any people or structures. As we were walking along we noticed a pond that was completely dry.

The *reason* that the pond was dry was not evident.

Perhaps there was a hole in the dam or in the drain pipe. Because we can't see the entire dam, it is possible that the dam is actually breached. Another possibility is that the region was suffering from drought conditions. Or perhaps an underground spring had dried up, or maybe someone upstream diverted water flow that previously fed the pond. Maybe it was pumped dry with an irrigation pump.

Depending on our access to pertinent information, we could debate, argue and wonder all day, or maybe forever, about *why* the pond is dry. But one thing is certain: *we know the pond is dry.*

Dry Equity

In a similar way, we know that farmers are going bankrupt or selling out every day and have been for many years. This is easy to prove by looking at the history of small farming operations all across the country. It is also easy to prove by asking questions of farmers who are still in operation.

I've discussed this with farmers many times and so far I've always gotten the same answers. When a farmer is ready to retire, his plan is to sell his land. If he sells his land to his son, his son cannot afford to farm it. If the father gives his land to his son, then the father has no retirement.

We know the equity has been stolen because the father cannot afford to give the land away and the son cannot afford to buy it. Their equity is all dried up.

Since we know for certain that the equity is gone, or certainly depleted to an unworkable level, perhaps we can identify the cause.

The Business of Farming

For the purpose of this analogy let's think of a farm as being like any machine that receives inputs and produces outputs. As with any other machine, the farmer has to *maintain* his farm so that it can remain productive and efficient.

In the production process, let's say that the farmer spends five dollars for his inputs and adds another five dollars to pay for labor and the maintenance of his farm. In order for the farmer to make a profit and do all the things that businesses do to maintain their machines and market their products, he needs to sell his output for fifteen dollars.

What actually happens is very different and is a national disgrace. Because of government intervention in the market the farmer gets paid $7.50 for a product that cost him $10 to produce.

The government taxes the American consumer $3 and then wastes half of what they collect. Out of this $3 the government pays the farmer a subsidy of $1.50, to add to his $7.50 income from his product.

The farmer now has an income of $9 from his product. Therefore he has a loss of $1. So how does the farmer make up for this one dollar loss?

The farmer pays himself a salary that is below the market value for the work that he does. The farmer learns how to be a mechanic, carpenter, metalworker, fence builder, machine operator, cattleman, animal doctor, weatherman, crop scientist, chemical specialist, businessman and whatever else is necessary to get the job done, while under assault by a money and legal system that is plundering his wealth and production.

The farmer becomes an expert in patching, binding and repairing all the tools of his trade. His equipment, his barns and his fences are old. As he nears retirement age, he makes plans in the back of his mind that he would rather not think about all.

He is a farmer because he loves the land. The farmer loves his family, his crops and livestock. The farmer sees the miracle of new life and growth in his calves and his corn. The farmer wants his children and grandchildren to experience the beauty of creation and to have the opportunity to produce. But the rulers who control the terms whereby the farmer has to trade real production for costless money have said: *No. There will be no next generation on your farm.*

Americans, and Christians in particular, have stood by and said nothing. We bleed our farmers dry while they work until their body or the bank says *no more.* Farmers take the abuse because they love what they do.

So the plans the farmer makes quietly in the back of his mind involve how he will maintain his farm as he approaches retirement. He calculates carefully to see that his fences, barns, tractors and planters will be just able to get through his last year. He can't afford to repair anything unnecessarily.

One of the ways the farmer rationalizes holding on for one more year is by looking at his land value according to its denomination in dollars. Because of the way we are taught to think about land and other real estate value, the farmer considers the increasing money value of his land to be his retirement. The unfortunate reality is that the land is not increasing in value, but instead the money is decreasing in value. The farmer is storing away money units by holding land to sell for his retirement. However, the purchasing power of these money units will be just enough to get by when it is time for the money to be spent in the future.

Farming Subsidies

Farming crops is not enough for a farmer to make a profit today. He must also know how to *farm subsidies*, maybe even better than he knows how to farms crops. Today's profitable farmer must also farm vast acreages, which require large and expensive equipment. The large acreage and expensive equipment in turn requires much debt, recorded as promises to pay in the ledger at the bank.

At the same time government regulation, increasing cost of inputs, and greater control over seed genetics puts farmers in a position of great risk relative to government and large corporations.

This environment drives small operators out of business and leads to a growing number of corporate farms that are skilled in *farming subsidies* and fleecing taxpayers.

Are there farming operations that are generating tremendous profits by f*arming subsidies*? Absolutely.

Some of these are the last of the family farms who are trying to hold on by seeking profits within a fraudulent system that has consumed many of their friends and neighbors across the country. However most of the farms that are generating tremendous profits by *farming subsidies* are corporate farms. These corporate farms are partners with government in transferring the wealth of rural America and crushing the heritage of agriculture and the family farm.

The American Consumer

Remember in our analogy that the farmer sold his product for \$7.50? And remember that the American consumer was taxed \$3? This means that the American consumer has \$10.50 in the farmer's product. This also means that the American consumer paid \$4.50 less than the farmer's product was worth. So what did the American consumer do with this \$4.50?

After the mortgage and groceries are purchased the American

family inspects their bank account. What do they find? $4.50 in disposable income!

This $4.50 adds up over time. It is used to purchase video games, movie tickets, sports tickets, vacations and $150 tennis shoes. Much of our media is filled with blood and gore, dishonesty and unfaithfulness, instant gratification, glitz, glamour and waste. This flood of entertainment tends to degrade our morals, weaken our relationships, damage our work ethic and reduce our productivity.

We purchase all of these things by spending the farmer's retirement while he works to feed us.

But there's more!

Because of the way our agricultural payment system is designed, farmers are paid for quantity not quality. This destructive system pays for pounds and bushels, not nutritional content. For this reason we have food that is *safe*, but not necessarily *healthy*.

Food that is highly processed, overloaded with chemicals and grown in nutrient depleted soils is weak and unhealthy. It doesn't take much of an imagination to suspect that the quality of our food is having a negative impact on the quality of our health. Health problems cost money, particularly in a system where costs are driven up by government intervention and third-party payment systems like ours.

Therefore, we have used the $4.50 that has been confiscated from the family farm to cheapen our minds and morals with entertainment and damage our bodies with highly processed and nutritionally deficient foods.

Summary

There should be no farm subsidies and government should not intervene in the market to reduce the price of farm commodities. The American consumer should not have to pay too much for their food, but setting the price for all goods and services is the role of the market. The American farmer should not have to give up his retirement and his farm and his family heritage to buy movie tickets and fancy tennis shoes for other people.

Driving families off the farm is costing us generational knowledge that cannot be recovered in an afternoon. We must work to enhance our food security by defending private property rights for everyone, including farmers. One of the rights they have in their property is the right to sell their production from their property and labor at a fair price on the market.

Some would say that American farmers cannot compete with imported foods from other countries. This sounds like a clever and sophisticated argument rooted in complex economics, but it is not. Producers exchange with producers. The paper money system that is pillaging the farmer is the same system that permits us to purchase agricultural products from other nations with costless money created from thin air. This system will completely fail sooner or later.

Private property, productivity and honest exchange are the solution for farmers and for all free societies.

4.7 Cause and Effect

Costless money production is the founding and enabling tool of stealth oppression, which is a cancer that eventually gives birth to open tyranny. Our ignorance of basic economic principles leaves us viewing effects as causes, while the causes always remain hidden from our mind's eye. We fund our own destruction while blaming each other for the pain caused by an ever present, yet unseen enemy.

One of the reasons that we cannot solve our social and economic problems is that we are trained to focus on effects rather than causes. We tend to recognize and focus on the pain, rather than looking to see what is causing the pain.

Let's consider a simple example. Suppose a fellow burns his finger on the eye of a stove. Since the stove is hot, he decides to solve the problem by pouring water on it to cool it off. The cause of the problem is that the stove is engineered to get hot. Pouring water on it doesn't solve anything. Of course, the only reason he would try to cool it with water is if he doesn't understand the cause and believes the water will make the stove cool and protect his finger.

Because we have knowledge, from our perspective, pouring water on the stove is an ignorant response. Unfortunately, because of the nature and reality of the world we live in, any similar response to effects, rather than causes is ignorant. Our opinion about things does not define reality or the nature of things.

An effect can be the cause of another effect, which is one reason this is such an important idea. We have to identify the root causes of a problem before there is any hope of solving it.

In the United States today, politicians do the opposite from what we the people want done. We are taught to look at what the politicians do as the cause of our problems, but that is bad thinking. The actions of the politicians are effects, not causes.

The ***effect*** is that they pass laws that limit what we can do with our property.

The ***effect*** is that they pass laws that increase taxes.

The ***effect*** is that they pass laws that put more people on welfare.

The ***effect*** is that they pass laws that grow government.

The ***effect*** is that they pass laws that ruin our savings, retirements and earning power.

The ***effect*** is that they pass laws that restrict our access to healthy food.

The ***effect*** is that they pass laws that weaken producers.

So the question is, what is the cause of these effects?

We must learn to start with the effect that is seen, and work backward until we discover the *root cause*, in a chain of cause and effect. If there is a problem to solve, the focus must be on the root cause of the problem. If the root cause is not removed, it will definitely produce the effect again.

Imagine having a small leak around an upstairs window in a house which causes a stain in the ceiling of a room. The cause of the stain in the ceiling is the water which came in through the roof, by the window and down on the ceiling. It caused the sheet rock in the ceiling to be wet.

The sheet rock could be replaced, plastered and painted, in which case the room would again have had a clean, clear nice ceiling. Until the next rain.

The next rain would lead to wet sheet rock and a new stain. To solve the problem, the leak in the roof must be stopped.

What is the chain of cause and effect that leads to bad law, corrupt actions, growing government, collapsing economies, etc?

Perhaps the reader would come up with a different chain of cause and effect than this author, but however it is done, root causes must be identified.

Please consider this chain of cause and effect. These are not definitive, but illustrative.

Root Cause: Men do not fear God and keep His commandments.

Effect: Men become slaves of sin and corruption. *"Do you not know that when you present yourselves to someone as slaves for obedience, you are slaves of the one whom you obey, either of sin resulting in death, or of obedience resulting in righteousness?" (Romans 6:16, NASB95)*

Effect: The sin nature of man is evident in the corruption that accompanies power. If man were naturally good, his goodness would be magnified by power. Instead we tend most often to see his corruption magnified by power.

Effect: Corruption and lust for power.

Effect: Failure of the Christian community to correctly translate important terms in Scripture. In particular the words *exousia*, *keseph* and *arguros*.

Effect: Failure to recognize that words have meaning.

Effect: Ignorance of the precise definitions of words which shape our thinking about important ideas like *money*, *law*, *justice* and *authority*.

Effect: Ignorance of economic teaching in Scripture.

Effect: We do not clearly see the role of production, which is the foundation on which legal plunder stands.

Effect: Legal plunder. Operationally, legal plunder is accomplished through various perversions of definitions, government and law.

Effect: The transfer of power, and therefore authority, from producers to non-producers, who having unlawful power will always, necessarily pervert justice and work destruction in society.

Effect: Control of social institutions including government, education and media.

Effect: Decades of efficient plunder.

Effect: World-wide financial collapse.

Effect: Complete subjugation of free men under the oppression and weight of corruption.

"The conclusion, when all has been heard, is: fear God and keep His commandments, because this applies to every person. For God will bring every act to judgment, everything which is hidden, whether it is good or evil." (Ecclesiastes 12:13–14, NASB95)

"He has told you, O man, what is good; And what does the LORD require of you But to do justice, to love kindness, And to walk humbly with your God?" (Micah 6:8, NASB95)

If a nation fears God and keeps His commandments, then such a nation will reject legal plunder and unjust law. This is what the Bible actually calls for by making authority subject to law and law subject to righteousness. The commandment against stealing prevents transfer of power and authority from producers to non-producers. The Biblical commands take care of the poor, prohibit excessive interest, cancel debts every seven years, restore land to families every fiftieth year, and let the land rest every seventh year, which is a year off from agricultural production. The health and prosperity in these actions is obvious.

On top of that, if the Bible is true, we will reap what we sow, which will be abundance and prosperity. God will bless our nation and repel our enemies.

Of course the Bible also explains that God sometimes uses one nation as a war club to punish another nation, even to the point of total destruction. I don't have any desire to learn how that comes about, but the fact that it is written in Scripture makes me think that if the God of the Bible exists, the passages about hell and the second death are real.

Perhaps you don't see anything related to God as the root cause. If we can agree that stealing production to empower non-producers is close to the root cause, we have plenty of common ground to eliminate most of the corruption and waste that is leading us toward collapse and greater oppression.

4.8 Evil Consumes Itself

Evil requires the means provided by good in order to pursue its destructive ends. If good did not produce, evil would continue to hate, but have no way to act. Our problems are not caused simply by motive, but by motive coupled with means. In simple terms, we are defeating ourselves with our own productivity.

In order to understand that evil consumes itself, we begin by observing a few things about good and evil.

Good and Evil

As C.S. Lewis noted, good exists in its own right. Only God is good and only God is self-existent. Following is the logic based on Scripture that I use to think through his point:

Only God is good.

"And Jesus said to him, "Why do you call Me good? No one is good except God alone." (Mark 10:18, NASB95)

"You are good and do good; Teach me Your statutes." (Psalm 119:68, NASB95)

Nothing existed before God.

"I am the LORD, and there is no other; Besides Me there is no God. I will gird you, though you have not known Me;" (Isaiah 45:5, NASB95)

"In the beginning was the Word, and the Word was with God, and the Word was God. He was in the beginning with God. All things came into being through Him, and apart from Him nothing came into being that has come into being." (John 1:1–3, NASB95)

And all that God created is good.

"God saw all that He had made, and behold, it was very good. And there was evening and there was morning, the sixth day." (Genesis 1:31, NASB95)

"For everything created by God is good, and nothing is to be rejected if it is received with gratitude;" (1 Timothy 4:4, NASB95)

In the beginning there was *only* God. Since God is good, there was no evil or bad thing in the beginning.

Since God created everything that has been created and all that God created was good, God did not create evil or badness.

Evil or badness is necessarily rooted in the actions taken by God's creatures, since the origin of all other things is God, whose creation and actions are good.

The thoughts, intents and actions of creatures *after being created* are sometimes evil. It is the *thought, intent* or *action* that is evil.

When the intent of the person is to do evil continually, then the person has chosen to pursue evil and may rightly be called evil or wicked. Actions include the intent of the heart. A person's actions make him guilty.

Stated another way, evil is the result of good things used for bad purposes. Evil is the twisting of good. Since people are sinful, they cannot be called good in the sense of being completely or thoroughly good. Only God is good in the sense of pure goodness, or holiness.

Another way of seeing this is that Satan is dependent on God for existence. Satan is also dependent on God to have the permitted power to act. Satan pursues evil, yet he is dependent on God to exist and to have the power to act in evil ways.

Another way of seeing that evil is not self-existent is to try to think of something evil that is not a bad use of something good. There will always be a good thing or collection of good things that serve as the foundation for evil actions and intents.

Evil is simply a perversion of good. Evil is a parasite that cannot exist apart from the source of its existence, which, at bottom, is always good.

Good, Evil and The Natural Order

The good God who created the universe organized things in such a way that those who pursue evil in any area are *net* destructive, rather than *net* productive. It is a very interesting process.

The natural order is so robust and sturdy that the world is continually healing, recycling and growing things. We can ruin sections of the earth for a time and we can see nothing grow but weeds, but the moment a man puts his hand to the plow or pick, he is able to begin producing the resources needed to sustain life. Of course the weather, bugs, diseases and people have to cooperate.

For example, one of the ways for people to become net destructive, or consume more than they produce, is for there to be drought, insects or sickness that overtakes a whole community of people.

"If I shut up the heavens so that there is no rain, or if I command the locust to devour the land, or if I send pestilence among My people, and My people who are called by My name humble themselves and pray and seek My face and turn from their wicked ways, then I will hear from heaven, will forgive their sin and will heal their land." (2 Chronicles 7:13–14, NASB95)

Another way is for too many people to consume, while too few people produce. The people who are not producing are necessarily pursuing evil because they are certainly stealing for life, wealth or power. The only three options within a society are for none to steal, few to steal or all to steal.

"Ill-gotten gains do not profit, But righteousness delivers from death." (Proverbs 10:2, NASB95)

Stealing is clearly possible in the physical world. In a similar way, violating spiritual law or God's law can, for a time, enrich one person at the expense of another. Being deceptive, hateful or a bully may have temporary gains, but the cost of those kinds of behaviors always exceeds the return. The person who is attacked may be wounded, but in many cases they become stronger. The attacker carries a burden of guilt, which leads to brokenness and despair.

"Do not be deceived, God is not mocked; for whatever a man sows, this he will also reap." (Galatians 6:7, NASB95)

Obeying The Laws of Nature

If I choose to grow corn, I must grow corn as corn grows. I cannot plant my corn in metal filings and water it with battery acid and expect to have a corn crop.

If I choose to raise cattle, I have to raise cattle as cattle are raised. I cannot pen them on the asphalt in a city and expect them to live, let alone reproduce or grow.

If I choose to melt steel, I must melt the particular steel at the temperature at which it melts. My opinion is meaningless. The laws of physics rule.

In other words, to the degree that I operate congruently, or in line, with the natural order of things, I am able to be net productive. To the extent that I reject the natural order of things and choose my own way, I will be net destructive. The same thing is true for individuals and a society with regard to justice.

If I grow corn as corn grows, I will have the production required to continue living. If I try to grow corn on my terms, I will have no production and will either receive gifts, steal or die.

People who take evil actions will reap evil, which often immediately takes the form of no production. A lazy man or a thief has no desire to plant corn or tend to herds. If the lazy man is told, *anyone who is not willing to work must not eat*, he will either stop being lazy or die. The same is true for the thief.

Optimal production is the fruit of individual life, liberty and property. Evil actions in the field or the court are destructive, not productive. If every person chose to acquire wealth by stealing, there would be nothing to steal and we would all starve and die. If every person chose to do what he could to be productive, we would have abundance.

If everyone produced, except *one* who chose to steal, then the society would prosper if the thief were caught and made to pay restitution through property or productive labor. If everyone worked, except one who was lazy, the lazy man would perish or be driven to work by his hunger.

The natural order of things requires us to produce to live and God commands that we work and do not steal. Therefore, the only way for evil behavior to continue is for the good producers to feed the evil thieves and the sluggards. In other words, in the natural order, evil depends on good for its survival and its strength.

Stated another way, the honest producer is funding his own temporal oppression, poverty and destruction.

An Example

The pattern is evident in social programs. Government and some businesses confiscate production from producers and use it to make the thieves wealthy and feed the lazy people who do not work. Production is the good source on which the evil of corporate subsidy and personal welfare depends. There is no other source.

Not only does evil depend on good, but those who give what they have stolen begin to believe it is theirs and they want the credit for giving away someone else's property. Consider the tempting of Jesus by the devil.

"And he led Him up and showed Him all the kingdoms of the world in a moment of time. And the devil said to Him, "I will give You all this domain and its glory; for it has been handed over to me, and I give it to whomever I wish. "Therefore if You worship before me, it shall all be Yours." Jesus answered him, "It is written, 'YOU SHALL WORSHIP THE LORD YOUR GOD AND SERVE HIM ONLY.' " (Luke 4:5–8, NASB95)

God is Creator and King, yet the devil is promising to give away what is not his to give. What the devil wants in return is to receive honor, glory and worship in exchange for giving away what would in effect be stolen property. Government does the same thing.

Evil Consumes Itself

Let's consider what would happen in a just society.

An able person who is not working will not eat. A person who works little will have little. A person who steals will pay restitution, meaning he will give back what he stole along with a penalty. A person who works hard, manages well and produces much will possess the means and resources to act. He will treat his fellows well because no theft, in any form, will be tolerated. He values others in the market to trade with and has regard for hard work and private property.

Since power comes from production, there will be a distribution of power throughout society so that the most productive people will have the power to act. However, they will never have more power than they can produce and there will always be others with similar power to balance their own. When the producer gets lazy, his power will decrease.

At no time will there be a centralization of power based on theft and never will the taxes be paid to rulers who pervert justice. There will be no wealthy people whose wealth is built by theft from the labor of others. To be clear, managing wealth and employing people to work is a good thing, as long as the wealth is from production and the labor market is uncoerced.

In an unjust society, theft is accomplished by legal plunder. Lazy people are fed. Producers are robbed. Wealth and power are in the hands of those who manipulate the system. Eventually, producers quit and the whole society collapses. The only people who survive are those who store up plunder and position themselves to plunder new producers. However, at some point, if everyone, everywhere, quits producing, the whole system will collapse into poverty and despair.

Bitterness and hatred consume a person from the inside. Theft and sloth consume a society from the inside. Unjust behavior cannot support itself. Unjust behavior consumes itself.

Evil Depends On Good

Evil depends on good for its very survival. For this reason it is clear that evil depends on good for its power.

The good, hardworking people in any society are the foundation that evil stands on to rule... the good, hardworking people.

The following chapters on *authority* further expand on this idea.

5. Understanding Authority

Authority is a force, not a standard.
Authority is a power distribution system.

5.01 Authority Charts

Now it is time to consider authority in detail. One of the great problems in society is the tremendous unlawful power held by supposed "authorities." This power is held because of a misunderstanding of authority.

For example, there is no great centralization of power and influence in the hands of burglars. Burglars claim the right to enter our homes and businesses and take what they want. We reject their claim. Their power is small. Their actions are risky and, when caught, costly. However, if we believe that they have the right to do this, then we would permit their actions and they would become wealthy and powerful. Our view of a practice (burglary) or institution (government) either grants or limits power and influence.

One of my favorite jokes is about the little boy who tells his father he wants to go into organized crime when he grows up. His Dad responds, "Government or private sector?" Some burglars rob us through the mailbox. We keep their records and haul their loot.

In order to get a good start on reorganizing our understanding of authority, we begin with pictures, because we all know a picture is worth a thousand words... (grin)

This section on authority begins with a series of charts which will be helpful in communicating important ideas about authority. People I have shared these with tend to find them useful. I have observed that non-Christians sometimes take exception to the basis of the claims, but tend to find the conclusions agreeable.

The following charts illustrate important aspects of the relationship between God, Creation, Labor, Property, Production, Justice, Law, Thrones, Rulers, Jurisdiction, Authority and Action.

The first chart explains the reading order and names the basic elements. The charts are read from the bottom up.

The reason the base includes God as well as Labor, Property and Production is NOT because they are equal. Rather these are foundations or distribution sources for authority. God is the Alpha and the Omega, the beginning and the end.

These concepts are being presented in terms of the Christian worldview. Therefore the chart begins at the bottom with God as Creator.

Labor, Property and Production are at the base because much authority is dependent on these three things.

It is important to note that people are made in the image of God, and God is a worker.

"But He answered them, "My Father is working until now, and I Myself am working." (John 5:17, NASB95)

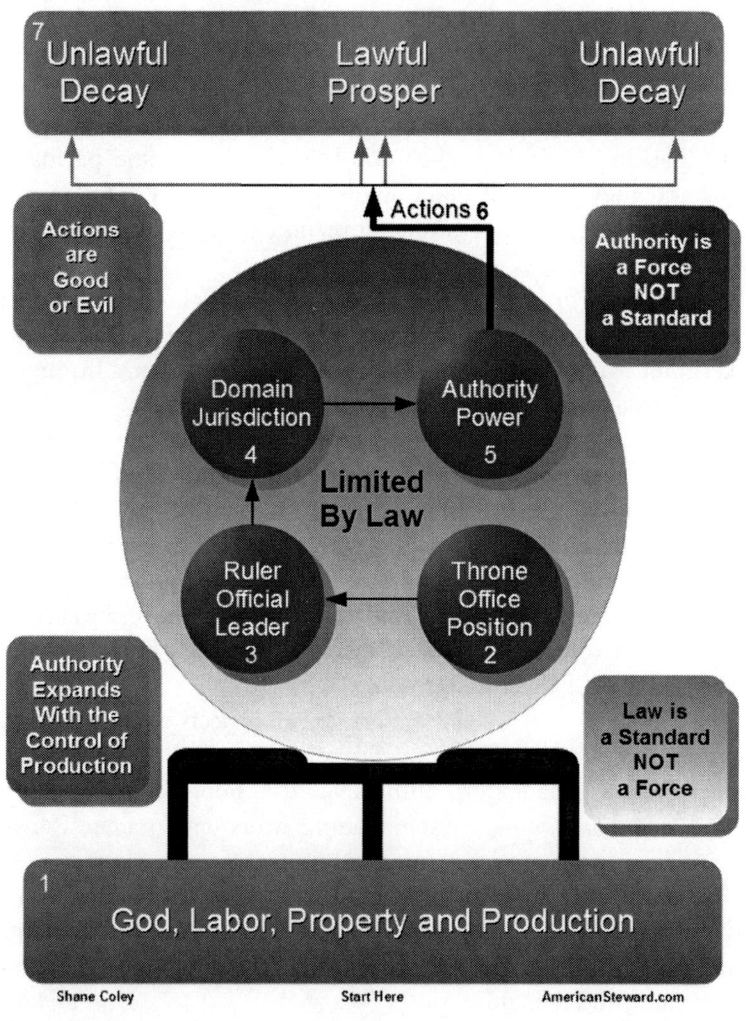

God regularly delegates specific original authority through labor, property and production. This is the starting point, numbered "1" in the left corner of the lower box.

The Creator is the foundation which supports the large circle. The circle *illustrates* the boundaries of law. Because Law is a standard, not a force, a person's actions can violate law, but the people/actors in the established framework are expected to behave lawfully. Unlawful action eventually leads to judgment under law.

According to Scripture, the *thrones*, *dominions*, *rulers* and *authorities* which are illustrated by the four small circles inside of law (the large circle) are created by God.

"For by Him all things were created, both in the heavens and on earth, visible and invisible, whether thrones or dominions or rulers or authorities—all things have been created through Him and for Him." (Colossians 1:16, NASB95)

These are simple and recognizable relationships.

A *Ruler* is seated on a *Throne*, which is over a *Domain* and has access to *Power*.

A *Governor* is seated in an *Office*, which is over a *State* and has access to *Power*.

When the *Ruler* takes action from the *Throne* over a *Domain* using available *Power*, his actions are either lawful or unlawful. The standard by which actions are judged is law.

Think of the chart as a fill-in model for all the cases where someone possesses authority. Following are a few examples, including some special cases which should be helpful in understanding the nature of authority.

The following case is a simplified generic version of the chart. We see here the *Office*, the *Actor*, the *Subject* and the *Authority*. These four elements are always present.

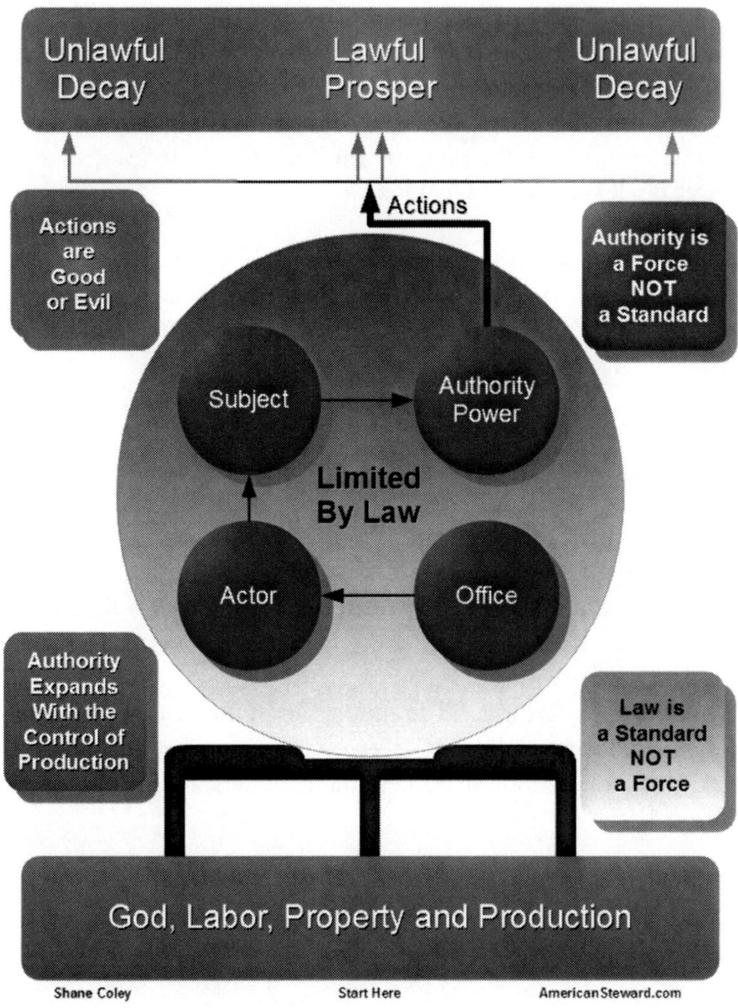

The following example illustrates that God is sovereign over all things and His actions are always lawful, but not for the reason one may think. This is discussed in greater detail in following sections.

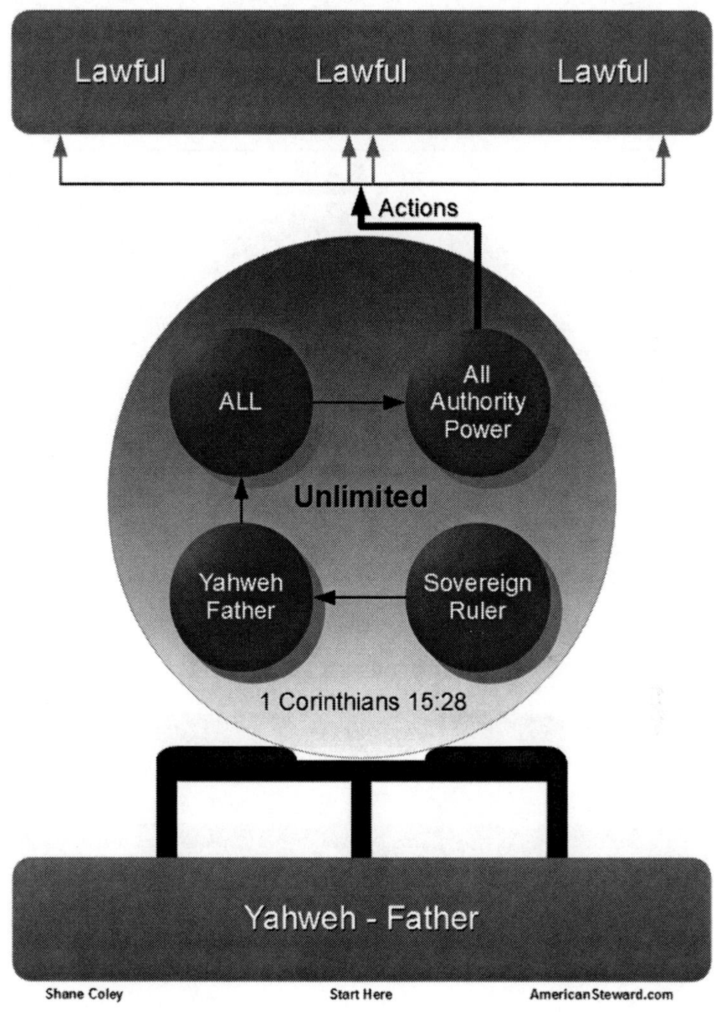

The following chart illustrates God the Son is subject to God the Father. This is clear in 1 Corinthians 15:27-28.

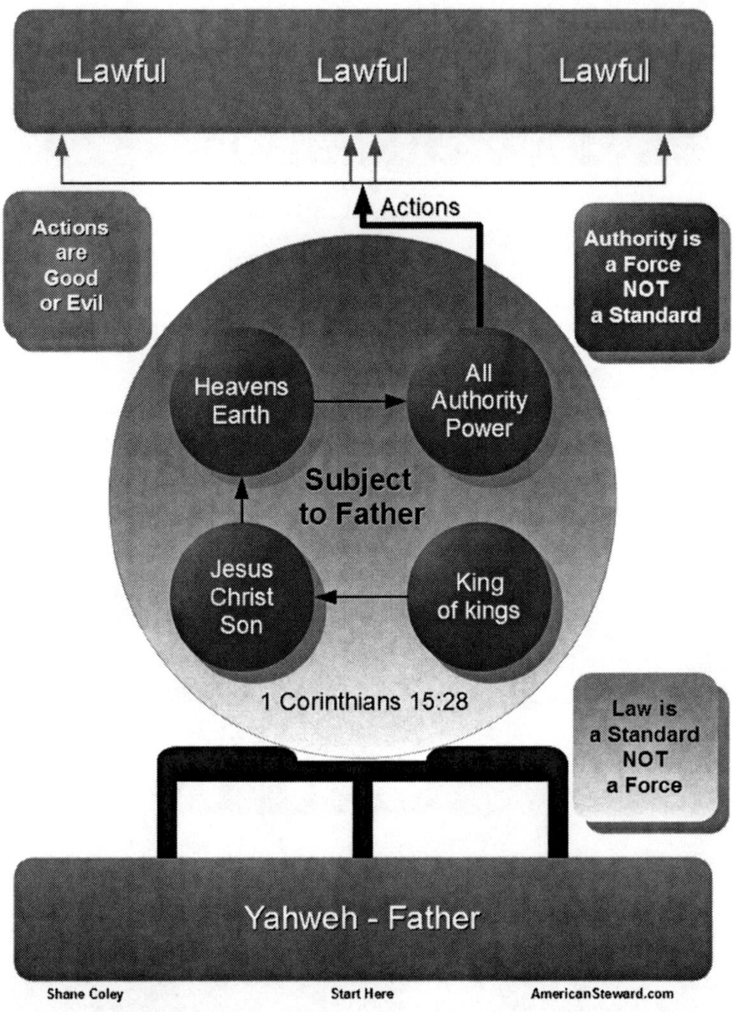

The following chart illustrates that individuals are <u>delegated</u> the authority to <u>*live*</u>. This will be clearer after discussing the definition and nature of authority.

Notice that *life* is given, *ruled* by the *individual* with *himself* as his *domain*, over and through which he exercises *authority* and *power*.

In very simple terms, I eat breakfast to sustain my life so that I may determine my next actions and do those actions with the energy I obtained from breakfast. The *Office* is life, the *Ruler* is me, the *Domain* is me and the *Power* is exercised through and by me. Individuals are equipped with all that is necessary to take action and be held accountable for those actions. This is a way of expressing *free will.*

Depending on how much property I own and how productive it is, I may have greater or lesser authority over my own life. In addition, I may choose to surrender authority over myself in exchange for wages or perhaps in exchange for a gift.

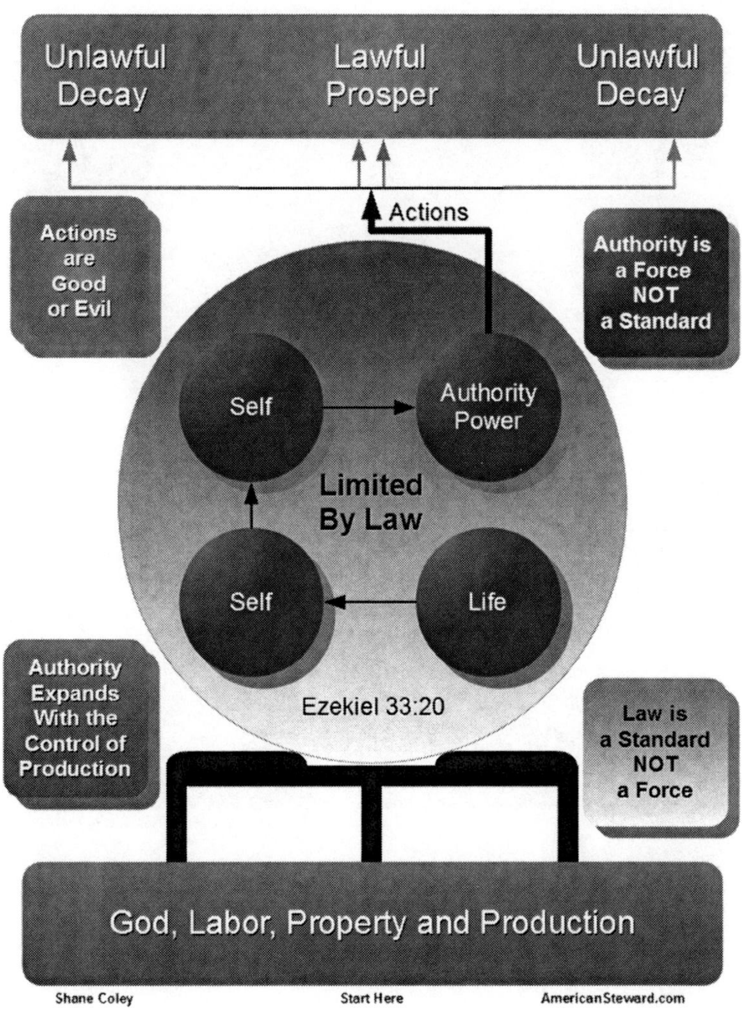

The following chart illustrates authority which is associated with property. This concept is incredibly important and interesting, since power comes from production and oppressive power comes from control of production.

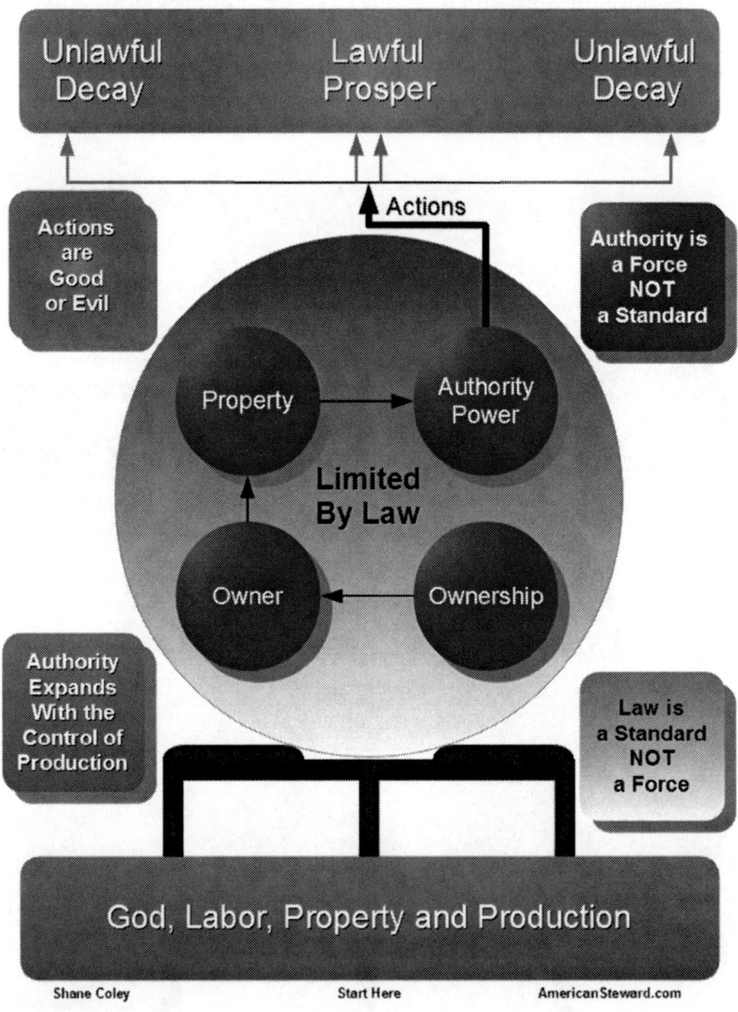

The following chart illustrates relationships in the judicial system.

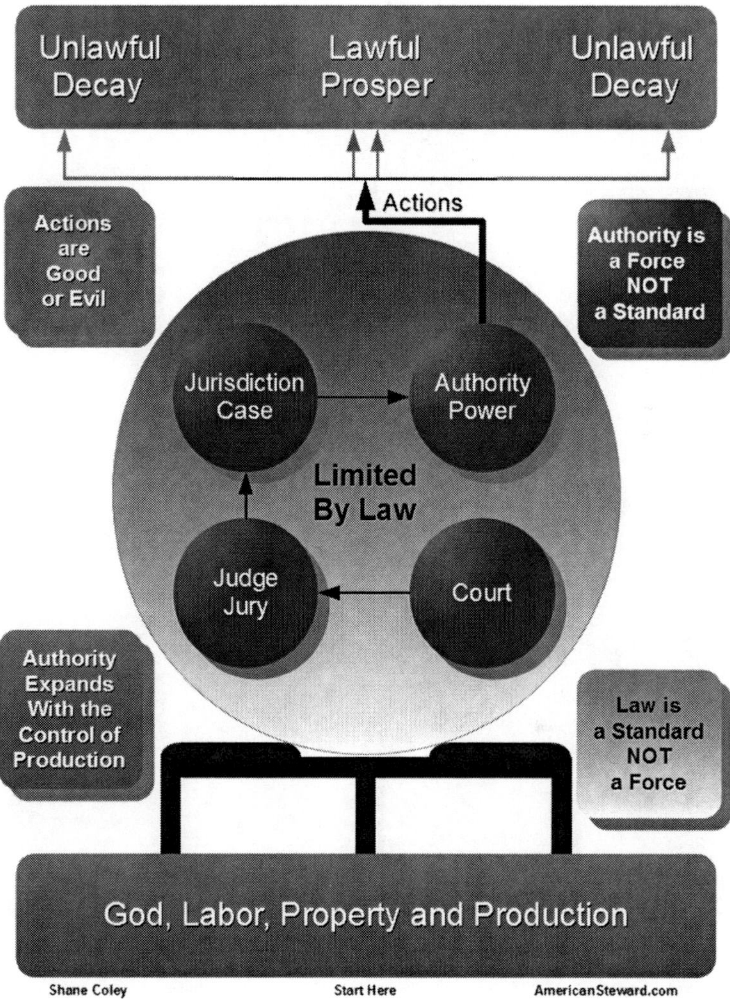

The following chart is an example of a government office.

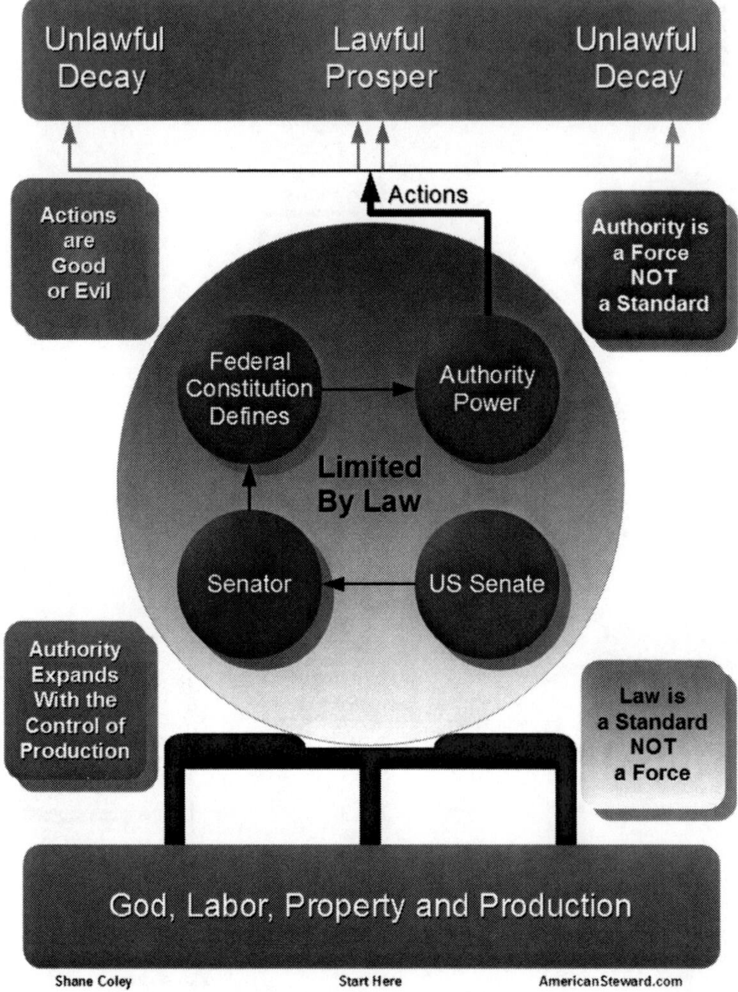

It may be helpful to remember these charts as you read the next chapters. They should be helpful in thinking through what authority is and how authority can be organized.

5.02 Introduction of 14 Observations

Authority is a complex and important thing that is typically misunderstood, even in scholarly Christian circles. My goal in this chapter is to prove this by presenting a collection of puzzle pieces that are intended to develop a clear and concise picture of authority. As with much of the material we are covering, some essential pieces may seem unimportant or unrelated in the beginning. I encourage you to patiently work with the pieces as this valuable and useful image of authority develops.

Please permit me to set expectations and state my purpose here. This chapter is like a friendly conversation on authority where thoughts are tossed back and forth to communicate ideas. Authority is a topic worthy of many whole books and at least years of research and study. Authority is a rich and multifaceted thing which plays a major role in human history and human affairs. My goal here is small and limited. Authority has dependencies, limits and boundaries and I want us to find as many of those things as we can in this conversational style text. I want us to identify what authority is – and what authority is not – so that we can use this knowledge of authority to limit destructive, centralized power and so that we can live free, fruitful and productive lives.

All people possess and are subject to various forms of authority. Authority is a word and idea that can give rise to strong emotion and firm opinion. Some people are appalled when authority is not respected, while others reject authority at every opportunity. For these and other reasons authority is a very difficult topic to discuss, yet a clear view of authority is essential for us to understand the principles and foundations of a free society. In fact, a free society cannot be sustained without a clear and correct understanding of authority.

Authority is Power

Please consider temporarily accepting the following assumption:

Here is the oversimplified assumption: *Authority is Power. Power is Authority.*

The above comparison is not complete, but it is correct as far as it goes. Scripture supports the notion that these terms are in some ways interchangeable.

For example, in the King James Version of the Bible (KJV) the Greek term *exousia* is translated mostly *power* and often *authority.*

In the New American Standard Bible (NASB) *exousia* is translated mostly *authority* and often *power*.

When studying *authority*, simply thinking of *authority* and *power* as roughly equal terms can help us understand much of what is wrong in our world today.

Confusing Authority with a Right to Rule

To put it mildly, misunderstanding the nature of authority is expensive. Current use of the term authority wrongly includes the idea that authority equals *the right to rule*. This idea aggravates man's natural tendency to resist being subject to anything other than himself.

As our image of authority develops, we will see that *properly distributed* authority is a necessary and healthy ingredient in any society, and we will discover how to recognize this *proper distribution* of authority.

Misunderstanding the nature of authority always leads to oppression and poverty. In practice, we give those in authority too much freedom and not enough respect. For example, many people incorrectly believe that because the government has the power to do a certain thing, it also has the right to do that thing. Please consider this next sentence carefully.

If we believe that authority equals the right to rule, then when anyone in authority claims the right to do the wrong thing, we lose respect for the very idea of authority.

This thinking leaves us with a serious problem. Healthy, law-abiding and lawfully organized authority gets a bad reputation because of the unlawful actions of malignant, unlawfully organized authority. The bad guys give the good guys a bad name because we don't know how to tell them apart.

A root of this problem is that we have a tendency to confuse authority with law.

Authority and Law

Consider the following two sentences:

Government has the authority to establish a welfare system.[82]

Government has the right to establish a welfare system.[83]

---

82 True

83 False

Many people would consider the preceding two sentences to be equal, but they are not. I hope we can agree that in a republic[84] the *right* to establish a welfare system is *limited by law.*

Therefore, since authority is not above law, authority is power that must be used lawfully.

Government does not have *the right* to establish a welfare system because a welfare system is dependent on unlawful forced wealth transfer, which is theft.

In order for the welfare system to exist, our society has to violate our *One Law* against stealing.

So while authority may say "yes," law says "no."

Following is a helpful way to think about a critical difference between authority and law.

Standard or Force

Please let the following ideas sink in before moving ahead.

Law is a standard, not a force.

Authority is a force, not a standard.

Law is standard.

Law has no power and takes no action.

Authority is power.

Authority has power and takes action.

Law is law, regardless of the subject of a particular law. Law against stealing a penny is the same law against stealing tons of gold. The law identifies the violation; the particular action determines the punishment. In determining punishment, the person robbed may demand payment in full, or forgive in part or forgive all.

Likewise, authority is authority, regardless of the degree or quantity of authority. A small amount of authority is like a small amount of water. Whether a teacup full or an ocean, water is water.

Unless authority is above law, then authority must be subject to law.

The preceding statement must be understood. A society cannot have it both ways. We cannot say that some authority is above law while other authority is not. Water is water, whether a little or a lot.

A law is a standard that does not increase or decrease in quantity or effect.

---

84 A republic is a society ruled by law, not by men.

Authority is power that does increase or decrease in quantity and effect.

Saying that a certain authority is above law, is to say that a certain authority has so much power that no one can or will hold it to account by law. A lawbreaking authority that is too strong to be held down by law has not somehow inherited a new right; it is simply a lawbreaker. Such an authority is usually considered above the law because it gives away plunder to those who defend it and crushes those who resist. Such an authority cannot exist when there is a proper balance of power in society.

Let's review our two sentences about government and a welfare system again in this light.

Government does sometimes have the authority (force) to establish a welfare system.

Government does not have the right (standard) to establish a welfare system.

The distribution and *force* of authority must be guided and limited by the *standard* of law.

Characteristics of Authority

Temporal or worldly power comes from production and oppressive temporal power comes from <u>control</u> of production.

The parable of *The Prodigal Son* illustrates that temporal power can influence the spiritual man, for good or for bad.

The next step is to consider the relationship between power and authority. We will begin by studying the text of the Protestant Bible, which the reader should consider as literature or Holy Scripture according to his personal worldview. In either case, the text says what it says.

At the end of the study from Scripture we will have a basis for making certain claims. Those of us who are Christian will be challenged in our understanding and thinking.

Those who see the Bible as no more than literature will have some very powerful material to work with. First, one can compare the practical claims and conclusions in the context of some other worldview. Second, one will have a basis for encouraging Christians to stop unlawfully yielding authority to government, since Christians are helping cause problems that people of every belief system have to live with.

Our study of Bible text will reveal the following:

1. Authority is best defined as *"the permitted power to act."*[85]
2. Authority may be used for good or evil.
3. Authority has limits or boundaries.
4. Authority is hierarchical and orderly.
5. Authority may be delegated.
6. Authority is singular over a jurisdiction.
7. Authority is knit into property and production.
8. Authority functions as a power distribution system.
9. Authority used properly under law is edifying.
10. Authority may be combined or aggregated unlawfully.
11. Authority that is properly delegated can be reclaimed at will.
12. Authority has characteristics that are dynamic and fluctuate over time.
13. Authority has ingredients that are difficult to identify and discuss.
14. Authority can include bad ingredients that generally can be identified.

5.1 Permitted Power to Act

1) Authority is best defined as "the permitted power to act."

Logic and reason must be used to identify the best definition of authority.

I recently spoke to an elected official who has been a pastor and is currently a lawyer. Given his unusual background I asked for his definition of authority. His first response was substantially "the ***right*** to [rule, control]."

I stated that authority does not include the right to rule or control. He then stated that there are other definitions of authority, which I interpreted to mean he had more to say on the subject in order to

85 This was previously defined as "the freedom and power to act," with commentary stating *Authority* is "the permitted power to act." I later noted that "permitted" retains the idea of "delegation," which is the only just method of transferring authority. "Freedom" suggests an autonomy that is not actually present under the standard of law.

qualify his definition, which is surely appropriate. We only had a few minutes and were not able to have a full discussion on the topic. I am confident he has excellent observations to make about authority and I perceive that he is a strong and principled leader who desires to do what is right. However, no following explanation could qualify including *"the right to act"* in a definition of authority. But that is exactly how we are trained to think.

If a good man who desires limited government, has served as a pastor, and is now a lawyer and elected official starts his definition of authority with the *right* to rule or control, then we clearly have a problem in our conventional thought on the subject of authority.

Given this gentleman's background, I was not surprised by his answer. Defining authority as *the right to act* is typical in many Christian commentaries I have studied. Following is a definition given in one such commentary:

[R]ightful, actual and unimpeded power to act, or to possess, control, use or dispose of, something or somebody.[86]

Returning to the definition I conclude to be correct, the idea of *"the permitted power to act"* can be seen in the phrase *"actual and unimpeded power to act."*

The next bit of the definition deals with jurisdiction or domain. Because the terms *rightful* and *unimpeded* are combined here, the definition seems to recognize no limits within the jurisdiction except *actual power.*

Associating *"the right to rule"* with authority is a huge mistake in understanding the nature of authority.

The Greek word in the New Testament that is translated authority is *exousia.*

In the following definition of *exousia* from the NASB Dictionary[87] we find *"power to act"* and *"authority,"* which are followed by the quantity of the specific English words which are translated from the Greek term *exousia* in the NASB.[88]

---

86 Wood, D. R. W., & Marshall, I. H. (1996). *New Bible dictionary* (3rd ed.). Leicester, England; Downers Grove, IL: InterVarsity Press.

87 Thomas, R. L. (1998). *New American Standard Hebrew-Aramaic and Greek dictionaries : Updated edition.* Anaheim: Foundation Publications, Inc.

88 In the word study chapter on authority there is a word count chart indicating the number of time exousia is translated various words in four English translations.

***1849.* ἐξουσία exousia**; from *1832; power to act, authority:*—authorities(7), authority(65), charge(1), control(1), domain(2), dominion(1), jurisdiction(1), liberty(1), power(11), powers(1), right(11).[89]

From Strong's Concise Dictionary[90] we get the following definition:

1849. ἐξουσία **ĕxŏusia**, *ex-oo-see´-ah*; from *1832* (in the sense of *ability*); *privilege*, i.e. (subj.) *force, capacity, competency, freedom*, or (obj.) *mastery* (concr. *magistrate, superhuman, potentate, token of control*), delegated *influence*:—authority, jurisdiction, liberty, power, right, strength.

1850. ἐξουσιάζω **ĕxŏusiazō**, *ex-oo-see-ad´-zo*; from *1849*; to *control*:—exercise authority upon, bring under the (have) power of.[91]

In both cases there is a reference back to Strong's Greek #1832, which is *exesti*. In the NASB Dictionary[92] *exesti* is defined as follows:

***1832.* ἔξεστι exesti**; from *1537* and *1510; it is permitted, lawful:*—lawful(26), may(3), permissible(1), permitted(2).[93]

God and Law

Please remember, we are studying the Christian worldview to see if Christians properly understand what the Bible says about authority. If the common Christian understanding of authority is incorrect, and we Christians therefore support unlawful government by our beliefs, everyone who desires freedom is benefited if we Christians correct our error.

In order to get authority and law sorted out clearly, it can be helpful to study the root words that *exousia* depends on, along with Bible teaching about God, authority and law.

---

89 Thomas, R. L. (1998). New American Standard Hebrew-Aramaic and Greek dictionaries : Updated edition. Anaheim: Foundation Publications, Inc.

90 Strong, J., S.T.D., LL.D. (2009). A Concise Dictionary of the Words in the Greek Testament and The Hebrew Bible. Bellingham, WA: Logos Research Systems, Inc.

91 Strong, J., S.T.D., LL.D. (2009). Vol. 1: A Concise Dictionary of the Words in the Greek Testament and The Hebrew Bible (30). Bellingham, WA: Logos Research Systems, Inc.

92 Thomas, R. L. (1998). New American Standard Hebrew-Aramaic and Greek dictionaries : Updated edition. Anaheim: Foundation Publications, Inc.

93 Ibid.

Strong's Greek #1832 above references two other root words for *exesti*, which are Strong's Greek #1537 and Strong's Greek #1510. *Exesti* bases *"it is permitted, lawful"* on the self-existence of God.

Strong's Greek #1537 is the idea of *"from"* or *"origin."*

Strong's Greek #1510 is *"I am"* or *"I exist."*

In other words, *exesti* is based on the idea of *"origin from self-existence"* or *"from I AM."* This reminds me of Moses and the burning bush where God makes the point that He is self-existent.

"God said to Moses, "I AM WHO I AM"; and He said, "Thus you shall say to the sons of Israel, 'I AM has sent me to you.' " (Exodus 3:14, NASB95)

When we understand God as the self-existent Creator of all things, then it follows that God is the source of law, which means God is above law. The power and authority of God permit Him to do whatever He chooses, which will be limited only by His nature. If Christians are correct about who God is, we are fortunate that God is just and consistent because law is whatever God chooses for it to be. God is the only lawgiver.

"For the LORD is our judge, The LORD is our lawgiver, The LORD is our king; He will save us—" (Isaiah 33:22, NASB95)

"There is only one Lawgiver and Judge, the One who is able to save and to destroy; but who are you who judge your neighbor?" (James 4:12, NASB95)

God's Power

Sometimes we want to stand in judgment of God, but before any basis for a charge can even be considered, we must understand that we don't have access to the same information as God. People also lack the ability to process all the information even if we had it. We are told in Isaiah that God's thoughts and ways are higher than ours.[94] Therefore,

94 *"Seek the LORD while He may be found; Call upon Him while He is near. Let the wicked forsake his way And the unrighteous man his thoughts; And let him return to the LORD, And He will have compassion on him, And to our God, For He will abundantly pardon. "For My thoughts are not your thoughts, Nor are your ways My ways," declares the LORD. "For as the heavens are higher than the earth, So are My ways higher than your ways And My thoughts than your thoughts. "For as the rain and the snow come down from heaven, And do not return there without watering the earth And making it bear and sprout, And furnishing seed to the sower and*

we can't even prepare to make a charge against God.

"For My thoughts are not your thoughts, Nor are your ways My ways," declares the LORD. *"For as the heavens are higher than the earth, So are My ways higher than your ways And My thoughts than your thoughts." (Isaiah 55:8–9, NASB95)*

God challenged Job with regard to man's limited knowledge and understanding:

"Then the LORD answered Job out of the whirlwind and said, "Who is this that darkens counsel By words without knowledge? "Now gird up your loins like a man, And I will ask you, and you instruct Me! "Where were you when I laid the foundation of the earth? Tell Me, if you have understanding, Who set its measurements? Since you know. Or who stretched the line on it? "On what were its bases sunk? Or who laid its cornerstone, When the morning stars sang together And all the sons of God shouted for joy?" (Job 38:1–7, NASB95)

And later God similarly speaks of His judgment, power and more. Consider all the ways God describes Himself based on His works and how He challenges Job to do the same things.

"Then the LORD answered Job out of the storm and said, "Now gird up your loins like a man; I will ask you, and you instruct Me. "Will you really annul My judgment? Will you condemn Me that you may be justified? "Or do you have an arm like God, And can you thunder with a voice like His? "Adorn yourself with eminence and dignity, And clothe yourself with honor and majesty. "Pour out the overflowings of your anger, And look on everyone who is proud, and make him low. "Look on everyone who is proud, and humble him, And tread down the wicked where they stand. "Hide them in the dust together; Bind them in the hidden place. "Then I will also confess to you, That your own right hand can save you." (Job 40:6–14, NASB95)

Right in the Eyes of the Lord

Again, when we understand that God transcends His creation, which is to say God is above and outside of creation, then we can

---

bread to the eater; So will My word be which goes forth from My mouth; It will not return to Me empty, Without accomplishing what I desire, And without succeeding in the matter for which I sent it." (Isaiah 55:6–11, NASB95) understand how law could come from God, which makes God the source of law and means He is above law. This is why the kings and the people of Israel were instructed and rewarded when *"they did what is right in the eyes of the Lord."*

In other words, God has all the information and gets to decide what is right or wrong, and no man can question Him. His judgments stand.

"So you [children of Israel] shall remove the guilt of innocent blood from your midst, when you do what is right in the eyes of the LORD." (Deuteronomy 21:9, NASB95)

"Nothing from that which is put under the ban shall cling to your hand, in order that the LORD may turn from His burning anger and show mercy to you, and have compassion on you and make you increase, just as He has sworn to your fathers, if you will listen to the voice of the LORD your God, keeping all His commandments which I am commanding you today, and doing what is right in the sight of the LORD your God." (Deuteronomy 13:17–18, NASB95)

God Will Not Pervert Justice

However, God does not decide arbitrarily what is right or wrong. Sometimes we don't understand the verdict because we don't have all the information, as indicated in Isaiah 55:8-9. Scripture tells us that God is not a respecter of persons and that the nature and character of God is such that He will not pervert justice.

"To show partiality is not good, Because for a piece of bread a man will transgress." (Proverbs 28:21, NASB95)

"Now then let the fear of the LORD be upon you; be very careful what you do, for the LORD our God will have no part in unrighteousness or partiality or the taking of a bribe." (2 Chronicles 19:7, NASB95)

"For there is no partiality with God." (Romans 2:11, NASB95)

"Therefore, listen to me, you men of understanding. Far be it from God to do wickedness, And from the Almighty to do wrong. "For He pays a man according to his work, And makes him find [consequences] according to his way. "Surely, God will not act wickedly, And the Almighty will not pervert justice. "Who gave Him authority over the earth? And who has laid on Him the whole world? "If He should

determine to do so, If He should gather to Himself His spirit and His breath, All flesh would perish together, And man would return to dust." (Job 34:10–15, NASB95)

God Cannot Be Called To Account

But even if God were unjust, there is nothing man can do about it. Whatever power mankind has is derived from God and there is no court to which God can be called.

"For He is not a man as I am that I may answer Him, That we may go to court together. "There is no umpire between us, Who may lay his hand upon us both." (Job 9:32–33, NASB95)

"Will you really annul My judgment? Will you condemn Me that you may be justified?" (Job 40:8, NASB95)

Only God Justifies

Therefore, at the end of all things, God will defend His children and no one will be able to bring a charge against them.

"Who will bring a charge against God's elect? God is the one who justifies; who is the one who condemns? Christ Jesus is He who died, yes, rather who was raised, who is at the right hand of God, who also intercedes for us." (Romans 8:33–34, NASB95)

"Who are you to judge the servant of another? To his own master he stands or falls; and he will stand, for the Lord is able to make him stand." (Romans 14:4, NASB95)

"Now to Him who is able to keep you from stumbling, and to make you stand in the presence of His glory blameless with great joy, to the only God our Savior, through Jesus Christ our Lord, be glory, majesty, dominion and authority, before all time and now and forever. Amen." (Jude 24–25, NASB95)

Permitted, Not Lawful

Note that the related word *exesti* can be translated either *"it is permitted"* or *"lawful."* Many people have *incorrectly* decided that the correct meaning to associate with authority is *"lawful."*

In defining the Greek terms *exousia*, only one of the two meanings drawn from its root word *exesti* can be chosen.

Authority is a form of power that can be used for good or evil, right or wrong. Since authority can be used for evil purposes, the only consistent meaning we can use from *exesti* is *"it is permitted."* Otherwise we are claiming evil or unlawful actions are lawful, which doesn't make sense.

Speaking based on the Christian worldview, God *permits*, but later judges, actions that are not lawful according to His standard of law. For example, people are *permitted* to sin, but that permission does not make sin *lawful*. Sin is the result of acts of the free will. Authority is, in a sense, one way of describing certain characteristics of free will. Each person has authority over himself up to a point, and that authority increases or decreases based on age, property, production, jurisdiction and other less tangible things.

Here is the proof, based on the Christian worldview, that authority is a force, not a standard and authority is not above law.

God Acts Lawfully

God is Creator and Lawgiver and is therefore above law, yet God does not pervert justice. God Himself chooses to act lawfully.

God could do anything He wants to do, because:

God is the source of all things, He defines what law is, He informs mankind through conscience, and He is answerable to no one.

Yet God acts lawfully.

God does not use ultimate authority or power to act unjustly. God Himself, who can do anything without penalty, does not put authority above law.

In fact, God could have reconciled people to himself by decree, but instead God the Son paid the full price, "being found in appearance as a man" and obediently dying on the cross to pay our sin debt, and He was raised on the third day.

God chose to work within the law to bring salvation to those who will worship and honor Him as Creator, Lord and Savior, even though He had the power to do whatever He wanted to do.

"Being found in appearance as a man, He humbled Himself by becoming obedient to the point of death, even death on a cross." (Philippians 2:8, NASB95)

Authority is a force, not a standard. Authority is not above law.

Therefore, if we take the definition of the Greek word *exesti* as *"it is permitted"* and the definition of the Greek word *exousia* as *"power to act,"* we come away with the definition of *exousia* being *"the permitted power to act"* or *"the freedom and power to act."* This will be even clearer as we move ahead in the review.

Authority is best defined as "the permitted power to act."

5.2 Good or Evil

2) Authority may be used for good or evil.

From a secular perspective we can easily see that authority IS used for good and for evil. The repeated scandal and lawlessness of people in power is obvious to all.

For a Christian this issue is more difficult because we are wrongly taught that authority is, in effect, a standard, like law.

Remember the definition from the preceding commentary above that said authority is the *"rightful ... power to act"*? If we see authority as *"rightful power"* and we are taught that we are to be *"in subjection to governing authorities"* then it follows that we must think of authority itself as having the *"right to rule."* But this thinking is seriously flawed. Consider the following two verses from Scripture:

Jesus has authority.

"And Jesus came up and spoke to them, saying, "All authority has been given to Me in heaven and on earth." (Matthew 28:18, NASB95)

The beast has authority.

"It was also given to [the beast] to make war with the saints and to overcome them, and authority over every tribe and people and tongue and nation was given to him." (Revelation 13:7, NASB95)

In both of the above verses the term *exousia* is translated *authority.* Authority is in relation to a jurisdiction. In these two cases the jurisdiction is clearly different. The degree, use and extent of the authority are *different*, but the authority is the same "stuff." Jesus and the beast both have authority.

Following is a simple analogy to illustrate. Let's use a farm tractor to think about *the permitted power to act.*

The *power* of our farm tractor can be used to plant and harvest corn to feed children, or it can be used to plow under and destroy the only food a family has to live on.

One use of the power is good, the other is evil. But the tractor is the tractor in both cases.

Likewise, authority is authority.

Authority was created for good, but it can be used for good or evil. *Authority is power which is permitted to be used for action.*

If a bulldozer were brought into the field and used to stop the tractor, then *the freedom to act* would be taken away from the tractor.

If the fuel were taken away from the tractor, then the source of its *power* would be gone.

If the maker of the tractor disconnected the right wire, the *power* would be unavailable and therefore *the freedom to use the power* is taken away.

Authority is the permitted power to act and the actions taken may be good or evil. Like anything else in creation, authority is good, but it can be corrupted and can be used for corrupt purposes.

I have heard the argument that because God created authority or because all authority flows from God, then authority is good. This sort of thinking is used to wrongly claim that we must be unconditionally subject to government. I agree that authority will be used for good up to the point that it is delegated by God to someone else. However, after authority is delegated, it does not follow that all uses of authority are good or that people should be subject to every authority.

There are two important ideas here. First, Christians are not instructed to blindly be subject to any and every authority. Second, we will see that just like any other lawless or sinful behavior; things that were created for good can be twisted and used for evil.

No One Is Subject To All Authority

First, an individual is obviously not to be subject to every authority. Here are examples:

When Christians refuse to worship the beast in Revelation, they are correctly rebelling against authority that is given by God.

"It was also given to him to make war with the saints and to overcome them, and authority over every tribe and people and tongue and nation was given to him. All who dwell on the earth will worship him, everyone whose name has not been written from the foundation of the world in the book of life of the Lamb who has been slain." (Revelation 13:7–8, NASB95)

In another act of defiance, Shadrach, Meshach and Abed-nego refused to worship the golden image set up by King Nebuchadnezzar.

"But even if He does not, let it be known to you, O king, that we are not going to serve your gods or worship the golden image that you have set up." (Daniel 3:18, NASB95)

Daniel quietly refused to stop worshiping God and refused to pray to King Darius:

"Then they answered and spoke before the king, "Daniel, who is one of the exiles from Judah, pays no attention to you, O king, or to the injunction which you signed, but keeps making his petition three times a day." (Daniel 6:13, NASB95)

Peter and John refused to stop preaching.

"And when they had summoned them, they commanded them not to speak or teach at all in the name of Jesus. But Peter and John answered and said to them, "Whether it is right in the sight of God to give heed to you rather than to God, you be the judge; for we cannot stop speaking about what we have seen and heard." When they had threatened them further, they let them go (finding no basis on which to punish them) on account of the people, because they were all glorifying God for what had happened;" (Acts 4:18–21, NASB95)

On the road to Damascus, Paul hears the following about *dominion* (and more) from Jesus:

"to open their eyes so that they may turn from darkness to light and from the dominion of Satan to God, that they may receive forgiveness of sins and an inheritance among those who have been sanctified by faith in Me.'" (Acts 26:18, NASB95)

The term *dominion* in the preceding verse is translated from *exousia*. We see here that there are competing authorities whom people are subject to either by ignorance or choice. The idea in focus is that a person can *"turn ... from the [authority] of Satan to God."* This is an example of being freed from a lesser authority that is acting unlawfully by making an appeal to a higher authority.

The preceding passages provide examples that make it clear that authority is not to be blindly followed.

Good Things Can Be Twisted For Evil

Secondly we will see that things that were created for good can be twisted and used for evil. Let's consider a simple example. Food is created to nourish and sustain health and activity and God called food good.

"Then God said, "Behold, I have given you every plant yielding seed that is on the surface of all the earth, and every tree which has fruit yielding seed; it shall be food for you; and to every beast of the earth and to every bird of the sky and to every thing that moves on the earth which has life, I have given every green plant for food"; and it was so. God saw all that He had made, and behold, it was very good. And there was evening and there was morning, the sixth day." (Genesis 1:29–31, NASB95)

However, if food is given freely to a man who will not work, he has no appreciation for it. In addition, he has free time to get into all manner of trouble because he doesn't have to work in order to eat. 2 Thessalonians 3:10 (quoted below) is not written to be unkind. It is written because people are created to be productive and each person has a responsibility to work. When people are not willing to do what they can, they decay spiritually and emotionally.

"For even when we were with you, we used to give you this order: if anyone is not willing to work, then he is not to eat, either." (2 Thessalonians 3:10, NASB95)

Imagine that a group of people in a society produce enough food to take care of themselves and the needy among them.

Now imagine that government in that society grows and over time takes away nearly all of their annual food production.

The government wastes most of what they take by letting it spoil, but the government officials have enough to be, quite literally, fat and happy with the remaining food they have confiscated.

Government has confiscated food which would have been used by the producers for good. Since production is limited and finite, what the government takes, the producers no longer have to use or to give.

Government causes the producers to be dependent on the government for their daily bread, with strings attached of course.

The government then uses the confiscated food to feed the government planners and the lazy people who will not work. Government uses the food to subsidize bad behavior.

So we see that food is created for good, but can be used for evil.

In fact, if food is used to feed a gang of criminals who are pillaging the city, then food is clearly being used for evil purposes.

We could say that food is created for good, but provides energy, which can be used for good or evil. Very much like the power of authority.

Authority may be used for good or evil.

5.3 Limits

3) Authority has limits or boundaries.

Please remember that this is a study of authority from Scripture and therefore from the Christian perspective. Whether you see the Bible text as literature or Holy Scripture, we are studying the text to see what this influential book has to say about authority. In addition, these chapters are like pieces of a puzzle.

In the following passage we see claims made about authority that help us understand the nature of authority based on Scripture. In this passage we are told that the Father delegates authority to the Son.

"For He has put all things in subjection under His feet. But when He says, "All things are put in subjection," it is evident that He is excepted who put all things in subjection to Him. When all things are subjected to Him, then the Son Himself also will be subjected to the One who subjected all things to Him, so that God may be all in all." (1 Corinthians 15:27–28, NASB95)

We can see from the above passage that God the Father possesses all authority, but He has delegated that authority to the Son, except for authority over the Father Himself. This indicates that authority is delegated, hierarchical and limited.

"And Jesus came up and spoke to them, saying, "All authority has been given to Me in heaven and on earth." (Matthew 28:18, NASB95)

Authority is *delegated* because God the Father *"put all things in subjection under His feet"* and the text is understood to refer to authority because people are instructed to be subject to higher authorities and because Matthew 28:18 states that all authority in heaven and on earth was given to Jesus.

We can see that authority is *hierarchical* because the Son is still subject to the Father.

We can see that authority is *limited* because the Son is still subject to the Father.

We know the Son is *subject* to the Father because of Luke 22:42 and other passages where the Son indicated His willing subjection to the Father.

"And He withdrew from them about a stone's throw, and He knelt down and began to pray, saying, "Father, if You are willing, remove this cup from Me; yet not My will, but Yours be done." (Luke 22:41–42, NASB95)

Other ways we know authority is *limited* is that a person in one city is not subject to the government in another city. Being a father doesn't give a man authority over *all* children. Police authority is *limited* by jurisdiction. Governments are *limited* in their authority by law.

Of course, some authorities behave badly. The limits on authority depend on either willing subjection to higher authority, as in the case of Jesus in the garden, or by the forceful limitation of a lesser authority by a higher, more powerful authority.

Authority has limits or boundaries.

5.4 Hierarchical

4) Authority is hierarchical and orderly.

We already observed from 1 Corinthians 15:27–28 that authority is hierarchical and orderly. In the parable of the talents recorded in Luke 19, we also see *hierarchy*, *orderliness* and *delegation*.

Before leaving on a trip to a distant country, a nobleman delegated authority over some of his property to ten slaves, in the form of pieces of silver.

"And he called ten of his slaves, and gave them ten minas and said to them, 'Do business with this until I come back.'" (Luke 19:13, NASB95)

When he returned he ordered that these slaves be called to him to give a report. Notice he is giving orders to the slaves to whom he gave authority over the pieces of silver. The authority he delegated was a *portion* of his authority. He also had authority over the slaves. We will observe later that the ability to reclaim authority is an important test in determining whether authority is properly delegated.

"When he returned, after receiving the kingdom, he ordered that these slaves, to whom he had given the money, be called to him so that he might know what business they had done." (Luke 19:15, NASB95)

As he received reports on the business they had done, he delegated greater authority to those who had been good stewards of the small authority previously delegated to them. A clear chain of command provides for an orderly environment.

"And he said to him, 'Well done, good slave, because you have been faithful in a very little thing, you are to be in authority over ten cities.'" (Luke 19:17, NASB95)

One of the slaves put his piece of silver in a handkerchief and hid it away. This caused the nobleman to call him a worthless slave and take away the silver and authority he had previously given to him.

"Then he said to the bystanders, 'Take the mina away from him and give it to the one who has the ten minas.'" (Luke 19:24, NASB95)

Therefore, because the authority was *delegated*, its use was judged. For some slaves greater authority was given and from others all authority was taken. In this parable we can see *hierarchy*, *orderliness* and *delegation*.

Authority is hierarchical and orderly.

5.5 Delegation

5) Authority may be delegated.

When authority is properly transferred the transfer is by *delegation*. A person or entity can only delegate authority which they possess and if properly delegated, the authority can always be taken back. This is clearly seen in Luke 19:24.

Whenever we see authority being given, it is given as a *subset* of the authority possessed by the one who is delegating. In 1 Corinthians 15:27-28 we see that the Father identified the limits of authority given to the Son as all authority, except over the Father himself. Therefore, the Father retains control over the original authority and He can take it back.

Of course, one person is subject to various authorities. For example, a child is subject to the authority of his parents, he is subject to the authority of the judge based on the standard of law, and he is subject to the authority of his employer with regard to his work.

Having said that, if a person or entity possesses authority that is supposedly delegated, but the one who supposedly delegated the authority cannot take it back, then the authority was not delegated. Instead it was captured by force or deception.

This is a very important concept that can help us determine if authority is lawfully and legitimately organized and held. As we continue assembling our puzzle, developing our image of authority, we will see that since authority is primarily based on power, and power comes from control of production, then, if the authority was aggregated or combined based on theft, that authority exists in an unlawful form.

You may wonder why I would say “the authority exists in an unlawful form.” Think of authority as being like matter and energy. We understand from the First Law of Thermodynamics that neither matter nor energy can be created or destroyed. Matter can only change forms. Einstein’s $e=mc^2$ equation is a mathematical explanation of this relationship between matter and energy.

Authority is the same as matter in the sense that authority cannot be created or destroyed, but the authority that exists can be transferred. After being originally delegated, authority may be delegated again, or it may be captured and combined. Authority is captured and combined using actions which are unlawful.

Authority may be delegated, but it may also be unlawfully captured and combined. If Authority is properly delegated, and not yet spent, it can be reclaimed. This is a powerful tool for understanding a particular authority.

Delegation of authority is the basis for nullification of unjust law and defense of “states rights,” which are actually state powers and individual rights.

Authority may be delegated.

5.6 One Authority

6) Authority is singular over a jurisdiction.

Stated another way, there is exactly one authority directly over everything and there are never two authorities directly over anything.

If we look at Luke 19 again, we see that the delegated authority was exercised by the nobleman’s slaves.

In this parable, the nobleman did not call on the people who the slaves did business with in order to judge the work of the slaves. He called on the slaves to whom he delegated the authority and he judged the work in terms of property.

The nobleman had mutually exclusive options. He gave the silver to his slaves to do business on his behalf. He could have never given the silver to his slaves to use in business. He could have momentarily given, then taken back the silver which was given to the slaves and done the business himself. At that point the nobleman would have exercised the authority associated with the silver.

But it can only be one case or the other. The nobleman either exercised or delegated the authority.

The reason I closely associate the authority with the silver in the preceding commentary is because authority is bound to property and production.

In chapter *5.5 Delegation,* there were three authorities noted as being over a child. In our example, the child is subject to parents, judge and employer.

However, the authority possessed by the parents and the judge is different from each other and different than the authority possessed by the employer.

The employer has authority over the child while he is on the job and with regard to the employer's property.

The parents cannot tell the child what to do with the employer's property and the employer cannot control the basic education of the child.

The judge cannot tell the child what to do with the employer's property, except to give it back if it was stolen. The judge does not have authority over the employer's property and therefore cannot exercise authority over the child in that regard.

So the point is that while an individual may be subject to various authorities, none of the authorities have the same jurisdiction or domain. In addition, if the child changes jobs, the old employer no longer has the same authority over the child. The child has come under a new authority.

Authority is singular over a jurisdiction.

5.7 Property

7) Authority is knit into property and production.

Let's consider a passage in the book of Acts from the story of Ananias and Sapphira to illustrate that there is authority associated with property.

"But a man named Ananias, with his wife Sapphira, sold a piece of property, and kept back some of the price for himself, with his wife's full knowledge, and bringing a portion of it, he laid it at the apostles' feet. But Peter said, "Ananias, why has Satan filled your heart to lie to the Holy Spirit and to keep back some of the price of the land? "While it remained unsold, did it not remain your own? And after it was sold, was it not under your control? Why is it that you have conceived this deed in your heart? You have not lied to men but to God." (Acts 5:1–4, NASB95)

This passage is about a piece of property that a husband and wife sold in order to bring all the proceeds to the apostles. The problem was that they claimed to bring all the proceeds, but actually kept back part of the proceeds for themselves.

Peter responds to each of them at different times and addresses this issue of deception. Peter condemns the lie and both Ananias and Sapphira fall down and die at his feet.

However, Peter also said to them that they had a right to do with their property what they chose to do. If they had kept the property for themselves, that would have been fine. If they had committed to give a portion in the beginning, that would have been fine. But lying about it was not acceptable.

There is a very important concept in Acts 5:4.

"While it remained unsold, did it not remain your own? And after it was sold, was it not under your control? Why is it that you have conceived this deed in your heart? You have not lied to men but to God." (Acts 5:4, NASB95)

Ananias owned his property and was free to do with it what he pleased. After it was sold the proceeds from the sale were *"under [his] control."* The English word *"control"* is translated from the Greek word *exousia*, which is most often translated *power* or *authority*. Ananias had *"the permitted power to act"* with regard to his property.

The NASB includes a footnote before the phrase *"under your control"* in Acts 5:4 which provides the alternate text *"in your authority."* Therefore, using the alternate text noted in the NASB, the passage could be written as:

"While it remained unsold, did it not remain your own? And after it was sold, was it not [in your authority]? Why is it that you have conceived this deed in your heart? You have not lied to men but to God." (Acts 5:4, NASB95)

This can be a little bit of a challenge to think about, but it is really simple. The idea of private property is expressed in the Eighth Commandment: *"You shall not steal." (Exodus 20:15, NASB95)*

Because people have a right to own property and no one has a right to take it away, except as a penalty for lawless behavior, clearly the owner has authority over his property.

Of course since stealing labor and property is the primary source of temporal power, in an unjust society property rights are always infringed on to varying degrees.

Power comes from production and oppressive power comes from control of production.

Production is the fruit of labor and property.

Authority is the permitted power to act.

Mixing these concepts together shows that a significant *domain* of authority is private property and a significant *source* of authority is the production that flows from private property.

Therefore, private property is a foundation from which further authority may be produced. If profits from production are confiscated, then there is a transfer of labor, property, production and authority.

When a farmer grows corn or cattle, he is, in part, producing authority.

Authority is knit into property and production.

5.8 Power Distribution

8) Authority functions as a power distribution system.

Authority as we know it is primarily comprised of power.

Our working definition of authority is *"the permitted power to act."*

As indicated by the authority charts, authority is one of four components that operate within the constraints of law. Among these four components is jurisdiction or domain, which is separate from authority.

Corrupt authority usually extends the use of power beyond its proper jurisdiction.

This is a simple concept, but it can be tricky to get straight in our thinking. If authority is power exercised over separate domains, then authority is a *power distribution system.* For example, imagine 1000 fathers with sons and daughters. The authority over those sons and daughters is distributed among the fathers.

Alternately, imagine 1000 farmers, each with a farm. Whatever authority is possessed based on property rights is distributed among the farmers, with equal authority over their property and relative authority based on the size and production of their farms.

Remember that power comes from production. If the farmers control their own property, then they develop greater or lesser authority based on the productive output of their farms. An easy way to think of this is to imagine a farmer purchasing more farmland with his profits. He is expanding his authority because he is expanding his production. For example, he will have authority over more production and laborers on his newly purchased farmland.

Now imagine that an outside group comes to the community and, through force or deception, the new group captures the profits from the farmer's production.

In that case the farmers are at continual financial risk because they are breaking even at best and can no longer survive a bad year based on their own resources. In addition, the group who has captured the profits from production has the resources with which to act, *without having the burden of having to produce them.*[95] Not only that, but the thieves are *insulated from losses* because they can confiscate profits <u>only</u> from the farmers who are profitable. See the Social Chart in the chapter *Two Social Models* for a good explanation of this process.

The farm example illustrates that power is distributed as an element of authority which is bound to property and production. When theft is permitted there is an unlawful power transfer. *Since authority includes power, a transfer of power is a transfer of authority.*

Our heading in this section is: Authority functions as a power distribution system.

---

95 This is an extremely important concept.

Here is the logic:

1) People have authority over their property
2) Labor and property are mixed to bear the fruit of production
3) Power comes from production
4) Oppressive power comes from control of production
5) Authority is significantly comprised of power
6) Preventing theft, i.e. No Stealing, maintains the lawful distribution of authority and power, which is based on property and production.

Since power comes from production, the only other alternative is a distribution of authority and power that is based on theft. This is easy to see if we consider the Social Chart or think about the following example.

Stewardship vs. Stealing

If a producer has a property and he uses this property in a system of honest exchange to produce profits, he will be focused on being a good steward of his business and his market relationships. This is certain because the natural order requires your attention to your property to prevent losses.

The Bible tells us we live in a world that is in *"bondage to decay"* or *"slavery to corruption."* Thermodynamics tells us the universe is subject to increasing entropy, which means increasing disorder.

In a free marketplace, people trade by choice, not force. If the producer doesn't take care of his property, production and relationships, they will decay and produce losses, rather than profits. Losses represent declining power and authority.

Because of the stewardship and management required to produce profits in an honest system of exchange, power is distributed based on production. However, this same system limits the scope and scale of a business to a level which produces the most desired combination of quality, price and service.

A high management demand and a limited profit potential ensure that a producer cannot oppress his neighbors.

First of all, he will not have a sufficient resource base (wealth) from which to exercise sustainable control over other people. If he tries to oppress his neighbor he will damage his market relationships and his business will become less efficient, which leads to losses, which equates to loss of power, which is a loss of authority. The authority he could have produced will belong to the person who profitably satisfied market demands.

The only way for this business owner or others to oppress their neighbors is for society to accept subtle tools for transferring, rather than producing, wealth. Only through theft can a person or institution maintain a sufficient stream of resources, i.e. profits from production, without the overhead of managing property and market relationships.

In other words, *No Stealing* can be thought of as an *insulator* between power sources or authorities. While this is not the sum total of authority, if we think of authority and power as being the result of the relationships between private property, labor and production, then we can think of property and production as power cells on a power grid and we can think of *No Stealing* as the *insulator* that keeps power from being unlawfully transferred from one power cell to another.

Remember that authority is bound up in property and production because we have authority over private property, and labor and private property lead to production, and power comes from production and oppressive power comes from control of production.

Power Plants – A Metaphor

Using our power grid analogy, think about this idea. If we transfer electricity from a magnificent power plant onto the power grid, the power flows and is used to make things happen at some endpoint. Lights come on, motors spin, computers calculate.

We tend to think of government and large corporations as being magnificent power plants and we are the light bulbs; but that is totally wrong. Remember that government produces nothing and wastes much, yet power is from production.

The proper analogy would be to think of individuals along with their labor, property and production as the *only* power plants.

The grid transfers authority and power from those humble power plants into the magnificent facilities (governments) that we are told are also power plants. The magnificent facilities are not generating power, but only *draining power from the producers.* This stolen power is then used to power the homes, recreation, wars and mega-corporations of the thieves, along with the redistribution of power (wealth) which buys more votes to maintain access to the *power draining plant.*

Corporations do produce, but their business model and profit structure depend on draining power from the humble power plants of productive individuals. If these corporations lost access to government bailouts, favors, competition stifling regulations, inflation and tax shelters, they could not compete. They would fail. They would go bankrupt.

If someone in a large corporation says this is not so, then ask them to cut all ties to government, ensure that their markets do not have competition stifling regulation, help protect small business from the courts, stop using debt to run the operation and pay their employees an inflation adjusted wage based on the real inflation rate, not the CPI. When they refuse, it is confirmation the mega-corporation owes its profits and market share to government intervention.

One last idea related to authority functioning like a power distribution system. Regardless of where on the grid the reader chooses to place the power plants, one thing is certain. *No one can harvest or steal power that has not been produced.*

Government can interfere with production, but cannot confiscate power that was not produced. Government cannot confiscate corn and cattle that were not grown.

The *power producers*, which are the *authority producers*, are the *source* of the *production*, *power* and *authority* that is used by government.

Our authority is transferred and centralized by theft. Our humble power plants are drained. The authority, like food, was created good. The authority at the time of its production was good. However, the unlawful aggregation of authority is evil in itself and the use of that authority is always evil and unlawful.

Redistribution of authority depends on differing weights and measures and violation of the eighth commandment, *"You shall not steal."*

Authority functions as a power distribution system.

5.9 Edifying

9) Authority used properly under law is edifying.

This section could be very long and involved, but I don't think that is necessary. We all have had experiences where a group of people are working together in some situation and either no one was *"in charge"* or two or more people were trying to be *"in charge."* When leadership is necessary and no one is in charge, there is no direction and nothing meaningful is accomplished. On the other hand, if more than one person is striving for the *"in charge"* position, then there is conflict, dissension, confusion and waste. Neither situation is productive.

Shopping and Dinner Parties

Of course there are situations where there is no need for a person to be in charge. If a group of ladies decide to go shopping, they can satisfy their general objectives by going to places of common interest and splitting and reconnecting at convenient times, etc. After all, the social aspect of the trip is the important thing.

On the other hand, imagine if that same group of ladies each had a dinner party coming up and the reason they were going to town was in preparation for their separate parties. Traveling together would not work very well then. They would each be trying to accomplish goals with conflicting requirements in terms of time, purchases to be made, priority, etc. The best thing for them to do is recognize that they each have authority over their own party, property and time. The proper use of the authority in this case is for it to be exercised separately, since the jurisdictions and goals are separate.

Now imagine the same group of ladies preparing for a party they will have together. In that situation they must coordinate their activities. They may agree together to the general goals of the gathering, but they will distribute authority over food, decorations, invitations, etc. to specific individuals. Someone will be in charge and others will assist based on the direction given from that person. When each person does their own part well and there is no undermining of leaders or vying for control, then the party planning and outcome will be successful.

This simple, non-political example expresses the idea that leadership, which is an exercise of authority, enables people to coordinate their activities in ways that are enjoyable and productive. No authority leads to confusion; multiple grabs at authority lead to conflict and properly distributed authority leads to productive and successful outcomes.

Notice that when the ladies are shopping together, they have agreed to pool their property for the purpose of travel. Each lady had to possess the resources necessary to be fed, clothed, rested and have the time to spend on the shopping trip. As they shop, they use their personal resources to purchase things for their individual purposes.

On the other hand, when shopping for their individual dinner parties, they are using their individual resources to meet a time sensitive, specific personal objective. This is an activity that needs purpose and direction.

And finally, when they are coordinating to have a single party, they are pooling their resources for the party and may shop or do other things as a group or individually in preparation for the party. In addition to purpose and direction this activity needs coordination, which requires leadership and distribution of authority.

In the above examples, personal property is a primary determining factor. Authority exercised under law would be authority that at the very least respects the property rights of the individual.

So the point is that authority has its place. This is also true in terms of government.

Divine Right of Kings

Authority used properly under law is edifying, but we seldom have a chance to see authority used properly under law. Rulers have incorrectly interpreted the Bible to claim various rights to authority and through authority over the centuries.

During the 16th and 17th centuries the idea of the *Divine Right of Kings* was used to influence the way that government was organized and operated. The idea was that kings were subject to no earthly authority and that they were seated on the throne and given the right to rule by God. In this way the king was subject to God alone, which also would indicate that the king has a high degree of accountability to God for how he rules. In practice, the king would ignore the accountability to God and focus on the idea that no person or institution had the right to question, let alone resist, anything the king chose to do. During some bits of history in some places the king was called to account by the Catholic Church, but this influence was limited or eliminated for various reasons.

The geopolitical history of monarchies, nation-states and the church is very interesting. However, for our purposes detailed history is not helpful because our focus here is on principle.

It is tempting to think that the idea of the Divine Right of Kings was rejected long ago and is no longer a factor in modern society, but that would be a mistake. The Christian view of government essentially treats whoever says they are the current government as being an "authority" ordained by God. There are now, and were then, passages of Scripture that were misused to support the idea expressed in the Divine Right of Kings, particularly Romans 13.

Government today behaves as though it is answerable to no one.

Regardless of what a government thinks about itself, if enough people treat government as having no earthly power to answer to, then it has no earthly power to answer to. Christians tend to transfer massive amounts of power to government because of our beliefs. If Christians think this way because of how we interpret Scripture, then our interpretation must be correct.

Kings, Law and Petty Theft

If a king sits on his throne because God seated him and gave him the right to rule, then his authority is from God. If a king claims that his authority is from God, then that king must also abide by God's law.

For example, a king cannot claim that God gave him the authority to violate the Eighth Commandment, *"You shall not steal."* That would be completely illogical. How can a king claim God has given commandments to all men, and God has made him king, but he does not have to obey the commandments given to all men?

At this point some would say that the king (government) is not subject to the law because he is king (government). The argument is ridiculous and illogical[96], but let's assume for a moment that it might be valid. The number one method for a king or any government to increase its power is to create a currency, force everyone to use it and then debase that currency. Currency debasement employs a form of theft known as *differing weights and measures*, which transfers wealth from producers to those who control the issuance of new money.

We have several problems now. First of all, if the king has authority from God, he should not have to use deception and theft in order to acquire the resources necessary to rule. How much sense does it make to claim kingship by the hand of God and then have to resort to petty theft to maintain or increase your kingship and power...?

The second problem is that currency debasement uses differing weights and/or differing measures. The Holy Scripture of the same God who has supposedly granted the king authority to rule says that differing weights and differing measures are an abomination to God.

Grain Trader

Consider this example of differing measure. Imagine a grain trader in a marketplace with a basket that is marked "one bushel," but the basket is actually larger than a bushel. The unsuspecting farmer selling

96 Remember that, according to Scripture, God Himself will not pervert justice. Jesus was obedient to the point of death, even death on a cross. His obedience was to God, who is the source of law.

his grain fills the trader's basket with too much wheat (more than a bushel) before being paid for only one bushel. The grain trader is stealing part of the grower's production.

Later, when the dishonest grain trader sells, his basket marked "one bushel" would actually be smaller than a bushel. The unsuspecting buyer leaves with less than a bushel of wheat, but this buyer paid for a whole bushel.

With each transaction the grain trader in the marketplace is stealing from those he is trading with. This would be an abomination since it is a deceptive and systematic method of violating the eighth of the Ten Commandments, "*You shall not steal.*" This form of theft, like all others, would also be illegal in a consistent secular system of law.

The following passages are clear that differing weights and measures are an abomination to God.

"'You shall do no wrong in judgment, in measurement of weight, or capacity. 'You shall have just balances, just weights, a just ephah, and a just hin; I am the LORD your God, who brought you out from the land of Egypt. 'You shall thus observe all My statutes and all My ordinances and do them; I am the LORD.' " (Leviticus 19:35–37, NASB95)

"You shall not have in your house differing measures, a large and a small. "You shall have a full and just weight; you shall have a full and just measure, that your days may be prolonged in the land which the Lord your God gives you. "For everyone who does these things, everyone who acts unjustly is an abomination to the Lord your God." (Deuteronomy 25:14–16, NASB95)

"Differing weights and differing measures, Both of them are abominable to the Lord." (Proverbs 20:10, NASB95)

"A false balance is an abomination to the Lord, But a just weight is His delight." (Proverbs 11:1, NASB95)

"Differing weights are an abomination to the Lord, And a false scale is not good." (Proverbs 20:23, NASB95)

"Is there yet a man in the wicked house, Along with treasures of wickedness And a short measure that is cursed? "Can I justify wicked scales And a bag of deceptive weights? "For the rich men of the city are full of violence, Her residents speak lies, And their tongue is deceitful in their mouth." (Micah 6:10–12, NASB95)

And to connect directly to the coins which kings debased, we read that Abraham made a purchase of land with silver according to the commercial standard measurement of weight. Debasing coins involves secretly reducing the weight of precious metal in the coins.

"Abraham listened to Ephron; and Abraham weighed out for Ephron the silver which he had named in the hearing of the sons of Heth, four hundred shekels of silver, commercial standard." (Genesis 23:16, NASB95)

At no time do the preceding Bible passages make an exception for some men, kings or government. But let's continue anyway to see if we can excuse the king from obeying the Eighth Commandment by using currency debasement, which is a form of differing weights and/or measures.

Involving Others Who Are Not King

So here is the ridiculous claim: "The king is not subject to God's law. It is acceptable for the king to profit and increase in power by using differing weights and/or measures, which is a form of theft and a violation of the Eighth Commandment."

Even if the preceding ridiculous claim was true, and it is not, we now have another problem. Currency debasement involves other people who are not king.

Currency debasement transfers wealth by theft to all early users of new currency. This means that in order for the king to use differing weights and/or measures to increase his power, he has to involve other people throughout society at various levels and of various characters in his scheme.

In other words, even if the king could justify disobeying God because he is king, the king cannot cause other people to disobey God's law because they do not have the Divine Right which the king claims as his excuse.

In addition, the people involved must agree to a system of theft that they know will pillage and rob their neighbors. This is integrating willful disobedience into the fabric of society. That does not sound like good leadership on the part of a king who God has placed in authority. In fact, history shows us that currency debasement always leads to the destruction of the society.

The Scripture that the king relies on to claim his "Divine Right as King" does not permit any man to steal, particularly not using differing weights and measures. In addition, because when the king engages in currency debasement he is involving other people in disobedience and he is pillaging the honest hardworking people in the society, the necessary affect on other people would prevent the king from using currency debasement to increase his wealth and power.

God's Model King, An Edifying Authority

Do other passages in the same Bible the king is relying on for his claims of power limit the king in any way? As a matter of fact, yes.

"When you enter the land which the Lord your God gives you, and you possess it and live in it, and you say, 'I will set a king over me like all the nations who are around me,' you shall surely set a king over you whom the Lord your God chooses, one from among your countrymen you shall set as king over yourselves; you may not put a foreigner over yourselves who is not your countryman. "Moreover, he shall not multiply horses for himself, nor shall he cause the people to return to Egypt to multiply horses, since the Lord has said to you, 'You shall never again return that way.' "He shall not multiply wives for himself, or else his heart will turn away; nor shall he greatly increase silver and gold for himself. "Now it shall come about when he sits on the throne of his kingdom, he shall write for himself a copy of this law on a scroll in the presence of the Levitical priests. "It shall be with him and he shall read it all the days of his life, that he may learn to fear the Lord his God, by carefully observing all the words of this law and these statutes, that his heart may not be lifted up above his countrymen and that he may not turn aside from the commandment, to the right or the left, so that he and his sons may continue long in his kingdom in the midst of Israel." (Deuteronomy 17:14–20, NASB95)

Let's review the preceding text conversationally. This passage indicates that, at least in some cases, God does indeed choose the king, which Scripture says in other places as well. We also see that the king should be from among the people, not a foreigner. He is also commanded not to multiply horses or wives. He is not to greatly increase silver and gold for himself. He is also commanded to physically write a copy of the law in the presence of the Levitical priests and he is to keep it with him and read it. He is to fear the LORD his God and observe the law so that his heart may not be lifted up above his countrymen and so that he may not turn aside from the commandment, so that he and his sons may continue long in the kingdom.

Therefore the king God calls is specifically limited.

Multiplying horses is to develop military strength, since horses were the tanks and airplanes of warfare in those days.

Multiplying wives was dangerous because they could turn the heart of the king away from God and justice.

When the king is commanded not to increase silver and gold for himself, the passage is referring to not laying a heavy burden of direct taxation of the people. It certainly leaves no room for draining all the wealth from society by differing weights and/or measures.

The king is commanded to write a copy of the law for himself in the presence of the Levitical priests. That task indicates that the priest at least has the role of ensuring that the king knows and correctly understands God's law. In addition, the task of writing the law on a scroll in those days was a big task that would have been an intense time of Scripture study for the king.

Writing and reading the Scripture would reinforce the king's fear of the LORD his God and would help him observe all the words of "this law and these statutes," which would then have a particular result, namely, the king's heart would not be lifted up above his countrymen and he would not turn aside from the commandment, to the right or to the left, which would be good for him and his children.

The king is to obey the law and he is not to think of himself as being above his countrymen.

Imagine a society where the government was a *partner* in defending the life, liberty and property of the individual. Suppose the government did not exercise authority outside its jurisdiction and the government did not steal from the people. Imagine the peace a society would have if the government did not build military strength for the purpose of conquest, thereby wasting the property and lives of its citizens.

As a Christian, I believe that knowing and following God's law is a prerequisite to these other things, but if the others could be achieved, western civilization would certainly be better off than it is now.

Authority used properly under law is edifying.

5.10 Unjust Aggregation

10) Authority may be combined or aggregated unlawfully.

There are various forms, combinations and assignments of authority. It is difficult to express all that makes up authority and this difficulty causes problems in personal relationships and in society.

Even if we cannot understand all that goes into healthy authority, with a little effort we can usually identify unlawfully organized authority.

Notice that we are not able to judge authority that exists as being right or wrong, because authority is power, not standard. Consider the following analogy.

A bolt of lightning is electricity and there is electricity in a power grid. A certain amount of electricity that is distributed on the power grid to power homes is healthy. The exact same amount in a single bolt of lightning may destroy a tree, kill a person or set a house on fire. The problem is not the electricity; the problem is the concentration of electricity in a single form, i.e. a bolt of lightning.[97] The units of electricity are no more good or bad in one case than the other.

The focus in this section is to find out if authority is being concentrated by men into something like bolts of lightning by stealing power off the producer's power grid.

Before going further, I want to note that some forms of authority operate outside the physical realm. Consider the following passage:

"Jesus summoned His twelve disciples and gave them authority over unclean spirits, to cast them out, and to heal every kind of disease and every kind of sickness." (Matthew 10:1, NASB95)

Whether or how intangible forms of authority may be aggregated is not what we are attempting to discuss here. But those ideas are very interesting.

The intent in this section is to observe that authority can exist in forms that are bad, such that authority becomes a lightning bolt, in the sense of concentrated power, which should be distributed.

All authority begins with original delegation that is healthy because it comes from God.

"Let every soul be subject unto the higher powers. For there is no power but of God: the powers that be are ordained of God." (Romans 13:1, AV)

---

97 Of course, in the case of lightning, no person purposely concentrated and released the power and lightning has positive effects, like fixing nitrogen. Any attempt to equate lightning and unlawfully concentrated authority in a good sense requires 1) unlawful actions of men to be lawful, since lightning is a natural event which obeys the laws of nature and 2) the lawful activity must be a net producer. Lightning is lawful according to the laws of nature and it fixes nitrogen which is well distributed and used freely by all. Concentrated authority is the fruit of unlawful actions and destroys many to benefit the few who possess the unlawfully concentrated authority.

"Every person is to be in subjection to the governing authorities. For there is no authority except from God, and those which exist are established by God." (Romans 13:1, NASB95)

While all authority necessarily begins with original delegation that is healthy, later transfers of authority are often unlawful and unhealthy.

Authority is in large part power. If original authority (farmer, father) is transferred to a central authority (warlord, government) by unlawful means (differing weights and measures), the central authority increases in power continually.

The transfer of authority is limited only by the availability of original authority. In other words, the government will confiscate the profits from whatever the people produce, whether crops, livestock, goods or children. One major problem with this transfer is that the central authority (government) will bleed the original authority (production) dry, which in the end leaves the people poor, while the central authority is still maintained in luxury. In other words, the transfer of authority leads to a feudal society with no middle class.

People depend on production and wealth is the fruit of production. Socialism, communism, fascism, etc. crush the productive capacity of a society, which decreases the wealth and power of the society. People often wonder why a ruling class that controls these systems of plunder would ruin the very foundation of their own power. The answer is simple. In this world and among men, power is a relative thing.

Those who rule want at least two things. First, they want to live in luxury. Second they want to possess more power than those they rule.

The ruling class can have luxury even if the people are destitute. In order to have relatively more power, the ruling class only needs to control profits from production. It doesn't matter whether the society is prosperous or poor, as long as the ruling class controls systems of plunder, regulation and law that give them control of whatever profits exist, whether large or small.

In other words, if we produce one acre of corn or ten thousand acres of corn, as long as the ruling class is able to control the profits, they have the ability to let you farm another year or drive you out of business, or out of your home. The rulers with control of legal plunder have tremendous control of the society and are able to manage the balance of power between nations.

Building Unjust Authority

Our topic is *unlawful aggregation of authority*. The best way to understand any authority is to see how it is formed and sustained.

People go to great length to judge the actions or jurisdiction of an authority, without even considering that just maybe the particular form of authority *should not even exist*. If the authority should not exist, then we need to deal with its source of power, not its use of power.

People think and talk about an authority, like government, police or an employer, based on how they see it behave. Someone may have training or knowledge which enables him to look at an authority and see things about it that are harmful (waste, fraud, corruption), but that same understanding may not be easy to explain to others who don't have the training or time to see the same problems.

While the institution can do bad or harmful things, it can also use its resources to do good things (feed a child) or favors (pave a certain road, sweet business deals). This leads to complex arguments, cases and discussions that in turn lead to confusion and uncertainty. So we need to begin by ignoring the actions and jurisdiction of authority and look at the way the authority was formed and is sustained.

The important question is should the authority even exist in a particular form?

For example, we know today that the modern nation state is extremely powerful and that most people believe "government has the right to rule." Many people simply conclude that since authority is from God and the state has authority, it should be obeyed.

This next statement is false and will seem silly, but in effect this is what we Christians are doing with the idea:

"Since authority cannot be stolen or corrupted and government authority does exist, it is given by God and must be obeyed" and then we quote Romans 13.

In effect, Christians are saying that everything in the earth is subject to corruption, except authority.

When we understand that we are, in effect, claiming authority cannot be corrupted, the common Christian view makes no sense. Of course there is the argument that Christians are not to resist authority. We have covered that misunderstanding in another place, but for now, rather than debating whether a particular authority should be obeyed, let's study how the authority was formed. Perhaps Christians have a responsibility to recognize and resist the unlawful formation of authority…

Studying how a particular authority is formed and sustained is a better approach for several reasons.

First, opposing authority is to oppose power and that can be costly. In fact, institutions with authority simply crush and consume those who resist because the institution has various advantages including time tolerance and a greater resource base. In other words, institutions don't have jobs, they don't die from old age and they have more resources. The institutions are supported by the systems (legal plunder) that take your labor and property away from you to subsidize the wealth of its benefactors. *Individuals are in many ways forced to oppose themselves.*

Second, the debate about opposing a form of authority which many people respect tends to be a fruitless exercise. People feel like you are attacking the good that they see in that form of authority, whether it is government, business or any other institution. Often people have friends or family inside the institution and any perceived attack on the institution seems like an attack on their friend or family.

In other cases, because a person has a positive view of an institution, if you speak against the institution, then the person listening feels like you are speaking against them, simply because they have unknowingly connected themselves with the institution by believing something good about it.

Until you can successfully explain why *the very existence* of a particular form of authority is bad or unlawful, you will stand alone against both the institution and the beliefs and resources of all those who empower it. This includes those who unwittingly believe lies, which permit themselves and others to be robbed to support the institution.

The third reason for studying how authority is formed is that most people are willing to judge theft if they can see it. This is important because most of the authority that causes us problems is formed through the unlawful control and confiscation of production. Remember that oppressive power comes from control of production.

Here is a summary of the three reasons to focus on how authority is *formed*:

Directly resisting bad authority is costly and institutions have more time and resources than an individual or small group. *The institution wins.*

People will react to any perceived attack on the legitimacy or actions of authority based on either propaganda about the institution, or based on the people they know inside the institution. *The institution wins.*

Unlawfully combined authority is necessarily formed based on theft. If we learn how to see and explain the source of the power held by an institution, and that source is pillaging and theft, then we can say the authority should not exist in that form, and perhaps not at all. *Law and Liberty win.*

Power Formed From Production

Let's begin by focusing on the reality that most power comes from control of production.

Imagine two opposing armies who were trained at the same time in the same place under the same leadership. If these two forces met in battle, but one army was fully equipped with food and the latest in military communication and gear, while the other army had no food and nothing but boxer shorts, who would win the battle? Obviously the army with resources would win the battle.

Now imagine that these two armies were different because one army lived in a productive and prosperous society that could provide the resources to support the army, while the other lived in a poor society suffering from sloth and famine. Since power comes from control of production, a poor society cannot equip an army with resources that have not been produced.

Here is a second example. Think of any modern day US president and imagine him both as president and as a drunken homeless man. In both cases we will say that he is the same person with the same beliefs, goals and objectives. It is easy to see that the beliefs, goals and objectives don't mean much unless there is also access to power and resources. Again we see power comes from control of production. And since authority is the permitted power to act, we see that power from production is a significant part of authority.

Oppressive Power Depends on Theft

Earlier we observed that in an honest system of exchange a business owner must pay attention to his business in order to produce profits.

But suppose one day a business owner decides he should be the boss of everybody. To be successful in ruling others he must either use force and plunder (open theft) or deceptive systems of law (hidden theft) to maintain the resource base (big bank account) from which to rule.

His business will not produce sufficient profits to cover the cost of oppressive governing. After all, to keep the people in check, he will have police, army and governors to support, along with all their wasteful bribes and habits.

If he tries to use the profits from his own production to rule others, he will fail. The business of ruling will take all his time, so he must stop managing the asset that provides the resources he is using to rule others. Without the time and energy to manage his business he will incur economic losses, which means he will lose his power and authority – that is, unless his power is based on stealing your labor and property.

Oppressive government depends on concentrated power, and concentrated power depends on theft. Theft by legal plunder in a society depends on real and perceived transfers of wealth to "leaders" in order to purchase their silence. Eventually they are also consumed by the system they help build.

Therefore the only way to sustainably oppress your neighbor is to have a continual stream of stolen resources. We have covered the mathematical and logical fact that costless money transfers wealth from producers to non-producers, which means that a key method of transferring power and authority is inflation.

Oppressive power comes from control of production. Authority is the permitted power to act.

Bringing this together

Following is a review of some ideas already covered:

The Greek word *exousia* is best defined as "the permitted power to act."

In the KJV translation of the New Testament, *exousia* is often translated *power* and sometimes translated *authority*.

In the NASB translation of the New Testament, *exousia* is often translated *authority* and sometimes translated *power*.

In the New Testament book of Acts, chapter 5 verses 1-10, the idea of authority being associated with property is clear. In fact, since power comes from control of production, clearly the transfer of property is a transfer of authority.

Since a business owner in an honest system of exchange does not have enough time or profit to oppress his neighbor, *oppression depends on theft*.

The Eighth Commandment states: "*You shall not steal.*" When people understand that their property is being stolen, they will resist. Stealing from people who know they are being robbed requires overwhelming force. This can come in the form of an invading army or the late stages of oppressive government.

The Bible tells us differing weights and differing measures are an abomination to God. Differing weights and measures are a deceptive form of the violation of the Eighth Commandment. Under an unlawful government, debased currency and unjust law are examples of differing weights and measures that are used to unlawfully transfer wealth, and therefore authority, from those who produce to those who rule unlawfully.

Laying aside the case of an invading army, here is the test:

Does the authority in question derive its power from stolen property?

If this authority had to either produce or humbly ask for the resources that give it power, would it continue to exist?

Since delegated authority can always be reclaimed, if the authority claims that it is operating based on delegated authority, can those who delegated the authority reclaim the authority?

Could our government exist in its current form without the power that comes from the unlawful confiscation of labor and wealth?

Could our government exist in its current form without inflation?

Could our government exist in its current form without payroll taxes invisibly taken out of the workingman's check before he gets it?

The good thing about authority which exists on the basis of theft is this:

If we stop supplying unlawfully organized authority with resources, it will wither and die. In other words we fund our own oppression unnecessarily.

If we stop the unlawful actions (theft) which result in centralized power (authority), the actions we are upset about will not exist. We will no longer have to debate the actions and proper use of unlawfully combined authority.

Authority may be combined or aggregated unlawfully.

5.11 Reclaiming

11) Authority that is properly delegated can be reclaimed at will.

Not only is this statement true, it is an incredible tool for understanding and analyzing authority. Since we are using a Biblical worldview to study authority, we should start at the beginning with the Creator. Please bear with me on this. It is interesting.

God created everything.

"In the beginning God created the heavens and the earth." (Genesis 1:1, NASB95)

"In the beginning was the Word, and the Word was with God, and the Word was God. He was in the beginning with God. All things came into being through Him, and apart from Him nothing came into being that has come into being. In Him was life, and the life was the Light of men." (John 1:1–4, NASB95)

And this includes authority.

"For by Him all things were created, both in the heavens and on earth, visible and invisible, whether thrones or dominions or rulers or authorities—all things have been created through Him and for Him. He is before all things, and in Him all things hold together." (Colossians 1:16–17, NASB95)

God the Father delegated all authority to God the Son, except authority over the Father.

"And Jesus came up and spoke to them, saying, "All authority has been given to Me in heaven and on earth." (Matthew 28:18, NASB95)

"For He has put all things in subjection under His feet. But when He says, "All things are put in subjection," it is evident that He is excepted who put all things in subjection to Him. When all things are subjected to Him, then the Son Himself also will be subjected to the One who subjected all things to Him, so that God may be all in all." (1 Corinthians 15:27–28, NASB95)

"I pray that the eyes of your heart may be enlightened, so that you will know what is the hope of His calling, what are the riches of the glory of His inheritance in the saints, and what is the surpassing greatness of His power toward us who believe. These are in accordance with the working of the strength of His might which He brought about in Christ, when He raised Him from the dead and seated Him at His right hand in the heavenly places, far above all rule and authority and power and dominion, and every name that is named, not only in this age but also in the one to come. And He put all things in subjection under His feet, and gave Him as head over all things to the church, which is His body, the fullness of Him who fills all in all." (Ephesians 1:18–23, NASB95)

The following passage indicates that in "the end" Christ will abolish *"all rule, and all authority and all power."*

Rule, authority and power cover all rights to act and all sources of the ability to act.

To abolish all rule would be to abolish all kingdoms and all governments and all forms of rule in all contexts.

To abolish all authority would be to abolish all *permitted power to act*. In other words one would be granted neither the freedom to act nor the power to act.

Power here is from the Greek term *dynamis*, which can be thought of as raw power. To abolish all power could be thought of as abolishing all distributions of accessible energy. In other words, no creature would be granted access to the willful command or control of any rule, authority, power, energy or action, except as delegated under specific control, and to a specific degree, by the Creator.

Of course there are important theological questions that follow, but we are not studying those things now. This is a study of the source and delegation of authority.

"then comes the end, when He hands over the kingdom to the God and Father, when He has abolished all rule and all authority and power." (1 Corinthians 15:24, NASB95)

Thinking in terms of power, not other aspects of theology, and viewed in the context of the preceding passage, we can see that if there is a Creator and He delegates all authority and is the source of all power, then for every knee to bow and for every tongue to confess that Jesus Christ is Lord is a small task for the One who is the source of all things.

"Have this attitude in yourselves which was also in Christ Jesus, who, although He existed in the form of God, did not regard equality with God a thing to be grasped, but emptied Himself, taking the form of a bond-servant, and being made in the likeness of men. Being found in appearance as a man, He humbled Himself by becoming obedient to the point of death, even death on a cross. For this reason also, God highly exalted Him, and bestowed on Him the name which is above every name, so that at the name of Jesus every knee will bow, of those who are in heaven and on earth and under the earth, and that every tongue will confess that Jesus Christ is Lord, to the glory of God the Father." (Philippians 2:5–11, NASB95)

Therefore, working from Christian literature and the Christian Biblical worldview, clearly the Creator is the source of all things. This includes thrones, dominions, rulers and authorities. No authority exists except that which is created by God. Since nothing exists except what God creates, no one can take authority from God by force. Therefore, if there is any authority distributed in creation, God had to distribute that authority willingly. Willing distribution of authority is delegation of authority.

From the top, God the Father delegated the highest level of authority to God the Son. Sometimes this is confusing because we expect that some forceful, visible change in everything would be evident, based on that assignment of authority. To clear this up a bit, think of a large business where a manager is assigned new authority. The role and the authority already existed and did not change after assignment. Instead the assignment simply changed who is the ruler seated in that particular throne or office. Many people in the business may never notice there was a change.

In the end Jesus Christ will abolish all lower distributions of authority. Another way to describe this to say that in the end Jesus Christ will reclaim all delegations of authority.

If God the father never distributed authority into creation by delegating authority, then no one but God would have authority over anything. Therefore a lawful transfer of authority will always be by delegation. Since God creates the authority, delegates the authority and will eventually reclaim the authority, we can see that properly delegated authority can always be reclaimed.

A Few Examples

If a property owner delegates authority over a certain field to an employee, the property owner can always reclaim that authority.

If a father delegates authority over the yard care to a son, the father can always reclaim the authority.

If a manager delegates authority over a project to an employee he manages, the manager can always reclaim that authority.

The only way for the employee or the son to decide to keep authority in the above examples is by force or deception. The same thing is true with the US Constitution and the states. The states conditionally delegated certain limited authority to a central governing body known as the US federal government. If the states are unable to reclaim the authority delegated to that central body, then the states are either deceived or held in check by force.

Remember that oppressive *power* comes from control of production and that authority is the permitted *power* to act.

Government produces nothing and wastes much, which means that every promise made by government must be kept by a producer.

Wealth is the fruit of production and the people are the producers.

Therefore the local, state and national governments are all dependent on the people for their power.

People established the local and state governments based on the private property that they possessed. Representatives at the state level created a landless federal coordinating governing body, i.e. The Federal Government. The local state and federal governments are created by the people and are dependent on the actions and resources of the people for their very existence.

Therefore, in practical terms, we can say that people create government and producers sustain government.

Production powers authority and authority is the permitted power to act. Authority is a force, not a standard. Law is a standard, not a force.

Producers give the government authority, which is the permitted power to act. Government action must be lawful. When government use of authority is unlawful, that authority should be reclaimed and the lawbreakers should be punished.

Since the people produce and delegate authority, the people should be able to reclaim their authority at will. In a Republic they can and do.

The marriage did not form the man and the woman. The man and woman formed the marriage.

Government did not create man. Man created government.

The federal government did not create states. The states created the federal government.

The production that powers government authority comes from the people. Authority is delegated by people to government, not by government to people.

If neither the individual nor the state can reclaim the authority that is exercised by the federal (or any) government, then that authority was taken by force or deception, and was not delegated. Taking authority by force or deception is either unlawful within a society, or the result of conquest at the hand of outsiders.

This is the test of lawfully organized authority:

Can the delegated authority be reclaimed at will?

Authority that is properly delegated can be reclaimed at will.

5.12 Dynamic

12) Authority has characteristics which are dynamic and fluctuate over time.

This topic could be covered in much greater depth, but for the present purposes we will just review the basics, which are reasonably simple.

Authority Can Increase or Decrease

Our first observation is that authority can increase or decrease over time. A very simple example is to think of an employee who is doing a better or worse job over time. An employee who is managing well is likely to receive increasing authority. An employee who is managing poorly is likely to lose authority. Matthew 25:14–30 is usually called the Parable of the Talents and serves as a good example of this idea.

Authority Can Be Consumed or Spent

We have to connect a few dots to make this point.

Remember that in Acts 5:4 we find the idea that authority is associated with property. The English word *control* is from the Greek word *exousia*, which is most often translated as *authority* or *power*.

"While it remained unsold, did it not remain your own? And after it was sold, was it not under your control?" (Acts 5:4a, NASB95)

Authority is best defined as *"the permitted power to act."* Oppressive temporal power comes from control of production. A farmer with one acre of land has less authority than a farmer with 1000 acres of land, simply because significant authority is bound up in property and production.

A man with wealth has greater authority than a man in poverty. This leads to the conclusion that a man who once had *wealth* that is now gone, also once had *authority* that is now gone.

Now imagine that the man of wealth delegated authority over some of his property to an employee. If the employee is a poor steward and his labor leads to losses, then the property owner is able to reclaim authority over all of the *remaining* property. However the property owner has lost the authority that is associated with the lost property.

Therefore we can see that authority can be consumed or spent.

Authority Can Be Produced

This is one of my favorite topics because it illustrates a method that God uses to delegate authority, which illuminates a seldom-noticed meaning in Romans 13:1.

"Every person is to be in subjection to the governing authorities. For there is no authority except from God, and those which exist are established by God." (Romans 13:1, NASB95)

The preceding passage is discussed in more detail elsewhere, but a short commentary here will be useful. The phrase "governing authorities" is best translated "higher powers" or "higher authorities."

Hyperecho is the Greek term that the NASB translates *"governing."* Referencing four Bible translations (KJV, NASB, NIV, YLT), the term *hyperecho* occurs in only five passages and is translated as follows:

"more important," "above," "surpassing value," "surpasses," "in authority," "the highest," "governing," and "higher."

Only in Romans 13:1 is *hyperecho* translated *governing*, which is an error.

Because authority is power and authority is orderly and hierarchical, for individuals to be subject to the higher authorities makes sense. To say *governing authorities* does NOT make sense because not all authorities are government. For example, for the employee to be subject to the employer in matters relating to his employment makes sense. This is an example of being subject to a higher authority which is not government.

Now consider the second and third parts of that passage:

"For there is no authority except from God, and those which exist are established by God." (Romans 13:1b, NASB95)

Since God created everything including authority, all authority necessarily comes from God. However, the relationship between man and God is fairly complex. *For example, God continues to directly delegate and distribute authority to men on a daily basis.* This is an incredibly important concept.

Remember that authority that is properly delegated does not cause problems in the world, but rather unlawful distributions of authority cause problems.

First let's review a few passages that indicate that God causes growth, increase, production, etc.

"'If you walk in My statutes and keep My commandments so as to carry them out, then I shall give you rains in their season, so that the land will yield its produce and the trees of the field will bear their fruit. 'Indeed, your threshing will last for you until grape gathering, and grape gathering will last until sowing time. You will thus eat your food to the full and live securely in your land. 'I shall also grant peace in the land, so that you may lie down with no one making you tremble. I shall also eliminate harmful beasts from the land, and no sword will pass through your land." (Leviticus 26:3–6, NASB95)

"He will love you and bless you and multiply you; He will also bless the fruit of your womb and the fruit of your ground, your grain and your new wine and your oil, the increase of your herd and the young of your flock, in the land which He swore to your forefathers to give you." (Deuteronomy 7:13, NASB95)

"He causes the grass to grow for the cattle, And vegetation for the labor of man, So that he may bring forth food from the earth," (Psalm 104:14, NASB95)

"They all wait for You To give them their food in due season. You give to them, they gather it up; You open Your hand, they are satisfied with good. You hide Your face, they are dismayed; You take away their spirit, they expire And return to their dust. You send forth Your Spirit, they are created; And You renew the face of the ground." (Psalm 104:27–30, NASB95)

"Indeed, the Lord will give what is good, And our land will yield its produce." (Psalm 85:12, NASB95)

"May the Lord give you increase, You and your children. May you be blessed of the Lord, Maker of heaven and earth." (Psalm 115:14–15, NASB95)

"Honor the Lord from your wealth And from the first of all your produce; So your barns will be filled with plenty And your vats will overflow with new wine." (Proverbs 3:9–10, NASB95)

"Then He will give you rain for the seed which you will sow in the ground, and bread from the yield of the ground, and it will be rich and plenteous; on that day your livestock will graze in a roomy pasture." (Isaiah 30:23, NASB95)

"I planted, Apollos watered, but God was causing the growth. So then neither the one who plants nor the one who waters is anything, but

God who causes the growth. Now he who plants and he who waters are one; but each will receive his own reward according to his own labor. For we are God's fellow workers; you are God's field, God's building." (1 Corinthians 3:6–9, NASB95)

"Otherwise, you may say in your heart, 'My power and the strength of my hand made me this wealth.' "But you shall remember the Lord your God, for it is He who is giving you power to make wealth, that He may confirm His covenant which He swore to your fathers, as it is this day." (Deuteronomy 8:17–18, NASB95)

"And He caused His people to be very fruitful, And made them stronger than their adversaries." (Psalm 105:24, NASB95)

Once again we need to connect power, production and authority. Power comes from production and authority is the permitted power to act. The preceding passages indicate that God is very active in causing his creation to be fruitful, especially when mixed with the labor of people who worship Him as Creator.

Either from intimate daily involvement or simply by virtue of the fact that God created everything, a good corn crop or good spring calving season is from the hand of the Lord. Increases in crops or livestock are an increase in property, which is an increase in the permitted power to act, which is an increase in authority. Therefore God renews and increases authority through labor, property and production.

"For there is no authority except from God, and those which exist are established by God." (Romans 13:1b, NASB95)

So now we see beginning with original creation and also daily through delegation of authority tied to production, all authority is established by God. The authority that is bound up in the corn and delegated to the farmer is now under the stewardship of the farmer. It is the responsibility of the farmer to see that his authority is not improperly used. This means that the farmer must use his authority lawfully and he must not permit his authority to be transferred unlawfully to anyone.

Authority has characteristics that are dynamic and fluctuate over time.

5.13 Hidden Ingredients

13) Authority has ingredients which are difficult to identify and include.

The Bible speaks about authority as it relates to husbands and wives, property owners, kings, governors, evil spirits, and other things. There are things about authority that are difficult to explain and difficult to understand. We are not trying to address those things in this text. Our purpose here is to identify the things that we can know and use on a daily basis to help us lead more productive lives.

Authority has ingredients that are difficult to identify and include.

5.14 Bad Ingredients

14) Authority can include bad ingredients that generally can be identified.

While some of the good things in authority can be difficult to understand and explain, many of the bad things can be clearly identified. For example, since we know that authority is the permitted power to act, and that oppressive power comes from control of production, then we can easily understand that authority which is formed based on theft of labor, property and production is an unlawfully formed authority. Since authority is a force which will always be used oppressively when unlawfully formed, we must understand the origin, nature and purpose of authority so that we can produce, maintain and defend a healthy distribution of authority.

Authority is intended to be used within the limits of just law. Recall that authority is a force, not a standard, and law is a standard, not a force. This helps us understand that when one in authority claims the right to act unlawfully, he is making a false claim. This is another indicator there is a corrupt ingredient in the authority of the one making the claim. The idea of the "divine right of kings" collapsed under the weight of this truth. After all, the Bible explains that God Himself does not use ultimate authority to do unlawful things. How can any man claim such a right, unless he believes himself to be above his Creator?

Authority can include bad ingredients which generally can be identified.

5.15 Thinking of Higher Authority

The 2003 Merriam-Webster collegiate dictionary gives us four definitions for authority. The first definition generally deals with the idea of authority being an expert in knowledge worthy of reference or citation. The second and third definitions of authority interest us and are discussed here. The fourth definition conveys an idea of credibility.

The second and third definition given by Merriam-Webster is as follows:

2 a: power to influence or command thought, opinion, or behavior

b: freedom granted by one in authority : RIGHT

3 a: persons in command *specifically* : GOVERNMENT

b: a governmental agency or corporation to administer a revenue-producing public enterprise ⟨the transit *authority*⟩[98]

Definition 2a includes the power to command behavior. This describes the relationship between the one having authority and the one subject to authority. The one having authority possesses sufficient power to cause or force specific behavior by the one subject to authority. This power will come from some combination of two sources which are discussed elsewhere.

Definition 2b includes the idea of freedom being granted by authority to one who is subject to that authority. In other words one in authority can command specific action or grant freedom to act. In this we also see delegation and levels or hierarchy in authority.

Definition 3a & b describes a person or institution as being an authority.

Our next step is to consider the Christian and secular view of authority.

The Christian View

One of the strong influences in our society with regard to authority is the Christian view of authority. When a Christian is asked how he should relate to authority, specifically government, he will typically refer to Romans 13. To put it very mildly, the typical Christian view of

98 Merriam-Webster, I. (2003). *Merriam-Webster's collegiate dictionary.* (Eleventh ed.). Springfield, Mass.: Merriam-Webster, Inc.

authority wrongly transfers tremendous unlawful power to government. We need to understand the concept of authority in Scripture in order to understand how faulty Christian thinking leads to unlawful and destructive government powers.

In addition, for a time, Protestant tradition flowing from Luther and Calvin rejected the idea that man can perceive natural law through reason. In this view, because man is imperfect and sinful, there is no way for him to rightly perceive the natural law. This is a foolish position to take since Paul writes in Romans 1 that *"since the creation of the world His invisible attributes, His eternal power and divine nature, have been clearly seen, being understood through what has been made, so that they are without excuse"* and in Romans 2 he explains that the Gentiles were *"a law to themselves"* who *"show the work of the law written in their hearts, their conscience bearing witness."* In addition, mankind proves every day the ability to reason and understand various aspects of God's creation. There is much more ground to cover here, but the bottom line is that when we take away our ability to reason, there is no way to develop an integrated Christian worldview from which to judge the actions of supposed "authorities."

"For the wrath of God is revealed from heaven against all ungodliness and unrighteousness of men who suppress the truth in unrighteousness, because that which is known about God is evident within them; for God made it evident to them. For since the creation of the world His invisible attributes, His eternal power and divine nature, have been clearly seen, being understood through what has been made, so that they are without excuse." (Romans 1:18–20, NASB95)

"For when Gentiles who do not have the Law do instinctively the things of the Law, these, not having the Law, are a law to themselves, in that they show the work of the Law written in their hearts, their conscience bearing witness and their thoughts alternately accusing or else defending them," (Romans 2:14–15, NASB95)

It is worth noting that over the centuries there have been terrible, murderous abuses of people and ideas by pseudo-Christian individuals and groups. Usually the abuses are born from wild eschatology mixed with a communist, workless view of society where everyone is equal; but as always, some are more equal than others.[99]

---

99 An Austrian Perspective on the History of Economic Thought (Murray N. Rothbard); Chapter 5.5 Communist zealots: the Anabaptists

In some cases the leaders confiscated all gold, silver, food, clothing and any other valuable things from the people, leaving them in poverty and starvation. Meanwhile the leaders lived in posh luxury from those goods while they lasted, always making promises about how things would be better soon, provided the leaders were strictly obeyed by the people. Those unfortunate enough to disobey the latest edict proved they were "unchristian" and were promptly put to death. These deadly and destructive episodes were bloody and brief. The Bible warns about such people calling them "wolves in sheep's clothing."

"Beware of the false prophets, who come to you in sheep's clothing, but inwardly are ravenous wolves. "You will know them by their fruits. Grapes are not gathered from thorn bushes nor figs from thistles, are they? "So every good tree bears good fruit, but the bad tree bears bad fruit. "A good tree cannot produce bad fruit, nor can a bad tree produce good fruit. "Every tree that does not bear good fruit is cut down and thrown into the fire. "So then, you will know them by their fruits." (Matthew 7:15–20, NASB95)

I mention this because we must be careful to separate true Christian behavior from the behavior of those who claim the Christian faith, yet bear fruit that is clearly contrary to the teachings of Christ. We Christians cause enough trouble by misunderstanding some important teachings of Scripture without being lumped in with those who intentionally abuse others, supposedly in the name of Christ.

Romans 13:1-7

This passage is often used to claim that Christians are to be subject to government, but that is not what the passage says. Government is only one authority to which individuals are subject. This concept is extremely important for us to understand.

Because government does not possess all authority, there are other authorities, including ourselves, which we must identify so that we are properly subject to each one. We will see that when government claims authority that is outside of its proper jurisdiction, government is seizing authority that belongs to others and that must not be tolerated.

When we accept an unlawful transfer of authority, we are no longer being subject to the higher authorities. In other words, the law of God, which is consistent with natural law, is the standard by which we must judge actions of authority. We will go into this in more detail, but our first step is to analyze Romans 13:1 to see what it actually says. Consider

Romans 13:1 as expressed in the NASB and KJV translations.

"Every person is to be in subjection to the governing authorities. For there is no authority except from God, and those which exist are established by God. " (Romans 13:1, NASB95)

"Let every soul be subject unto the higher powers. For there is no power but of God: the powers that be are ordained of God. " (Romans 13:1, KJV 1900)

In the two preceding passages, it is clear that each individual is to be in subjection to something. The New American Standard Bible (NASB) indicates that we are to be in subjection to the *"governing authorities"* while the King James Version (KJV) states that we are to be subject to the *"higher powers."* At this point we need to study two of the original words which are being translated to English a few centuries apart.

First we will consider the meaning and use of the Greek word translated either *"governing"* or *"higher."* After that we will consider the meaning and use of the Greek word translated *"authorities"* or *"power."*

hyperecho

Our first Greek term is *hyperecho* or *huperecho* which is derived from the base words *huper* and *echo. Huper* means *over* or *beyond. Echo* means *to hold* or *to have.* Therefore *hyperecho* is acceptably defined as "*to hold above, to rise above, to be superior."*

Hyperecho is the one, single term translated *governing* or *higher* in the two Bible translations noted above.

5242. **ὑπερέχω huperechō**; from *5228* and *2192; to hold above, to rise above, to be superior:*—authority(1), governing(1), more important(1), surpasses(1), surpassing value(1).[100]

The Greek term *hyperecho* appears in only five passages in the New Testament. To help convey the ideas, in the following passage list, Philippians 2:3 is repeated from the NIV translation, and 1 Peter 2:13 is repeated from the YLT translation.

You will notice that in the following passages the term hyperecho (governing in the NASB) is translated "more important," "above," "surpassing value," "surpasses," "in authority," "the highest," "governing," and "higher."

Hyperecho is not translated *government* or *governing* in any other

100 Thomas, R. L. (1998). New American Standard Hebrew-Aramaic and Greek dictionaries : Updated edition. Anaheim: Foundation Publications, Inc.

passage. Notice the different English words which are translated from the Greek term *hyperecho*:

"Do nothing from selfishness or empty conceit, but with humility of mind regard one another as more important than yourselves; " (Philippians 2:3, NASB95)

"Do nothing out of selfish ambition or vain conceit. Rather, in humility value others above yourselves, " (Philippians 2:3, NIV)

"More than that, I count all things to be loss in view of the surpassing value of knowing Christ Jesus my Lord, for whom I have suffered the loss of all things, and count them but rubbish so that I may gain Christ, " (Philippians 3:8, NASB95)

"And the peace of God, which surpasses all comprehension, will guard your hearts and your minds in Christ Jesus. " (Philippians 4:7, NASB95)

"Submit yourselves for the Lord's sake to every human institution, whether to a king as the one in authority, " (1 Peter 2:13, NASB95)

"Be subject, then, to every human creation, because of the Lord, whether to a king, as the highest," (1 Peter 2:13, YLT)

"Every person is to be in subjection to the governing authorities. For there is no authority except from God, and those which exist are established by God. " (Romans 13:1, NASB95)

"Let every soul be subject unto the higher powers. For there is no power but of God: the powers that be are ordained of God. " (Romans 13:1, KJV 1900)

Using a layman's approach to identify the best English word to use in Romans 13:1, we will do a test using a single substitute English term in place of *hyperecho*. If all the passages make sense using one English word, this is a good indication it may be the best word for us to use in translation. The term we will use for our test is *"higher,"* which happens to be the way the KJV translates *hyperecho* in Romans 13:1 already.

"Do nothing from selfishness or empty conceit, but with humility of mind regard one another as [HIGHER] than yourselves; " (Philippians 2:3, NASB95)

"Do nothing out of selfish ambition or vain conceit. Rather, in humility value others [HIGHER THAN] yourselves, " (Philippians 2:3, NIV)

"More than that, I count all things to be loss in view of the [HIGHER VALUE] of knowing Christ Jesus my Lord, for whom I have suffered the loss of all things, and count them but rubbish so that I may gain Christ, " (Philippians 3:8, NASB95)

"And the peace of God, which [IS HIGHER THAN] all comprehension, will guard your hearts and your minds in Christ Jesus. " (Philippians 4:7, NASB95)

"Submit yourselves for the Lord's sake to every human institution, whether to a king as the one [HIGHER], " (1 Peter 2:13, NASB95)

"Be subject, then, to every human creation, because of the Lord, whether to a king, as the highest," (1 Peter 2:13, YLT)

"Every person is to be in subjection to the [HIGHER] authorities. For there is no authority except from God, and those which exist are established by God. " (Romans 13:1, NASB95)

"Let every soul be subject unto the higher powers. For there is no power but of God: the powers that be are ordained of God. " (Romans 13:1, KJV 1900)

When we use the one English term *higher* every time we see the one Greek term *hyperecho*, each of the passages are understandable and sensible. If we went back in each of those verses and tried to insert some form of the term *govern* or *governing*, at least three of the passages would make no sense.

Even though the term *"higher"* is not a perfect translation in each case, the ideas that are conveyed are consistent. Recalling that there are other authorities beside government, it is evident that the KJV translation *"higher"* is more correct than the NASB translation *"governing."*

In review, these two translations (NASB and KJV) clearly indicate in Romans 13:1 that every person should be subject to the *"higher" powers* or *authorities*. It is not correct to use the term governing here.

If we try to translate the original Greek term *hyperecho* to *"governing"* in other places, several of the passages make no sense.

In our study of authority we found that authorities operate by levels in a chain of command, with one being higher than another. We also observed that there are various authorities other than government which individuals are commanded in the Scriptures to be subject to, which makes sense when we look at the way things actually work in "the real world." Two simple examples are the authority of parents over children and the authority of employers over their own property and in a limited way over employees.

In addition, all authorities, by definition, rule in their jurisdiction. The jurisdiction is indicated by hierarchy, which is the reason that we are to be subject to higher authorities. There are many authorities distributed around individuals that the individual is not subject to, like employees who are not subject to other employers besides their own, as we have discussed previously.

To use the phrase *"governing authorities"* is to suggest there is another kind, but there is not a different kind of authority. For example, an employer has authority with specific jurisdiction to govern his property and an individual has authority with specific jurisdiction to govern himself. The actions of both of these are to be judged based on the standard of law. Authority is like water. One may have more or less of it, but it is always water.

Having said this, there is reference to rulers in Romans 13, so the idea of rulers is definitely part of Romans 13, but not in the way we are taught.

exousia

The next Greek term is *exousia* which is translated in various places in the New Testament as *authority*, *power*, *domain*, *right*, *jurisdiction*, *control*, *liberty* and *dominion*. The most common translation of *exousia* in the KJV is *power*, while the most common translation of *exousia* in the NASB is *authority*, as the following chart explains.

exousia	KJV	NASB	ESV	NRSV
authority	29	71	72	71
power	69	12	12	15
right	2	11	11	9
domain	0	2	1	0
jurisdiction	1	1	2	1
liberty	1	1	0	1
control	0	1	1	1
putting…in charge	0	1	0	0
be in authority	0	1	0	0
dominion	0	1	0	0
strength	1	0	0	0
charge	0	0	1	2
disposal	0	0	1	1
claim	0	0	1	1

Based on root words, context and reason, the best definition for *exousia* is *"the permitted power to act."*

1849. **ἐξουσία exousia**; from *1832; power to act, authority:—* authorities(7), authority(65), charge(1), control(1), domain(2), dominion(1), jurisdiction(1), liberty(1), power(11), powers(1), right(11).[101]

For further explanation of *exousia,* please refer to the chapter *Characteristics of Authority* and the section *Permitted Power to Act.*

Summary

For the Christian, since A) all authorities are established by God, and B) one authority is higher than another, and C) there are authorities other than government, and D) the individual is to be subject to all higher authorities, we must not read Romans 13:1 as being *limited* only to ruling authority.

In fact, in Romans 13:1-7 the term government does not appear at all. This makes sense because the English word *govern, governed, governing* and *government* only occur 10 times in the NASB and 8 times in the KJV in the whole Bible, and none of those cases are from a word which means government. Therefore we see that there are various authorities, all of which we are to be subject to, including, but not limited to, rulers who are servants of God and who are not allowed to steal.

5.16 In Search of a Consistent View

Romans 13:1-7 tends to give Christians a hard time because we misunderstand the nature and purpose of authority. The passage is written in such a way that we must mix the clues it contains with logic and reason to sort out the meaning. The first goal in this chapter is to identify inconsistencies in the standard interpretation of this passage, then to search for a consistent interpretation. Before we begin, it is worth mentioning the words of Peter regarding Paul's writing.

"Therefore, beloved, since you look for these things, be diligent to be found by Him in peace, spotless and blameless, and regard the patience of our Lord as salvation; just as also our beloved brother Paul, according to the wisdom given him, wrote to you, as also in all his letters, speaking in them of these things, in which are some things hard to understand,

[101] Thomas, R. L. (1998). New American Standard Hebrew-Aramaic and Greek dictionaries : Updated edition. Anaheim: Foundation Publications, Inc.

which the untaught and unstable distort, as they do also the rest of the Scriptures, to their own destruction. You therefore, beloved, knowing this beforehand, be on your guard so that you are not carried away by the error of unprincipled men and fall from your own steadfastness, but grow in the grace and knowledge of our Lord and Savior Jesus Christ. To Him be the glory, both now and to the day of eternity. Amen." (2 Peter 3:14–18, NASB95)

A much more detailed, word by word study could be done, but for now we will focus on only a few words and the ideas which are presented in the passage from Romans 13. Following are some simple divisions of the text into one or more sentences. After discussing various possible meanings for sections of the text, I explain my understanding of Paul's intent in the passage.

Overview

It is necessary to remember that the proper distribution of authority, as arranged and appointed by God, results in a balance of power between individuals in a society. Lawful government is a healthy and valuable institution that benefits law-abiding individuals. However, a government that is fueled by theft always leads to destruction of the good in a society. Theft is a transfer of power, which is derived from the profits from production, which is also a transfer of authority.

These verses in Romans clearly describe something that God established for our good. Therefore, what is being described is a balanced and complete system given by God for the use and benefit of mankind. Otherwise the unqualified cause and effect statements about good being praised and evil being punished could not be true. In other words, in a perfect system with a perfect distribution of authority, good will always be praised and evil will always be punished.

This is true because all people depend on (someone's) production and power comes from control of production. Authority is the permitted power to act, which means that both *exousia* and *dynamis* power would reside in the hands of producers, except as delegated to government, by producers, for lawful purposes.

If (when) government abused the delegated authority, the authority would be reclaimed and put in the hands of new officials.

The use by mankind of a perfect system will never be perfect because someone will always be prepared to abuse the system. However, if a society makes it a point to understand and employ such a system, evil will be suppressed and good will be encouraged and rewarded.

"When the righteous increase, the people rejoice, But when a wicked man rules, people groan." (Proverbs 29:2, NASB95)

"The king gives stability to the land by justice, But a man who takes bribes overthrows it." (Proverbs 29:4, NASB95)

"The righteous is concerned for the rights of the poor, The wicked does not understand such concern." (Proverbs 29:7, NASB95)

"When it goes well with the righteous, the city rejoices, And when the wicked perish, there is joyful shouting. By the blessing of the upright a city is exalted, But by the mouth of the wicked it is torn down." (Proverbs 11:10–11, NASB95)

"When the righteous triumph, there is great glory, But when the wicked rise, men hide themselves. He who conceals his transgressions will not prosper, But he who confesses and forsakes them will find compassion." (Proverbs 28:12–13, NASB95)

"A leader who is a great oppressor lacks understanding, But he who hates unjust gain will prolong his days." (Proverbs 28:16, NASB95)

If we see that what we call government, or any other authority, is punishing good and rewarding evil, we know immediately that this authority derives its power from unlawful actions including theft or plunder. We know this because that is the way the world, as God organized it, works.

Producers know how hard it is to take care of property and produce profits. Producers also understand the natural order of things and recognize their dependence on the God of creation, or at least the natural order, for the increase from, and fruitfulness of, their labor and property. In other words producers have respect for one another, respect for the good and expect evil to be punished. There is no benefit for a producer to promote theft, unless he believes he will be the recipient of the stolen property, in which case his profits are once again derived from theft and he is on the path of becoming an oppressor.

Romans 13 also communicates that we are to be subject to all rulers in the same way regardless of their faith or worldview. Christians are not to respond any differently to rulers based on the ruler's belief system. In other words, if there is a ruler who claims to be a Christian, yet who wants to rob producers, he is to be treated exactly the same way as an atheist, agnostic or one who practices any other form of religion. In all cases, producers would say: *"No sir. Your actions are unlawful and will not be permitted."*

God gave us a perfect working system which functions for our good, but it has been replaced by an imposter that punishes good and rewards evil. An imposter can only remain until his identity is revealed. Once his identity is revealed he must be rejected as an imposter or accepted as a better replacement for the real thing.

Fortunately for us, we are not called to be subject to the imposter. Our job is to expose the unfruitful deeds of darkness. Wise, productive, law-abiding citizens will approve and support the exposure of evil and corruption.

"Do not participate in the unfruitful deeds of darkness, but instead even expose them;" (Ephesians 5:11, NASB95)

So here is the key: We are to be subject to all authority, including rulers, whether the rulers are Christian or not *and* we are to expose and resist unlawful actions which lead to unlawfully formed authority that will pervert justice and destroy the good in a society. This is true even if it is a Christian doing the unlawful thing, and even if he doesn't understand that what he is doing is wrong.

As clearly stated in Romans 13:1-7, the distributions of authority ordered and arranged by God do not pervert justice. If an authority perverts justice, it is taking unlawful actions which we must resist, rather than be subject to.

Authority is not above law. Lawfully organized authority will not pervert justice.

While people are subject to various authorities, all authority is subject to law. Since law is above authority, law is the basis on which the actions of authority are to be judged.

Because authority is power, when power is centralized it affects and controls much in society. If a theft-based, overgrown authority is challenged it will call on dependent people and institutions for support. This places custom and public opinion above law.

Therefore, when a person resists the unlawful actions of authority which are ratified by custom and public opinion, he is accused of resisting authority, which is false. He is actually being obedient to the standard of law, which when followed would maintain a distribution of authority that is balanced, perfect and substantially based on production.

A lawful distribution of authority would include small authority in the hands of rulers and great authority in the hands of those who are productive. With a lawful distribution of authority, custom and public opinion would be in agreement with law in defending individual life, liberty and property.

As you read Romans 13:1-7, think in terms of ALL forms of authority, not just the case of rulers or "government." When you think of "government" authority, think of that authority in a form and at a scale limited by the standard of law, including *No Stealing*.

Remember that according to God's distribution of authority, producers would be the entry point for renewed authority, which producers would possess based on their profits from production. Corn crops, calf crops, mines and manufacturers would produce the means and resources to act according to efficient management and strong market relationships with other producers.

All people are expected to be willing producers to a degree greater than or equal to their consumption. The power or authority held by rulers would be delegated by producers so that rulers can be partners in defending individual life, liberty and property, according to the standard of law and without partiality.

Wealth producing individuals would care for those unable to care for themselves, primarily through family and church relationships. Wealth transfer from producers to rulers and favored business would be treated as the illegal act that it is, according to the standard of law.

Bad Ole Producers

One of the arguments I hear about producers having power is that producers are bad, mean, greedy, immoral, evil people who hate the environment and other people, especially their employees. This is the kind of thinking that is expected in a society that honors those who play and castigates those who pay. There are many problems with this line of reasoning.

Last time I checked, people depend on production. People eat food and use things. Food and things must be produced. Government produces nothing and wastes much. Therefore every promise made by government must be kept by a producer.

It is the government that is wasting our labor, property, sons and daughters. It is the government that is bankrupting nations around the globe. Government is able to do so because of its unlimited access to the means and resources to act through legal plunder, beginning with the money system.

Even if these exact same people who are now causing havoc in the world from their positions in government were the producers, I would be pleased. The reason? They would have to produce what they use to do whatever they choose to do. They would protect their own property and produce efficiently to have the means and resources to act. These rulers turned producers would have limited power and authority and they would learn to respect the private property of other people. These people who previously wielded central power, fueled by theft, would now have to contend with one another, since power, authority, labor and property would be distributed among individuals.

The most important point is this:

When producers keep their own production to use as they see fit, there is no centralization of power or authority. There is a distributed balance of power in society, which is based on the good stewardship of property, time and relationships.

Romans 13:1-7, NASB

"Every person is to be in subjection to the governing authorities. For there is no authority except from God, and those that exist are established by God. Therefore whoever resists authority has opposed the ordinance of God; and they who have opposed will receive condemnation upon themselves. For rulers are not a cause of fear for good behavior, but for evil. Do you want to have no fear of authority? Do what is good and you will have praise from the same; for it is a minister of God to you for good. But if you do what is evil, be afraid; for it does not bear the sword for nothing; for it is a minister of God, an avenger who brings wrath on the one who practices evil. Therefore it is necessary to be in subjection, not only because of wrath, but also for conscience' sake. For because of this you also pay taxes, for rulers are servants of God, devoting themselves to this very thing. Render to all what is due them: tax to whom tax is due; custom to whom custom; fear to whom fear; honor to whom honor." (Romans 13:1–7, NASB95)

Following is a section-by-section review of the preceding verses.

"Every person is to be in subjection to the governing authorities."

Inconsistent View

This sentence is taken to mean that every person is to be subject to government without any limitations. However, we have already seen that the Greek term *hyperecho*, which is being translated "governing," actually means *"higher."* Rather than *"governing authorities,"* the KJV translates the Greek as *"higher powers."* The best definition for *exousia* is *"the permitted power to act,"* so *"higher powers"* makes sense. It is inconsistent to translate *hyperecho* as some variation of *"higher"* in every other place and *"governing"* here.

Consistent View

Suppose that this first sentence means that every person is to be in subjection to the authority which is directly above him in each jurisdiction, whether as son, employee, citizen under law, etc.

"For there is no authority except from God, and those which exist are established by God."

Inconsistent View

In the standard interpretation, it has already been established in the preceding sentence that authority is *government*, or at least the authority being discussed here is *government*. The standard definition of authority says that authority has *the right to rule*.

By extension, the standard interpretation then says that all *government* is from God and the point is restated by saying that those authorities (*governments*) which exist are established by God.

The first error in this reasoning is that we have incorrectly associated *authority* and *government*. There are *other* authorities besides government. People are to be subject to *ALL* higher authorities. The Greek term in the verse means *higher*, not *government*.

The second error in this reasoning is that we have associated *"the right to rule"* with authority, which falsely leads to the idea that authority is a *standard* like law. Beyond these errors we will see the conflict and inconsistency that follows based on the next verses.

The English term *"established"* in the preceding sentence is from a Greek term, which means *"to draw up in order"* or *"arrange."* The following definition is from the NASB Dictionary.[102]

5021. τάσσω tassō; from a prim. root ταγ- tag-; to draw up in order, arrange:—appointed(2), designated(1), determined(1), devoted(1), established(1), set(1).

102 Thomas, R. L. (1998). *New American Standard Hebrew-Aramaic and Greek dictionaries : Updated edition*. Anaheim: Foundation Publications, Inc.

Consistent View

Suppose instead we say that all *permitted power to act* is from God, because only God is self-existent and all of creation depends on God for existence. Apart from God, there is no existence and no power to act.

Authority includes power and temporal power comes from production. The corn crop and the calf crop are specific examples of authority being refreshed and renewed by the hand of God. God created the corn and the calf, caused them to grow and ordered the creation in a way that production renews and increases authority.

Furthermore, all authorities are ordered and arranged by God so that the hierarchy and jurisdiction of all authority is well organized according to the power and sovereignty of God.

"Therefore whoever resists authority has opposed the ordinance of God; and they who have opposed will receive condemnation upon themselves."

Inconsistent View

Once again, the standard view suggests that anyone who resists government has opposed the ordinance of God and will receive judgment on themselves for having resisted authority.

In this translation we see the term *"ordinance"* which tends to lead our mind to the idea of law. However, the underlying Greek term means *"ordinance"* or *"institution."* Since the Greek term translated *"established"* means *to order or arrange*, it follows that *authority* is something that is *instituted* by God.

Consistent View

Suppose we say that whoever resists authority has opposed the institution and organization of the permitted power to act which is created and ordered by God.

When we recall that people depend on production and that power comes from control of production and that property is protected by the eighth commandment, then we see that only producers, and those with whom producers are willing to share, will be sustained. Recall 2 Thessalonians 3:10:

"For even when we were with you, we used to give you this order: if anyone is not willing to work, then he is not to eat, either." (2 Thessalonians 3:10, NASB95)

Those who are unwilling to work will either die or change their attitude and behavior. In addition, individuals who do not respect the property rights of others or who behave badly in the marketplace will have a very difficult time in exchange and therefore would be very limited in their ability to produce.

It seems clear then that those who resist God's well ordered distribution of authority will indeed incur judgment on themselves. Notice this judgment is not only because of law or "government," but rather it includes a simple outworking of natural penalties associated with resisting God's natural order and God's distribution of the permitted power to act.

Stated another way, if I am lazy I will not refresh or renew my own authority. If I am abusive toward my fellows, they will cease to trade with me, thereby limiting my profits and therefore my authority.

If I am unwilling to work and unable to steal, my authority, or *"permitted power to act,"* will melt away as I approach death. If I am a law-breaker, properly distributed authority will judge and penalize me by the *standard* of law.

This brings to mind sowing and reaping, which other worldviews recognize by the label "karma."

"Do not be deceived, God is not mocked; for whatever a man sows, this he will also reap." (Galatians 6:7, NASB95)

"For rulers are not a cause of fear for good behavior, but for evil."

Inconsistent View

Now we have reached a key point of inconsistency in the standard interpretation of this passage.

We are told that authority is government, and government has the right to rule, and that individuals are to be subject to government without reservation because government was created by God, and every government that exists was established by God.

This reasoning defies logic and is contrary to Scripture and the idea of law. Remember that *exousia* has a root word *exesti*, which carries the two meanings *"it is permitted"* or *"lawful."* From this we get the definition that authority is the *"permitted power to act."*

Suppose one claims that *exousia*, which is *authority*, is the *"lawful power to act."* This leads to the idea that all *actions* of *authority* are *lawful*. This poor reasoning creates untenable problems since authority is often used to perform *unlawful actions.*

Consistent View

This passage says that rulers *"are not"* a cause of fear for good behavior, but for evil. The passage does not say that rulers *"should not be"* a cause of fear for good behavior.

This means that rulers who are exercising authority as distributed by God through production and law *will not be* a cause of fear for good behavior and *will be* a cause of fear for evil. In other words this is a good test for determining whether a particular authority or ruler is lawfully seated, organized and empowered.

If a ruler punishes good behavior and praises evil, we can be confident he possesses authority that has either been stolen or will soon be lost if he is operating in a society that rewards the good and punishes evil.

"Do you want to have no fear of authority? Do what is good and you will have praise from the same; for it is a minister of God to you for good."

Inconsistent View

According to the standard interpretation we could translate this to "Do you want to have no fear of government?" which is a mistake. The proper interpretation would be "Do you want to have no fear of the permitted power to act which is lawfully organized and behaves lawfully?"

According to the standard interpretation, the next sentence again indicates a contradiction between our *correct understanding of authority* and our *experience with government.*

The standard interpretation suggests *authority* and *government* are essentially the same thing. This passage says that if we do what is good, we will *actually be praised* by authority. However government as we know it regularly does just the opposite. We live in societies today that punish producers and reward sluggards and thieves.

Consistent View

According to our interpretation, if an employee is *"doing good,"* we can easily understand the employer exercising authority in that relationship and praising the employee for his good actions. After all, that authority is exercised to the mutual benefit of both parties in an honest system of exchange. The same would be true between a father and son or a citizen and the court.

Government would also reward good, lawful, productive behavior if the resources that rulers depended on came from producers who would reclaim their authority if rulers behaved unlawfully.

Once again the standard interpretation fails us when we read this next phrase:

"[F]or [authority] is a minister of God to you for good."

Inconsistent View

If this passage is talking about *government*, and we view *authority* as *the right to rule* and therefore determine that it is wrong to resist government, then the standard interpretation requires us to believe that a government that ***punishes good, rewards evil and behaves unlawfully is a minister of God for our good.*** Not only is this implied and backwards idea contrary to our understanding of the purpose of authority and the nature of God, it directly contradicts the preceding verses which say good will be praised and evil punished.

Consistent View

On the other hand, according to our interpretation, all authority is from God and the distribution and organization of authority is developed by God, so that if we *"do good"* we will receive praise from authority because it is a minister of God to us for good.

A power distribution system which is rooted significantly in production, organized according to the natural order and constrained by natural law, will reward good, productive behavior and punish evil, lazy, destructive behavior. Rulers who are operating in keeping with that distribution of power will sometimes even voice praise for the good.

"But if you do what is evil, be afraid; for it does not bear the sword for nothing; for it is a minister of God, an avenger who brings wrath on the one who practices evil."

Inconsistent View

According to the standard interpretation, we again see that *government* is the one who bears the sword and it is a minister of God that punishes those who do evil. But we are again faced with this contradiction: We know government regularly rewards evil, even to the degree that government is often the most unlawful actor in society, promoting evil in government, law, business, family life and education.

Consistent View

On the other hand, our interpretation remains consistent. First, the phrase *"bearing the sword"* indicates the power to punish. Even if we take the passage to be talking about rulers, we know that lawful punishment is often something less than death. Authority exercised under law is capable of punishing up to and including capital punishment.

Therefore, we must ask: Is the authority that is based on a lawful distribution of power capable of being *"an avenger who brings wrath on the one who practices evil"*? The answer is a resounding yes! The one unwilling to work is lead by the command in 2 Thessalonians 3:10 to his death. The sluggard will harvest little and his authority will diminish. The thief or murderer will be caught and will be made to pay restitution according to the standard of law.

"Therefore it is necessary to be in subjection, not only because of wrath, but also for conscience' sake."

Inconsistent View

According to the standard interpretation this tells us that we are to be in subjection to *government*, not only because government can punish, but also to keep our conscience clear. However, if this is talking about government we can only conclude from experience that the Apostle Paul was confused (which I do not believe) because government punishes good and rewards evil. How can a person's conscience be bothered by rejecting and resisting lawless behavior?

Consistent View

On the other hand, if Paul was talking about people being in subjection to authority so that we do not resist God's order and reap punishment, then we can see that being in subjection protects us from wrath and keeps our conscience clear.

After all, how can our conscience be bothered by refusing to obey commands which are unlawful?

Or how can our conscience be clear if we obey commands that are unlawful?

"For because of this you also pay taxes, for rulers are servants of God, devoting themselves to this very thing. Render to all what is due them: tax to whom tax is due; custom to whom custom; fear to whom fear; honor to whom honor."

Our consistent view of authority includes rulers and the particular authority delegated to rulers. When we think about rulers and the actions that they may take under the standard of law, we recognize that the unlawful centralization of power and authority in the hands of rulers is not permitted.

Therefore rulers who are supported by the taxes of the producers will have adequate, yet limited authority, suitable for maintaining order under the standard of law.

We must not confuse resisting unlawful actions with resisting authority. Authority is subject to law, so when we hold authority accountable to the standard of law, authority maintains a lawful and healthy distribution that will reward good and punish evil.

Some Bible translations put far too much emphasis on government. Consider the following section title and translation:

Bizarre Passage Heading:

"A Christian's Duties to the State"

"Everyone must submit to the governing authorities, for there is no authority except from God, and those that exist are instituted by God. 2 So then, the one who resists the authority is opposing God's command, and those who oppose it will bring judgment on themselves. 3 For rulers are not a terror to good conduct, but to bad. Do you want to be unafraid of the authority? Do what is good, and you will have its approval. 4 For government is God's servant for your good. But if you do wrong, be afraid, because it does not carry the sword for no reason. For government is God's servant—an avenger that brings wrath on the one who does wrong. 5 Therefore, you must submit, not only because of wrath, but also because of your conscience. 6 And for this reason you pay taxes, since the authorities are God's public servants, continually attending to these tasks. 7 Pay your obligations to everyone: taxes to those you owe taxes, tolls to those you owe tolls, respect to those you owe respect, and honor to those you owe honor." (Romans 13:1–7, HCSB)[103]

I generally like the Holman Christian Standard Bible (HCSB) translation of Scripture. However, this is a very poor translation of these verses. First of all the word *government* is not in any original term in the passage.

Secondly the key term from which the idea of government is drawn in verse one is *hyperecho*, which means *"higher."* It does not mean government.

Thirdly in verse 4, the Greek refers to authority, as in "authority is God's servant for your good," not "government is God's servant for your good." The terms "government," "it" and "government" should all be referencing authority from verse 3.

Fourthly this translation says *"since the authorities are God's public servants,"* when it should say *"since rulers are God's public servants."* By placing the word *authorities* in that translated verse we have now incorrectly made *authorities* a synonym for <u>*government and the rulers in government*</u>. Authority is neither a person nor an institution. Authority is *the permitted power to act.*

Of course the section title takes the cake: *"A Christian's Duties to the State."* The modern nation state is built on theft, which is a violation of the eighth commandment *"You shall not steal."*

The Christian owes no duty to obey lawless powers. It is the Christian's duty to be obedient to the law of God, which is consistent with the law of nature, which will limit the unlawful organization of power which forms the state.

---

103 *The Holy Bible: Holman Christian standard version.* 2009. Nashville: Holman Bible Publishers.

In place of the state we would have lawful government, with limited power delegated to it by producers who possess the authority that is created, organized and renewed through production by God.

I recognize that there are other forms of authority and other ingredients in authority. However, if we get a proper handle on the authority that is bound to production, many of the problems that man brings upon himself will be solved. Things will be better. Liberty and law will become stronger. Lawlessness, theft and oppression will become weaker.

"When the righteous increase, the people rejoice, But when a wicked man rules, people groan." (Proverbs 29:2, NASB95)

5.17 Authority Conclusion

Authority is "the <u>permitted</u> power to act."

Authority is NOT "the <u>right</u> and power to act."

If we treat authority as a standard, like law, the problems that follow will destroy any free society.

Authority is a force, not a standard.

Law is a standard, not a force.

When we associate *government* and *the right to rule* with authority, we create a second body of law. If government has the right to rule, then it cannot be called to account and whatever actions it takes are lawful, because it is a standard unto itself. In other words, there would then be a second standard and second law.

There would be the standard of just law, and the standard of government law, known as positive law. That is, there would be two separate bodies of law and two separate standards - until one considers that there are hundreds of governments in history and around the world. Every government becomes a standard unto itself and defines law according to itself. Chaos, waste and destruction follow.

If authority is *government* having *the right to rule*, the body of law will reflect the government, which means the body of law and the standard will be as inconsistent, arbitrary and corrupt as the government.

Since only one body of law can be applied at any one time, *authority as the right to rule* negates just law, otherwise commonly known as natural law or Biblical law.

If the authority decides what law is without holding to a standard of justice and righteousness, then it displaces justice and puts tyranny and corruption in its place. From a Biblical standpoint this makes no sense. Why would the Creator grant government, which is not even a word mentioned in Scripture, the right to violate God's law, which is just? Why would God permit government to violate His law, when God Himself will not pervert justice? Permitting two standards is inconsistent with God's nature.

In addition, if God permits a nation to create its own law, apart from justice and righteousness, then the basis for judging nations or the actions of rulers is eliminated. How can God tell a nation or government that it has the right to rule and whatever its rulers do is lawful, and then judge them for their actions? That makes no sense. The rulers would then be able to exercise authority using free will which cannot be judged.

These problems would make Scripture inconsistent with itself. Even Romans 13 is internally inconsistent if the passage is considered to be about government, rather than about the principles surrounding properly defined authority.

Following are the problems restated if authority is *wrongly* defined as *"the right and power to act"*:

1. Authority becomes second law
2. Authority becomes second standard
3. Authority negates law
4. Two standards are inconsistent with God's nature
5. Nations cannot be judged
6. Authority and Free Will become inconsistent
7. Scripture conflicts with itself under this line of reasoning
8. Romans 13 is inconsistent with itself and other Scripture

Authority is the permitted power to act. Actions taken with the force of authority will be judged by the standard of law. Authority is power and power is from production. Authority is distributed by God in creation based on production. Think about calves and corn. A transfer of labor and production is a transfer of authority. Properly delegated authority can be reclaimed at will. Central power can only be concentrated by theft. There are many authorities besides what we commonly call government.

The sun rises and the rain falls on the evil and the good, but those who are blessed by God are most productive. If they will hold onto what they produce, there will be a healthy balance of power in society.

1. Authority is best defined as "the permitted power to act."
2. Authority may be used for good or evil.
3. Authority has limits or boundaries.
4. Authority is hierarchical and orderly.
5. Authority may be delegated.
6. Authority is singular over a jurisdiction.
7. Authority is knit into property and production.
8. Authority functions as a power distribution system.
9. Authority used properly under law is edifying.
10. Authority may be combined or aggregated unlawfully.
11. Authority that is properly delegated can be reclaimed at will.
12. Authority has characteristics that are dynamic and fluctuate over time.
13. Authority has ingredients that are difficult to identify and discuss.
14. Authority can include bad ingredients that generally can be identified.

"The LORD will command the blessing upon you in your barns and in all that you put your hand to, and He will bless you in the land which the LORD your God gives you. "The LORD will establish you as a holy people to Himself, as He swore to you, if you keep the commandments of the LORD your God and walk in His ways. "So all the peoples of the earth will see that you are called by the name of the LORD, and they will be afraid of you. "The LORD will make you abound in prosperity, in the offspring of your body and in the offspring of your beast and in the produce of your ground, in the land which the LORD swore to your fathers to give you. "The LORD will open for you His good storehouse, the heavens, to give rain to your land in its season and to bless all the work of your hand; and you shall lend to many nations, but you shall not borrow. "The LORD will make you the head and not the tail, and you only will be above, and you will not be underneath, if you listen to the commandments of the LORD your God, which I charge you today, to observe them carefully, and do not turn aside from any of the words which I command you today, to the right or to the left, to go after other gods to serve them." (Deuteronomy 28:8–14, NASB95)

So much could be written about all the ways Scripture backs up the ideas of authority, justice, law, production and prosperity, but that will have to be for another time.

6. Important Ideas

Restoration is out of reach of our mind.
Restoration is within the reach of our hand.

6.1 Truth Takes A Minute

To be an expert in details and current events is to be a slave of the propagandist. Master principle, teach others and restore liberty.

Some say we are too far gone as a nation to recover and prosper. One of the common arguments is that people don't know how to work anymore and that we have generations of people who have unknowingly been indoctrinated with false teaching and bad ideas.

I, on the other hand, am confident we can recover and prosper. The argument about work and sound thinking is valid in one sense and invalid in another.

Work Ethic

It is true that people generally don't know how to work these days. One of the reasons is quite simply that kids grow up in a ready-made, disposable, urban society. Few people are raised on the farm and few people are exposed to manufacturing or repair of any sort. We don't build the things we use, we buy them. When our things break, it is often cheaper to replace than repair. How can a person learn the basics of work when there is little work to do?

Then there is every generation's undying complaint, *"kids these days...,"* which is usually accompanied by the idea that kids are irresponsible and will not work. I consider the complaint to be misplaced for many reasons, two of which I will share here.

First, the kids are not the problem; we are. Our generations have either taken away or have not restored the opportunity for kids to work. How can we complain about our children not learning to work?

Second, when a proper work environment exists, the kids show that they are willing. Think about all the young people who work as waiters and waitresses. They are paid a small base salary and make their money tokens based on tips. They are paid well because they are accountable to serve well. Remember the Parable of the Prodigal Son? Tie behavior to results and good behavior usually comes in the end.

Lies Are A Burden

Now let's consider confused thinking which is brought about by false teaching and bad ideas. Whether you see error in our common thinking or not, please indulge the following argument as a possibility.

The focus here is not on what is taught, but on the kind of system required to teach things that are false.

Parents teach kids many things. For example, we teach our children that one lie leads to another. A person who tells a lie eventually forgets who he told which story, which leads to being found out. What parents are essentially saying is that the liar has to control all access to all relevant information, which is much like creating a make-believe alternate reality. There is the truth about the thing and the liar's deceptive version of the thing. The truth is ever-present. The liar has to be certain that those being deceived only see the alternate reality, not the true reality. This is a lot of work and can be very expensive to maintain.

The false alternate reality has to be carefully monitored and maintained. This story has to be told over and over for as long as a person might be thinking about the lie. If the truth is recognized even once, then the whole story collapses and cannot be rebuilt.

High Cost of Infrastructure

With that backdrop, let's think about the K-12 and college education system[104], along with government, foundations and the media.

Those who look at our idea-shaping system as a problem, believing that false teaching and bad ideas prevail, often despair because they see the enormous system and vast resources which are dedicated to promoting unsound thinking. The natural response is to imagine a *competing system* that teaches the "right" ideas. This is a task that requires the buy-in of at least hundreds of thousands of people for generations, during which time these people and organizations spend decades taking over the systems that are causing us problems. There are many things objectively wrong with this approach.

First, the people who have the wealth to accomplish this are dependent on the false teaching and bad ideas for their gain, much like our ship owner in *A Ship Story*. They will never follow through with reshaping the system. The plan will collapse along the way, every time.

Second, the problem is not properly understood. This "equal resource" and "long-term" view looks at effects, not causes. *It places truth and untruth in the same category.*

Even one individual expends significant resources, especially time and energy, in order to create and maintain an artificial alternate reality

104 Regarding education, I strongly encourage the reader to read The Abolition of Man by C.S. Lewis

regarding a small thing that people will forget in a short time. How much more planning, resources and energy are necessary to progressively and perpetually deceive an entire society?

Truth Is A Foundation

On the other hand, when a person always endeavors to tell the truth, there is no energy spent remembering who has been told which story. In addition, rather than spending time and energy controlling access to information to maintain the lie, the truth-teller is able to point to reality and invite whoever to dig in to whatever, whenever. In other words, the truth-teller is cooperating with and depending on reality. It is a very inexpensive proposition.

In addition, a sophisticated group of people can expend tremendous resources constructing an elaborate lie, only to see the whole thing collapse by a revealing, innocently made remark from a five year old running through the kitchen after bedtime. Millions of dollars, elaborate schemes and years of work can be undone with simple truth.

So here is the category mistake. Untruth requires tremendous, continuous resource allocation to create and maintain an alternate reality and control access to information, so that truth on the topic is not revealed. Truth has no such overhead. Truth is inexpensive to support because reality is relied on and access to information is unrestricted.

"When there are many words, transgression is unavoidable, But he who restrains his lips is wise." (Proverbs 10:19, NASB95)

Truth is accessible and clear. Our understanding of truth is reinforced by reality. Untruth requires excuses, distractions, diversions, deceptions, demands, certifications, peer pressure and other forceful human or social intervention.

Earth-shaking, life-changing truth can be communicated in a moment and, like a seed planted in good soil, will bear good fruit.

The Natural Order Classroom

There are many people today who are lazy and will not work. We could build special schools all across the country to teach these people, young and old, how to work and be decent in their behavior. This would be a very expensive proposition. It would cost hundreds of millions of dollars each year to build and maintain such a network of education to address the problem of the unwilling worker.

It would take years of teaching and testing to determine the success rate of the program, which would, of course, be designed to keep the program going. Reported results would always be in doubt.

On the other hand, we could introduce a system based on 2 Thessalonians 3:10 which says in part *"if anyone is unwilling to work, he is not to eat, either."* This classroom is inexpensive, very fast and has a high success rate. Students who fail starve and die. Those who pass the class remain among the rest of the living.

The natural classroom is what the Prodigal Son was exposed to. As a matter of fact, that is the world we have been given to teach us the truth about things. When we take people out of the natural classroom, we condemn them to decay and brokenness.

Competing False Systems

Without equal resources, one system of untruth is powerless against another system of untruth. If a group of people decided to change the particular deception being propagated through a society, they would indeed require tremendous resources and *decades* to replace the old lie with the new one.

But truth only takes a minute.

Amazing Reality

So here is what we have observed. Propaganda and lies are dependent on other lies, which are all expensive and time consuming to maintain. Everything that is true has to be lied about in order to create and maintain a false alternate reality. Developing a lie has to be done slowly over time in order to succeed. The artificial classroom is not only time consuming and expensive, but very ineffective. Lies can compete successfully against other lies, but not against truth.

Since lies are so expensive and are mostly intended to steal, the false systems are built on lies and theft. In fact, a producer cannot afford to work and maintain a lie. Besides, producers tend to have an appreciation for truth, having spent considerable time in the Natural Classroom.

The only way to gather enough resources to build and maintain a lie is to steal from producers. There is no other source. The primary tools for stealing from producers are armies, authority, money and law.

Armies comprised of men who are producers protecting their property tend to be peaceful. Armies built by plundering producers are engineered for war.

Authority is falsely considered to be the right to rule.

Money is a system of plunder based on differing weights and measures.

Unjust law is used to plunder and control producers.

Our understanding of authority is based on a lie. Our understanding of law is based on a lie. Law is subject to righteousness and authority is subject to law.

Therefore, if we make our laws subject to righteousness and make actions of authority subject to law, then we will necessarily eliminate money, all forms of differing weights and measures and all forms of theft.

When that happens, the resources required to build and sustain the lies that are flowing through social institutions will be gone nearly overnight. Instead of a housing bust, there will be a propaganda bust. There will be an institutional bust. A plunder bust. An elite power structure bust. Almost overnight these things will disappear.

At the same time, we will be putting the Natural Classroom in place, which is FREE. Dominion over the earth was given to man by God. We already have the classroom. Operating the classroom is FREE. If we will abide by the law, *No Stealing,* and we *Know Stealing* when we see it, power will be distributed according to stewardship, production and relationships. There is no need for any one person to judge another person's progress in the system, except as a direct report under properly distributed authority. The Natural Order will judge. According to the Bible, God Himself gets involved and a man reaps what he sows.

Truth is low-cost because it is freely available. Truth is a fast teacher because everything reinforces every other thing when we build our understanding based on truth. Truth is consistent and effective. The Natural Classroom and Natural Order are effective disciplinarians, if people don't interfere in the process.

Lies that cost billions of dollars and take decades to build with theft, war and plunder can be replaced by truth and justice in a moment.

Lies take decades. Truth takes a minute.

6.2 Energy and Liberty

Even though a farmer produces a product that has a high demand in the market, his profits are confiscated by distorting market values through a complex web of law, regulation, fiscal policy and monetary policy. In other words, if a farmer's prices can be kept low and his cost of inputs high, then his profits go to others based on allocations of value on paper within the money system.

Since power comes from production and oppressive power comes from control of production, then anything that can be used to meter or limit production is valuable to the oppressors. We do much of our work with machines. Therefore production can be metered to a great degree by metering and controlling energy.

There are at least four ways to meter energy in order to meter, manage, limit or increase production.

One method is to use the monetary system along with law, regulation and military power to influence the relative value of energy to other goods and services.

A second method, which is also used to influence the first, is to limit access to available energy sources. For example, preventing oil drilling or the use of nuclear power is a way to limit access to energy sources, which limits overall production and increases the relative cost of energy as compared to other goods and services.

An example of a third method is to block the production, importation or sale of low cost, highly fuel-efficient automobiles into the United States through tariffs and regulation.

A fourth method is to undermine the research and development of alternate energy technologies. Simply interfering with the production of high fuel efficiency automobiles in the United States is a great example of this. The importance of energy in our ability to produce should cause energy research to rank high in investment compared to all other kinds of research.

Because agriculture, mining and manufacturing are under assault in the United States, we can know for certain that the intentional undermining of productive capacity is an explicit goal of those non-producers who control the means and resources to act through legal plunder. This is confirmed because a farmer has to sell his land to retire and a farmer's son cannot afford buy land and farm it. The equity has been leached out of the family food production enterprise. Similarly manufacturing businesses are not profiting. They are either moving offshore, just holding on, shutting down or going bankrupt. This also proves that productive business that produce real goods and services are under assault in the USA.

Because we know production is being suppressed and essentially outlawed, and because production in this age depends on energy, we can be certain that energy is controlled to control people, liberty, production and prosperity. There is a movement that has been around for decades which has a goal of replacing money with energy credits. This would be a disaster for individual liberty.

Another big tool in the energy control bag is global warming. This whole climate change propaganda machine is based on lies and designed to create an environment where popular opinion will support government action that is in direct contradiction to what is best for the people whose opinion is being managed. Global warming is about controlling access to natural resources and energy. It is all about control of production, because power comes from production. Authority is distributed through production. In order for government to possess overwhelming power, people must be prevented from being productive. A productive nation is extremely difficult to conquer. A non-productive nation will barely put up a fight because they are hungry and have no resources to equip an army.

Remember that when production ceases, goods and services begin to be depleted. All people depend on production. The ruling class is small in number and they have the authority, meaning power, to force many to produce a little so that the elite few will have abundance. At the same time, the many are depleting their resources because the producers have been prevented from producing. This causes a shift in the balance of power in favor of the ruling class who can overcome the many with force, because the many are fighting on two fronts. On one side the producers face disappearing resources, goods and services, food and fiber, means of production, etc. Producers are working to survive and keep their businesses afloat. On the other side, they face the force of arms possessed by a ruling class that is fat because the producers feed them.

Another important point about energy and production is that modern machines and technology make people so productive that wasting enough to make a productive nation weak is extremely difficult. This is the reason for the welfare and warfare state created by the managers of the US government. The ruling class limits our access to energy and natural resources, which limits our ability to produce. As many people as possible are encouraged not to work, while the output of those who keep working is wasted faster than they can produce. This is why we are in debt and the reason there is no hint of slowing down the spending, war or waste. The USA is being conquered with our own resources and complicity from within. The ruling class will still be in control, but the idea is for the USA to be a vassal of a global empire.

That only works if we are weak. We will only be weak if Americans are taught not to work or are prevented from having access to the natural resources with which to work.

Always remember that any discussion of energy is also a discussion of liberty.

6.3 Information Age

The PEN and the PRESS

Young Genius walked out by the mountain and streams,
Entranced by the power of his own pleasant dreams,
Till the silent – the wayward – the wandering thing
Found a plume that had fallen from a passing bird's wing,
Exulting and proud, like a boy at his play,
He bore the new prize to his dwelling away,
He gazed for a while on its beauties, and then
He cut it, and shaped it, and called it – a PEN.

But its magical use he discovered not yet,
Till he dipp'd its bright lips in a fountain of jet;
And O! What a glorious thing it became,
For it spoke to the world in a language of flame;
While its master wrote on, like a being inspired,
Till the hearts of the millions were melted or fired; -
It came as a boon and a blessing to men,
The peaceful – the pure – the victorious PEN!

Young Genius went forth on his rambles once more,
The vast sunless caverns of earth to explore!
He searched the rude rock, and with rapture he found
A substance unknown, which he brought from the ground;
He fused it with fire, and rejoiced in the change,
As he molded the ore into characters strange,
Till his thoughts and his efforts were crown'd with success;
For an engine uprose, and he call'd it – the PRESS.

The Pen and the Press, blest alliance! combin'd
To soften the heart and enlighten the mind;
For that to the treasures of knowledge gave birth,
And this sent them forth to the ends of the earth;

Their battles for truth were triumphant indeed,
And the rod of the tyrant was snapp'd like a reed;
They were made to exalt us – to teach us to bless
Those invincible brothers – the PEN and the PRESS[105]

Edmund Burke (1729-1797) was an Irish elected official serving in the British House of Commons. Burke became an influential thought leader by writing broadly into an information vacuum. At a time when people were usually left in the dark, Burke published speeches and other writings which informed the people about certain actions of government. For example, Burke was a vocal supporter of the cause of the American Revolutionaries.

Edmund Burke published papers where there were none, and the people received vital information that was otherwise unavailable.

Today we have just the opposite problem. We live in the information age where people are flooded with information. The result is that people are unable to receive vital information because it is lost in a flood of trivial information.

In the days of Edmund Burke the ruling class simply agreed together to be silent. Today the ruling class controls information in part by flooding us with entertainment, propaganda, trivia, misguided teaching and worthless news.

Today the task of conveying true and useful information involves much more than simply publishing it.

The first great challenge in the information age is to find the ancient paths and foundational truth that are buried under the rubble of institutions, education, propaganda and entertainment. The second great task is to focus foundational knowledge like a laser which will penetrate the barrier of trivia, entertainment and diversion, so that people may again receive vital information that is otherwise lost.

Fortunately, wisdom, knowledge and understanding are capable of filtering out most of the noise, propaganda and lies which flood our information, entertainment and education systems. Liberty will never have a louder voice, brighter colors or a bigger foot print than the institutional media, but liberty can take away their audience by education. The more one learns about the history and nature of systems of plunder, the dumber the media and pundits look.

---

105 Sanders, Charles W. and Joshua C. Sanders, A.M., *Sanders' Series The School Reader, Fifth Book*, Ivison & Phinney, 321 Broadway, New York, 1855 p.85 Anonymous

"Buy truth, and do not sell it, Get wisdom and instruction and understanding." (Proverbs 23:23, NASB95)

6.4 Institutions

Any government that grows, eventually kills; first productivity, then wealth, then people.

There are good institutions in every category, but they are rare.

I define a corrupt institution as any organization whose survival depends on coercively receiving someone else's labor, property and production, usually for institutional self-preservation or in pursuit of legal plunder, particularly while effectively ignoring or working against the interest of those providing the resources.

A few examples are trade associations, cooperatives, religious associations, religious ministries, political groups, subsidized business, and of course government. When these institutions are funded through a chain of events that are dependent on plunder and deception, bad things happen.

Of course these institutions have member benefits or do some good things, but the benefits are often like buying a thousand dollar hamburger. It is a bad trade. Over time the institution becomes focused on itself, rather than those it was originally organized to serve.

Institutions Are Net Consumers

With rare exceptions, institutions are net consumers. Institutions depend on producers in order to survive. Within a social order that prevents stealing, if producers willingly and freely contribute resources to an institution, then that institution is valuable to society. If the survival of an institution depends on forcefully confiscating profits from production, then that institution is a parasite that is draining valuable life from the society.

Institutions Outlast Individuals

With rare exceptions, institutions outlast individuals.

Institutions which are part of the network of plunder in a society have *effectively* unlimited resources.

Since an offending institution is supported by the plunder of producers, when resources are transferred, there is a two to one power transfer between the institution and the producers who support it. In other words, because there is no exchange of production, the transfer of resources moves in one direction. For example, every time one unit of money is transferred from the producers to the institution, there is a relative change of two units. If there was an exchange of production, like corn for wheat, both parties would benefit. Without mutual benefit, why would anyone ever exchange one thing for another?[106]

Most often, one or only a few producers attempt to resist a particular institution at any one time, which means that through the institution the resources of many neutral producers are focused like a laser on one or a few resistant producers. For example, a farmer or manufacturer may be unwittingly helping crush his neighbor.

In addition, if producers lose their profits to plunder and are at risk of losing their capital, they are in no position to fight the institution. Even in an honest system of exchange, most of a producer's capital is tied up in his productive enterprise. In a costless money system, the producer's real property is subject to loss because he is out of balance on paper, in terms of the money system. A farmer will lose his farm because of ledger entries at the bank. Productive land, buildings and machines are wealth and capital. Ledger entries are not wealth or capital.

On the other hand, the institution's access to resources, in terms of the money system, is liquid, refreshed annually and not dependent on the *productive* thought or labor of those who operate and receive salaries from the institution.

If one million producers annually contribute $100 each to an institution, then the producer who resists is facing an opponent funded annually to the tune of $100 million dollars. The institution influences producers who do not yet see the problem. While producers are out producing, the institution gives gifts, hires lawyers, gains experience in using an unjust legal system, lobbies government for more resources and generally outlasts the producers who have the gall to complain about being plundered.

Since authority is power and power comes from production, institutions are able to easily overpower the *supposedly* insubordinate producers.

---

106 This is a great truth in economics. Exchange does not occur because two things are equal in value. It occurs based on what can be called a *double inequality of value.* From some combination of a variety of reasons, item A is more valuable to me and Item B is more valuable to you. I may give up a few bushels of corn, from the tons that I produce, in exchange for a few bushels from your tons of wheat. We *both* gain from the trade.

Institutions Force Producers To Fight Themselves

Because institutions are fueled by production confiscated from producers, producers are in effect forced to fight themselves. To draw a simple analogy, in World War II the United States was at war with Germany. Of course there were many other countries involved on the sides known as the Allies and the Axis, but for the sake of analogy we will focus on the United States and Germany.

Imagine if the United States was required to gear up engineering and manufacturing to supply military gear and soldiers for our own army, and also was required to do exactly the same thing for the German army.

Even worse, we would be required to multiply the relative strength of the enemy. For every one military resource we produced for ourselves, we would have to give ten resources to Germany.

It sounds dumb to supply the enemy at a rate of 2 to1 or 10 to 1, but that's what we do with most institutions. Who in their right mind would provide any resources to an enemy that was trying to establish or maintain a relationship based on force?

Institutional Conflict Breeds More Institutions

Resisting one institution with another institution is a worthless exercise. While resisting an institution with an opposing institution is effective, the end result is not an improvement.

Suppose *Institution B* is created to resist *Institution A*. The problem is that over the course of time producers go from *Institutional Oppressor A*, to both *Institutional Oppressors A and B*, and finally to *Institutional Oppressor B*. The process consumes their time, energy and resources in exchange for no improvement in their condition.

In other words, the situation goes from *bad* to *worse*, and then if you're lucky enough to defeat Institutional Oppressor A, in the end you just go back to *another version of bad* under Institutional Oppressor B. Institutions by their very nature engage in internal and external self-preservation at the expense of producers who unwillingly provide the resources for the institutions to exist. This is especially true because *the general systems of plunder depend on institutions* to control producers and keep the people fighting amongst themselves.

Institutions Are Defeated By Behavior

The most important thing to understand about institutions is this:

The only way to defeat unlawful plundering institutions is by individual *behavior*.

Let's identify flaws in the two typical ways in which we are trained to resist institutions.

The first method is to support an opposing institution, which, as mentioned previously, is a waste of time.

The second way is to encourage movements.

Movements absorb the energy of the particular individuals who are actively resisting because they are currently upset about some aspect of the systems of plunder and oppression to which they are being subjected.

Movements come and go because movements are *expensive,* and producers do not have the *time* or *energy* to stay involved in movements indefinitely. They have work to do. The producers who are upset with the plundering institutions are not supported by theft like the plundering institutions are, so these producers have to keep working.

It is worth noting there is the *artificial movement* that is externally sustained by institutions within the system of plunder. For example, the Soros Open Society Institute was one of the major contributors to the media campaign that was designed to play to an audience of 535, meaning the US Congress[107]. This was an *artificial movement* designed to project itself as a mass movement on the part of various voting constituencies which would influence congressmen to vote a certain way on a certain issue.

In this case, the *artificial movement* was populated by those who were deriving their livelihood from the system of plunder. Workers in the *artificial movement* were sustained by institutions and favored business whose resources are derived from plunder, based on differing weights and measures, which enable the manipulation of labor and property on paper.

Sustained Cultural Impact

But producers who are trying to protect their property rights have no such support. This next statement will seem very oversimplified, but it helps to explain why movements are not sustainable. The first order of business for a producer is to secure food, shelter and clothing for himself and those for whom he is responsible. Unless the movement will

107 http://www.renewamerica.com/analysis/vernon/061002 Will George Soros rule America (with a little help from his friends, McCain-Feingold)?

put food in the stomach, a roof over the head and a shirt on the back, the movement is not sustainable.

The only way for anything to have a sustainable, long-term impact on society is for the thing to be tied to the stomach. There are two pieces to this puzzle.

The first piece is required and will always be present in every society. It is quite simply some level of production. A society that defends individual life, liberty and property will be highly productive, which leads to abundance and prosperity. A society that is highly oppressed will produce what it can under adverse conditions. The greater the oppression; the greater the poverty, disease, hunger and death.

The first puzzle piece, noted above, is about work that leads directly to some level of production. The second puzzle piece is not production in a direct, tangible sense.

The second puzzle piece secures the ability to produce without interfering with the ability to produce.

This is different from a *movement*, which is expensive, time consuming and takes people away from their productive work. To overcome the corruption and plunder of institutions, we need a tool that lets us keep working so that we are able to continue producing. Otherwise resistance leads to our poverty, not liberty and prosperity. Finally, this tool must also be inexpensive and easy to use.

It may sound like the tool I am describing is too good to be true, but it is not. What I am describing is a collection of behaviors which are driven and shaped by belief, which is founded on truth.

If, as a community of free people, we are all willing to actively *confront* stealing in all forms, at all times, and we are willing to set a standard that says if anyone is not willing to work then he is not to eat, we will completely separate the connection between the producer and the stomach of those who plunder.

Think of separating the connection between the producer and the stomach of the plunderer with this allegory. Suppose you were king of the United States and you called in the head of the Internal Revenue Service (IRS) to give him new powers. You inform him that the IRS may use any resources, any new systems, any laws, police force or any other thing they desired without limits, except one. No person who works for or supports the tax collection, investigation or any other aspect of the IRS work, directly or indirectly, is allowed to eat any food, drink any water or take any form of nutrition ever again, no exceptions.

By disconnecting the stomach from the plunder, there remains no one to do the plundering. They either quit and produce, or starve. Either way, the IRS is no longer a problem. This is a picture of what happens when stealing is outlawed. No honest system of funding a government that defends individual life, liberty and property depends on theft. Without theft there remains a balance of power in society, which is a balance of authority, which is distributed based on production.

I guarantee that if free people will stand together and say *"No more!"* the institutions will try to regain their position by force. The thieves and their minions will use all manner of propaganda, violence, force, and threats of impending disaster to frighten people into submission. I would expect what are sometimes called false flag operations. But if producers know the truth about how the world really works and are committed to liberty and righteous law, the thieves will not succeed. The thieves will be overcome.

Once the thieves understand that the producers will stand together on the principle that the individual has the right to his own life, liberty and property, then they will become producers, or they will perish.

According to the Bible, God has given able-bodied people the right to choose to work and eat or not work and die. Far be it from me to deprive them of their God-given right to choose life or death.

6.5 Media

We have a problem with the media because it is controlled by those who control access to profits via the money system, and who therefore control rules, regulations and laws. This statement is not directed at any ethnic group or oriented around any conspiracy theory. This is a reality of the social and economic system to which we are subject. Consider the media in terms of the Two Social models and the non-producer's control of the means and resources to act.

The media will not advance ideas that threaten the systems of plunder to which the media and its supporters owe their profitable existence. This is true and should be expected based on the combination of theft and human nature.

Thomas Jefferson is quoted as saying something along the lines that he didn't read the newspaper because he would rather be uninformed than misinformed. I can't explain why, but that has been my position from childhood. I did read a few newspaper articles during my state senate race in 2010, but otherwise I can count on one hand the other articles I have read in a newspaper.

I rarely watch television and don't subscribe to any service that includes the major news networks. I don't watch the news or follow it on the Internet, unless a topic catches my attention via email or conversation.

The news media has no vested interest in informing people of the things that increase personal liberty and security. Important information is regularly suppressed. A notable current example is the clear message of liberty and overall presidential campaign of Ron Paul. Congressman Ron Paul tells the truth and has tremendous support across the country, but the media ignores him and think their own actions are funny.

Remember that if the truth about our system is commonly known, the stealing will end. The stealing is required for the media and its supporters to remain in power. There is no way that the media will tell people the truth about things that matter.

Henry Kissinger wrote a book that I read many years ago called *Diplomacy.* Either in that book or from that starting point I came across the idea of *foreign availability*. As I recall, the idea is when an enemy will definitely have access to certain technology, your nation should be the supplier for at least two reasons. First, your nation will know the technology because your citizens or government produced it, which is an advantage in geopolitical maneuvering and war. Second, if there are profits to be made, it is better to make them than to leave the business to someone else, provided the enemy will gain access to the technology with or without your nation doing the work.

This same thinking about *foreign availability* is employed by the media. If those who control the media know that the people will have access to certain information anyway, then the media must be the supplier and must have credibility on the material in order to shape conventional thought on the subject matter. In other words, if people know a certain set of facts, the media must admit to those facts or lose all credibility.

The goal of the media after admitting the facts is to recast the information to lead people away from truth. This is accomplished in a variety of ways based on a keen understanding of human nature. Common tools for the deceptive purpose are entertainment, ridicule, complex explanations, diversions from the real issue, focus on effects or generally anything to cause people to waste time, waste energy, fight each other or do anything except learn about the root causes of the problems we face.

Much more could be said and these comments are no more than a rough outline to indicate that the media is a problem which must be understood and addressed. I concluded years ago that the solution is education. Producers will never have a bigger footprint, brighter colors or a louder voice than the media. We will never be able to beat them at their game of confusion and misdirection by opposing the media institutions with other media institutions. As explained in the chapter on Institutions, the proper way to defeat institutions is with behaviors that are driven and shaped by belief, which is founded on truth. To know truth requires education.

We cannot be stronger than the media by using other media, but we don't need to be. Producers provide the resources that the media depends on for survival. We can educate their current audience, in which case that audience will disappear. An audience educated in the truth about money and production will either mock mainstream media, or turn away in disgust. More importantly, the people will know how to defend individual life, liberty and property, and that is the only thing that will put the media in its place.

Media companies in a society that makes plunder and stealing illegal will have producers for subscribers. Since the media will not be supported by a system of plunder, they will have to satisfy their subscribers or go out of business. Real producers respect private property and truth. Our media will again serve the public good by reporting things of substance and shedding light on the tiny little sprouts of corruption that always come up, so that we can crush and burn that weed while it is small.

6.6 Moral Law

I am going to attempt to make a point about government, law and morality by choosing a divisive issue. Since the issue is likely to get a person's dander up, it should work well as an example.

Americans live in a country with over 300 million people having a variety of different worldviews. There are various issues that divide public opinion. For example, some people think that it should be legal to grow, sell and use marijuana. Others are completely opposed to marijuana and believe that it should be illegal. I am not writing this chapter to support or oppose either view. Instead, I want to consider who has the right to make the decision about marijuana.

The first step is to introduce a new term to go alongside of legal and illegal. The new term is *silent*. For an example of the concept of silent in law, we will look at the First Amendment to the US Constitution.

"Congress shall make no law respecting an establishment of religion, or prohibiting the free exercise thereof; or abridging the freedom of speech, or of the press; or the right of the people peaceably to assemble, and to petition the government for redress of grievances."[108]

The phrase "Congress shall make no law" is a way of saying that the government shall be silent on the issue. So the question is not simply should marijuana, for example, be legal or illegal, but we must also ask if it is something that the government should be *silent* about. Our Constitution already requires the government to be *silent* on religion, the freedom of speech, the freedom of the press and the right of the people to peaceably assemble and to petition the government for redress of grievances.

There is a very glaring and obvious question that we must ask at this point. If government law makes society better and government acts in our best interest, then why would we prevent government from making laws about these most important and precious rights?

Let's ask that question again. If we call on government to address moral issues and to uphold a high moral standard and bind people to good behavior for their own best interest and in the best interest of society as a whole, then why would we not ask government to pass good laws about religion, speech, the press, free association and the methods whereby we speak to government when we think the government may (imagine that…) have made an error?

For instance, the government could write a law that says each person may practice any religion he chooses, provided he does so peacefully. Or the government could write a law that says the press can report on anything they want to, as long as it is true. Those laws sound okay. Why not let government, who has our best interest in mind, write good laws for us on these subjects?

Obviously, we do not trust government to do the right thing with regard to these exceptionally important issues. Why would we trust government with anything else of value?

---

108 First Amendment, US Constitution

A Brief Tangent

At this point I want to make a distinction between government and The State. Because the following two issues are related, let's also consider the distinction between the Institutional church and the Biblical church. The way I would identify an Institutional church is by determining if the attributes and properties that most clearly define the church in question are its institutional attributes.

So here is our comparison:

The Institutional church is to the Biblical church as The State is to government.

Church

In the Institutional church, the people serve the leaders and the leaders rule by centralizing authority and controlling access to information.

In the Biblical church, the leaders serve the people and the leaders have limited influence due to a natural distribution of authority and free access to information.

The Institutional church acquires power through force and deception, hiding these activities under the cover of darkness.

The Biblical church ministers in the open through labor and teaching, which are conducted in the light.

State

The State is characterized by at least the following properties. It is always a monopoly of force organized for legal plunder and serves the purpose of enriching the few at the expense of the many. The State rules by centralizing authority and controlling access to information. The State acquires power through force and deception, hiding these activities under the cover of darkness.

Government, on the other hand, administers just law, based on natural law, and defends the life, liberty and property of the individual. Government leaders serve the people and the leaders have limited influence due to a natural distribution of authority and free access to information.

According to the Christian worldview there is no place for a theocracy today.

"Jesus answered, "My kingdom is not of this world. If My kingdom

were of this world, then My servants would be fighting so that I would not be handed over to the Jews; but as it is, My kingdom is not of this realm." (John 18:36, NASB95)

Romans 13:1-7 indicates that the religion or worldview of the ruler is not a criterion we can use to determine whether or not we should be subject to higher authorities, including government.

Silent

It should be obvious at this point that we are currently ruled by The State, which is lawless, not by lawful government. This has been the case since at least 1607 on this continent.

So now we have two questions. First, there is the question of whether The Lawless State has the moral understanding necessary to pass moral law. Second, there is the question of whether government that defends life, liberty and property would pass moral law.

Let's deal with the second question first. Let's consider something that no one would think to outlaw, like spinach. Actually, our lawless government is working toward outlawing home-grown vegetables, but we will ignore that attack on our life, liberty and property for the moment[109].

Do I have the right to eat spinach? I think we would all say yes.

Do I have the right to steal from you in order to buy spinach?
Do I have a right to steal your spinach?
Do I have a right to make you grow spinach for me?
Do I have a right to make you eat spinach?
Do I have a right to tell you what to do with your spinach?

No.

Do I have the right to eat spinach, even if I am violently allergic to spinach?

Yes.

We can see from considering spinach that the real issue is not the spinach. The issue is your rights and my rights. Lawful government would defend our right to choose what to do with our property, beginning with our own body, provided we did not infringe on the rights of others.

---

109 http://www.opencongress.org/bill/111-s510/show S.510 - FDA Food Safety Modernization Act

So if lawful government should and would be silent on religion, speech, the press, voluntary association, the redress of grievances, and would defend our private property rights in all cases except when we infringe on someone else's property rights, then how could The Unlawful State have any basis for passing law that infringes on any of these rights?

Consider a brief history of The State since the US Constitution was ratified.

The State sanctioned cruel slavery, robbed the farmers, merchants and blacksmiths that supported the Revolutionary war, went to war against its own people, is responsible for the Trail of Tears, led in eugenics research, sterilized Americans who were considered to be unfit, was cited by Hitler as an example in handling "undesirable people" because of the way The State handled the Indians, robbed the American people by debasing the currency, created three unlawful money systems including the unlawful Federal Reserve System, passed the unlawful income tax, instituted conscription in the form of the draft, stole land, broke treaties, still slaughters babies around the globe through abortion, drove production off of our soil with GATT and NAFTA, has destroyed the family farm through market manipulation, subsidy, income tax, regulation, and inheritance tax, is destroying our right to grow our own food through Senate Bill 510, has destroyed the health care market through regulation, with the latest destructive blow being Obama-care.

Those are just for instance...

So even if it were the role of government to pass a law about spinach or marijuana, and it is not, The State is absolutely and totally devoid of the moral sensibility required to decide what moral law should be passed or to enforce that law. The State is the most violent and egregious offender of natural law on the continent.

But The State *does* make law about these moral issues. What is the result?

Some say that moral law restrains immoral behavior. Some say that *as the laws have relaxed* the problems in society have gotten worse.

However, I believe that we have our cause and effect mixed up. It is the unlawful intervention of The State in society, particularly through education and media, which has degraded our culture, degraded the character of our people and degraded our morals.

The State secures and increases its relative power by making the people dependent, simple-minded and docile. The absence of moral law or presence of unjust law does not cause our morals to degrade. Government intervention in education and the media, government propaganda, the subsidizing of bad behavior, and penalizing of production all combine to degrade our morals.

It is our degraded morals that allow The State to make perverse and destructive laws, which control the minutest detail of good behavior, while making perverse and destructive behavior lawful.

In other words, a moral society would never permit The State to get away with trampling their rights, interfering with their production and stealing their property, all while at the same time making perverse behavior lawful. Only ***after*** morals have been undermined will increasingly perverse and destructive laws be incrementally accepted.

In the end, what we have are laws that control producers and protect non-producers in their destructive and perverse behaviors. The laws restrain producers while protecting systems of plunder. If lawful government were silent about behaviors and protected private property rights, then producers would be free to help who they wanted to help while those who engaged in destructive and perverse behavior would have to stand on their own two feet. If the moralist is truly correct about what is good and what is bad, those who engage in unfruitful behavior will go down the path of the prodigal son. Liars and thieves would reap what they sow.

When The State begins making moral law, the end result is the subsidy and encouragement of bad behavior combined with penalties on production and producers, which leads to sloth, violence, poverty, moral decay and ultimately the collapse of the society.

If marijuana and spinach were treated the same, then the profit motive would be the same for both. There would be the same number of people slaughtered in gang warfare over marijuana as there are today over spinach. If you want a simple proof, look at the passage of the 18th and 21st amendment and the history of violence between the dates of their passage.

Alcohol & Income Tax

Prohibition of alcohol did nothing to slow the flow of alcohol, but it did cause enough blood to flow that the 18th amendment was repealed by the 21st. The irony is that Christians in effect supported the income tax in exchange for prohibition, because the only way to get government to accept Prohibition was to have a replacement for the substantial revenue from the excise tax on alcohol. Later, Prohibition was repealed and we were left with the income tax, which has destroyed more property and lives than alcohol ever has.

Grapes have naturally occurring yeast on the skins which turn grape juice into wine. In other words, one of the purposes for which God created grapes was to produce wine. Therefore Christians condemned alcohol outright, which God created, while supporting a tax and money system that employs differing weights and measures, which are an abomination to God. It is hard to imagine a better example of backward thinking.

No Stealing

If a person were to steal to support their marijuana consumption, they would have to steal less if the price for marijuana was simply the cost of production plus whatever profit the market would bear. That means there will be less crime as a result of marijuana consumption. Not to mention the fact that a person could freely grow their own spinach and marijuana at home, just like people could make and drink alcohol at home, even during Prohibition.

Summary

So here is what we have discovered.

Lawful government would *defend* individual life, liberty and property.

The State is a monopoly of force designed to control people and steal property and production through the guise of legal plunder. The State *steals* individual life, liberty and property.

Building from our sin nature, the corruption of our character and morals as a society is the result of government intervention, not the result of bad law. Destructive and perverse law that controls the producer and forces him to subsidize bad behavior, is only permitted in a society that is sufficiently corrupt to tolerate the next incrementally bad law.

When The State has the gall to attempt writing moral law, the result is theft, violence, death, chaos, moral decay and destruction of property.

We can easily see why this is the necessary outcome if we understand the moral depravity and evil nature of The State, whose power comes from force, coercion and theft. There is no way an immoral overlord would have any reason or moral foundation to pass moral laws that are genuinely good for the society. The State always and only does those things which will increase its power and reward its minions.

If we truly want a moral society we must defend private property rights and punish stealing even when The State is the thief. We must permit producers to keep their own production, thereby rewarding production, investment and efficiency. Production leads to abundance which leads to prosperity. Those who are engaged in behaviors that are unfruitful and destructive will no longer be rewarded with the fruits stolen from the producers.

The State is unfit to write or enforce moral law because it owes its entire existence to violations of natural law and all of its power comes from a mixture of force, deception, theft, propaganda and lies. When we understand the nature of The State we no longer have to wonder why moral law harms more people and destroys more property than the behavior that is being outlawed ever could.

6.7 Absolute Truth?

This chapter will delight some and enrage others. Please, take this chapter with a grain of salt. The intent is to present a view of truth that I consider valuable, but which I also know will be rejected by some. I respect your right to believe and act according to your own thinking and will, up to the point of infringing on another person's right to do the same. Stated another way, please humor me...

We should expect conversations about truth to be emotionally charged and filled with excitement! After all, the central claim about truth is that truth is a standard by which actions may be judged to be right or wrong. Opportunities for conflict abound!

Even worse, sometimes people confuse truth claims and preferences, which adds fuel to the fire. For example, if something is a preference, yet I treat it as true, and demand you do the same thing, a conflict arises between individuals. Or conversely, if something is a truth claim and I treat it as a preference, I am trying to create a standard that the natural order of things will not ultimately support.

For example, if a person thinks that drinking alcohol is wrong and demands that you don't drink alcohol, he is treating his preference as a truth claim.

On the other hand, if a person thinks that murdering someone is a choice and demands the right for himself or others to murder, he is treating a truth claim as a preference.

It is not my intention to make a case for specific preferences or truth claims. Instead, I simply want to make some observations about *truth*.

One Truth, Two Preferences

Our culture suffers under a confusion called relativism, which claims that I have my truth and you have your truth. This argument falls apart very quickly under mild scrutiny.

In order for two people to each have a different truth, then truth must change. However, truth by its nature is unchanging, which means the different things that we each have cannot both be truth.

Instead what we are saying is I have my error and you have your error. Or perhaps we are saying I have my preference and you have your preference.

Absolute Truth

To help illustrate the point let's consider the idea of *absolute truth*. Some people say that there is no such thing as absolute truth. I would work to refute this argument, except that the job is already done. The argument refutes itself. Consider the following dialogue between Truth-Seeker and Worldly-Wise.

Truth-Seeker: Do you believe that there is such a thing as absolute truth?

Worldly-Wise: No.

Truth-Seeker: So there is no such thing as absolute truth?

Worldly-Wise: No, there is no such thing as absolute truth.

Truth-Seeker: So there is absolutely no absolute truth?

Worldly-Wise: Um… Well, I don't really know.

To say that there is absolutely no absolute truth is to make a statement of absolute truth.

In fact, truth is absolute by its nature.[110] There is a very interesting

---

110 A friend asked me about the case where a person answers "I don't know." This answer leads to the same outcome, but the path is a bit more obscured. Consider a) Aristotle's Correspondence Theory of Truth noted below, b) the first law of logic, A is A, and c) the fact that one must rely on truth to argue against truth. Mr I Don't

line of reasoning which follows the realization that *truth has identity.* But that will have to be addressed another time.

Since truth by its nature is absolute, then truth is unchanging. The nature of a thing cannot be changed. Otherwise the thing becomes something else.

Things that are true are not true because I think them. That which is true existed before me and will exist after me. I cannot think of a way to even imagine the beginning of truth. Truth doesn't get old. Therefore, there is no basis to claim that truth has a beginning or an end. I conclude truth is eternal. If truth is unchanging and eternal, then it cannot originate from within a person.

Since truth is unchanging and eternal, and since truth cannot originate from within me, truth is also external to me. Therefore, in order for me to have truth, I must *receive* it.

Can Truth Be Known?

This brings us to another obstacle in the discussion. Some people believe that truth exists, but it cannot be known. This is really a rather foolish argument, which also defeats itself in conversation. The person who claims that truth cannot be known will rely on truth to make their point that truth cannot be known. The argument goes something like this:

"I am telling you that it is true that truth cannot be known. Therefore, since truth cannot be known, whatever we think is true, is in fact and by definition false. This means that my thought that truth cannot be known is actually false. Therefore truth can be known."

C.S. Lewis makes a good point in The Funeral of a Great Myth[111] when he discusses the idea of reason as an absolute. Here he is referring to origin from evolution, which he calls a myth. Lewis writes "*But at the same time the Myth asks me to believe that reason is simply the unforeseen and unintended byproduct of mindless process at one stage of its endless aimless becoming. The content of the Myth thus knocks from under me the only ground on which I could possibly believe the Myth to be true. If my own mind is a product of the irrational - if what seem my clearest reasonings are only the way in which a creature conditioned as I*

Know is surrounded by and using the thing of which he is questioning the existence. Besides, a person who argues they don't know if absolute truth exists has no basis to question your understanding that it does exist. How would they know?

111 Lewis, C.S., Christian Reflections, The Funeral of a Great Myth, 1967 p. 89

am is bound to feel - how shall I trust my mind when it tells me about Evolution? They say in effect 'I will prove that what you call a proof is only the result of mental habits which result from heredity which results from biochemistry which results from physics.' But this is the same as saying: 'I will prove that proofs are irrational': more succinctly, 'I will prove that there are no proofs'"

I was recently in a discussion with an individual who said that he never likes to use the word always. So I asked him this question: "Is it always wrong to use always?" He understood immediately that he had refuted his own argument and we moved on to another point.

When a person claims that truth cannot be known, he must use truth claims to make his case. So even a person that vehemently denies that truth exists, must rely on truth to tell you about it.

The Claims of Scripture

People believe different things about the Bible. Some see it as just old literature, while others consider the Bible to be the inspired, inerrant, infallible and sufficient word of God. Regardless of how you see the Scriptures, there is a particular story told in the text.

On one hand, we can ask, "is it true that the story makes certain claims?," and on the other hand, we can ask "are the claims that the story makes true?"

For our purposes here we are only observing *the claims that the story makes.*

Exodus 3:14 is commonly understood as an indication that God is self-existent.

"God said to Moses, "I AM WHO I AM"; and He said, "Thus you shall say to the sons of Israel, 'I AM has sent me to you.' " (Exodus 3:14, NASB95)

We also find in Isaiah 57:15 that God lives forever, which is to say that he is eternal.

"For thus says the high and exalted One Who lives forever, whose name is Holy, "I dwell on a high and holy place, And also with the contrite and lowly of spirit In order to revive the spirit of the lowly And to revive the heart of the contrite." (Isaiah 57:15, NASB95)

We also see that that same eternal life is said to be in Christ Jesus.

"For the wages of sin is death, but the free gift of God is eternal life in Christ Jesus our Lord." (Romans 6:23, NASB95)

In Psalm 51:6 we see that truth can be known.

"Behold, You desire truth in the innermost being, And in the hidden part You will make me know wisdom." (Psalm 51:6, NASB95)

In Psalm 119:142 we see that God's law is truth. Since truth can be known, God's law can be known.

"Your righteousness is an everlasting righteousness, And Your law is truth." (Psalm 119:142, NASB95)

In Psalm 119:160 we see that the sum or totality of God's Word is truth. In John 14:6 Jesus says that He is the way, and the truth, and the life. In I John 5:20 we see again that God is also called the true God. In John 10:30 we see one of the indications of the Trinity when Jesus says that He and the Father are one.

"The sum of Your word is truth, And every one of Your righteous ordinances is everlasting." (Psalm 119:160, NASB95)

"Jesus said to him, "I am the way, and the truth, and the life; no one comes to the Father but through Me." (John 14:6, NASB95)

"And we know that the Son of God has come, and has given us understanding so that we may know Him who is true; and we are in Him who is true, in His Son Jesus Christ. This is the true God and eternal life." (1 John 5:20, NASB95)

"I and the Father are one." (John 10:30, NASB95)

In Colossians 2:6 we see that Christ Jesus must be received.

"Therefore as you have received Christ Jesus the Lord, so walk in Him," (Colossians 2:6, NASB95)

In 1 John 3:23 we see that in order to receive there is an element of belief.

"This is His commandment, that we believe in the name of His Son Jesus Christ, and love one another, just as He commanded us." (1 John 3:23, NASB95)

"that if you confess with your mouth Jesus as Lord, and believe in your heart that God raised Him from the dead, you will be saved;" (Romans 10:9, NASB95)

Finally we see that Scripture claims that Jesus Christ is the Word of God who was with God in the beginning and through Him all things came into being.

"In the beginning was the Word, and the Word was with God, and the Word was God. He was in the beginning with God. All things came into being through Him, and apart from Him nothing came into being that has come into being. In Him was life, and the life was the Light of men. The Light shines in the darkness, and the darkness did not comprehend it." (John 1:1–5, NASB95)

And again we see that God's words are truth.

"Now, O Lord GOD, You are God, and Your words are truth, and You have promised this good thing to Your servant." (2 Samuel 7:28, NASB95)

Truth is self-existent, eternal, can be understood, is not from within, must be received, must be believed, and must be accepted. These ideas correspond closely to Scriptural explanations of God and Salvation.

The Correspondence Theory of Truth

The Correspondence Theory of *Truth* postulated by Aristotle says that *"Truth is that which corresponds to reality."*

There is a reality that our thoughts and words cannot create, destroy or change. In order for us to think or say something true, the thing we think or say must rightly correspond to reality, otherwise our claim or belief is false.

Summary

Truth by its nature is absolute. The God of Scripture, as explained by Scripture, claims to be the truth. Even if we don't attempt to identify the source of truth, the *Correspondence Theory of Truth* effectively lays sufficient groundwork to judge some things as being objectively true or false. People cannot learn everything or remember everything they learn. Even so, there is truth and truth can be known.

6.8 The Truth About Property Tax

It is my belief that we can fund government without violating individual rights.

Property Tax

Property tax makes us Renters, not Owners.

What we call property tax, the Communist Manifesto calls rent. The first plank of the Communist Manifesto says there shall be: *"Abolition of property in land and the application of all rents of land to public purposes."*

If we study closely we find that property tax is really an indirect consumption tax. Let's think about how this works. What is the reason that government relies so heavily on property tax?

Government can associate the tax bill with the property. If you don't pay, you lose your property.

"Government is not reason. It is not eloquence. It is force. Like fire, government is a dangerous servant and a fearful master."
~ George Washington

Example:

Consider an elderly lady who is living on a fixed income with declining purchasing power. Each year the choice between food, energy (for heating and cooling), medication and property tax becomes more challenging.

There comes a time when she cannot afford everything and property tax is the first thing to go.

Our government, which is charged with defending the Life, Liberty and Property of Georgians, will take her property.

She will be moved to an assisted living home that she cannot afford, which means the taxpayers will pay the difference. The bill to taxpayers will be more each year than if we simply paid her property tax and let her keep her home.

What will happen to the property?

The government will sell the property on the courthouse steps. Someone who has the cash to purchase the land and pay the government rent, in the form of property tax, will now own the land. Otherwise, the government agency will purchase the land with new money created from nothing that transfers the cost to producers.

Where does the cash come from?

The cash for property tax will come from people who are active in the marketplace, especially in the centers of business like the larger cities.

So what have we really done?

1. We steal the home of an elderly lady or at least force her to sell her home against her will.
2. We spend more on professional services for her in an assisted living home each year than the tax bill.
3. The property is sold to an active business person at a discount - instant profit.
4. The business person's cash comes from business conducted in the larger cities where the consumption tax should be collected.
5. We have indirectly collected a consumption tax from that business person by selling the land at a discount to someone who can afford to pay the government rent in the form of property tax.

Why not simply collect a consumption tax to begin with and let the people keep their property?

To our shame, if there is anything government is good at, it is wealth redistribution.

We can use a consumption tax to fund our local governments without violating the rights of our citizens.

Tax Equity

Some will complain that sending taxes from populated counties to rural counties is unfair.

I do enjoy that conversation. If we are going to talk tax equity, can we discuss restoring the family homes and family farms that have been taken away and broken up by declining real prices for agricultural products, rising property tax burdens and the destructive death tax?

That tends to end the conversation about tax equity.

Simple First Step Solution

Our property tax bill is set by millage multiplied by the assessed value of the property. We need to add one more element.

We need to set a cap on the property tax remitted by declaring that no person's property tax remittance can exceed two percent of their after tax income.

Of course the government officials will say that will deprive them of tax revenue. But think about what these government officials are actually saying.

If grandma can't pay because she doesn't have enough cash, that is her problem, not the government's problem. Cough up the cash or give up the property. It doesn't matter that you and your family worked for a lifetime to pay for it.

The government gets their money and then grandma goes into a retirement home that costs the taxpayers more than if we simply found another way to cover her property tax.

Property tax is an indirect consumption tax engineered to transfer the means of production from individuals to government and favored business.

6.9 Marque and Reprisal

In the US Constitution, under Article 1, Section 8 the powers of Congress are named. Consider the following item:

To declare War, grant Letters of Marque and Reprisal, and make Rules concerning Captures on Land and Water;

I interpret a Letter of Marque and Reprisal to be:

Written authorization granted by a government to a private party, granting authority to go beyond the borders of that country, in order to retaliate against foreign enemies by killing or capturing individuals or taking plunder as compensation for damages. A proper use of this defensive power is clear with regard to the cause that engendered the reprisal, it is specific in its objective, and limited in the time, type and degree of retaliation.

Executive Power

There are two important ideas here.

First, a study of the debates during the founding makes it clear that the executive branch was never delegated the power to commit soldiers for any purpose, except to repel an imminent invasion.

Most of the founders rightly feared any delegation of war powers to the executive. They knew the damages and cost that would accompany the certain abuse of war powers vested in one individual. Unfortunately this power has been abused for most of US history.

One of the ways the US Constitution confirms the limit on war power is that the power to grant Letters of Marque and Reprisal are delegated to congress and ***not*** to the executive. If congress is delegated the power to declare war *and engage in actions which are short of war*, then there is no way to claim the president has the power to engage in war, except when under imminent threat of attack.

This is worth restating. If the constitution did not delegate the power to issue Letters of Marque and Reprisal to congress, then one could make a weak argument that the president has the power to do this smaller thing. However, this specific power is delegated to congress and is not delegated to the president.

Under the US Constitution, congress can declare war. This is an all-out commitment of troops and treasure to violent and deadly conflict with other peoples and nations. Clearly the US Constitution does not grant the president the power to declare war.

In addition, congress is given the power to grant Letters of Marque and Reprisal. The executive is not granted this or any like power.

Letters of Marque and Reprisal are acts short of war. If congress is delegated the power to take military action short of war, then there is yet another barrier between the executive and the commitment of the troops and treasure of the people of the United States to war or any military conflict.

Defending Life, Liberty and Property

The war on terror currently which is being waged against non-state actors should be executed through Letters of Marque and Reprisal or similar narrow, surgical assaults which employ US military assets.

This same approach should be used to eliminate any unlawful threat to the individual life, liberty and property of US citizens.

The other unsustainable thing the US government does is maintain troops and bases around the globe. Americans pay to maintain over 700 bases in at least 130 of the 190 or so[112] countries in the world. This is bad policy, unjust, unfriendly and unsustainable.

The US has eighteen Trident nuclear submarines, any ***one*** of which being capable of simultaneously destroying all the major cities in very large countries. So we need military bases all over the world, why?

The military industrial complex that Eisenhower talked about is plundering the American people at home and plundering others around the globe in the name of the American people.

---

112 The country count fluctuates over time and differs based on who is counting.

Letters of Marque and Reprisal

The following two bills are examples of attempts to get the US Congress to authorize the president to issue Letters of Marque and Reprisal in response to the attacks on September 11, 2001. These bills never became law.

In 2001

H.R.3076 — September 11 - Marque and Reprisal Act of 2001

HR 3076 IH
107th CONGRESS
1st Session

H. R. 3076
To authorize the President of the United States to issue letters of marque and reprisal with respect to certain acts of air piracy upon the United States on September 11, 2001, and other similar acts of war planned for the future.

IN THE HOUSE OF REPRESENTATIVES

October 10, 2001

Mr. PAUL introduced the following bill; which was referred to the Committee on International Relations

A BILL

To authorize the President of the United States to issue letters of marque and reprisal with respect to certain acts of air piracy upon the United States on September 11, 2001, and other similar acts of war planned for the future.

Be it enacted by the Senate and House of Representatives of the United States of America in Congress assembled,

SECTION 1. SHORT TITLE.

This Act may be cited as the `September 11 Marque and Reprisal Act of 2001'.
SEC. 2. FINDINGS.

The Congress finds the following:
(1) That the terrorist attacks on September 11, 2001 upon the United States were acts of air piracy contrary to the law of nations.

(2) That the terrorist attacks were acts of war perpetrated by enemy belligerents to destroy the sovereign independence of the United States of America contrary to the law of nations.

(3) That the perpetrators of the terrorist attacks were actively aided and abetted by a conspiracy involving one Osama bin Laden and others known and unknown, either knowingly and actively affiliated with a terrorist organization known as al Qaeda or knowingly and actively conspiring with Osama bin Laden and al Qaeda, both of whom are dedicated to the destruction of the United States of America as a sovereign and independent nation.

(4) That the al Qaeda conspiracy is a continuing one among Osama bin Laden, al Qaeda, and others known and unknown with plans to commit additional acts of air piracy and other similar acts of war upon the United States of America and her people.

(5) That the act of war committed on September 11, 2001, by the al Qaeda conspirators, and the other acts of war planned by the al Qaeda conspirators, are contrary to the law of nations.

(6) That under Article I, Section 8 of the United States Constitution, Congress has the power to grant letters of marque and reprisal to punish, deter, and prevent the piratical aggressions and depredations and other acts of war of the al Qaeda conspirators.

SEC. 3. AUTHORITY OF PRESIDENT.

(a) The President of the United States is authorized and requested to commission, under officially issued letters of marque and reprisal, so many of privately armed and equipped persons and entities as, in his judgment, the service may require, with suitable instructions to the leaders thereof, to employ all means reasonably necessary to seize outside the geographic boundaries of the United States and its territories the person and property of Osama bin Laden, of any al Qaeda co-conspirator, and of any conspirator with Osama bin Laden and al Qaeda who are responsible for the air piratical aggressions and depredations perpetrated upon the United States of America on September 11, 2001, and for any planned future air piratical aggressions and depredations or other acts of war upon the United States of America and her people.

(b) The President of the United States is authorized to place a money bounty, drawn in his discretion from the $40,000,000,000 appropriated on September 14, 2001, in the Emergency Supplemental Appropriations Act for Recovery from and Response to Terrorists Attacks on the United States or from private sources, for the capture, alive or dead, of Osama bin Laden or any other al Qaeda conspirator responsible for the act of air piracy upon the United States on September 11, 2001, under the authority of any letter of marque or reprisal issued under this Act.

(c) No letter of marque and reprisal shall be issued by the President without requiring the posting of a security bond in such amount as the President shall determine is sufficient to ensure that the letter be executed according to the terms and conditions thereof.

In 2007

110th CONGRESS
1st Session
H. R. 3216

To authorize the President to issue letters of marque and reprisal with respect to certain acts of air piracy upon the United States on September 11, 2001, and other similar acts of war planned for the future.

IN THE HOUSE OF REPRESENTATIVES

July 27, 2007

Mr. PAUL introduced the following bill; which was referred to the Committee on Foreign Affairs

A BILL

To authorize the President to issue letters of marque and reprisal with respect to certain acts of air piracy upon the United States on September 11, 2001, and other similar acts of war planned for the future.

Be it enacted by the Senate and House of Representatives of the United States of America in Congress assembled,

SECTION 1. SHORT TITLE.

This Act may be cited as the `Marque and Reprisal Act of 2007'.

SEC. 2. ISSUANCE OF LETTERS OF MARQUE AND REPRISAL.

The President of the United States is authorized and requested to commission, under officially issued letters of marque and reprisal, so many of privately armed and equipped persons and entities as, in his judgment, the service may require, with suitable instructions to the leaders thereof, to employ all means reasonably necessary to seize outside the geographic boundaries of the United States and its territories the person and property of Osama bin Laden, of any al Qaeda co-conspirator, and of any conspirator with Osama bin Laden and al Qaeda who are responsible for the air piratical aggressions and depredations perpetrated upon the United States of America on September 11, 2001, and for any planned future air piratical aggressions and depredations or other acts of war upon the United States of America and her people.

SEC. 3. SECURITY BOND REQUIRED.

No letter of marque and reprisal shall be issued by the President under this Act without requiring the posting of a security bond in such amount as the President shall determine is sufficient to ensure that the letter be executed according to the terms and conditions

Summary

The president does not have the authority to commit our troops to war and he does not have the authority to issue Letters of Marque and Reprisal.

Letters of Marque and Reprisal are effective methods of dealing with enemies of Liberty. At the end of the day, the enemy is the one who controls access to the means of production through theft.

If the enemy has to steal by force, free people can identify their enemy and choose to fight or submit. In the process, free people get to keep and use their resources for their side of the battle and the enemy has to find a way to confiscate necessary resources for his side of the battle. Production alone will not support armies. There must also be theft, because producers will not leave home to go kill other producers. They have work to do. They have homes already. What will they do with another one in some foreign land?

Only tyrants who feed soldiers with the fruits of the labor, property and production of producers will draft the sons and daughters of producers to go to war.

There will always be manipulation, hatred, wars, conflict and theft. However, the scale, scope and sustainability of tyranny and oppression are limited by defending individual life, liberty and property. This necessarily eliminates the use of money systems, because money systems are engineered to centralize power through control of production.

When we discover an enemy, we should notify him that we will not tolerate his pillaging, plunder, theft, murder, and disrespect of individual life, liberty and property. He may choose to stop or he will be stopped.

This is the purpose of rulers who are to bear the sword, as ministers of God for good to those who do good, and as an avenger to punish those who do evil, based on just law subject to righteousness.

A people should be strong in defense and just in their actions.

Only when people are faced with using their own lives and property to engage in war will wars be limited. When the tyrant can steal your property and then use it to provoke your neighbor to war, your blood and that of your children must be spilled to entertain him and satisfy his lust for power. We are ignorant and foolish if we permit this to continue.

6.10 Regulation

It is critical that we understand the true purpose of regulation. Propaganda says that regulation protects us from big bad business, but that is a lie. The easiest way to understand the purpose of regulation is to understand the following concept:

Regulation is cheaper and more profitable than competition.

First of all, can one really believe that large corporations who are paying billions to lobbyists are failing to meet their objectives? If what they were doing did not work, it would stop.

Second, a large corporation is already in a certain business and has economy of scale. "Regulatory burdens" are a line item on their balance sheets which would otherwise be replaced by decreased prices due to efficient competitors. Decreased prices or higher quality products from a competitor reduces the corporation's profits.

If a large corporation can prevent small companies from entering the market, then they are able to maintain higher prices on lower quality goods. Regulation is a barrier to entry for competitors.

Following is a blog post I wrote in November 2008 which makes the point through allegory.

Br'er Rabbit

The stories of Br'er Rabbit are said to trace back to Cherokee Indian myths. The stories illustrate types of behavior we observe in people.

In one story Br'er Fox has captured Br'er Rabbit with a Tar Baby as a trap.

The Tar Baby is a doll covered in sticky tar that Br'er Rabbit gets tangled up with. When Br'er Fox comes out of hiding to gloat over his capture of Br'er Rabbit, he begins thinking of the things he can do to Br'er Rabbit. The story includes a variety of different possibilities ranging from hanging the poor old rabbit to roasting him for dinner.

Now we get to the point of the story that interests us.

Caught in the tar trap, Br'er Rabbit says "You can roast me, hang me, skin me, do anything at all, but PLEASE don't throw me in the briar patch!"

Well the fox wants to do the worst thing he possibly can to this wily, aggravating old rabbit, so Br'er Fox throws Br'er Rabbit right into the briar patch. And then silence...

But soon Br'er Rabbit is seen sitting up the hill on a log, cleaning the sticky tar out of his fur and smiling.

"I was born and bred in the briar patch!" said the sly old rabbit.

Briar Patch and Government Regulation

We have a tendency to think of Government Regulation as being bad for big business because we believe regulations keep them in check. We are told regulations punish big business when they operate "unfairly."

Br'er Rabbit and Big Business

Br'er Rabbit was "bred and born; born and bred" in the briar patch.

The briar patch provided a home and protection to the rabbit and his ancestors.

Regulation provides a home and protection to Big Business and its ancestors.

Br'er Fox, do anything to Br'er Rabbit, but PLEASE don't throw me in the briar patch!

Br'er Citizen, do anything to Br'er Business, but PLEASE don't Regulate me!

Greed and Control

Remember that for large corporations, Regulation is CHEAPER and more PROFITABLE than Competition.

Regulation is a tool used by those at the top of the economic system to reward favored corporations and punish troublesome corporations.

Small business and the consumers pay the price for these elite games. Consumers are rewarded with higher prices and lower quality services. Small business finds increasingly large barriers to entry in the marketplace.

In the end, regulation protects and benefits large corporations and powerful people, while harming citizens. Both consumers and small business are harmed by the very regulation that benefits big business; which is exactly opposite to what we are told.

Regulation to big business is like Br'er Rabbit in the Briar Patch!

They love it!!!

It is their home.

It provides them the protection to which they owe their very existence.

6.11 Generational Knowledge

One of the most dangerous problems we face today is the loss of generational knowledge. Some things are learned through experience and maintained from generation to generation. This is particularly true with regard to the natural order and natural world. A simple example is agriculture.

There are many things children learn from parents and grandparents on the farm. These things take time to see, learn and practice. A farmer must become competent in a wide array of skills. As the young man matures, he will transitionally take over the role of production manager from the elders in his family.

As the world population grows, the worldwide dependence on efficient and quality agricultural production will continue to increase. Today agricultural production is at great risk because we are crushing the family farm, destroying wealth, forcefully commercializing agriculture, corrupting seed with GMO technology, permitting patents on living organisms, protecting corporations and assaulting small farms in courts, eliminating the manufacturing base necessary to support efficient agricultural practices, depleting the soil, producing food that is safe, but not healthy, and more.

It is true that society currently faces serious problems from an economic standpoint, but the problems are different than most people think. In some ways our problems are far more serious than realized, and in other ways the problems are simple deceptions which are easily overcome with knowledge.

Idle Resources

One of the problems we have is that our productive enterprises are sitting idle. Our machine shops, farms and manufacturing are under constant assault. Small business is being crushed, equity is being leached away, property is being confiscated, and regulation makes production nearly impossible.

The bright spot is that we can get them going again. Since people eat food and use things and producers exchange with producers, this must happen.

The dangerous weakness is decreasing generational knowledge, which I will return to in a moment.

Problems on Paper

Another bright spot is that other than our plants sitting idle and our loss of generational knowledge, most of our problems are on paper. Our debt, national and personal, is on paper. Our bank balances are on paper. Our obligations are on paper.

In a just court, if a con artist is discovered and convicted, whatever was owed to him based on his scam is no longer owed. In fact, he is now forced to pay restitution, to the extent that he has anything with which to pay. The productive people in the world have lost home and business as dupes in a scam that make Bernie Madoff look like a typical dime store shoplifter.

Differing weights and measures, which transfer wealth, are systematically employed through the money system. The money system, combined with purchased influence, is responsible for transferring wealth from producers to non-producers.

Non-producers value things that producers hold in contempt. When non-producers are put in charge of educating the population, there is no way they will call their own activities wrong. In fact, since theft and lies are clearly known to be wrong when noticed, the non-producers justify their actions by glorifying themselves and vilifying producers.

Have you ever noticed the non-producer's definition of greed? Greed to non-producers is when you want to keep your own labor and property.

And the non-producer's definition of generosity is giving away the fruits of the producer's labor.

Since the non-producer doesn't produce anything to give, and there is no other source besides production, the only thing they can give away is what someone else worked hard to produce, whether product or service.

So again, the bright spot is that most of our business problems which prevent producers from having *access* to real property to use in production is a *problem on paper*. We need to develop a plan to wipe the unlawful debt off the books by simply deleting ledger entries. The banks as we know them need to be closed, not bailed out.

The Setup

Western civilization has gotten itself into a really bad place, with the United States being a primary bad actor in the situation.

The reality of the world, which will always reassert itself, is that producers exchange with producers. All the talk of trade imbalance is deception and manipulation. There is no way to have a trade imbalance if people are trading real goods and services. In an honest system of exchange, no business owner will permit himself to be overextended with regard to customer credit. In an honest system of exchange, international trade is no more than an accumulation of these small transactions.

But we don't operate in an honest system of exchange. We have a money system that plunders producers and gives non-producers effectively unlimited access to the profits from production.

Therefore, we have exchanged paper for production during a phase in history when the US Dollar was acting as the world's reserve currency. We send paper dollars to other countries in exchange for labor, property and production.

The money managers know this practice is unsustainable, but then their goal is not for the exchange of paper for production to go on forever. The goal is to severely restrict or eliminate the productive capacity of western nations, particularly the US. A strong and prosperous nation and people is nearly impossible to subject.

Shutting down a factory or farm is a serious problem. However, taking away the knowledge and skill required to make them produce is a far worse problem and much more difficult to overcome.

The Effect

By planning and having the past forty years to exchange paper for production, which enables the people of the USA to acquire goods and services with worthless paper, a window of opportunity has been created to destroy generational knowledge. By driving a series of overlapping generations out of the manufacturing facility and off the farm, the transfer of knowledge and skill that takes a lifetime to develop is being lost.

Instead of people learning to care for durable goods, they learn to recycle disposable goods.

Instead of learning how to do productive labor and manage real property, they are sent to college in droves, thereby increasing debt and loading the market with generic diplomas having no additional earning potential. The jobs that students were supposed to get are going away, since, temporally speaking, production will always be the source of wealth and security for a nation.

The jobs of previous generations of students were supposed to lead to greater prosperity. They were promised reliable savings, retirement and wealth. But that was just an illusion on paper.

Instead of honoring production, which has to occur if people continue to eat food and use things, we vilify producers and honor those who either play or acquire wealth through systems of plunder.

Restoration

If those who love liberty get our government back under control and return to an honest system of exchange, we will face false flag[113] attacks from the centuries old cadre of thieves, our systems of production must be restored, genetically modified organisms must be purged from our soil and crops, and generational knowledge must be reclaimed. The US is in an excellent position to restore what has been lost.

If anyone wants to complain about the bad shape we are in, have them think about rebuilding after a season of burning heretics at the stake, Stalin's Russia and the slaughter of 20 million Russians, Hitler's Germany and the Holocaust, Pol Pot's Khmer Rouge and the killing fields of Cambodia where over 20% of the population was killed, think about war torn Europe... Then be thankful for the opportunity we have to restore liberty and production.

We have technology and teaching tools that will transform western civilization for the good if we use these tools to build and not to destroy. We can prove that knowing the truth about money and production is necessary to sustain a free and prosperous society. I personally believe we must also honor God and seek His favor.

We must learn again how to produce food and things. One of our most precious natural resources is the knowledge possessed by our older generation. Honor them by learning from them so that you too can help preserve and pass along precious generational knowledge.

---

113 False Flag operations are covert actions by one group designed to deceive the public so that the operations appear to be carried out by some other group.

6.12 Borrowed Credibility

One of the most dangerous manipulations of government and other organizations is *borrowed credibility*. There are many subversive organizations having a series of inner circles whose primary objectives run contrary to the interests of each successive outer circle. The outer circle includes you. The inner circles are employees and favored members of the organization.

Think of a bulls-eye target with a center dot and a series of larger rings. Each circle has a relationship with its neighboring circles. The greatest power is held at the center.

In some cases the inner circle is populated by those who founded the organization. More often, an organization is started by individuals with good intent, but over time the organization is captured through large donations, attrition or management by professional bureaucrats.

The objective of subversive organizations may range from simply keeping the gravy train rolling, to plans involving decades, centuries and geopolitical power structures.

Organizations are built to centralize power, in some cases for good, and other times for evil. Since power comes from production, to have great power it is necessary for the organization to have access to resources from many producers. The solution is concentric circles.

Each circle has a relationship with its own inner and outer circle. Influence is exercised by elevating people through the system slowly, placing just enough bridging individuals in key positions to transfer messages and credibility. There is a great deal of manipulative psychology that is brought to bear on people in this way.

In addition, the farther the circles are from the center, the less power the individuals and circles have, and the more wealth and power they are responsible for supplying to the organization.

Power comes from control of production and production is limited by head-count and machinery. Therefore, a large number of people do the work, and a small number of people control the direction and use of the profits, otherwise known as the means and resources to act.

In order to control resources, the organization must control individuals. Isolated and laser focused threats of harm or loss to a small number of individuals will cause them to radiate the desired message out through the circles.

The threat of loss can be in the form of job, recognition, sweet deals, political office, etc. The threat of harm can be physical, peer pressure, black balling, legal pressures, financial pressures, etc.

The next key tool is the ability to sway and direct public opinion. This is where *borrowed credibility* works its magic.

The organization will do some good thing for a family, school, community, etc.

The organization will give out awards and accolades to outer circle individuals.

The organization will have stated goals that are positive and emotionally satisfying.

Onlookers see the organization through these other people and actions. What is seen is like a whitewashed tomb. The good people and the (stolen) gifts are the paint.

At the same time, the organization is run or controlled by people who understand power structures and long-term thinking. These people know they can get away with saying one thing, while doing another. Because people farthest from the center have the least knowledge of the real tools of power, the scheme works. Remember the quote from Keynes?

."..The process engages all the hidden forces of economic law on the side of destruction, and does it in a manner which not one man in a million is able to diagnose."

The Economic Consequences of the Peace, John Maynard Keynes, 1919

And one of the Rothschild brothers?

"The few who understand the system, will either be so interested in its profits, or so dependent on its favors that there will be no opposition from that class. The great body of people, mentally incapable of comprehending the tremendous advantages will bear its burden without complaint."

Rothschild Brothers of London in a private letter

Generally speaking, people don't understand how violation of basic principles will lead to the destruction of a free society. This same lack of knowledge empowers subversive organizations.

Borrowed credibility works something like this:

"I heard that such and such organization was bad, but Uncle Joe and Mr. Smith are part of the organization and they are fine, upstanding members of the community. They would never be part of something like that."

Or:

"I heard that such and such organization was bad, but they just gave a thousand dollars to the school and the homeless shelter. They can't be all bad."

In the first case, credibility is borrowed by using the good name of the people in the outer circles. The organization gets the benefit of the hard earned good name that people know, and is left unharmed by the theft and pillaging people are trained to not see.

In the second case, credibility is borrowed by giving away resources that have been coerced and stolen from producers. The organization gets credit for giving away what it did not produce.

The Point

Be careful to whom you lend your good name.

Watch out for organizations who want to honor you, so that they can spend your credibility for purposes that are subversive.

Don't give organizations the credit for the life work and good name of its members. Assign to the organization the name that it has earned, good or bad.

Don't help the organizations that are tearing apart free societies by lending them your name.

"A good name is to be more desired than great wealth, Favor is better than silver and gold." (Proverbs 22:1, NASB95)

7. Solutions

Said the father to his son,
"I gave you liberty. Have you secured it for your sons and daughters?"
Said the son to his father,
"No, I just used it for me."

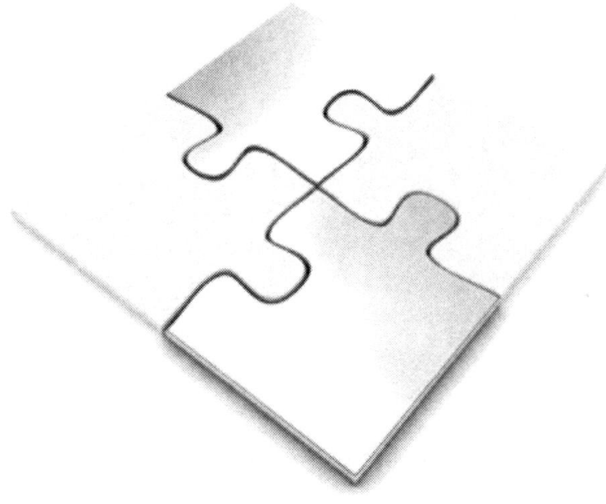

7.1 HB3 Constitutional Tender

Following is the testimony I gave regarding sound money. The setting was a State of Georgia, House of Representatives, Banks and Banking Committee, Financial Institutions & Services Subcommittee.

I have included this material because it is an example of specific state level legislative action that can help restore our republic and move us toward a healthy balance of power in society. Please become informed about the details of this and other similar legislation at the following website:

http://constitutionaltender.com/

In addition, this is an excellent example of good Christian men who apparently don't understand the effects of what they are doing or why their actions violate just law.

I should mention that I have very good friends who currently or previously worked in the banking business, including my wife. They are my friends and family whom I love and respect. However, they are not the standard by which right and wrong are to be judged. The banking business doesn't produce the things people eat and use. It only helps transfer wealth, which ultimately destroys any free society. That reality doesn't change simply because I have friends and family associated with banking.

My Testimony - HB3 Constitutional Tender Act

The video of this can be found at:

http://blog.soundmoneycafe.com/2011/03/video-coley-testimony-hb3.html

Coverdell Legislative Office Building (CLOB)
18 Capitol Square SW Atlanta, GA 30334
Atlanta, GA

Monday, March 7, 2011 • 9:00am – 12:00pm

Good morning. My name is Shane Coley.

I have studied history and economics extensively. I was raised in the cattle business, I can operate or rebuild heavy equipment and I am a professional software architect. I am self-employed. I was recently a candidate for state Senate in the 47th District where I carried my home county. My positions here today match my positions during the campaign.

The laws of Georgia are created and modified by our state legislature. The legislature is made up of individuals, like you, who analyze legislation in the context of your personal belief system, which makes your belief system very important to Georgians.

The majority of the banking and finance committee members publicly claim to be Christian. Therefore, I will talk about some of the general constraints or limits of the Christian belief system, and then about secular belief regarding theft or stealing.

In at least nine places the Bible tells us about differing weights and differing measures. In at least four places the Bible says that differing weights and differing measures are an abomination to God. A Christian must not ignore this.

Here is an example of differing measure: Suppose I were in the market buying wheat and I had a basket marked one bushel, but the basket was secretly larger than one bushel. My oversized basket would enable me to steal part of your wheat.

Differing weights and differing measures deceptively cause theft, which is a violation of the Eighth Commandment, "You shall not steal."

Since 1971, the only way to create a new US dollar is to record an entry in a ledger of the Federal Reserve System, or in a ledger of your local bank. Producers have to work years for new Dollars that the bank creates instantly with the stroke of a key.

When new US dollars are created in this way, there is no new wealth created, but the purchasing power of all previously existing dollars is decreased. This is an example of using differing measures to steal labor and property from producers.

This is clearly, undeniably, objectively a form of theft. To support fiat or fractional money is to support theft.

Some claim that our money system makes us wealthy. This is false. Wealth is the result of production.

Many of us notice that People depend on Production. People eat food and use things. Food and things must be produced. Government Produces nothing and wastes much. Since people depend on production and government interferes with production, there is no way that government has any solutions for us. We must remember that every promise made by a government official has to be kept by a producer. There is no other way.

It is impossible to confiscate a loss. Only profits or capital from past production can be confiscated. It is logically impossible for the creation of new US Dollars to make us wealthy. If I had time, I would prove that creating costless money will first make us poorer and eventually crush our free society.

The reality is that the creation of costless money can only lead to the destruction of a free society.

For those who are not constrained by the Christian belief system, if you oppose theft then you must oppose creating new US dollars from nothing.

Please listen carefully to the following quote from an old banker.

"The few who understand the system, will either be so interested in its profits, or so dependent on its favors that there will be no opposition from that class. The great body of people, mentally incapable of comprehending the tremendous advantages will bear its burden without complaint."

To the Christians and those who oppose stealing: I respectfully ask that you vote for the Constitutional Tender Act as a small step toward eliminating differing weights and differing measures and theft from our monetary system.

And finally, let's recall a bit of what John Maynard Keynes wrote in 1919: "while [creating costless money] impoverishes many, it actually enriches some" and also "[Inflation] engages all the hidden forces of economic law on the side of destruction, and does it in a manner which not one man in a million is able to diagnose."

To those members who hold stock in banks or have otherwise profited from the banking business: Since our loss is your gain, I respectfully ask that you recuse yourself from this vote and from the vote on the final bill.

The Following Dialog

After presenting testimony, I engaged in a dialog with Representative Bruce Williamson on fractional reserve banking. Bruce Williamson was a gentleman. Representative Williamson lives in a neighboring county and we have mutual friends. He opened with a prayer that I would be blessed to hear and concur with any time. The problem we have is that neither Bruce, me, nor government is the standard. A good man's character does not make an objectively immoral practice moral or right.

The bankers of the world may be upset with those of us who explain the truth about the effects of costless money and money systems on society. Are those of us who simply want to keep our property permitted to be upset about being robbed through unjust money systems?

Representative Williamson claimed that Georgia banks don't create money, yet he later said:

I'm not disagreeing with the fact that it expands the money supply, but I don't see that that's inherently unhealthy.

But "expanding the money supply" does create new dollars and is inflation.

When I said that banks create dollars from nothing, Representative Williamson disagreed yet again, stating:

"It's not nothing. Its promises to pay that provides the liquidity to shop keepers, to home owners..."

And:

"All you're doing there is allowing these promises to pay, that when you come to borrow the money to buy the automobile or piece of land or buy new shelving for your hardware store, all the bank's doing is turning around and lending you those dollars... It's not the collateral, it's your promise to pay back."

In other words, his stated view is that the money is not created from nothing, rather it is created because the borrower promises to use his land, labor and capital to produce enough to pay the loan back, plus interest to the banker. The banker has essentially no skin in the game.

If *"it's not the collateral,"* why does the banker take the borrower's collateral if the borrower doesn't pay? Explain this to the people who have lost homes and businesses.

In an honest system, the banker would have to loan out property that *actually exists* in order to *earn* interest. In the fractional reserve system, he creates money from thin air and then essentially loans your property back to you - and gets paid interest for doing it. The bank brings nothing to the table except the legal privilege to create money.

When you borrow money for a piece of land, the money that you use to pay the seller comes from a ledger entry at the bank which is made because you agree to pay the money back. The only real asset in the transaction is the land. The banker has no equity or asset in the transaction at all. If you default, he gets the land.

Of course that ledger sheet trick works until the bubble pops, particularly when the bubble is combined with Sarbanes-Oxley and federal regulators.

Representative Williamson also stated plainly that leaving the gold standard was a mistake.

"It all goes back to fiat inflation. I do not disagree one bit with the fact we should never have gotten off the gold standard. I think Steve Forbes has got it right, but all we are is dealing with the Federal Reserve Notes that our Federal Treasury is [unintelligible] the currency of the nation."

However, the Gold standard simply limited the amount of new money created from nothing by the Federal government. Creating money from nothing is always a problem because the mechanism makes an economy unsustainable. The economy is unsustainable because costless money causes a breakdown in the price mechanism and distorts the allocation of resources. It also pillages and weakens the producers.

The banks create new money from nothing, much the same as the Federal Reserve. In fact, the banks are able to create nine new dollars for each one new dollar created by the Federal Reserve. Which is bigger? Nine or One?

If costless money is a problem and the banks create more than the Federal Reserve, then the banks are not innocent. They participate in inflating the money supply, or to use Representative Williamson's phrase in "expanding the money supply," which IS inflation. Creating new money units from nothing disproportionately harms the weak and frugal. It enriches those who are granted a special privilege by government (banks) to create those new money units from nothing - at least from nothing that the banker owns. In the bank's view, your property gives them the right to create money that didn't exist in order to charge you interest for using the money. What a racket.

There is so much more that can be said and the problems are far reaching and complex, but the bottom line is that fractional and fiat money cause theft and lead to poverty and oppression.

In the Bible, the Greek term *trapeza*, which means *table*, is translated *bank*. Banks have come a long way... now they are complex and deceptive tools of plunder, housed in magnificent buildings with *trapezas* inside.

7.2 A Resolution

Declaration of Knowledge of and Commitment to The Foundations and Principles of Liberty

LET IT BE KNOWN that the undersigned believe governments are to be instituted among men to SECURE the NATURAL RIGHTS of LIFE, LIBERTY and PROPERTY.

Citizens of the United States of America have been deprived of the knowledge of the Foundations and Principles of Liberty over at least the past Century. Today even our older generation lacks wisdom, knowledge and understanding that our younger generation and our nation need. With extremely rare exceptions, none of us, including our business leaders, elected officials, ministers, doctors, lawyers or farmers have the understanding needed to secure our Liberty and our Future as a state or nation.

Essential knowledge and understanding has been trained out of our public speech and thought.

We must learn to think in terms of centuries, production and human nature.

No nation which institutes a system based on Differing Weights, Differing Measures or Unjust Judgments has ever remained intact; these nations always collapse.

We have been trained by government schools and media to focus on effects, rather than causes.

We must learn that whoever understands root causes will rule.

We must learn that those who do not understand root causes will be ruled.

We must learn that power comes from possessing or controlling the means and resources to act.

The means and resources to act come from Producers.

Differing Weights, Differing Measures and Unjust Judgments grant free and unrestricted access to Production, which is Unlawfully Confiscated and used to Rule the People.

No other issue matters as long as the Government and favored business has unrestricted access to the Labor and Property of a nation's Producers. Those who believe the answer is found in worshiping the God of Abraham, Isaac and Jacob can be certain that mature worship is not present in a nation which permits legal plunder, without so much as a whimper in protest.

A renowned banker once said "*Give me control of a nation's money, and I care not who makes its laws.*" He was right.

A Legislature that can silently and deceptively take your Property without your Consent, *will take your property without your consent*, and often without your knowledge.

Essential Knowledge

WHEREAS Scripture says "*My people are destroyed for lack of knowledge. Because you have rejected knowledge, I also will reject you from being My priest. Since you have forgotten the law of your God, I also will forget your children." (Hosea 4:6, NASB95)*

WHEREAS Thomas Jefferson stated "*If a nation expects to be ignorant and free in a state of civilization, it expects what never was and never will be.*"; and

WHEREAS George Washington stated "*Government is not reason. It is not eloquence. It is force. Like fire, government is a dangerous servant and a fearful master.*"; and

WHEREAS Ronald Reagan communicated in his first inaugural address that Government is the Problem and Productivity is the Solution; and

WHEREAS excessive Government size, scope and power destroy Life, Liberty and Property; and

WHEREAS excessive Government size, scope and power are the result of Theft and Deception which grant unhindered access to Production through Costless Money, which leads to Corruption of the Legislature; and

WHEREAS the stated goal of George Washington's Treasury Secretary, Alexander Hamilton, was to Confuse the People and Corrupt the Legislature; and

WHEREAS Alexander Hamilton was successful in Confusing the People and Corrupting the Legislature because he was allowed to use Differing Weights, Differing Measures and Unjust Judgment to gain unhindered access to other people's Production; then

BE IT HEREBY RESOLVED that BECAUSE the SECURITY of the LIFE, LIBERTY and PROPERTY of Citizens of GEORGIA and the UNITED STATES depends on a widespread and popular understanding of MONEY SYSTEMS and PRODUCTION; and

The importance of the CONTROL of PRODUCTION to LIFE, LIBERTY and PROPERTY demands an explanation;

Life, Liberty, Property, Production, Abundance and Prosperity have relationships that we must know, understand and remember to live well and govern well;

Therefore these important ideas which are required to establish the foundation for a strong and prosperous Georgia are herein stated:

Life, Liberty, Property

WHEREAS Life, Liberty and Property are gifts from God which precede all human legislation and are superior to it; and

WHEREAS Individual Liberty necessarily includes secure ownership of private Property; and

Authority

WHEREAS Authority is the Permitted Power to Act; and

WHEREAS Power comes from Production; and

WHEREAS Oppressive Power comes from Control of Production; and

WHEREAS Transfer of Production is transfer of Authority; and

Production

WHEREAS People depend on Production for Life, Health, Happiness and Security; and

WHEREAS Liberty and Property are combined with Labor which results in Production; and

WHEREAS Production is the only source of our Food, Shelter and Clothing; and

WHEREAS Production is the source of the Means and Resources to Act; and

WHEREAS We must eat to live and live to think, therefore Thought relies on Production; and

WHEREAS People depend on things which are Produced to meet all physical needs; and

WHEREAS People desire Prosperity; and

WHEREAS Production results in Abundance, and Abundance leads to Prosperity; and

WHEREAS Prosperity comes before popular access to Leisure, Luxury and Learning; and

Government

WHEREAS A Prosperous society must understand the difference between Government and Law, let us therefore know and understand that;

WHEREAS People depend on Production, but Government Produces nothing and Wastes much; and

WHEREAS Excessive Government power is founded on Differing Weights, Differing Measures and Unjust Judgments which are an abomination to God and which violate the 8th Commandment and secular law against theft; and

WHEREAS The Natural Order dictates that things which are useful for the General Welfare can ONLY come from Producers who ACTUALLY make useful things; and

WHEREAS Service jobs and leisure activities are dependent on Production; and

WHEREAS Government imposed Taxation, Regulation, Litigation and Inflation reduce Production which destroys Prosperity and makes society poorer; and

WHEREAS Excessive Taxation, Regulation, Litigation and Inflation are DESTRUCTIVE to LIFE, LIBERTY and PROPERTY; and

WHEREAS Inflation rewards theft and deception while punishing thrift and savings; and

WHEREAS Inflation harms the most vulnerable in our society; and

WHEREAS It is not the Right, Role or Purpose of government to reduce Production or Confiscate Property from Producers to give to others; and

WHEREAS Authority is a FORCE and Law is a STANDARD; and

WHEREAS Authority is subject to Law and Law is subject to Justice; and

WHEREAS Centralization of Power and Authority by force and deception are Unjust and therefore Unlawful; and

WHEREAS Government is authority which is subject to Just Law; and

Producers

WHEREAS Production retained in the hand of the Producer ensures a Balance of Power in society based on efficient use of scarce resources and voluntary market relationships; and

WHEREAS Most genuine Producers are Generous and Wise people; and

WHEREAS It is the Right of the Producer to willingly give gifts to those in need; and

WHEREAS Government Produces nothing and Wastes much; and

WHEREAS Confiscated Property is necessarily the Fruit of Another Person's Production; and

WHEREAS Production necessarily requires Time; and

WHEREAS The confiscation of Time is equal to the confiscation of Life; and

WHEREAS The confiscation of Life includes the confiscation of Liberty; and

WHEREAS Producers are being forced to fund both our society's destruction and the unlawful actions of unrestrained Government; and

WHEREAS Government is not Securing individual LIFE, LIBERTY and PROPERTY; and

THEREFORE Government is Stealing and Destroying LIFE, LIBERTY and PROPERTY; thus

LET IT BE KNOWN that unlawful interventionist GOVERNMENT is the PROBLEM and PRODUCTIVITY retained in the hands of the PRODUCER is the SOLUTION; and it is the NATURAL RIGHT and DUTY of each person to search out a BASIS upon which a JUST SOCIETY that defends Individual LIFE, LIBERTY and PROPERTY can be organized.

7.3 What Can I Do?

As I look over this book I see many more things that could be said. There are quotes and ideas that reinforce arguments... But it has to end sometime. There will be another day for the things that I will undoubtedly wish were included. I have studied and written when I would have enjoyed fishing, but time and priorities would not permit. If I had a research team and no other responsibilities, this could be a better work. As such, I humbly present much of the best of what I have learned over years of study in hopes that it will benefit others who love liberty and production. Even more so, I am hopeful that my Christian brothers and sisters will find new treasures in Scripture as these ideas sink in and begin to bear fruit.

I encourage everyone to learn the truth about money and production. I encourage each person to learn about useful and honorable things of personal interest. We need you and your special skills and insights. Our situation will change only if we are informed about things that really matter. We must look for root causes. We must be honest with ourselves. We must learn how the world really works.

I work diligently to eliminate error from my thinking, so I strongly encourage everyone to help me by challenging the claims made in this book. Please be bold in offering criticism. Surely there will be errors, omissions or poorly framed ideas that I have overlooked.

However, I am confident these central arguments will be proved and refined under scrutiny. When that work is done, we all need to begin challenging any error we can identify in Bible translations. I encourage everyone with a Bible software program like Logos Bible Software 4 to report *money*, *bank*, *governing*, *belt* and any other poorly translated words as typos in each translation of the Bible. I request that we all begin with the term *money* in Genesis 43:21 and the term *money* in 1 Timothy 6:10.

Imagine if hundreds of thousands of people flood the publishers with these comments... We can participate in correcting a centuries old problem in western and Christian thought. Christ came to set the captives free.

"The Spirit of the Lord is upon Me, Because He anointed Me to preach the gospel to the poor. He has sent Me to proclaim release to the captives, And recovery of sight to the blind, To set free those who are oppressed, To proclaim the favorable year of the Lord." (Luke 4:18–19, NASB95)

The captives cannot be free if they feed their oppressors and ask the oppressor to teach them what is true.

For those with no Bible software, write the publishers or call them. Let them know that we expect correct translations of Scripture. Information has come to light that indicates there are some errors to correct.

Perhaps even more importantly, ask your pastors, Bible teachers and professors to either show the error in this work, or begin introducing Biblically sound economic teaching in church and class.

After considering the density of economic terms used to describe Salvation, no pastor can justifiably walk away from the duty to teach people rational, Godly economics. Our misunderstanding of economics is a serious problem. A pastor that will preach in a church that uses at least one economic term in Sunday School, music or his own sermon nearly every Sunday, yet will do nothing to develop a correct understanding of economics among his congregation, is not doing his duty as a preacher, teacher and leader. A fun exercise is learning to listen for economic terms on Sunday.[114]

Of course some people will accuse me of focusing too much on this one thing in Scripture. I usually respond with this brief analogy: Imagine that a young Boy Scout troop is going on their first long wilderness camping trip. Let's say that there are five things that they must master to safely, responsibly and successfully complete this trip.

Imagine the scout leader had a sudden commitment that took him away for six months, beginning two weeks before the camping trip, and you were the new scout leader. When you meet these scouts for the first time you begin asking questions and discover that they have mastered four of the five essential things that they must know to literally survive this camping trip. What will you do?

The answer that always comes back is this: the new scout leader would focus on the one essential thing the boys don't know anything about. The selected focus is not because this one thing is more important than the other four things. It may be less important than some or all of the others. *Yet, because it is essential and the boys don't know it, that thing is most important to them - on that day.*

Our economic understanding from Scripture and generally in the western world is very confused. It is the essential thing that is not being addressed. This needs to be corrected and churches have no excuse to fail to lead in this effort. Our ignorance of Biblically sound economics causes us to fund on Monday what we preach against on Sunday. We have to teach the truth about money and production.

Teach your children, family and friends. Learn what your elected officials need to do to restore liberty and prosperity, then find people who will do those things. Help them get elected and support them when they do what is right.

Summary

Authority is the permitted power to act. Authority is NOT the right to rule. Authority is a force, not a standard. Authority is subject to law.

Law is a standard, not a force. Law takes no action and has no power. Law is subject to righteousness, rightness, justice.

---

114 To get an idea of the number of hymns which use economic terms, go to google.com and in the search box type the following, minus the brackets: [site:hymnlyrics.org price] You may want to use the list of terms from Economics of Salvation to get started.

People eat food and use things. Food and things must be produced.

Government produces nothing and wastes much.

Every promise made by government must be kept by a producer.

No Stealing maintains a healthy balance of power in society, with the means and resources to act controlled by those who are too busy working and too dependent on market relationships to oppress their neighbor. People who work and own property respect other people's property.

No Stealing cannot be achieved in a society unless the society *Knows Stealing* when it occurs.

If we subsidize bad behavior, we get more of it. If we penalize production, we get less of it. This caused the fall of the Roman empire.

I personally believe that only a society that honors and worships God the Father, Son and Holy Spirit will have the belief system and favor of God that will lead to Godly peace and prosperity. Perhaps you know of a different foundation. Whatever the foundation, the above facts about Authority, Law, Justice, Wealth, Production, Power, and Control remain true.

Let's Get This Done

The most satisfying thing I have had the pleasure and privilege of experiencing is seeing these ideas grow in the hearts and minds of people. The material in this book typically has two effects.

First, there are amazing ideas that hit you right away.

Second, and even better, there are ideas which will find good soil, sprout, grow and produce good fruit, gradually over time. After a few months most readers will suddenly realize their view of the world has been radically changed.

"He has told you, O man, what is good; And what does the LORD require of you But to do justice, to love kindness, And to walk humbly with your God?" (Micah 6:8, NASB95)

8. Other Illustrations

The following short articles are sample blog posts from 2008

8.1 Comparing Keynes and the Austrians

We labor under the ideology of the Keynesian school of economics. John Maynard Keynes is the system's namesake and is the "highly revered" economist and intellectual who is credited as the founder our current economic system.

This chapter compares two facets of the Keynesian school of thought to the Austrian school of thought. The first item involves the respective views of the "crisis."

We Have This Under Control!

In the Keynesian view the current crisis should never occur because the central banking system has the sophisticated tools necessary to prevent any such crisis from occurring. Consider Fed Chairman Bernanke's comments about the control the Fed has over the economy and your spending decisions.

"Like gold, US dollars have value only to the extent that they are strictly limited in supply. But the US government has a technology, called a printing press (or, today, its electronic equivalent), that allows it to produce as many US dollars as it wishes at essentially no cost. By increasing the number of US dollars in circulation, or even by credibly threatening to do so, the US government can also reduce the value of a dollar in terms of goods and services, which is equivalent to raising the prices in dollars of those goods and services. We conclude that, under a paper-money system, a determined government can always generate higher spending and hence positive inflation."

(Ben Bernanke, "Deflation: Making Sure 'It' Doesn't Happen Here" [Remarks before the National Economists Club, Washington, D.C., 21 November 2002])

And when things do break, the apologists have been trained to suggest that it would really be worse if the Fed hadn't saved us.

"David Henderson and Jeff Hummel have managed to ruffle quite a few Austrian feathers with their recent Cato briefing paper, and no wonder: that paper claims not only that Alan Greenspan's Fed was

innocent of any role in encouraging the housing boom but that Greenspan had actually managed to do something Austrian monetary economists have long claimed to be impossible, namely, solve the monetary-central-planning problem. Greenspan, by their assessment, managed to mimic the kind of money-demand accommodating money supply growth that would occur under free banking, thereby achieving (according to their paper's executive summary) 'a striking dampening of the business cycle.'" Guilty as Charged, Mises Daily Article , November 7, 2008 by George A. Selgin

Never mind the factors that systemically dampen the business cycle like JIT inventory, changing ratios of non-cyclical sectors in the broader economy, or foreign trade and dollar holdings. We are expected to believe that any dampening of the business cycle is because of the stellar performance of the Fed.

Fundamentally the Keynesian view says there should not be any more business cycles and those in the past were caused by the Fed having inadequate "tools" to prevent the crisis. *The answer has always been more power in the hands of the Fed.*

Austrian Solutions

The Austrian view, on the other hand, *predicts*, *explains* and offers *solutions* to the Business Cycle.

The Austrian view recognizes that Fractional and Fiat money, enjoying legal monopoly through the coercive power of government, causes money to be unrealistically cheap.

Cheap money leads to malinvestment because the signal given by abundant, low cost money is that there are real savings present which will sustain longer term or lower margin investments.

Because creating Fiat or Fractional money *ex nihilo* is not the same as creating real savings, the investments are overpriced and are not sustainable. In addition, the explanation shows how and why the cheap money primarily affects capital goods.

The solution involves several components, but in simplest form, one could say the Austrian view is that natural money as private property without government intervention essentially solves the problem.

Now, on to our second comparison.

State First

The Keynesian view begins with the *primacy of the state* and therefore seeks to justify state action, thereby rendering a fragmented and conflicting series of economic models. Suffice it to say that when one needs to justify actions in any context, something is amiss.

In addition, the lack of a single, unified economic model suggests that for Keynesianism to earn the accolade of being a credible "school of thought" should be out of reach. Instead Keynesianism is glorified by the government, education system, and media.

Individual First

The Austrian view, on the other hand, begins with the *primacy of the individual* in economic and social affairs. As such, the effort is made to observe and seek an accurate and true explanation of economics and related social order. The result is a single, unified economic model at its core.

Who is Right?

On one hand there is the Keynesian crowd who say the business cycle should never exist because the central bank has the "tools" to prevent a crisis. Keynesians always begin by justifying state actions. They never see bubbles until a few years *after* the bubble pops. *Truly brilliant thinkers...*

On the other hand there are the Austrian scholars who *predict*, *explain*, and *resolve* the business cycle and, with a unified core model, rigorously explain specific realities of economic and social order. The Austrian school recognizes and defends principles which are beneficial to individual life, liberty and property.

Who should we believe?

Do we believe the Keynesians who are responsible for the policies that are leading to the economic collapse of countries around the globe? Do we believe people who make claims which are constantly out of line with reality and are clearly destructive to liberty and private property? No way. Not me.

Between these two, my pick is the Austrian School[115] of economics, which matches reality and identifies principles that protect individual life, liberty and property.

---

115 http://mises.org – Go there often.

8.2 Inflation & Moral Decay

Another destructive aspect of Inflationary monetary systems is the overall effect on morality. This will in no way be a thorough treatment or even a substantial review. The intent is simply to raise the point.

Consider this Bernanke quote for reference:

"We conclude that, under a paper-money system, a determined government can always generate higher spending and hence positive inflation." Ben Bernanke, "Deflation: Making Sure 'It' Doesn't Happen Here" Remarks before the National Economists Club, Washington, D.C., 21 November 2002

First note that the Federal Reserve actions are linked to "a determined government."

Next we see that this determined government, acting through the Fed, "can always generate higher spending." In other words, the government can use the inflationary monetary system to, in effect, force citizens to spend, rather than save.

Keynesians claim that the key to economic vitality is spending, while Austrian economists contend that the key is savings. Since one would be hard pressed to produce widgets with no production tools and production tools are capital intensive, it makes sense that before a low cost, high quality, efficiently produced good can be made available for purchase, someone had to save enough to build the widget factory.

In addition, savings is not the destruction of natural money, it is the deferral of spending. The natural money simply is held for future purchases. In addition, savings in a sound money economy lowers interest and enables the production of consumption goods in the future.

Enough of that. Effect on morality is the question we are considering.

If a determined government forces consumers to spend (as their only defense to rising prices caused by the government inflating the money supply), then consumers can only buy cheap goods or go in debt to buy before prices rise. In either case, a "consumption economy" is created. The market churns out large volumes of cheap goods that are replaced every few years. Durable goods are not very durable any more.

The *virtues* of saving and planning are replaced by the *vices* of irresponsible spending and debt.

This fosters an instant gratification mentality. Because no one looks forward in time considering what can be bought in the future, planning and frugality become a mockery. Because we are trained not to look forward, we certainly lose any basis for looking back to discover and maintain tradition.

Consider the present conditions in the United States. Households and businesses are in deep debt. The family is under assault. Integrity seems to be in decline. Instant fixes to every problem are on the shelf. Morality and frugality are mocked. Durable goods are gone. Disposable goods are everywhere.

Inflation transfers wealth and productivity into the hands of the propagandist. The declining dollar trains people to seek instant gratification and live in perpetual debt. That is more than an unhealthy combination; it is a recipe for disaster.

8.3 Fiat Money and Growth

One of the arguments for the central banking model is that we "need more money" for a growing economy. This is a popular fallacy. In simple terms, if all cars cost $300 or $3,000 or $30,000 or $300,000 why do we care one way or the other, as long as wages have a similar relative value to the car as now?

The *price* of the good and *quantity* of money is meaningless.

What is important is the relative value of goods and labor. In its finest form, money is simply the common commodity used in exchange which enables economic calculation. With a common unit of account one can compare the value of an acre of land and a tractor, for instance.

Suppose an acre of land is equivalent in value to one tenth of a tractor. If the land costs 1 ounce of silver and the tractor costs 10 ounces of silver, this works just as well as if the land costs 100 ounces of silver and the tractor costs 1,000 ounces of silver. The relative value is unchanged.

In addition, since we know a car in the past cost $3,000 and a car today costs $30,000, we can clearly see that the same good can sell for a higher price in the future. If it can sell for a higher number of monetary units (price) in the future, why not a lower number? It's just math...

In a sound money economy, a car would actually cost less today than in the past. Because of increases in production efficiency, your gold and silver would have greater purchasing power today than 100 years ago or even 20 years ago.

If the purpose of printing new money tokens is only to be sure everyone has some, then all prices should have remained stable. But prices are much higher. The US Dollar has lost more than 95% of its purchasing power. Why?

Since the quantity of money is not important *and* since we have seen with the *Five Guys Analogy* that inflation serves no purpose if everyone gets the new money on the same day *and* since we know that the purpose of inflation is to cause a hidden wealth transfer, we can draw a few simple conclusions.

First, in our inflationary monetary system, one is either pillaging or being pillaged. There is no middle ground.

To make the argument that we *need more money* in order to have a healthy, growing economy is to make the following ridiculous argument:

A productive and independent business person just can't make it unless a significant portion of what he produces is stolen from him.

He can never be expected to succeed unless his profit is forcefully taken away from him through the process of inflation; the confiscated money must be used to bury him in regulation, while burdening the workforce and consumer with destructive lies and propaganda, paid for out of their own productivity.

One must never expect an increase in wealth if people are allowed to keep what they earn.

Sounds like a bad idea when one discovers that the architects of this monetary system actually expect us to believe that we will grow wealthy by allowing ourselves to be robbed...

8.4 What Is The Goal?

The greatest temporal challenge we face as a nation is our money system.

Destruction and Robbery

We labor under a monetary system which is designed to destroy.

Lenin plainly stated that the system we now operate under would end in our destruction as a free society. The *Five Guys Analogy* illustrates that the process of inflation causes a wealth transfer. Keynes, speaking about Lenin as well as Keynes own views, stated the following:

"Lenin is said to have declared that the best way to destroy the capitalist system was to debauch the currency. By a continuing process of inflation, governments can confiscate, secretly and unobserved, an important part of the wealth of their citizens. By this method they not only confiscate, but they confiscate arbitrarily; and, while the process impoverishes many, it actually enriches some... Lenin was certainly right. There is no subtler, no surer means of overturning the existing basis of society than to debauch the currency. The process engages all the hidden forces of economic law on the side of destruction, and does it in a manner which not one man in a million is able to diagnose."

The Economic Consequences of the Peace, John Maynard Keynes, 1919

Our nation is being robbed. You are being robbed, or you are robbing others. There is no middle ground. We must understand this as a nation. It is true.

The Printer and the Producer

In terms of money, consider this very simple illustration. We will remove all the middle men and rules in order to have a clear picture of what is happening to us.

Imagine you own a house, which you worked hard all your life to pay for. Let's say it cost $100,000.

Now imagine that you are going to sell that house. There are two buyers who are interested in purchasing your home. One offers you paper money and the other offers you gold.

The paper money is identical to the dollars you use every day, but was printed in the garage of the first buyer the same morning he came over to make an offer.

The gold was mined from the ground and refined by the second buyer. The gold came from property the second buyer worked for and the mining and processing was done using labor and equipment he owned or leased.

To which one will you feel better about handing over your house keys?

Would you sell to the producer or the printer?

If you sell to the printer you are exchanging your labor and productivity for an illusion of value.

If you sell to the producer, you are exchanging labor for labor, productivity for productivity.

Crisis Pregnancy and Planned Parenthood

Suppose you have a desire to protect unborn children. Maybe you hold the view that those female fetuses, young ladies who are a few days old, also have a right to life. Maybe they should have a choice. The Fifth Amendment in the US Constitution states:

"No person shall be held to answer for a capital, or otherwise infamous crime, unless on a presentment or indictment of a Grand Jury, except in cases arising in the land or naval forces, or in the Militia, when in actual service in time of War or public danger; nor shall any person be subject for the same offence to be twice put in jeopardy of life or limb; nor shall be compelled in any criminal case to be a witness against himself, nor be deprived of life, liberty, or property, without due process of law; nor shall private property be taken for public use, without just compensation."

Our first property rights are for our own person. It seems that abortion would be illegal based on the Fifth Amendment, if for no other reason. Surely an unborn baby has broken no law worthy of death.

In any case, suppose you hold the view that abortion is wrong, as I do. If that is the case, then you want to work to protect the unborn.

The current environment we operate under is as follows:

Local Crisis Pregnancy Centers are under-funded and staffed by volunteers. They are strictly limited with regard to presenting the pro-life position in schools.

On the other hand, Planned Parenthood is provided with millions of dollars each year by the government, in order to promote the practice of abortion. They have open doors in the schools. In some places school officials can assist young girls with an abortion without parental notification. Their cause is promoted in the media and by the government.

Best Protection

The most effective action we can take is to cut off their funding and keep our own productivity. In this way the crisis pregnancy centers are strengthened, the propaganda is dramatically decreased and Planned Parenthood will have to raise money based on merit, rather than pillaging and coercion of people by government.

So... What is the goal?

Abolish the Federal Reserve and return to a sound money system.

Here is what we can do now: We can tell the truth. We can educate our fellow citizens. We can help people understand what government has done to our life, liberty and property.

Once we do that, let's see what follows. Maybe people will object to being robbed and demand real change.

8.5 What Else Have We Lost?

Today is Thanksgiving Day 2008 and I have the great privilege and pleasure of being in South Georgia with family. I am thankful for many things that are easy to be thankful for. I try to be thankful in all things, in accordance with the teaching of my Christian faith.

During the critical coffee cup selection process this morning I found a cup decorated with a Norman Rockwell image. The scene is of a father and son with fishing gear standing in front of the door to a business. Dad is hanging a sign that says "GONE on BUSINESS"; and one can cipher "will return tomorrow." Dad is happy to hang the sign and go, while the son peeks around a corner in delight as they "sneak off" to fish.

Andy Griffith first comes to mind. And then I recall talk of the days when neighbors would regularly, commonly, often visit on Sunday or raise a barn together. People had time for other things in life than work and a tight schedule.

But today, one of my dearest young friends, barely in her twenties, tells me she would be lost without her Blackberry calendar.

What changed?

As I recall from memory, in 1910 about 70% of all business expansion was self-funded. In those days the monetary system allowed a business to save for its own expansion.

After 1913 this steadily became impossible. A business could not compete without debt funded expansion. Cheap credit made debt cheaper than savings for expansion. In fact, if one saved, inflation would destroy one's wealth faster than any interest that was earned and your competitor would use debt to encroach on your market share while you saved...

Someone will say; "so invest in the stock market for better returns..."

But the stock market is a scam, unless one takes the view that having wealth on paper is the same as having real property. As we have seen clearly (once again) in the past few weeks, wealth on paper can disappear in a flash.

Even if the economy were healthy, what would happen if everyone decided to "cash out" on the same day? The whole system would collapse and most people would get pennies on their dollar (which is only worth about two pennies to begin with) if they were lucky.

Meaning in this context

Because business and individuals have been put in a position in which spending is believed to be cheaper than saving, and because saving provides negligible returns, we have become a debtor society. Remember Bernanke stated plainly that a determined government could, in effect, force people to spend rather than save by forcing higher inflation through government deficit spending:

"We conclude that, under a paper-money system, a determined government can always generate higher spending and hence positive inflation."

Ben Bernanke, "Deflation: Making Sure 'It' Doesn't Happen Here" Remarks before the National Economists Club, Washington, D.C., 21 November 2002

To The Point

Not only does our monetary system cause a literal and actual wealth transfer through the process of inflation, it also reconfigures the use and application of factors of production. In other words, that which is valuable in a system which relies on ever increasing levels of debt, is different than that which is valuable in a system of honest exchange.

In our false prosperity economy there is no time for the typical US citizen to slow down and enjoy friends, family and fishing.

Someone may think of golf or video games or our entertainment flooded society. Perhaps even leisure time and vacations.

However, the picture is not complete unless we think about how burned out we feel when we vacate. Who is paying for the leisure and the entertainment? What is not paid for in its place? What about the tenuous (at best) condition of our savings, investments and retirement?

As a nation, is our leisure usually cash or credit?

In other words what is the real cost of the "leisure" we consume?

How leisurely is what we do for entertainment? Is our entertainment typically edifying or destructive? Do kids go and consume entertainment when they would be better off and healthier to have productive chores to do? Or to spend time with friends and a fishing pole?

We have lost our quality time. We have lost simple things, simple times, time for family, fishing, and growing old within a community. We have lost the opportunity to really enjoy each other and the world around us. We have lost relationships and friendships.

As a nation, we have debt instead of savings. Our retirement and wealth are at the mercy of a system that will fail.

We have little real wealth. What we seem to own requires our continuing participation in the system or we lose our property; for example, we must pay property taxes or the government will confiscate our property. Based on law and regulation, the government is the senior controlling partner in anything we own.

If we rest, we lose.

What else have we lost?

The Federal Reserve System and our complicit government have stolen our property and have stolen our quality time with family and friends.

8.6 Fundamentals and Accountability

This is an essay I wrote in November 2008.

Banking Conference

I attended a banking conference last week which was held at a university. The conference and the people will remain unnamed for the following reasons. Many of the ideas presented, by students and professionals alike, are rooted in the reality that the people are trapped in a system which dares anyone to step out of line.

The teaching they have received, the workplace they enter and the system in which they labor; all present, indeed demand, their defense of a facade which is founded on lies and deception. Some of the people may understand the truth but feel unable to acknowledge it. Others may be under the false impression that what they have been taught is ethical. And, of course, there will be some who know the truth and join in to defend the system because of self interest, benefiting themselves at the hidden expense of other people.

In any case, names will be left out of this discussion because our interest is not to assail or offend, but rather to support those who long for an ethical system of exchange and especially to support those who, if they understood the system we have is quite simply founded on theft and bent on destruction, *would* desire an honest system.

I believe that many of those who were present do want a system that is ethical and edifying, or would, provided they understood our current monetary system is the opposite.

I will simply refer to this event as *the banking conference.*

Much was said during the banking conference about banks, government, Government Sponsored Enterprises (GSE), Wall Street, rating agencies, the Fed, borrowers, business and greed.

The commentary and focus were rather intriguing. Not only did we hear from panels involved in banking and financial planning, but we also heard from the students, and therefore have some sense of how students are integrating the teaching they receive, the leadership that is provided and the news that they consume into an understanding of our present monetary system.

There was a good bit of talk about solutions, greed and accountability. I was struck by the clarity of the propaganda and deception on display.

The Heroes

In this confused and deceptive narrative, the government, the FED and GSEs were the heroes.

The government made cheap housing available; the GSEs provided long term financing which enabled Savings and Loan operations, and later, banks to keep loaning money to enable the American dream of home ownership. The Fed provided the cash.

The Greedy

The rating agencies were bad because Wall Street was a client and so the agencies received revenue from Wall Street firms. To make matters worse, the agencies were facing increasing competition, and therefore they succumbed to issuing inaccurate ratings for fear of losing business.

Wall Street, of course, is just greedy.

The Bad Guys

But the real bad guys were the borrowers and businesses who *"borrowed money they knew they could not repay."*

Lucky for us, the Government is *working hard* to save us!

Another Perspective

Maybe the preceding views are lies born of propaganda and economic ignorance. Maybe there is a different way of looking at this whole situation…

Government regulation created a regulatory minefield which replaced the free market with central planning, corruption and moral hazard.

A root cause of the crisis is unjust law, like the 1977 Community Reinvestment Act (CRA), which forced banks to loan in increasingly unsustainable ways.

Cheap money issued by the FED causes bubbles, which uniformly create financial disasters, which in turn bankrupt the small banks and hardworking people. At the same time the FED issues more of the same dollar poison that caused the problem, in order to save the favored banks and businesses.

Moral hazard created by the FDIC and GSEs, like Fannie Mae and Freddie Mac, exacerbated the effect of the poor lending policies. A bank is more willing to transact loans that it knows will be immediately moved off its books, transferring the obligation onto the balance sheets of the GSEs; which actually means transferring onto the balance sheet of the US taxpayer… These are genuine moral hazards.

Regarding the rating agencies, supply and demand is a terrible scapegoat to enlist as a cover for ethics violations. If the trusted rating agencies were issuing bad assessments, this is to be blamed on ethics violations, i.e. lies and dishonest business practices, not competition and loss of revenue. In a system of honest exchange a dishonest ratings agency would fail quickly.

And finally that *bad ole borrower…* Here he is in a system that is *designed* to keep working people in debt. This is a system which conveys the false idea that banks are conservative in their lending practices in order to keep from making bad loans and losing money. The system is filled with propaganda that completely deceives worker and small business owner alike regarding money and the overall system of plunder.

Of course Mr. Borrower is not to be completely excused for making bad economic calculations, even though much of the information he receives is secretly rooted in fraud. However, he was drawn into bad transactions through a government policy which all but demanded that banks make loans with no money down, with no proof of income, with no rigorous appraisals, etc.

The system set many people up for failure so that they have neither a home today, nor credit capable of purchasing a home in the future.

Good Ole Government

The panelists primarily acted as apologists for government while wagging a finger at borrowers.

However, in certain obvious cases of error, such as in describing the lending policies of a small bank which was recently confiscated by the bank regulators, the banks were acknowledged to have made a few bad choices...

BUT!! Don't get the wrong idea!! Listen carefully now... the system works and the government came in and saved the day and not one depositor lost a dime!! (This is classic propaganda, theft and lies.)

This raises many questions. Why is the government *saving* or *taking over* a bank? Why not leave the bank to be purchased like any other business in the market, at a discount which reflects its supposedly poor management? Is its management poor in fact, or only according to some ever-changing policy superimposed by government?

In addition, it should be noted that the ONLY way for the depositors to *not lose a dime* is for the government to devalue everyone else's money tokens enough to transfer a certain number of fiat dollars back into the hands of the *saved* accounts of the *saved* depositors.

In any case, the only entity that was uniformly instructed to act ethically, consider fundamentals, meet obligations, not over extend, make good decisions, was the small business and the individual borrower. In this imaginary world, everyone else was above reproach and not guilty of failure or subject to criticism.

The government and favored business rob the American people blind, and teach us to blame ourselves for the problems they create.

Addendum

Future Plans

My plans for this book are to receive feedback and challenges from readers, which I will use to update the work and publish revisions, clarifications or additions. This work will never be perfect, but it is ready to come under critical eyes and begin the next stage of refinement.

After a short time *Know Stealing* will be available as a physical book.

There are several other projects in the works which will follow *Know Stealing*. The purpose is to advance ideas which are capable of strengthening the defense of individual life, liberty and property. If you would like to support or participate in the work, please consider watching for updates regarding the American Steward Initiative at the website listed below.

While I don't anticipate significant changes, there will surely be small adjustments. For those who obtain an early copy, the updated content can typically be downloaded again from the book seller. Kindle users can get an updated copy by contacting Customer Support at Amazon.

More information can be found at the following website:

http://www.KnowStealing.com

Updates – 1.0 through 1.04

The primary updates have been for the correction of missing or misplaced words. There have been a few sentences rearranged for readability.

Chapter *3.7 A Simple Test* has an improved introduction.

Chapter *6.4 Institutions* is edited for clarity. In defining problem institutions, the term *corrupt* needed to be added.

Chapter *4.6 Robbing Farmers* has been edited for clarity.

Chapter *5.01 Authority Charts* has been edited for clarity.

The section on *Authority* has a significant change that tightens the definition of *Authority*. Upon review I noticed that *permitted power to act*, which has been part of the definition from the beginning, is more thorough than *freedom and power to act*. There is further explanation in a footnote in Chapter *5.02 Introduction of 14 Observations*.

Updates – 1.05 through 1.06

These two updates are primarily for small grammar and spacing adjustments. Edits of some substance include better comments in *Words Have Meaning* and an edit to an opening sentence in *Economics of Salvation.*

Acknowledgments

To write a proper acknowledgment would require another book. Please know that these words are completely inadequate to describe all the people, relationships, good things, and hard things, in my life which have worked together for my good, and hopefully for God's glory.

To all my friends, family and encouragers, thank you.

To all who worked in or supported my 2010 State Senate campaign, thank you.

To Rob Jordan and Craig Fischer of WJJC radio, 1270 AM, in Commerce Georgia, thank you for standing up and speaking boldly where others fear to whisper. The opportunity to share ideas through the Liberty and Production radio program exists thanks to Craig suggesting the idea. Rob and I have a great time on Monday mornings talking about... Liberty and Production. Both Rob and Craig are exceptionally knowledgeable about our history and the problems we face. Thanks guys.

WJJC radio is small, but these gentlemen produce several home grown, untarnished, politically incorrect programs that may be of interest. Tune in sometime at wjjc.net on your PC or with an android app.

Karen Watkins is a good friend who helped complete the title *Know Stealing*. After considering many possibilities, I settled on the title *No Stealing*, but I knew something was missing. When I shared the name with Karen, she asked: "*Know or No?*" Her question immediately resolved the issue.

Bob Machen has been a friend for many years. He is the person who calls to ask about some problem no one knows about, or he gives a push when something should be done, or he connects people at just the right time. Bob is a friend and blessing.

Dan Blechinger has also been a friend for many years. Twice a week for the past seven years we have traveled together to a company in Atlanta where he is a Vice President and I do consulting work. In all that time we have never been without topics of substance to discuss. Dan is a brilliant person who always says just what he thinks, which is a character trait I value highly. His contributions, feedback and challenges regarding various arguments found in *Know Stealing* have been invaluable. Dan has always been an unwavering encourager, supporter and friend.

Bob Bailey is a relatively new friend who loves God and people, like all those mentioned here. He has great knowledge and a wonderful collection of old books that he has put to good use. Bob has exerted effort to connect me with people who could challenge my thinking, which for me is like being a kid in a candy store. He took time to read and challenge my writing in the past few weeks, having questions and suggestions which were excellent and led to positive edits in *Know Stealing*. Bob is also one of my banker friends. I love bankers, but fractional banking I oppose.

Coleman Porter and Mike Strickland represent the kind of thinking that is necessary to restore liberty. They are the two people who most clearly exhibit a willingness to be honest with themselves, even when it is uncomfortable. They both amaze me with their desire and ability to set aside the implications of certain knowledge and seek to know what is true and right. I am thankful they are my friends.

Cody Murray is another sharp young man who has experienced significant hardship and yet works hard to overcome obstacles, seeking wisdom and understanding along the way. We both enjoy breaking things down, so our conversations are stimulating and fruitful. Our intellectual mining expeditions turn up useful ideas and improved understanding.

I had the pleasure of meeting Dr. John Feezell, a professor of Business Administration at LeTourneau University, when my daughter was a LeTourneau student. Meeting John the first time was more like seeing an old friend. John was successful in business before working as a professor, which, combined with his educational credentials and unique style of viewing problems, has enabled him to be a priceless resource and sounding board for me. Our conversations remind me of digging for hidden treasures.

Dr. Brent Baas is head of the computer science department at LeTourneau University. Brent is one of those brilliant people whose words are few and meaningful. His encouragement, insights and open mind always lift me up. He too was as a familiar friend from our first meeting.

My Dad thinks of things *as they could be*, rather than *as they are*. He left home for college with less than two dollars in his pocket and earned a PhD, which he used to do what had never been done in the cattle industry. His vision and labor gave me opportunities that few in my generation had. He put me to work from a young age, for which I will always be grateful. Thanks to my Dad, I was operating a tractor all day in the hayfield by the time I was eight. I did all the things that people do on a farm, which is another one of my treasures in life. I rode and slept on a working D7 Caterpillar as a small child, and operated it as a teenager. Thousands of acres, in one place or another, cattle, horses, fences, fish, deer, woods, equipment, old trucks, jeeps, shops, welders, ponds, fields – were my back yard. Can life get better than that? Thanks Dad.

I also want to give a special thanks to my Dad for offering to read the final draft, if I would wait to publish. I have gladly waited a few days and he has almost finished. His excellent suggestions for clarification have been applied, and after reading two thirds of the material, he encouraged me to go ahead with publication. I am thankful for his time and honored by his confidence.

My Grandmother Coley inspires me beyond words. She was bedridden for twenty years and was cared for by her mother and daughters. The story goes that <u>*one*</u> day for a <u>*few minutes*</u> she had a <u>*little bit*</u> of a sour attitude. Though severely crippled with arthritis, she was always concerned about other people. Without fail, pastors reported that she encouraged them, when they had visited to encourage her. She *never* complained. She would not tolerate unkind words. She is a tremendous and rarely matched example of faith, peace, grace and love. Her favorite Bible verse was Psalms 119:75.

"I know, O LORD, that Your judgments are righteous, And that in faithfulness You have afflicted me." (Psalm 119:75, NASB95)

I am thankful for my Grandmother, her prayers, her example and the high standards she set. Even bedridden, I count her among the producers.

Then there is Leesa. Words will never do. If there is such thing as a perfect wife, mother, partner and friend, she is. I dreamed of Leesa before I knew who she was, and my dreams fell short. I have spent my whole life taking things apart to see what is inside. Leesa has always helped me keep doing just that. She has never been the smallest weight or obstacle. She has always been more than I could ever ask, and I have never had to ask.

Finally, I am thankful that I am a child of God and privileged to participate in His creation. What an amazing treasure we find in the economics of salvation. Children of God have the true, eternal free gift of life, paid for by the Giver, rather than a false and consuming free gift, founded on theft, offered by thieves and paid for by producers.

"And you also were included in Christ when you heard the message of truth, the gospel of your salvation. When you believed, you were marked in him with a seal, the promised Holy Spirit, who is a deposit guaranteeing our inheritance until the redemption of those who are God's possession—to the praise of his glory." (Ephesians 1:13–14, NIV)

About The Author

Shane and his wife of 25 years have two adult children and have resided in north Georgia since 1983. Shane is a Georgia native who was raised in the beef cattle business. He attended Abraham Baldwin Agricultural College and studied Agricultural Engineering at the University of Georgia.

While he has spent the past fourteen years building and managing computer data systems for Agricultural and Document Management services, his overall life experience is broad and deep. Until 1991 Shane managed the family farm and logging operation. At age 25, he opened a hydraulics and heavy equipment repair business as a stepping-stone to international export, manufacturing and computer technology business opportunities. Although Shane has never taken a computer class, he has had continued success building large server-based computer applications.

Shane has a love for liberty, truth, and understanding, which drives him to study the world in which we live. As a committed Christian Shane is active in church and ministry.

Shane has spent years studying apologetics, history, economics, personality, organizational behavior, science and more. One of his favorite short debates is with people who say there is no absolute truth. The point is made simply by asking if the claim being made is that *"there is absolutely no absolute truth..."* The argument refutes itself.

Shane was a candidate for the Georgia State Senate in 2010 and earned sufficient support to be in a runoff after a primary season with five candidates. While the race was lost, Shane carried his home county and was less than 50 votes short of a tie in the next most populous county of the district.

Shane is the host of Liberty and Production, a radio show based in Commerce Georgia at WJJC, 1270 AM and WJJC.net.

Know Stealing is the written culmination of fifteen years of research and an extension of the message of Liberty and Production he vigorously presented during the 2010 Senate campaign.

Shane and Leesa share a top priority of personally returning to productive agriculture. Their vision is of a farm combined with teaching facilities which have the purpose of producing for today and promoting knowledge that will help defend individual life, liberty and property for generations to come.

Knowledge, wisdom and understanding can lead the American people from debt to savings, which will enable us once again to enjoy time, and build a legacy, with family and friends. At every opportunity Shane will use his time and resources, alongside family, to learn, write, and teach; grow trees, crops and livestock; build machines, work horses, raise mules, fish, hunt, and spend a little more time on his Harley.

CPSIA information can be obtained at www.ICGtesting.com
Printed in the USA
LVOW121300240212

269999LV00002B/2/P